THE POLAR T\

THE POLAR TWINS

Edited by Edward J. Cowan
and Douglas Gifford

JOHN DONALD PUBLISHERS LTD
EDINBURGH

© The Editors and Contributors severally 1999

All rights reserved.
No part of this publication may be reproduced
in any form or by any means without
the prior permission of the publishers
John Donald Publishers Limited,
Unit 8, Canongate Venture,
5 New Street, Edinburgh, EH8 8BH.

ISBN 0 85976 513 X

British Library Cataloguing in Publication Data

A catalogue record for this book is available
from the British Library.

Typesetting and origination by Brinnoven, Livingston
Printed and bound in Great Britain by Redwood Books, Trowbridge

Preface

This collection is partly based on a year-long seminar series at the University of Glasgow. Our thanks go to Mrs Dorothy Mallon for processing the typescript. Also to Hazel Hynd, who provided the index.

Edward J. Cowan
Douglas Gifford

Notes on Contributors

Cairns Craig is Professor of English Literature, University of Edinburgh.

Thomas Owan Clancy is Lecturer in Celtic, University of Glasgow.

Sonja Cameron is Co-ordinator for CTI Centre for History, Archaeology and Art History, University of Glasgow.

George Brunsden recently completed his Ph.D in Scottish Studies at Glasgow and has returned to his native Canada.

Martin MacGregor is Lecturer in Scottish History, University of Glasgow.

Fiona Black is nearing completion of her Ph.D in Scottish Literature, University of Glasgow.

E. Mairi MacArthur is an independent scholar based at Inverness.

Edward J. Cowan is Professor of Scottish History, University of Glasgow.

Owen Dudley Edwards is Reader in History, University of Edinburgh.

Kirsten Stirling is completing her Ph.D in Scottish Literature at the University of Glasgow and is presently Assistante in the section d'anglaise, Université de Lausanne.

Johanna Tiitinen of Helsinki University, Finland, is visiting Research Fellow in Scottish Studies, University of Glasgow.

Douglas Gifford is Professor of Scottish Literature, University of Glasgow.

Glasgow School of Scottish Studies

Glasgow School of Scottish Studies exists to facilitate and oversee a whole range of inter-disciplinary scholarly activity from the three-year undergraduate MA in Scottish Studies through the postgraduate degrees of MPhil, MLitt and PhD to the post-doctoral levels. Based on the four core departments of Scottish History, Scottish Literature, Celtic and Philosophy, the School also enjoys representation from the departments of Archaeology, History of Art, Politics, Philosophy, English Literature, English Language, Social and Economic History, Theatre Film and Television Studies, the Hunterian Museum, Music, Sociology, Divinity, Law, Adult and Continuing Education, the Archives and Business Records Centre, the University Library, St Andrews College, the Royal Scottish Academy of Music and Drama and the Mackintosh School of Architecture. The School has agreements, to further research as well as student and faculty exchange, with the Centre for Scottish Studies at Germersheim, part of the Johannes Gutenberg University of Mainz and the University of Brest as well as with a number of other European and North American universities. The Director of the School is Professor Ted Cowan and the Convener of the Executive Committee is Professor Alex Broadie.

The School also offers the distance-taught MPhil in Scottish Literature. Members are also involved in the exciting Abbotsford Project on Sir Walter Scott's Library in collaboration with the Faculty of Advocates under the supervision of Professor Douglas Gifford. In addition to publishing several Scott manuscripts the School is currently sponsoring some six publications on a wide range of topics, essay collections derived from conferences and seminar series. It also sponsors the successful poetry broadsheet *Skinklin Star* under the editorship of Matt Ewart. It has attracted financial support from the Scottish Arts Council and from the private sector. Annually the School promotes a series of conferences, themed seminars, Come-All-Ye Evenings, visiting speakers, pre-sessional courses for overseas students and Summer Schools.

A wide range of choice is available at the postgraduate level. All degrees may be pursued in individual subject disciplines or through the inter-disciplinary programme. The M.Phil., either taught or by research, is a one-year degree, the M.Litt. which is examined by thesis, normally takes two years and the Ph.D involves a three year programme of intensive research and the presentation of a thesis.

A recent development with the University of Strathclyde is the Glasgow-Strathclyde School of Scottish Studies which facilitates collaboration in teaching, research, publication, joint conferences and seminars and the exchange of faculty supervision at the postgraduate level. There is no greater concentration of talent, expertise and resources in this field anywhere in the world. Glasgow, with a long and distinguished track record in Scottish Studies, is well placed to contribute to the cultural life of Scotland in the 21st century.

For further information contact Mrs Dorothy Mallon at:
 Tel and fax: 0141 330 4576
 e-mail: D.Mallon@scothist.arts.gla.ac.uk

Contents

	Preface	v
	Notes on Contributors	vi
	Glasgow School of Scottish Studies	vii
1	Introduction: Adopting and Adapting the Polar Twins *Edward J. Cowan and Douglas Gifford*	1
2	The Fratricidal Twins: Scottish Literature, Scottish History and the Construction of Scottish Culture *Cairns Craig*	19
3	Personal, Political, Pastoral: The Multiple Agenda of Adomnán's *Life of St Columba* *Thomas Owen Clancy*	39
4	Keeping the Customer Satisfied: Barbour's *Bruce* and a Phantom Division at Bannockburn *Sonja Cameron*	61
5	Aspects of Scotland's Social, Political, and Cultural Scene in the Late 17th and Early 18th Centuries, as Mirrored in the Wallace and Bruce Traditions *George M. Brunsden*	75
6	'Surely one of the greatest poems ever made in Britain': The Lament for Griogair Ruadh MacGregor of Glen Strae and its Historical Background *Martin MacGregor*	114
7	A Taste of Scotland: Historical Fictions of Sawney Bean and his Family *Fiona Black*	154

8	Among Sublime Prospects: Travel Writers and the Highlands *E. Mairi MacArthur*	171
9	'Intent upon my own race and place I wrote': Robert Louis Stevenson and Scottish History *Edward J. Cowan*	187
10	John Buchan's Lost Horizon: An Edinburgh Celebration of the University of Glasgow *Owen Dudley Edwards*	215
11	The Roots of the Present: Naomi Mitchison, Agnes Mure Mackenzie and the Construction of History *Kirsten Stirling*	254
12	A World at the End of History? *A History Maker* by Alasdair Gray *Johanna Tiitinen*	270
13	'Out of the World and into Blawearie': The Politics of Scottish Fiction *Douglas Gifford*	284
	Index	304

1

Introduction: Adopting and Adapting the Polar Twins

Edward J. Cowan and Douglas Gifford

When Gregory Smith wrote his pioneering *Scottish Literature: Character and Influence* (1919), he distinguished 'two moods' inherent in the Scottish character and psyche, coining the term 'Caledonian Antisyzygy' (later taken up by Hugh MacDiarmid and thenceforward grossly overused) to denote what he saw as a fundamental Scottish dualism. On the one hand was a predilection for emphasising 'actuality', 'grip of fact', 'sense of detail' and 'realism'; on the other, 'the airier pleasure to be found in the confusion of the senses, in the fun of things thrown topsy-turvy, in the horns of elfland . . .'. Smith did not restrict his observations to creative writing, but implied that these antithetical characteristics informed all of Scottish culture and were to be discerned throughout Scottish history as well as in present everyday life.

> There is more in the Scottish antithesis of the real and the fantastic than is to be explained by the familiar rules of rhetoric. The sudden jostling of contraries seems to preclude any relationship by literary suggestion. The one invades the other without warning. They are the 'polar twins' of the Scottish Muse.[1]

The essays here adapt Smith's idea of 'the polar twins' to explore the uneasy relationship between Scottish history and Scottish literature throughout the centuries.

At birth the twins were indistinguishable; our earliest historical sources were literary, while the first Scottish poem was historical in content. Tacitus's *Life of Agricola*, in Latin, which was written about 98 A.D., described the Roman campaigns in North Britain culminating in the great defeat of the Caledonians at the battle of Mons Graupius. The native leader, Calgacus, famously but fictitiously pronounced that the invaders created a desert and they called it peace. Some five hundred years later a poet named Aneirin composed *The Gododdin*, in Welsh, to celebrate another glorious defeat, this time at Catraeth where the Men of the North were slaughtered by the

Northumbrians. It was the function of the singers to commemorate 'The old and the young, the bold and the meek True is the tale, death confronted them'.[2] One of the earliest Scottish prose compositions, Adomnán's Latin *Life of Columba*, is discussed below by Thomas Clancy who neatly demonstrates the gulf between authorial intent and critical expectation; Adomnan sought to construct an account of his subject's holiness and saintliness while historians attempt to ransack his work for biographical and historical information.

Literature is as elusive as history during the first millennium or so of the Scottish past though we are gradually gaining some impression of what has been lost or ignored.[3] Much must have circulated in the oral traditions of the early peoples – Picts, Scots, Britons and Angles – which is now irrecoverable. A Scandinavian infusion, in the shape of the Vikings, contributed invaluable poems and sagas, long prose narratives in the Old Norse vernacular, about the lives of the peoples of the northern and western isles. Indeed it could be argued that the Icelandic saga tradition represents the most consummate fusion of history and literature in the medieval world. From the twelfth century the Normans preserved fragments of native tradition in their chronicles and *romans*.

The twins were reborn, in a sense, in the late thirteenth century when Scotland's earliest known vernacular poem lamented the catastrophic death of Alexander III in 1286 – an event which transformed the nation's gold into lead:

> Crist, borne in virgynyte,
> Succoure Scotlande, and remede,
> That is stade in perplexite.

At almost the same moment, on the eve of the Scottish Wars of Independence, the first major Scottish chronicle was produced, though until now it has been unnoticed, embedded as it is in the well-known *Chronicle of the Scottish Nation* by John of Fordun, compiled around 1370.[4] Fordun does not reveal what motivated him to put together his lengthy and supremely important compilation, but his contemporary, John Barbour, was more forthcoming in composing his epic chivalric poem, *The Bruce*, a heroic account of the life and adventures of Robert I who freed his people from the tyrannical ambitions of the two English Edwards in the period 1306–29. Barbour introduces his poem of some 9000 lines with the statement:

> Storys to rede ar delatibill
> Suppos that thai be nocht bot fabill,
> Than suld storys that suthfast wer
> And thai war said on gud maner
> Have doubill plesance in heryng.[5]

Introduction

Truthful, well-told history was his aim, to show 'the thing rycht as it wes', so that before it was forgotten it would be implanted in memory for all time. His 'true story' owed much to the conventions of medieval romance and, despite his optimistic protestations, as Sonja Cameron demonstrates in her study of the battle of Bannockburn, literature won out over history, as she believes it always will. She also makes the telling point that sober historians, who have tended to be highly suspicious of literary sources, have nonetheless been dazzled by Barbour's achievement, to the detriment of their craft.

The first sustained vernacular account of Scottish history is to be found in the ultimately tedious rhyming couplets of Andrew Wyntoun's *Orygynale Cronykil of Scotland* which was written for a Fife laird circa 1420. Andrew was attempting to make sense of the confused traditions about his country's past.

> As men ar be thare qualyteys
> Inclynyd tyl dyversyteys,
> Mony yharnys for tyll here
> Off tymys that befor thaim were,
> The statys chawngyde and the greis.
> Quhar-for off swylk antyqwyteys,
> Thai that set hale thare delyte
> Gest or story for to wryte,
> Owthir in metyre, or in prose,
> Fluryside fayrly thaire purpose
> Wytht queynt and curious circumstance . . .

His intention in writing was to make 'reliable chronicle historical narratives', hitherto preserved only in the medium of Latin, available in his own language. He drew in part from Barbour whose views he shared on the delightful yet fabulous qualities of *romans*, but he was adamant that he would neither embroider nor detract from the 'stories', that is, the histories upon which he depended, though he admitted that 'few wrytys I redy fande/ That I couth drawe to my warande'.[6] It is clear that throughout his ambitious, and today somewhat under-rated account, he made free use of *gestes*, ballads and oral tradition.

In the 1440s Walter Bower, abbot of Inchcolm, set himself the task of completing Fordun's *chronica* which he named *Scotichronicon* and which has recently been made available in a splendid new edition and translation by Professor Donald Watt and his highly distinguished team of scholars, surely one of the most outstanding accomplishments of twentieth-century Scottish medieval scholarship. Bower tells us that he was urged to undertake the project by Sir David Stewart of Rosyth, another laird who, like

Wyntoun's patron, belonged to a section of Scottish society which demanded access to the nation's past and which also increasingly thirsted after the poetry of the makars in the Scots vernacular. Walter, who wrote his massive chronicle in Latin, was also concerned about the tension between 'suthfastnes', or truth, and style.

> In particular I shall not aim in my writings at beauty of style with brilliant diction, but I shall try to devote my attention to the true riches of different historians and to events known to me otherwise. Indeed the chronicles by themselves are so brilliant, vouched for by the names of the writers, that they do not need the lustre of an elaborate style to delight the hearts of readers. In addition to this the artlessness of an uncultivated style has usually removed all suspicion of falsification. For how could any one who is quite unable to produce a polished style know how to fabricate fiction?

He expressed the same point elsewhere in poetic form:

> Read therefore the page written for you
> in a firm fashion and unadorned,
> not bound with the knots of flowery eloquence,
> but variegated with the true chronicles of the Scots.[7]

Needless to say, despite his best intentions, the good abbot could not avoid some measure of fabrication as is reflected in his concluding comment on the entire project – 'Christ! He is not a Scot who is not pleased with this book'.

In Bower there is much quotation of Scottish poetry composed in Latin but little awareness or acknowledgement of the vernacular tradition. The legacy of fifteenth-century poetry included the hugely influential Blind Harry's *Wallace* which has been described by Matthew McDiarmid as 'the greatest single work of imagination in early Scots poetry'.[8] That the career, and indeed the legend, of William Wallace was already quite well known is indicated by the enthusiastic description of his adventures in Bower who believed that through his martyrdom in 1305 Scotland's greatest patriot entered the ranks of the immortals. Harry (if such was his name – the matter is in doubt, as is his blindness) owed a great debt to Barbour's poem, parts of which he plundered in elaborating the legend wherein Wallace becomes a bloody-minded anglophobe intent on the liberation of his country, whatever the cost. In orchestrating his hero's epiphany Harry removed him from the confines of history, though ever since he wrote historians have vainly scrutinised the poem, searching for a history that never was.[9] George Brunsden's examination of the publishing history of the two poems concludes that *The Wallace* was to become one of the most popular publications of the seventeenth and eighteenth centuries, far outstripping *The Bruce* in editions and appeal. William the supposed 'common man' or 'the man from nowhere' was to be preferred to Robert the aristocrat and king.

But by now the aims of historians and creative writers were diverging. As early as the first decades of the fifteenth century, in *The Kingis Quair,* James I had turned the epic away from history and politics towards the personal, in a fusion of the courtly, the amatory, and the consolations of philosophy. By the end of the century poets like William Dunbar, Robert Henryson and Gavin Douglas were similarly concerned with new metaphysical and moral issues, with Dunbar particularly interested in his place in the hierarchies of the court. While one of his most ambitious poems, 'The Thrissell and the Rose', does celebrate a crucial historical event, the marriage of James IV to Margaret Tudor in 1503, like its companion piece, 'The Golden Targe', it is far more concerned to show how the poet has mastered the medieval dream genre of Chaucer, Lydgate and Gower, and indeed rather anticipates the *literati* poets of the Scottish Enlightenment in its elimination of Scottish history in order to honour Chaucer as 'the flour imperiall' of 'Britaine' and 'oure Inglisch'. Henryson, if more rooted in native experience, nevertheless refashions classical and European material such as the fables of Aesop and the love story of Troilus and Cressida – admittedly with a reductive anti-courtly Scottish twist – in 'The Testament of Cresseid'; while, in the same period, the major achievement of Gavin Douglas, Bishop of Dunkeld, is his Scots translation of Virgil's *Aeneid*. Something, however, remained of the old relationship of history and literature; their old didactic aims are to the fore in work like Sir David Lyndsay's *Ane Satyre of the Thrie Estaitis,* with its urging that the young King James V 'mak reformatioun' on the eve of the more drastic Reformation, and Robert Wedderburn's angry condemnation of his apathetic countrymen in *The Complaynt of Scotland*. Both Lyndsay's early morality play, with its ferocious mixture of comedy and instruction, and Wedderburn's appeal for unity against the English after the ravages of the 'Rough Wooing' (arguably the first major work of Scots prose) are rooted in the *speculum* tradition of moral instruction of the Middle Ages; both share a profound concern for Scotland's welfare, with a resounding echo of Harry's foregrounding of a national heroic symbol-figure in Lyndsay's impressive creation of a Scottish heroic Everyman in the towering presence of John the Commonweal, and Wedderburn's suffering representative of wasteland Scotland, Dame Scotia. Both contain evidence of a democratic, populist, and frequently reductively egalitarian strand in Scottish thought which runs back to Barbour and Harry and forward to the regenerative and satirical myth-fictions of Scott, Stevenson, Munro, Gunn and Gibbon. But it is worth noting that Lyndsay's epic *The History of Squire Meldrum* is already bending history and instruction into comic parody, so that actual history and characters are inflated and distorted and the aim of moral instruction deflated. A continual tendency in Scottish creative writing hereafter is towards parody of romance and the reduction of heroic national epic. With the honourable exceptions of a few poets and poems hereafter, like Allan Ramsay's (mock-medieval) 'A Vision', or Robert Fergussons's 'The Ghaists' (both taking their inspiration from the eighteenth-century sentimental Jacobitism which followed the Union), Scottish poetry withdraws from consideration of the whole matter of Scotland until MacDiarmid and Soutar in the 'Scottish Renaissance' of the early twentieth century. It is significant that Burns, the National Bard, in his 'The Vision', reduces Wedderburns's 'Dame Scotia', and Ramsay's Guardian of Scotland, Wallace, to 'Coila', a maiden embodiment of Kyle and Burns's Ayrshire, with nothing of Ramsay and Fergusson's specific anger against historic injustice to Scotland. And later poets like James Hogg, William Tennant and Robert Pollock move the epic further towards escapist comedy or religious polemic, while, as Cairns Craig and Douglas Gifford examine in their essays, Scottish fiction and culture generally increasingly finds itself at odds with Scottish history, either as fact or in interpretation.

This is, however, to anticipate the ever-increasing parting of the ways of the twins. When Henryson in The Testament of Cresseid asked 'Wha wat gif all that Chauceir wrait was trewe?', asking if his classical history was 'authoreist or feignit of the new', he posited the essential question to be addressed about all writers and historians. The first of Scotland's 'speculative historians' of the sixteenth century, John Mair, recalled that during his childhood Harry 'fabricated a whole book about Wallace, and therein wrote down in our native rhymes all that passed current among the people of his day', and he confessed that he could give only 'partial credence' to such writings. Mair, the great schoolman and scholar of international renown, was determined to test his historical hypotheses. He was more inclined to trust Latin sources, though he admitted that even they might prove fallible. It is the supreme irony of Scottish historiography that at the moment when Mair seemed to promise a more scientific, that is a more experiential or common-sensical type of history, the indefatigable and ingenious Hector Boece intervened with his hugely influential *Scotorum Historiae* (1527). In his introduction Boece, a native of Dundee and principal of Aberdeen University, explained that the world and everything that it contained was subject to change; nothing was permanent. He claimed that his *History* included only what was known to him through personal study and industry or by consulting 'richt trew and faithful auctoris'. Hector was undoubtedly one of the great Renaissance Scots yet he confounded posterity by including hefty dollops of myth, legend, tradition and sheer invention in his chauvinistic narrative. That his account was to be preferred to the more sober observations of Mair is indicated by a royal commission to John Bellenden for translating Boece's work into Scots (1531), a process overseen by the author himself. The Scots it seems, given the choice, have always opted for the more colourful and more flattering version of their country's past. John Knox's *History of the Reformation in Scotland* (1559), divinely inspired testament though it supposedly was, knowingly incorporated the liberal use of fictitious anecdote and literary flourish. John Leslie and George Buchanan in their respective histories celebrated a period of over two thousand years during which language, custom, costume and manners had survived as recognisable entities, so anticipating those writers who in the aftermath of James Macpherson's revelation of Ossian, rejoiced in a culture that was believed to be as old, or older, than that of Greece and Rome. Leslie regarded history as 'the witnes of tymes, the maistres of lyfe, the lychte of truthe'; not for him misty fables and the painted colour words designed to obfuscate rather than clarify.[10] Buchanan, following his old teacher Mair, believed in the supreme authority of the classicists upon whom he was dependent for information about large chunks of Scottish time. He dismissed as ridiculous the view that the void had been filled by native bards and seanachaidhs ignorant of letters and learning who relied upon fallible memory and the expectant patronage of their chiefs. Buchanan, probably the greatest intellect of sixteenth-century Scotland, was severely dismissive of all fabulists, particularly those who composed in the vernacular.[11]

Robert Lindsay of Pitscottie could well have been one of the inventive vernacularists condemned by George. The Fifer's *Historie and Chronicles of Scotland* (1565) shared some of Knox's fascination for personality and character but it mostly revealed its author's fondness for story rather than history. Knox founded a minor school of Scottish historiography which blended narrative with the reprinting *in extenso* of significant primary documents. There were not many historians of the Reform but the technique was followed by Archbishop Spottiswood and David Calderwood as well as by the mainly royalist chroniclers of the Covenanting upheaval and the subsequent wars. Such writers did not entirely eschew the fabulous though they were intensely interested in marvels. At least their methodologies permitted the reader to scrutinise authorial interpretation though, as with all historians, there was often a problem of selection of evidence.

There can be little doubt that in the Lowlands the Reformation cast something of a blight upon creative literature but Protestantism did not have a comparable impact upon the the *Gaidhealtachd*. Gaelic literature, in the main but not exclusively, had been transmitted through the oral medium. In the late seventeenth century Neil MacMhuirich, a member of a distinguished kindred of hereditary bards and historians which flourished from the thirteenth to the eighteenth century, concluded his Gaelic history of the Montrose wars with the observation,

> I had many stories to write on the events of the times if I undertook to do it, but what induced me to write even this much was, when I saw that those who treated of the affairs of the time have made no mention at all of the Gael, the men who did all the service.[12]

The 'Book of Clanranald', to which MacMhuirich contributed, contained much other material, including history, tradition, genealogy and poetry. As Professor Derick Thomson has indicated, 'Scottish Gaelic literature throughout its history has been dominated by verse to an unusual extent'.[13] Much of that poetry was concerned with the tempestuous historical events of the period in a way that has no parallel in Lowland Scotland. In his discussion of 'The Lament for Griogair Ruadh MacGregor of Glen Strae' Martin Macgregor brilliantly restores history to the poem, thus vindicating not only its remarkable composer, Marion Campbell, widow of the victim, but also the authority and veracity of Gaelic oral tradition.

The talented court poets of the reign of James VI, such as Alexander Montgomery, were replaced by less accomplished and more Anglicised successors after the king succeeded to the English throne in 1603. Some political and historical awareness can be seen behind the symbols of 'The Cherrie and the Slae', in which the Cherrie represents Catholicism and the Slae the bitterness of the new Protestantism – but the national significances are overlaid with heavy medieval allegory, together with the ambiguities which afterwards will proliferate in Scottish poetry and fiction. And while William Drummond of Hawthornden is a considerable poet who also wrote *The History of Scotland* (1655), he works in a Petrarchan tradition which confines his themes to lost love, the transitoriness of life, and the consolations of religious belief, only occasionally allowing his Royalist and anti-Covenanter feelings to escape into verse. That same period, however, witnessed much ballad composition, often inspired by contemporary events. It is often forgotten that the Lowlands also enjoyed a vital oral tradition which was to be harvested by early collectors such as John Watson and Allan Ramsay in the early eighteenth century, by Robert

Introduction

Burns, by Walter Scott and William Motherwell and a host of others devoted to the preservation of popular heritage. The very act of conservation was a source of literary inspiration for those men and others of their ilk, though they often depended upon female informants; women, it seems, were often the tradition bearers in the Lowlands as in the Highlands. Folklore literature and popular tradition, important entities in their own right, have for too long and too often been ignored or neglected by mainstream or 'establishment' authorities suspicious of media they did not care to comprehend.

The use made of historical events by the ballads, rendering them timeless and archetypal in the manner of folk memory, reminds us that both 'literature' on one hand and popular story-telling on the other are equally guilty – or skilful – in manipulating history for aesthetic and political effect. Shakespeare's version of the Macbeth story, making a barbaric travesty of whatever the realities of the Celtic king's life actually were, in order to pay a back-handed compliment to his new master James VI and I, is a fine, if second-handed Scottish, example; Harry's rectification of Barbour's omission of Wallace from his epic is probably the outstanding example of the *vox populi* insisting that history be re-fashioned to give back the kind of hero desired, as well as hitting back at aristocratic bias in previous story-telling. Harry comes midway between 'literature' and popular, oral history. And if we move from the popular creation of such elevated icons as Mary Queen of Scots and Bonnie Prince Charles (the necessity of including his soubriquet indicating the power of popular myth-making), to consider the iconising of lesser figures such as Rob Roy or, even less historically identifiable, The Gaberlunzie Man, we can see just how potent a force such legend-making can be, in that it, in a sense defeats history. In her essay here Fiona Black studies a comparable piece of popular invention in her examination of the origins and growth of the legend of Sawney Bean, the archetypally repulsive and horrific Scottish cannibal who, in his early versions as nightmare Scot sums up for many English chroniclers the worst aspects of Scotland – and who almost certainly never existed, but developed as an embodiment of repressed fears and prejudices. If it is now impossible to disentangle the origins of the legend of Sawney Bean, we can see that through time the Scots adopted him as one of their own pet hates, a symbol of what lay beyond the pale of religious orthodoxy. People see what they wish to see – and as Mairi MacArthur demonstrates, many people visited the 'Land o Cakes' seeking confirmation of their preconceptions, a quest in the fulfilment of which Scottish tourist agencies were only too happy to lend their assistance.

By the nineteenth century such folk-history – but with very different political and national motivations – can be seen to perpetuate itself in the folk-romances of James Hogg, especially in his defiant riposte to Scott's *Old Mortality* in *The Brownie of Bodsbeck* (1817), with its legendary view of Claverhouse as a destroying devil, and its hiding Covenanters seen throughout through folk-perception as mysterious Brownies, or elsewhere as in *The Three Perils of Man* (1822), with its totally anachronistic and unapologetically confused folk-view of Scottish-English Border history, which easily merges the historical and the supernatural. Even the arch-realist John Galt can be seen to enter the realms of folk-history and mythology with his version of Covenanting tradition in the grim account of the sufferings of the man ordained by Providence to kill Claverhouse, the eponymous representative of folk-suffering in *Ringan Gilhaize* (1823).

The discipline of History has been under attack for a couple of decades now by, among others, Hayden White, author of *Metahistory: The Historical Imagination in Nineteenth Century Europe* (1973) and several other books and articles in which he argues that paradigms for history, literature and science were developed in the nineteenth century but while science and literature have moved on, have evolved in new ways, history has not. Historians, he claims, in seeking to simplify the past, hopelessly distort it. To quote, 'Since the second half of the nineteenth century history has become increasingly the refuge of all those "sane" men (and he meant women as well) who excel at finding the simple in the complex and the familiar in the strange'.[14] Historians delude themselves into thinking that while they deal in facts, creative writers deal in fiction. According to White, historians employ the literary trope of Irony to shape the narrative structure of their works. In other words they know more than the people they describe and to whom they are thus superior. Scottish historians, we may think, stand guilty as charged; they have not progressed far from the Rankean school and the British empirical tradition and many of them to this day positively eschew the potential historical value of literary sources. Nonetheless, as we have tried to indicate above, the debate in Scotland has a lengthy pedigree. In the aftermath of the Scott phenomenon the German poet and essayist Heinrich Heine remarked:

> Strange whim of the people! They demand their history from the hand of the poet and not from the hand of the historian. They demand not a faithful report of the facts, but those facts dissolved back into the original poetry whence they came.[15]

Ironically Heine had long been anticipated by an anonymous commentator on *Old Mortality* (as yet unacknowledged by Scott), the descriptive passages of which showed that though the author 'has the imagination and feeling of a poet, he is deficient in the judgement and discriminating taste of the historian'.[16] The critic is known to have been Thomas McCrie, biographer of John Knox, a man much distressed by Scott's unsympathetic and disrespectful depiction of the Covenanters. As Stevenson observed in 'A Humble Remonstrance' (in *Memories and Portraits* (1897)), 'the art of narrative, in fact, is the same whether it is applied to the selection and illustration of a real series of events or of an imaginary series'. Henry James had written of the sanctity of truth, but in the opinion of Stevenson 'truth will seem a word of very debateable propriety, not only for the labours of the novelist but for those of the historian'. Here Stevenson seems to anticipate White's conclusion that, in the final analysis, history and creative literature share the same basic tropes and the same organising principles which manipulate their material to suit author and audience.

In the intellectual ferment of the Enlightenment thinkers of all kinds – creative writers, historians, philosophers, social scientists, economists and assorted theoreticians united in a common interest in 'manners'. David Hume the philosopher (well known in his own day as a servant of Clio), rejoiced that he lived in 'the historical age, and [that] we are the historical people'. His own *History of England to the Revolution of 1688* (1763) treated initially of the sixteenth and seventeenth centuries; he thereafter worked backwards to complete his history from the time of Julius Caesar. Despite the book's title, which was of course diagnostic – already in his view England equated with Britain – he did discuss Scottish history, but Hume's main concern was twofold, to investigate the nature of causation and to demonstrate the constancy of human nature. In this historical age Adam Smith reflected on the relationship between rhetoric and narrative, the former associated with persuasion and the latter with facts. 'The design of historical writing is not merely to entertain', he wrote.

> It sets before us the more interesting and important events of human life, points out the causes by which these events were brought about and by this means points out to us by what manner and method we may produce similar good effects or avoid Similar bad ones . . . In this it differs from a Romance the Sole view of which is to entertain, This being the end, it is of no consequence whether the incidents narrated be true or false.[17]

It did not seem to occur to Smith that in attempting to recreate the manners, institutions and beliefs of the past, historians and imaginative writers might be engaged upon a similar quest, namely the construction of a conjectural history, which as we suggested above, had been anticipated by their sixteenth-century predecessors.

The most influential Scottish historian of the century was William Robertson, principal of Edinburgh University and leader of the Moderate party in the kirk. He published his *History of Scotland* in 1759 and followed it with his *History of the Reign of Emperor Charles V* (1769), the *History of America* (1777) and *An Historical Disquisition ... of India* (1791). His *History of Scotland* treated the period of 1542–1603, with a Preface on the medieval period, and was received with rapturous applause. He observed that 'no period in the history of one's own country can be considered altogether uninteresting' – although Robertson then dismissed the first 900 years of Scottish history as 'pure fable and conjecture' which 'ought to be totally neglected or abandoned to the industry and credulity of antiquaries'. He also took a pretty dim view of much of the rest of Scotland's past which he saw as having been bedevilled by an over-weening aristocracy whose power was finally broken by the Union of 1707. Commerce defeated them, and at that point 'the people acquired liberty'. There was perhaps an inconsistency in Robertson's attitude, for he felt compelled to admit that Scotland's 'mountains and fens and rivers, set bounds to despotic power and amidst these, is the natural seat of freedom and independence'.[18] With this point of view, though very little else of what Robertson and Hume wrote, Gilbert Stuart agreed; he rejoiced that he lived 'in this enlightened age of philosophy and reflection' but he chose to seek his inspiration in a more distant Scottish past, in 'the democratical genius of the Scottish constitution' by which subjects could resist the tyranny of the monarch and 'making him a sacrifice to justice, and an instruction to posterity, conduct him from the throne to the scaffold'.[19] Yet Stuart, like most of his contemporaries, subscribed, above all, to the idea of progress.

Enlightenment historiography is complex,[20] but equally complex is the situation of creative literature during the eighteenth century. At least three individuals who were arguably the greatest Scottish writers of the period made their careers in the south – James Thomson, author of *The Seasons* and 'Rule Britannia', Tobias Smollett the novelist, and James Boswell, the memorialist of Samuel Johnson. Of those who remained at home Robert Fergusson was almost alone in explicitly condemning creeping Anglicization. Without doubt one of the major literary events of eighteenth-century Scotland was the publication of James Macpherson's *Fragments of Ancient Poetry* (1760) which seems to have confirmed Adam Smith's dictum that 'the Poets were the first Historians of any'. The debate about the relationship between history and literature which had rumbled on for centuries was greatly reinvigorated by Hugh Blair's *A Critical Dissertation on the Poems of Ossian* (1763/65), a hugely influential treatise which also fostered waves of Celtomania still crashing on the shores of the late twentieth century to deposit an apparently irresistible flotsam amd jetsam of bards, druids, heroes, clans, mysticism, scenery, lamentation and loss. It was this heritage which combined in abundance with that of the Enlightenment to produce the ambivalent genius of Sir Walter Scott.

Scott's contribution was immeasurable. He was deeply read in the literatures of Europe as well as Scotland and the British Isles, knew the ballads intimately, and had an acquaintance with the sagas. He was also a collector, a poet, a novelist and a historian. He strove to reconcile the dichotomous elements of his country's past while formulating his own idiosyncratic vision of Scotland's present and thus its future. He created some of the world's greatest historical novels, unashamedly quarrying his materials from Scottish experience – yet in his *Tales of a Grandfather* (1828) he distorted and trivialised his national history, stressing at every opportunity the barbarism and violence of Scotland and the Scots before they were rescued by the beneficent political union of 1707. This Tory Unionist, whose imagination was fixated on medievalism, nevertheless confronted crucial issues for modern Scotland, as in his *The Letters of Malachi Malagrowther* (1826), in which he fought successfully for the right of Scottish banks to issue their own bank-notes, as well as for the rights of Scotland generally. That said, there is no doubt that he helped in the creation of an anachronistic and alternative Scottish identity of bogus tartanism – and yet, as the great Marxist critic George Lukacs pointed out, he was the first writer to involve ordinary women and men in the historical process. His impact upon posterity world-wide was enormous. Even Leopold von Ranke whose 'scientific history' was to dominate and almost smother the subject for a century, not least in Scotland, claimed that it was the novels of Scott which first interested him in historical investigation. One of us has argued that Scott resolved personal and national problems of dissociation through a process of mythic regeneration worked out in successive novels[21]; the other deplores Scott's squandering of his enormous talents, thus perhaps further illustrating Cairns Craig's provocative discussion of 'The Fratricidal Twins' which opens this collection.

What, however, of Scottish fictional history? History is arguably psychology writ large, psychology the microcosm of history's macrocosm. Scott's 'new history' has been extensively examined. What does his – and William Robertson's – 'new history' principally amount to? It is surely that history must be understood as springing from comprehensible human motivations, rather than from incomprehensible human 'badness' or error. As scholars have shown, when David Hume dealt with the Covenanters in his *History of England,* he described them as though they were simply barbaric fanatics who raised civil war in the nation; they are to be denounced. He attempted little diagnosis of the deeper, and what later historians came to perceive as the understandable, motives of the Covenanters – and certainly with none of the understanding (*pace* McCrie) of their grievances which Scott shows in *Old Mortality*. Scott's Covenanters are made human and comprehensible, as are his Jacobites, or his Edinburgh rioters, and later, his Cavaliers and Roundheads, Crusaders and Saracens, Normans and Saxons. Thus, whatever one may deplore as his 'escape to Scotland', as Edwin Muir termed it, Scott in his fiction returned the relationship between psychology and history, handing down new ways of exploring people in history to innumerable novelists, from Flaubert and the Brontës and Thackeray and Eliot, to Fenimore Cooper and Henry James. And modern criticism is revaluing Scott, realising that much of his achievement lies in the juxtapositioning of fictional romance and historic realism, with realism ironically undercutting romance. Francis Hart in *The Scottish Novel* (1978) put forward the interesting view that, rather than treating historical periods separately, Scott imposed a recurrent pattern upon history, a pattern which emerged from his own polarised view of Scottish past versus present, with older social disorder against present attempts to assert social order. Such a dualistic and Coleridgean view of history as the opposition of two mighty principles, of conservatism and progression, may be argued with; but it is not to be dismissed as simplistic escapism or evasion, and it provides the dynamics and patterns of the school of Scottish fiction which follows, with Hogg's dualisms of *The Private Memoirs and Confessions of a Justified Sinner* (1824) and Galt's 'theoretical histories' such as *Annals of the Parish* (1821) and *The Provost* (1822), down to Stevenson's *The Master of Ballantrae* (1888), the neglected and embittered historical studies of the Highlands of Neil Munro, and the more localised and sardonic view of social change in Brown's *The House with the Green Shutters* (1901). Such fiction may disengage from overt discussion of Scotland's challenges in politics and history, as Craig and Gifford argue here; but it nevertheless puts forward an important diagnosis of destructive dualism in Scottish mind and psyche.

After the deaths of Scott, Hogg and Galt in the 1830s, Scottish literature and historiography alike entered a slough of despond. In 1834 John Carlyle wrote to his not-yet-famous brother, Thomas:

> I believe that a man possessed of any real Wisdom and Belief never had larger scope than in our times. There is poor Scotland lying in deepest darkness and Unbelief, fettered and festering. It were a most glorious office to instruct her in better things. There is more courage in Scotchmen – right Scotchmen – and more devotedness than anywhere else, but now they are without any to guide them. The humblest means of clearing up their darkness and instructing them in truth is desirable above all other things.[22]

Tom departed for Chelsea that same year whence he did his best to instruct his fellow countrymen in his own inimitable fashion, but no-one else took up the challenge. Much popular, and populist, literature and history was published but little of great note; otherwise for much of the nineteenth century interest was served by numerous reprints of Scott who still held sway when Robert Louis Stevenson tested his prentice pen in the 1860s and 70s. Stevenson's health drove him into exile as well. Ted Cowan explores the life-long tensions between history and literature which engrossed the author of *Kidnapped* and *Catriona* as he rescued Scottish literature from the worst excesses of the kailyard school. By the advent of the twentieth century Scott's mantle had descended to John Buchan, a public figure whose busy life did not preclude the publication of fiction and popular history which was seldom very thoroughly researched. Owen Dudley Edwards's chapter on the complex changes in John Buchan's view of himself in relation to his own and Scotland's history conceals its major points behind the guise of a tribute to the University of Glasgow. Buchan, after 'selling his birthright for English Establishment pottage', and abetting in Oxford's refusal to acknowledge his Glasgow achievements, went on as a 'recruit from the periphery' to create extremely subtle propaganda for England and Britain in the Great War – but in the latter part of his career fundamentally changed his loyalties, returning to mythic Scottish roots and taking his revenge on English historical supremacy. Edwards makes his most profound point regarding Buchan's, and the historical novelist's, main challenge. 'The historian's best hope must be that historical fiction will illuminate the parts of the past which formal history cannot reach. The historian should finish reading a successful piece of historical fiction feeling that it may well have been so . . .'. Thus Edwards pays the final compliment to successful historical fiction; it can work where history cannot, the creative imagination replacing absence.

The development of a new relationship with history in the work of the modern novelist is taken up by Kirsten Stirling and Joanna Tiitinen. Stirling explores the work of the great twentieth-century novelist Naomi Mitchison; working from the premise that all history is a construction, and that 'history is the manner in which the events of the past are narrated', and juxtaposing the different approaches to history-making of Agnes Mure Mackenzie and A. J. Youngson, together with contemporary theories of narration, she shows just how dependant both history and story are on teller, audience, and the organisation of material. And if Stirling's analysis of Mitchison's great post-war novel, *The Bull Calves* (1947) reveals the mutual dependency of history and story-telling, then Johanna Tiitinen's exploration of a contemporary text, Alasdair Gray's *A History Maker* (1994), goes even further in its conclusion that Gray's emphasis on the subjectivity of history is a positive strength. Taking issue with Fukiyama's notion of contemporary Western society as post-historical as argued in *The End of History and the Last Man*, she and Gray insist on a continuing, creative and dynamic notion of history which relishes the possibilities of divergent interpretation.

And divergent interpretation is just what Cairns Craig offers with his challenge to conventional and negative readings of the relationship between Scotland's history and Scotland's literary creativity. Defending the validity of Scott's romantic history as a significant exploration of the mythic patterns which underlie the supposed 'reality' of history, patterns 'which may be more fundamental than the socio-economic', Craig reverses the usual view which sees Enlightenment as cultural betrayal, and finds a holistic maturity regarding the real kinship of history and literature in Enlightenment historians, in Scott and his successors, and in nineteenth-century thinkers such as J.G. Frazer. While Gifford's description of withdrawal by creative writers from political engagement might seem to clash with this, it will upon reflection emerge that such withdrawal was not an evasion of serious analysis, criticism and parody of Scottish history and society, but contained within its very negativism a slow re-alignment of serious literature with Scottish realities, with the work of Alasdair Gray and other contemporaries marking a very positive return to the matter of Scotland.

If these essays share any common ground, it is in their recognition that both history (either as what actually happened or as how what happened is relayed to us) and the imaginative exploitation of it in fiction, drama, and poetry, matter and are of value.   While not pretending that history is simply story-telling, and while recognising that at one end of the spectrum lies the immensely important work of the recorder of events, and at the other end the more simple activity of diversionary and escapist entertainment, we can surely allow that, somewhere in the middle ground in which lie committed but unavoidably biased and didactic history, propaganda, and imaginative and emotional recreation of the past, the two human activities meet, not in fratricide, and not just as polar twins, but as interpreters of human experience. In this middle ground the twins work together with the past, the present and even the future, never achieving final truth, but equally trying to lend validity to the human experience.

Notes

1. Gregory Smith, *Scottish Literature: Character and Influence* (London 1919) 20.
2. *Tacitus on Britain and Germany* (trans.) H. Mattingly (Harmondsworth 1948) 80; *The Triumph Tree: Scotland's Earliest Poetry 550–1350* (ed.) Thomas Owen Clancy (Edinburgh 1998), 48. See also Kenneth H. Jackson *The Gododdin The Oldest Scottish Poem* (Edinburgh 1969) 56–7.
3. Thomas Owen Clancy and Gilbert Márkus, *Iona The Earliest Poetry of a Celtic Monastery* (Edinburgh 1995); Benjamin Hudson 'Historical Literature of Early Scotland' *Studies in Scottish Literature* 26 (1991) 141–55.
4. Information kindly communicated by Dauvit Broun whose discovery this is.
5. *John Barbour: The Bruce* (ed. and trans.) A.A.M. Duncan (Edinburgh 1997) 47.
6. Andrew of Wyntoun, *The Orygynale Cronykil of Scotland* (ed.) David Laing 3 vols. (Edinburgh 1872) i, 3–6.
7. *Scotichronicon, by Walter Bower* (ed.) D.E.R. Watt 9 vols (Aberdeen and Edinburgh 1987–98) ix 7–9, 17.
8. *Harry's Wallace*, (ed.) M.P. McDiarmid 2 vols. *Scottish Text Society* (Edinburgh 1968–9) i, vi.
9. Edward J. Cowan, 'The Wallace Factor in Scottish History' in *Images of Scotland* (eds.) Robin Jackson and Sydney Wood *The Journal of Scottish Education: Occasional Paper, Number One* (Dundee 1997) 5–17.
10. John Leslie, Bishop of Ross, *The Historie of Scotland* 2 vols. Scottish Text Society (Edinburgh 1888) i, 40–41.
11. See Edward J. Cowan, 'The Discovery of the Gaidhealtachd in Sixteenth Century Scotland' *Transactions of the Gaelic Society of Inverness* (1999) forthcoming.
12. 'The Book of Clanranald', in *Reliquiae Celticae Texts, Papers, and Studies in Gaelic Literature and Philology left by the late Rev. Alexander Cameron Ll.D.* (eds.) Alexander MacBain and John Kennedy 2 vols (Inverness 1894) ii 203.
13. Derick Thomson, *An Introduction to Gaelic Poetry* (London 1974) 11.
14. Hayden White, *Tropics of Discourse: Essays in Cultural Criticism* (Baltimore 1978) 50. For a useful discussion see Lloyd S. Kramer 'Literature, Criticism, and Historical Imagination: The Literary Challenge of Hayden White and Dominick LaCapra' in *The New Cultural History* (ed.) Lynn Hunt (Berkeley 1989) 97–128.
15. Quoted George Lukacs, *The Historical Novel* (Harmondsworth 1969) 61–2.
16. *A Vindication of the Scottish Covenanters* (Glasgow 1824) 22.

17. See the useful section on Historiography in *The Scottish Enlightenment: An Anthology* (ed.) Alexander Broadie (Edinburgh 1997) 649–82.
18. William Robertson, *The History of Scotland* 3 vols. (London 1759) iii 186, i 222–3.
19. Gilbert Stuart, *The History of the Establishment of the Reformation of Religion in Scotland* (London 1780) 278, 199.
20. For discussion see Colin Kidd, *Subverting Scotland's Past* (Cambridge 1993) and David Allan, *Virtue, Learning and the Scottish Enlightenment Ideas of Scholarship in Early Modern History* (Edinburgh 1993).
21. Douglas Gifford, 'Scott's fiction and the Search for Mythic Regeneration', in *Scott and his Influence* (eds.) J.H. Alexander and David Hewitt (Aberdeen 1983) 180–9, and 'Myth, Parody and Dissociation; Scottish Fiction 1814–1914' in *The History of Scottish Literature* vol. 3 *Nineteenth Century* (ed.) Douglas Gifford (Aberdeen 1988) 217–59.
22. Edward J. Cowan, 'Icelandic Studies in Eighteenth and Nineteenth Century Scotland' *Studia Islandica* 31 (1972) 126.

2

The Fratricidal Twins: Scottish Literature, Scottish History and the Construction of Scottish Culture

Cairns Craig

There is a moment in Scottish cultural experience when Scottish history and Scottish literature are deeply and creatively interwoven: it is, of course, the moment when Sir Walter Scott, building on the work of the Enlightenment historians, invents the 'historical novel'. Scott's achievement was the culmination of the exploration of the relationship between narrative and history that had been conducted by the Scottish Enlightenment writers throughout the second half of the eighteenth century. Those Enlightenment historians had seen themselves as 'men of letters', contributing to a literary culture, while their successors, the novelists, saw themselves as 'conjectural historians', filling out through the imagination the lacunae of our knowable past. If the development of narrative history was in part a response to the rise of the novel, its techniques were in turn to shape the possibilities of historical narration by the novelists. Rarely can an interchange between disciplines have been so productive of new forms of understanding and a new understanding of the potentialities of form: the historical narratives of Hume, Robertson and Smollett flow into the narrative exploration of history in the work of Scott, Galt and Hogg, an influence that can still be discerned in the work of Stevenson, Gibbon and Gunn. Narrative history and the historical novel are two of the towering achievements of the Scottish Enlightenment and its aftermath, each benefiting from the terrain for imaginative reconstruction of the past opened up by 'philosophical' and 'conjectural' history and by the stadialist conception of social progress, and together they were to precipitate the engagement with national histories that was fundamentally to shape not only nineteenth century literature from Balzac to Tolstoy, but also the construction of new national identities across the world.

Despite the enormous influence of Scottish conceptions of history and its literary portrayal throughout Europe and North America, the interplay of history and fiction was to have, according to many later analysts, only destructive consequences within Scottish culture itself: Marinell Ash points to this problematic outcome when she identifies the influence of Scott in Scotland as being entirely different from his influence in Europe:

> Why, given the immense influence of Scott on historical scholarship in nineteenth century Europe, did Scottish history go so badly off the rails in the second half of the nineteenth century? The answer lies in Scotland itself. Many historians have remarked on the change in the middle decades of the nineteenth century from a distinctively Scottish society to one (or several) societies with a British or even imperial orientation. Yet the time that Scotland was ceasing to be distinctively and confidently herself was also the period when there grew an increasing emphasis on the emotional trappings of the Scottish past. This is a further paradox and its symbols are Bonnie Scotland of the bens and glens and misty shieling, the Jacobites, Mary Queen of Scots, tartan mania and the raising of historical statuary.
>
> What occurred was an historical failure of nerve.[1]

'The emotional trappings of the Scottish past' are substituted for real Scottish history, and the reality of the Scottish past is undermined by its fictional representation by generations of Scottish novelists. Scottish fiction narrates Scottish history only to neutralise it, both as a discipline and as an effective part of Scottish cultural life.

Allan Massie provides a similar version of the relationship between history and literature from a novelist's perspective when he writes of nineteenth-century Scottish novelists that, it is clear that [they] either only found themselves competent to deal with scenes of rural life or were attracted to Romance as it appeared in a more glamorous Past. It is not . . . unfair to see this as a failure of both nerve and imagination . . . And this posed a real problem which nobody in Scotland has answered satisfactorily. How do you write about a second-hand society?[2]

Scotland is a 'second-hand society' precisely because of the confusion between the real world that Scots live in and the romantic glamour with which the Scottish past is invested and with which Scotland itself has come to be identified. The reality of Scotland, past and present, has been made invisible because of the dominance of novelistic 'romance', concealing the real history of the nation. Far from providing a fulfilment of the work of the historians, the nineteenth-century Scottish novelists are seen as infusing Scotland's history with literary genres that substitute romantic or comic evasion for effective and realistic understanding.

In twentieth-century Ireland W.B. Yeats could invoke his own literary creations as playing an integral part in the heroic struggles of modern Irish history –

> When Pearse summoned Cuchulain to his side,
> What stalked through the Post Office? What intellect,
> What calculation, number, measurement, replied?
> We Irish, born into that ancient sect
> But thrown upon this filthy modern tide,
> And by its formless spawning fury wrecked,
> Climb to our proper dark, that we may trace
> The lineaments of a plummet-measured face.[3]

– and could present himself as the bard of a nation with a historic mission to challenge the nature of modernity. Irish literary invention and Irish national self-definition could be seen to stand together in the moment of the 1916 Rebellion. In Scotland, far from the Scottish past being the medium through which the nation could rediscover and remake its identity, Scottish history had ceased, in the view of the nation's most significant writers, to have anything but destructive implications: a warped and distorted history had failed to sustain a literature adequate to the requirements of a full national identity and, as a consequence, literature had failed to come to grips with the realities of the nation's history. It is a conflict which travels in both directions: history is perverted by becoming infused with literary elements which distort the reality of the past, while at the same time literature is distorted by becoming entirely obsessed with a 'historical' Scotland at the expense of the presentation of its modern reality. Scotland as a whole becomes subject to the perversion which Peter Womack analyses in relation to the Highlands:

> The Highlands, then, are imaginary. It follows that the non-Highlands (the Scottish Lowlands, or the metropolis, or anglophone Britain generally) are real. The consumer of the myth partakes of 'the pleasing enthusiasm which these wilds impart' and then quits them 'with regret': to move back across the Highland line is to leave Fancy's Land and re-enter, sadly or thankfully, but in either case inevitably, the realm of factual truth.[4]

Scottish history becomes, on one side, 'Fancy's Land', disengaged from reality, or, alternatively, it is seen as being so appalling and so resistant to the imagination that it cannot help but undermine every effort of the artist to come to terms with it. Edwin Muir spoke for generations of analysts of the relationship between Scottish history and Scottish literature when he envisaged Scotland's history as a destructive wasteland, negating the powers and purposes of literature:

> ... Knox and Melville clapped their preaching palms
> And bundled all the harvesters away,
> Hoodicrow Peden in the blighted corn
> Hacked with his rusty beak the starving haulms.
> Out of that desolation we were born.

The 'desolation' out of which the modern writer must create is the product of a self-destructive history, but precisely because the history has been so destructive no sustained or effective literary creation is possible: writers can engage only with an alternative and illusory past for the nation, and a fake nation is substituted for a real one:

> Now smoke and dearth and money everywhere,
> Mean heirlooms of each fainter generation,
> And mummied housegods in their musty niches,
> Burns and Scott, sham bards of a sham nation.[5]

A 'sham' nation narrated by 'sham' authors is the only outcome of the conflict between the fratricidal twins of Scottish history and Scottish literature.

II

Muir's dispirited view of Scotland was, of course, part of the general 'modernist' despair over the nature of contemporary society and the perversion of values that had been brought about by industrialisation, but the underlying structure of the conception of Scottish history which Muir presents has continued to play a crucial role in constituting the narrative of the Scottish nation – not simply in the mythologies of the poets and artists, but in the work of the historians as well. The structural elements of this vision are two linked conceptions which derive from the analysis of what went wrong with Scottish culture after Scott and which are related to the mutually destructive interaction of history and literature. The first is that Scottish history is characterised by a series of disruptions that absolutely break all sense of continuity with the past and make it incapable of construction into a coherent narrative: Scots are born not out of a rich inheritance but out of a desolation in which each new era destroys the 'harvest' of the past. The second is that Scottish history – whether in terms of the actual course of events or in terms of the discipline of history as the narration of those events – is a false version of a true Scottish history which never managed to make itself manifest. Such tropes are pervasive in those analyses of Scottish culture from the 1960s to the 1980s which focused relentlessly on that multitude of illusory discourses – tartanry, highlandism, kailyard, Clydesidism – by which a real Scotland had been betrayed by a combination of unrealised history and literary falsification.

The opening, for instance, of Bruce Lenman's *Integration, Enlightenment and Industrialization* turns even one of the most cataclysmic moments of Scottish history, the last civil war and battle fought on British soil, into no more than the afterecho of a finality already completed, a conflict become irrelevant to the established identity of the country:

> The defeat of the Jacobite army commanded by Prince Charles Edward Stewart at the battle of Culloden, fought a few miles to the west [*recte* east] of Inverness in April 1746, finally laid to rest an issue in Scottish politics which most Scotsmen as late as 1744 assumed had been settled 30 years previously.[6]

The whole Jacobite Rebellion becomes, quite simply, the belated re-enactment of a conclusion already reached, part of a past already wiped out and made irrelevant to the present. Jacobitism is not a politics to be rejected on principle or to be seen as a serious influence on Scottish culture: it is dismissed as without significance to a present that has established a new agenda and a new set of values. Already redundant in the moment of its occurrence it has nothing to link it to the future. The same elision of the past is also prepared for by the book's conclusion: 'By 1832 Scotland was poised on the verge of momentous changes in her economic life', we are told, changes which would be shaped by the 'harsh impersonality of a market society, shaped by class relationships' (p.164). In this case, however, it is not that one form of society will utterly supplant another, it is that the harsh world will be made bearable by aesthetic conceptions of Scotland which conceal and make invisible its industrial reality. If the structure of Scottish history has previously been one in which the past is continually obliterated, then in the era of modernity the arts of Scotland would enact an equivalent negation, obliterating the real, contemporary Scotland in favour of Scotland as a non-industrial 'land of mountain and of flood': 'Like Scott's evocation of a safely-dead pre-Union Scotland, this vision was ultimately less a tourist lure than an emotional salve for North Britons uneasily conscious of also being Scots' (p. 167). 'Scotland' as an identity is nothing more than an escape hatch through which people living in Scotland flee from the appalling and unacceptable nature of the environment in which they have to live into false histories which are irrelevant to modern circumstances.

For Lenman, as for many others, the Scottish Enlightenment represents the most important achievement of Scotland as a cultural formation only to the extent that it undermines and negates the nature of Scottishness. The Enlightenment intellectuals of the eighteenth century are internationally successful figures precisely to the extent that they cast in doubt their roots in Scottish culture, precisely to the extent that their work denies – indeed destroys – the last vestiges of an authentically Scottish culture. The romantic efflorescence of Scotland in the nineteenth century is then nothing more than the 'emotional salve' of a people who no longer have any connection with a past which they can identify with and which gives them their identity as Scots. A similar structure dominates one of the most influential post-war analyses of Scottish culture, David Craig's *Scottish Literature and the Scottish People*. In Craig's presentation, Scottish experience is a slow dissolution of a real and unified culture, each achievement of Enlightenment Scotland being no more than a stepping stone towards the destruction of any authentic Scottish culture. For Craig, Scottish culture is 'doomed' to failure by history, geography, by ideology – producing a desert where once there had been a fertile landscape: 'After the decline of the Edinburgh of the *Review* and of Scott, Scotland does not again have a resident literary class who can be taken as representing the best mind of their society'.[7] As he put it in an essay on Burns in Hugh MacDiarmid's *The Voice of Scotland*:

> In a culture so thin and so badly placed as the Scottish there were few conflicts in society that did not lead to waste and confusion. Much of the national spirit, often in rabid form, went into the Low Kirk religion, but its spirit – utterly uncompromising and literally exact resistance to worldliness and worldly power – was irreconcilable with the cultivated ethos. . . By 'grace' a man's religious belief was justified by his own consciousness of God-given salvation and inspiration – and the right of the community to apply it for themselves in judging who should be their minister, constituted the main issue over which the religious life of contemporary Scotland was divided: it led directly to the Disruption of 1843. This is another of the deep dis-unities which ran off the energies of 18th century Scotland into dispute and partisan bitterness, in a way characteristic of the race, which made a stultifying monotony of idiom, religious, political, poetic – an inhumane extreme of partiality, in which positions defined themselves more by violence of opposition than by their positive natures.[8]

Scotland's culture is a 'waste', a 'confusion': the elements of that culture are irrelevant to modern definitions of culture because of their 'rabid form' and incapable of producing anything cultivated because of the 'partisan bitterness' that is 'characteristic of the race'. The narrative of Scottish culture can only be the narrative of the gradual dissolution of a real culture into a false one: we live in the aftermath of the doom which fell upon an authentic but now lost Scottish culture.

The impact of this conception of Scotland is manifest in the work of the historian who has probably had the greatest popular influence on modern perceptions of Scotland, T.C. Smout, for his two studies of Scottish history, *A History of the Scottish People 1560–1830* and *A Century of the Scottish People*, enact between them a paradigmatic version of these constructions of the Scottish past. The first volume rises towards a culmination in 'The Golden Age of Scottish Culture', which recounts the take-off of industrialisation and an early entry into the world of potential plenty which it promises, while the second volume tells of the failure of Scotland to benefit from the consequences of that industrialisation, producing the iron age of Victorian poverty and misery to which 'culture' is almost irrelevant. Smout's first volume concludes with the question, 'How can we account for the unprecedented cultural achievements of the Scots in the century after 1740?',[9] as though Scotland's achievement of any kind of cultural success is a miracle incapable of rational explanation; while the second begins,

> The age of great industrial triumphs was an age of appalling deprivation ... I am astounded by the tolerance, in a country boasting of its high moral standards and basking in the spiritual leadership of a Thomas Chalmers, of unspeakable urban squalor, compounded of drink abuse, bad housing, low wages, long hours and sham education.[10]

The rhetoric of Smout's presentation sets the two epochs against one another, as though these two 'ages' of Scotland's experience were not joined together across the impositions of the historian's divisions, as though no one had lived from one epoch into the other and as though the second had utterly erased all traces of the first, leaving modern Scotland totally detached from the achievements of its 'golden age'. The word 'sham' points to the roots of this view in Muir's poetry, and the way in which, for Smout, industrial Scotland disowns and erases Enlightenment Scotland replicates the paradigm that Muir provided for such versions of Scottish culture in his account of John Knox, whose life becomes for Muir a synecdoche of the culture which he 'fathered':

> The life of John Knox is broken in two. For the first forty years we can vaguely discern a devout Catholic; for the next twenty-seven we see another character, with the same name, the same appearance, and probably the same affections and passions, but with entirely different opinions. This new figure is born at the age of forty, and seems to have no ancestry. For Knox left no record either of his early life or of his conversion: the one is like an absolute event which had existed from eternity, the other is as if it had never been.[11]

Scotland is a country always erasing itself, turning its past into falsehood, or falsifying its present by disconnecting it from its past. Scotland, like Knox, is a self-negating nation, one whose history moves by a series of obliterations of its previous existence and therefore in denial of the very premises of history, which assumes a continuing object called Scotland to be narrated. Undiscerned by history and unrealised by literature, the reality of Scotland, past and present, remains invisible to both.

The same motifs appear forcefully in the second edition of Chris Harvie's *Scotland and Nationalism*, in an autobiographical section in which Harvie seeks to see Scotland through the synecdoche of his home town of Motherwell. This is a place where, in the title of one of his chapters, 'nothing abides' and from which the Scots journey to 'no sure land' – and once again Edwin Muir is the ghost haunting the present:

> In 1936 a visit to Motherwell decided Edwin Muir to write his *Scottish Journey*. The sprawling, silent, steel-manufacturing town seemed to him to exemplify, in its total subordination of community to material development, the fatal impact of industrialisation on Scotland. With the slump it had ceased both to work and to exist as a community . . .
>
> Nine years later Motherwell gave the SNP its first election victory, and fifty-seven years later it remains a paradigm of the Scottish predicament. Few of the houses of 1936 still stand. New housing schemes and multi-storey blocks, a new civic centre, a new station have opened. The Clyde valley is now a huge recreation park . . . A town has been created which Muir would hardly recognise, a town which is strange to me, and I was born and brought up in it between 1944 and 1949.[12]

The Scottish predicament is not simply the lack of jobs or the residue of a harsh industrial world: it is the total elision of the past and its replacement by a novelty that radically dislocates the present, depriving the individual of the essential foundations of personal identity in a continuous cultural narrative. The destruction of personal identity in turn makes it impossible for there to be a shared national identity:

> What is true for Motherwell applies to the other settlements of the Scottish central belt, from the former colliery villages of Ayrshire to the textile towns of Strathmore. A combination of policies to attract work to areas of unemployment and to disperse the congested population of the Glasgow conurbation has created a new Scotland, neither urban nor rural, which straggles westwards from the fringes of the Firth of Forth to the lower Clyde. It is this unknown Scotland, not in the guidebooks, away from the motorway, seen fleetingly from the express, that holds the key to the modern politics of the country.[13]

A 'new' Scotland, an 'unknown' Scotland: not a culture travelling somewhere but one travelled through, by-passed, defining itself not in terms of a potential future but by a grim reluctance to enter the modern world of political and social rationality: 'Battered by economic decline and the ineptitude of their own representatives, the people of the tower blocks and the bleak estates – the Scotland that no one ever visited – responded to the old loyalties and the old songs. Fletcher's prophecy – that ballads and not laws made a nation – seemed to be coming true.'[14] The Scots are either erased by the changes in their environment, or lurk in ancient loyalties resistant to the processes of history: they are negated by change or endure in a primitive hostility impervious to any kind of transformation.

Scottish culture has, of course, always lived under the shadow of its possible annihilation. Scott, charged so often with being responsible for Scotland's loss of its real identity, was also deeply conscious of the threat of cultural extinction, a fear recorded, most famously, by Lockhart in his biography of Sir Walter, who is described as having

> walked across the Mound, on his way to Castle Street, between Mr Jeffrey and another of his reforming friends, who complimented him on the rhetorical powers he had been displaying, and would willingly have treated the subject-matter of his discussion playfully. But his feelings had been moved to such an extent far beyond their apprehension: he exclaimed, 'No, no – 'tis no laughing matter; little by little, whatever your wishes may be, you will destroy and undermine, until nothing of what makes Scotland Scotland shall remain.' [15]

Fear of cultural extinction is something which can be resisted: to be living in the aftermath of cultural extinction is to be trapped in impotence. The threat of discovering that we have moved from a possible future extinction to an actual extinction ran through the rhetoric of Scottish political culture in the 1980s in the form of the 'doomsday scenario' – the continued victory of Thatcherite policies in defiance of the democratic wishes of the Scottish people. The consequence was an anticipated apocalyptic end to Scottish cultural distinctiveness: '. . . there is a danger that Scotland's national character and characteristics become lost . . . a danger of becoming simply "Region 11" (or whatever the furthest from London is being called)'.[16] And if the series of electoral and referendum defeats from 1979 to 1992 were not enough to bring about this apocalypse, cultural 'entryism' by people from England would achieve the same effect of wiping out all connection with the Scottish past: 'the more general danger is that Scotland's political culture – our hostility to Thatcherism, and our scepticism regarding the activities of powerful establishments – could be diluted by influxes of those whose lived experience gives them little reason to oppose the status quo . . . people for whom the 1979 referendum has no meaning, for whom pieces of history like the Clearances and the Highland land question have no relevance, for whom the hardships of industrial society (past and present) strike few chords'.[17] The threat was sufficient that when the next general election was due in the early 1990s, *Radical Scotland* could announce it as Doomsday II, a disaster with as many sequels as any Hollywood blockbuster. In the 1980s the 'doomsday' scenario recapitulates the analysis of Scottish culture as a history is undone by literature, a literature unsupported by history that had been the burden of Anthony Ross's analysis in 1971 in *Scottish International* – the most prestigious Scottish journal of its era:

> Scotland is sick and unwilling to admit it. The Scottish establishment at least will not admit it. The tartan sentimentality, the charades at Holyroodhouse, the legends of Bruce and Wallace, Covenanters, Jacobites, John Knox and Mary Stuart, contribute nothing towards a solution. Small wonder that so many of the ablest people she produces emigrate rather than face the struggle of living here in the fog of romantic nostalgia for a world that never existed, and lies and half-truths about the world that does exist.[18]

Decade by decade the pervasive trope of Scottish culture remains the same: overwhelmed by its fictional versions, the real Scotland has disappeared and become invisible to modern eyes. Sick, warped and deceitful: not a national culture but a shame of sham.

III

So deep-rooted has this model of Scottish culture become that it defines the very questions which are asked of the Scottish past and therefore determines the valuations that are made of it. The most recent application of this model is in Colin Kidd's *Subverting Scotland's Past: Scottish Whig Historians and the Creation of an Anglo-British Identity, 1689 – c.1830*. For Kidd, Scottish history, both as social process and as discipline, is defined – as always within this structure – by something which failed to happen, since the 'ready acceptance of English ideals in Scottish political culture is almost certainly connected to an ideological non-occurrence in Scotland's modern history'.[19] This non-occurrence is the fact that Scotland 'missed out on the development of a full-blown "romantic" nationalism' (p.1) despite the fact that 'the Scottish whigs in 1689 possessed all the ideological ingredients out of which European intellectuals a century and a half later were to create nationalist movements' (p.28). The failure to develop a romantic nationalism Kidd ascribes to a complex series of deconstructions of the traditions by which the Scottish past had been defined: the country had 'a defiantly ethnocentric tradition of political discourse in which, for

Scottish whigs, national independence and domestic constitutional freedom from tyrannical kings were closely identified' (p.28–9). This tradition, however, is undone in the course of the eighteenth century by the undermining of three of its fundamental elements: first, the ancient origins of the Scottish monarchy, as described in Fordun's chronicle, and on which rested Scotland's claims to ancient independence from the English crown, were revealed to be mythic; second, Buchanan's definition of the nature of kingship and the rights of the people to regicide if tyrannised, became increasingly embarrassing in the context of a more settled political culture; and third, the Scottish Whig historians identified the traditions of English constitutionalism as the ones which had helped develop both economic and political freedom. The consequence was that Scottish intellectuals became increasingly 'conscious of the historic failures from which they had been rescued by incorporating Union' (p.98) and conscious, therefore, of the extent to which 'Scottish history pre-1707 could not explain the present; the long sweep of English history could' (p.206). The Scottish past 'as a repository of political and institutional value remained empty' (p.215), and no matter how 'vivid and distinct', it was 'denuded of ideological significance' (p.210). That Muir's conception of Scottish culture haunts this argument is revealed by the return of the word 'sham' at the moment when the Scottish traditions of kingship are finally overthrown: 'although the Fergusian ideology proved to have remarkable staying power, Innes ultimately succeeded both in ruling out of bounds the principal theatre of conflict, and in exposing a vital dimension of national identity as a sham' (p.107). And what this leaves behind is a culture which could only offer 'a sterile historiography of local colour and romance' (p.210), an insignificant past which could not be overcome even by 'the "tory" mythmaking of Sir Walter Scott' (p.247).

Kidd's argument begins from the exceptional 'non-occurrence' of romantic nationalism in the nineteenth century and explains it in terms of the self-subversion of Scottish history by Scottish intellectuals in the eighteenth century. And yet, what country provided more stimulus to romantic nationalism than Scotland did, from Macpherson's 'Ossian' to Scott's novels? What country was more associated in the European mind with romanticism than Scotland was – from its Highland landscape to the songs of Robert Burns? What is 'missing' in Scotland is not the tokens of romantic national culture but a nationalist politics, and that nationalist politics was unnecessary because of Scotland's role within the British empire. As Graeme Morton has argued,

> it is invalid to judge Scotland in terms of a nation-state to be, because it was an issue that had little relevance. The nature of the Victorian state was not a

centralised one. It was anathema to contemporary thought to campaign for a Westminster-style Scottish state (that is, centralisation). Scottish nationalism, Scottish cultural sub-nationalism and Scottish culture, if they can be separated at all in the nineteenth century, must be understood in terms of a bourgeoisie that had all the power it needed to govern its own society . . . . Scottish nationalism and politics could be satisfactorily combined by the Scottish bourgeoisie at the local level.[20]

Remove the 'non-occurrence' as something exceptional and to be explained and what one can see is something very different from the 'subversion' of Scotland's past: Scottish culture was relentless, as Kidd demonstrates, in its search for both the historical 'truth' of its own past and for the principles which governed the development of 'progressive' history. Those principles it found exemplified in England's history rather than in Scottish history because England represented the most advanced economic nation, just as the Lowlands of Scotland were regularly presented as 'progressive' in comparison with the Highlands. Those same Scottish Whig intellectuals were, however, no less relentless in subverting the 'myths' of English culture and insisting, as Hume did, that English 'liberty' had more to do with luck and accident than it had to do with a providential destiny, and could be lost as easily as it had been found. Far from being 'subverters' of Scotland's past, those Scottish whig intellectuals were 'subverters' of *all* pasts based on fanaticism and enthusiasm rather than on moderation and reason. Far from being focused on destroying the Scottish past, they sought a universalist explanation for historical progress to which Scotland could not but be marginal – except, of course, in themselves and in their own contribution to the history of Europe. Part of the driving force of their intellectual endeavour was precisely that they could not substitute a 'national' truth for a universal one, could not – like the intellectuals of major cultures – read their own nation's particularity as 'representative' of all nations: their subversion is not an act of national betrayal but an attempt to locate Scottish history within a universal system and to learn the lessons of that system for how history can be ordered and controlled towards the betterment of humanity. If, for a time, England provides the model for such betterment that does not mean that at some future time the model might not be France, or the United States or the Soviet Union: what is at stake is not the meaning of national histories but the meaning of history-in-general, and how nations can guide themselves in relation to it.

If Kidd's argument has a characteristic false beginning in its search for a non-occurrence whose lack is irrelevant to the real history of Scotland, it has a characteristic conclusion in the way that it effectively severs the Scottish past from the Scottish present. The Scottish Enlightenment thinkers are dramatised as subverting Scotland's past rather than being themselves the culmination of it: Scotland's history and the value of its culture, in other words, are not allowed to be represented by the achievements of those who debated its past, only by the past which they debated. Scotland thus comes to be defined by a certain 'past' – one which has been shown to be false – while the continuation of what was Scotland is incorporated into something that is no longer identifiable as Scottish, in this case 'Anglo-British identity'. A sham Scotland haunts a Scotland which has become infused with an identity that makes it no longer Scottish. 'Anglo-British identity', however, is something produced in Scotland, by Scots: it becomes one of the defining elements of Scottishness, since it is not something which is subscribed to in the same way by English intellectuals. To call it 'Anglo-British' is to make it seem as though Scottishness has been wiped out by the importation of an English identity: but it is precisely the construction of a Scoto-British identity that Kidd is tracing, one which, in its foregrounding of the value of English history, nonetheless relates to that English history, and to the Britishness which emerges from it, quite differently from how English intellectuals would relate to their own history, and constructs 'myths' of English culture which English people may subscribe to, but cannot be subscribed to in exactly the same way by Scots. For Kidd, however, the 'dissolution of Scottish historical confidence' (p.7) is prelude to 'the emergence of a culture in which the national past was usable only as part of a sentimental or reactionary politics of nostalgia' (p.79) and in which real history will give way to the 'mythmaking of Sir Walter Scott' (p.247), rather than prelude to the construction of a confident Scoto-British identity which Scotland will impose on its more powerful neighbour as the cultural requirement of its political subservience. To treat 'Anglo-British' culture as something alien to the nature of Scottishness and Scottish cultural history is to draw a boundary round Scottish culture which necessarily deprives it of its most vigorous and creative element in the period of imperial expansion. It is precisely through its interaction with English culture that Scotland is defined in the nineteenth century: the effort to locate some kind of fundamental and purely Scottish culture simply ignores the very terms on which 'culture' was being constructed and, as David Morse discovered when he tried to define 'Englishness' in the Victorian period, ignores the extent to which exactly the same issues afflict any attempt to describe 'Anglo-British' culture in an English context:

> It was Hume and Mackintosh who laid the foundations for a modern history of England. It was Adam Smith who elaborated an economic theory that could serve as a framework for England's destiny as a trading nation. It was James

Mill who in his classic *History of British India* (1818) mapped out Britain's failure as an imperial power and legislator for mankind. It was Sir Walter Scott who in *Ivanhoe* produced the definitive myth of a proud Saxon race indomitably struggling against the Norman yoke. It was Thomas Carlyle who extended and developed this into a philosophy of the English character and critique of industrialisation, and while Macaulay, who was perhaps the one single writer to produce a view of England that was more influential than Carlyle's, was not himself Scottish, but was deeply influenced by the ideals of the Scottish Enlightenment, the foremost protégé of Francis Jeffrey at the *Edinburgh Review* from 1839 to 1847, and from 1852 to 1856 MP for Edinburgh itself.[21]

In Scotland, the works of these figures might be constructed as 'Anglo-British'; in England they could equally be constructed as 'Scoto-British', and a whole tradition of nationally-based analyses of English culture from F.R. Leavis to Roger Scruton has regularly sought to exclude precisely these Scoto-British writers from any account of what constitutes English culture.[22] In both cases, the real nature of the complex interactions of Scottish and English cultures in a post-Union environment are being contrasted with a supposedly 'pure' national culture which did not exist, *could* not exist and cannot be used as a yardstick for judging either culture's success or failure. Kidd's 'non-occurrence' was the absence of a Scottish culture separate and self-sustaining, precisely because no such Scottish culture would have been possible in the period, and the model of such a culture is an irrelevance to our understanding of what actually did happen.

Inevitably, the issues of Scotland's identity in the nineteenth century go back to Sir Walter Scott. It is significant that the recuperation of Scott's reputation as a novelist was founded not on the work of a Scottish critic but on that of a European Marxist – Georg Lukacs – and in a reading of Scott's works that emphasises their fundamentally 'realist' mode. Against the local insistence on Scott's 'mythmaking', Lukacs presented Scott as the first novelist to engage with the real dynamics of history, with those forces which would later be understood fully only from within a marxist perspective. Scott's 'realism' is founded, for Lukacs, on his awareness, despite his own politics, of the economic forces which shape cultures and generate historical change:

> Scott portrays the great transformations of history as transformations of popular life. He always starts by showing how important historical changes affect everyday life, the effect of material and psychological changes upon people who react immediately and violently to them, without understanding their causes . . . Like every great popular writer, Scott aims at portraying the totality of national life in its complex interaction between 'above' and 'below'; his vigorous popular character is expressed in the fact that 'below' is seen as the material basis and artistic explanation for what happens 'above'.[23]

Lukacs's reading of Scott reasserted Scott's place not as the creator of evasive national myths but as the fulfilment of the Scottish Enlightenment understanding of the material bases of history and as a prefiguror of Marx: Scott, for Lukacs, is the real foundation of the European novel in the nineteenth century because he reveals the 'real foundations' of the history in the material circumstances of the mass of the people: 'Scott, by disclosing the actual conditions of life, the actual growing crisis in people's lives, depicts all the problems of popular life which lead up to the historical crisis he has represented' (p.39). And Scott's version of history, far from being the evasion of real history that is implied by Kidd, is seen by Lukacs as prefiguring the disenchanted terror of Benjamin's 'Angel of History': 'Scott sees the endless field of ruin, wrecked existences, wrecked or wasted heroic human endeavour, broken social formations etc. which are the necessary preconditions of the end-result' (pp.58–9).

That Scott the realist, as opposed to Scott the romantic mythmaker, could only be seen from a European marxist perspective, is symptomatic of how limited has been – and in many cases still is – the view of Scott from a Scottish context. Far from a betrayal of Scottish history, from a Lukacsian perspective Scott's use of Scottish history ennobles it as the base from which the universal principles of the historical process can be discerned. Scott's novelistic presentation of history parallels Hegel's philosophy and prefigures Marx: a more profound engagement with history, more profoundly rooted in the presentation of Scottish history, could not be imagined. To regard this as the failed outcome of Scotland's engagement with the processes of history in the eighteenth century is the real subversion of Scotland's past, a subversion which negates the enormous significance of Scottish culture's effort to understand the very foundations of the historical process in and through Scottish history, and by comparing that history with the history of other cultures. If Scotland's particular history is 'placed' as a minor statement of the major processes of history-in-general it is nonetheless a statement without which the universal principles could not have been discerned: the real history of Scotland which is not subverted by those eighteenth century Scottish Whig theorists is the enormous contribution that they, and Scotland, made to the understanding of history, an understanding which could not but acknowledge its own minor role in the historical process – except, of course, as the very source from which all history was to be understood.

IV

The issue of what happened to Scottish history and Scottish literature in the nineteenth century remains and, however significant the Scottish contribution to the understanding of history has been, it is still arguable that the outcome made the Scottish past unusable and irrelevant to the modern world, even to modern Scotland. Scott, it might be argued, could only be read as a 'realist' by ignoring the extent to which his work opens the way to those romantic falsifications of the Scottish past which are symptomatic of a culture no longer in touch with its present reality.[24] To understand this dimension of Scott's work, however, one has to challenge the very basis on which 'historical' and historically-oriented of readings of Scott are made, and the assumption of almost all historians and cultural analysts reading Scott that only 'realism' and historical fidelity can count as serious engagement with the world. Whenever Scott deviates from the course of historical probability he is charged with committing crimes against the 'real' – and, thereby encouraging the conspiracy to evade the real which then dominates nineteenth-century writing in Scotland.

Such arguments, however, are based on the supposed priority of 'realism' over all other modes of presenting human experience, and the conformity of 'realism' with the requirements of 'history'. History, as the discovery of what really happened, has a natural tendency to approve of novels which claim to deal with history in a realistic fashion and an equal aversion to texts which are non- or anti-realist, texts which implicitly deflect and subvert the purposes of history as the reconstruction of what really happened. But all histories are texts and as texts are driven as much by the requirements of textuality as by the requirements of 'reality': it is precisely this tension between the textual and the real that is one of the fundamental driving forces of Scott's fiction, foregrounding as it does both its search for historical accuracy and its awareness of the metaphoric and generic structures by which that reality is constructed into the artifice of a narrative, whether historical or literary. Where the historian, by and large, attempts to suppress the awareness of the tropes which structure historical narrative and the textual forms of its presentation, Scott emphasises the disjunction between the historical 'facts' and the modes of writing through which they are re-presented. Scott's 'mythmaking', far from being an evasion of the real, is an acknowledgement of just how limited our conception of the real is when conveyed through the conventions of literary 'realism'. Scott was well aware – and indeed was a central example – of what Northrop Frye describes as the relationship between realism and myth in *The Anatomy of Criticism*:

Realism, or the art of verisimilitude, evokes the response 'How like that is to what we know!' When what is written is *like* what is known, we have an art of extended or implied simile. And as realism is an art of implicit simile, myth is an art of implicit metaphorical identity...We have then, three organizations of myths and archetypal symbols in literature. First, there is undisplaced myth, generally concerned with gods or demons, and which takes the form of two contrasting worlds of total metaphorical identification, one desirable and the other undesirable. These worlds are often identified with the existential heavens and hells of the religions contemporary with such literature. These two forms of metaphorical organization we call apocalyptic and demonic respectively. Second, we have the general tendency we have called romantic, the tendency to suggest implicit mythical patterns in a world more closely associated with human experience. Third, we have the tendency of 'realism' (my distaste for this inept term is reflected in the quotation marks) to throw the emphasis on content and representation rather than on the shape of the story.[25]

Scott's romanticism is not an evasion of the 'real': it is the exploration of those 'mythic' patterns which underlie the supposedly 'real' of history. Coming to terms with Scott is not, as Lukacs proposed, simply a matter of seeing how his narrative parallels the 'real' conflicts of the historical world: it is a matter of grasping the conflicting interpretive structures which constantly displace the 'real' of history into a 'mythic' environment which may be more fundamental than the socio-economic, and may offer a more fully explanatory causal structure of what history considers to be the 'real'. As Ian Duncan has argued,

> We may interpret two valences of romance in Scott, in fruitful tension with each other. First, romance signifies an individualist estrangement from real life, a puerile narcissism and egotistical delusion; in the progressive, rationalist ethos of a narrative of socialization, it is a condition to be outgrown and cured. This, the anti-romance theme of the modern novel, rhetorically governs the frame of *Waverley* and other novels. Second, however, romance signifies the heritage of a cultural identity that is lost but ethically true, an historically alienated ancestral patriarchy recalled in vision or legend. The field of tension or contradiction between these versions of romance and history alike is the individual imagination: hence Scott's delivery of the subjective meaning of romance as a map of the imagination, continent of the aesthetic and the sentimental springs of a rational morality.[26]

Denial of the value of the 'mythic' and of 'romance' in favour of the real may be the natural gesture of a historiography committed to the 'real', but it is not therefore an evasion of reality: it may be, in fact, that it is the 'realistic' frame of modern history which is too narrow and too circumscribed – too ideologically committed to certain presuppositions about the world – to grasp the fundamental issues with which Scott's fiction, and the fiction of his successors from Hogg to Stevenson, were engaged.

To see the outcome of Scott's engagement with Scottish history we should not be looking at the 'failure' of Scottish history in the nineteenth century, its 'strange death', its 'non-occurrences': we should be looking back from what *did* occur to see how it is founded on Scott's achievement and on the developments of Scottish thought from the Enlightenment. And what did occur was a continuation of the historical imperatives of Scottish eighteenth-century thinkers beyond the boundaries of what had come to be defined as 'history', a continuation of the search for the organising principles of human evolution not in the frame of knowable history, however filled in with 'conjectural' hypotheses, but beyond that frame towards the origins of human society and of modern consciousness in the pre-historic, knowable only through its survival in myth. If we see the Scottish nineteenth century retrospectively through the work of J.G. Frazer what we can see is that 'history', as defined by modern historiographers precisely as a development of Scottish Enlightenment theories of progress, had ceased to be the relevant context in which Scottish thinkers were working: having made sense of history, the dynamic left to nineteenth-century Scotland by the Enlightenment drove onwards to apply the principles of empirical psychology, founded on the work of Hume and Reid, and the principles of conjectural history, as developed by Hume and Robertson, to the prehistory of civilisation, to the subconscious structures by which the human mind was still governed, no matter how rational our civilisation had claimed to become. It is not to the understanding of history that Scottish culture in the nineteenth century was committed – that had already been achieved by the eighteenth-century thinkers – but to the understanding of what preceded it, and to understanding that pre-history as itself part of the logic of progress, even when it seems most alien to the rational mind:

> For when all is said and done our resemblances to the savage are still far more numerous than our differences from him; and what we have in common with him, and deliberately retain as true and useful, we owe to our savage forefathers who slowly acquired by experience and transmitted to us by inheritance those seemingly fundamental ideas which we are apt to regard as original and intuitive. We are like heirs to a fortune which has been handed down for so many ages that the memory of those who built it up is lost, and its possessors for the time being regard it as having been an original and unalterable possession of their race since the beginning of the world. But reflection and enquiry should satisfy us that to our predecessors we are indebted for much of what we thought most our own, and that their errors were not wilful

extravagances or the ravings of insanity, but simply hypotheses, justifiable as such at the time when they were propounded, but which a fuller experience has proved to be inadequate. It is only by the successive testing of hypotheses and rejection of the false that truth is at last elicited. After all, what we call truth is only that hypothesis which is found to work best.[27]

Frazer's refusal to treat the savage mind as 'irrational' but simply as an early stage in the development of those forms of understanding which characterise the modern mind is the continuation of Scott's (and Hogg's and Galt's) analyses of how the structures of myth are not only a constitutive element of what happens in history but, more importantly, shaping forces in how history is narrated.

To ask 'what happened to Scottish history in the nineteenth century', or to ask if the lack of Scottish history is a sign of cultural failure, is simply to ask the wrong kind of question. To begin from these questions is to set out on a search for the wrong kind of evidence, for it is to begin from the assumption that Scottish culture is self-negating and doomed to failure, and from the expectation that there is a history Scotland *ought* to have had rather than the one that it did have. In effect, to start from these questions is precisely to subvert the past and to evade the 'real', because it requires us to search for what is absent, trying to explain what did not happen, rather than trying to explain the real Scotland which actually happened. The real Scottish history of the nineteenth century is a history rich enough in intellectual achievement to require serious efforts to understand it, rather than pre-emptive strikes designed to empty it of any Scottish significance. If the Scots were no longer interested in writing histories of Scotland in the nineteenth century, or applying Scottish history to their current political objectives, it was because they had their eyes focused on more significant issues, ones which were to be as much the foundation of twentieth century culture as their theories of history had been the foundations of nineteenth-century culture.

Notes

1. Marinell Ash, *The Strange Death of Scottish History* (Edinburgh 1980) 10.
2. Alan Massie, review of Francis Hart, *The Scottish Novel*, *The London Magazine* (October 1979).
3. W.B. Yeats, 'The Statues', *Collected Poems* (London 1950) 375.
4. Peter Womack, *Improvement and Romance* (London 1989) 166.
5. Edwin Muir, 'Scotland 1941', *Collected Poems* (London 1963), 97.
6. Bruce Lenman, *Integration, Enlightenment and Industrialization: Scotland 1746–1832* (London 1981) 1.

7. David Craig, *Scottish Literature and the Scottish People* (London 1961) 287.
8. 'Burns and Scottish Culture', in Hugh MacDiarmid (ed.), *The Voice of Scotland: A Quarterly Magazine of Scottish Arts and Affairs*, Vol VII, Nos 3–4, 28.
9. T.C. Smout, *A History of the Scottish People 1560–1830* (London 1972) 470.
10. T.C. Smout, *A Century of the Scottish People* (London 1986) 2.
11. Edwin Muir, *John Knox: Portrait of a Calvinist* (London 1929) 11.
12. Christopher Harvie, *Scotland and Nationalism: Scottish Society and Politics 1707–1994* (2nd ed., London 1994) 115.
13. Ibid. 116.
14. Ibid. 167–8.
15. J.G. Lockhart, *Memoirs of Sir Walter Scott* 5 vols (London 1900) i, 460, for a discussion of this passage in relation to Scott's views on Scottish culture see Paul H. Scott, *Walter Scott and Scotland* (Edinburgh 1981) 70 ff.
16. *Radical Scotland* (25, Feb/Mar 1987) 3.
17. *Radical Scotland* (35, Oct/Nov 88) 11.
18. Scottish International (1971) 6.
19. Colin Kidd, *Subverting Scotland's Past: Scottish whig historians and the creation of an Anglo-British Identity, 1689–c.1830* (Cambridge 1993) 1.
20. Graeme Morton, *Unionist-Nationalism in Scotland 1830–1860*, unpublished thesis, University of Edinburgh (1984) ch.3.
21. David Morse, *High Victorian Culture* (Basingstoke 1993) 47–8.
22. See my own analysis of this tradition in *Out of History* (Edinburgh 1996), chapter 5, 'George Orwell and the English Ideology'.
23. Georg Lukacs, *The Historical Novel*, trans. Hannah and Stanley Mitchell (Harmondsworth 1969) 52.
24. Kidd's fundamental argument is that 'Scotland's literati rendered their native country in a sense a 'historyless' nation': it is an argument which I myself gave voice to in 'The Body in the Kit Bag', *Cencrastus*, 1, 1980 (not cited by Kidd) but revised in *Out of History* (Edinburgh 1996) Chapter 2, 'The Body in the Kit Bag', and Chapter 3, 'Out of History'.
25. Northrop Frye, *Anatomy of Criticism* (Princeton NJ 1957) 136, 139–40.
26. Ian Duncan, *Modern Romance and Transformations of the Novel: The Gothic, Scott, Dickens* (Cambridge 1992) 59.
27. J.G. Frazer, *The Golden Bough: A Study in Magic and Religion* (London 1922) 264. The cultural contexts that bind Scott to Frazer have been analysed in detail by Robert Crawford, *Devolving English Literature* (Cambridge 1992), Chapter 3, 'Anthropology and Dialect'.

3

Personal, Political, Pastoral: The Multiple Agenda of Adomnán's Life of St Columba

Thomas Owen Clancy

Adomnán's *Vita Sancti Columbae* is rightly famous, though probably more as an historical work than a literary one.[1] Much work has been done in recent years on Adomnán's technique as a hagiographer, his sources, the historical background and purposes of his work, and the evidence for the monastery of Iona in it.[2] A certain amount has also been done on his Latin style, and a recent paper by Jennifer O'Reilly has pushed forward our sense of Adomnán as scholar, exegete, and careful author.[3] In the following, I will concentrate on an examination of how Adomnán is present in the *Life* as narrator and author, and on the varying agenda we can see him working towards in the construction of the *Life*. On the whole, the questions I want to ask of the work are literary ones, though they have import for how we read this essential early medieval text, and hence for how we interpret its historical information.

As an historical document, there is no denying the importance of the *Vita Columbae*. Though we need to supplement its witness with that of the Irish Annals (partly made up of a chronicle from Iona), Bede, and later tradition to arrive at something approximating to a biographical sketch of Columba, without it we would be left with a sizeable gap in our understanding of sixth- and seventh-century society in Northern Britain and Ireland. We would not know with any conviction that there were then Picts in Skye (*VC* I.33); we would not know that Iona had rights to seals on a certain nearby island (I.41); would not know that Iona had an English baker (III.10); that the Pictish king in Columba's time had jurisdiction over the king of the Orkneys, still less that he (at least sometimes) resided near Inverness (II.42, 34). We would know no proto-Nessie, nor the strange beasts the size of frogs who threaten to scupper the third voyage of Cormac Úa Liatháin (II.27, 42). This is a random harvest: more sober examples could be provided. They are selected merely to show over what a range Adomnán's witness is crucial for any picture, social, political or zoological, of the early medieval north.

If then our view of Columba's time, and our view of Columba is predominantly mediated through Adomnán's voice, we need to be more acutely aware of that voice and its own interests. Columba is a saint we encounter, by and large, through Adomnán, though I do not think this would have been the case for most early medieval Gaels, who possessed a vast stock of legend and poetry concerning the saint, no doubt largely disseminated by mouth and ear, little of which is directly based on Adomnán's work.[4] In exploring Adomnán's own voice and concerns in *Vita Columbae*, I am not aiming to deconstruct the *Life*, nor to dismiss its value as evidence, still less to provide another paper on 'The Purpose of Adomnán's *Vita Columbae*'. Rather, I think the *Life* has a multiple agenda, and is far from a simple document. It is an elusive text that resists certain types of investigation, and greatly resists pigeon-holing.

First, some facts. Adomnán's *Vita Columbae* has been preserved for us in two manuscript traditions, which themselves have some significant minor differences, few of which concern us here. The A-text is preserved in a rare contemporary copy, by the author's successor Dorbbéne (†713), the famous Schaffhausen manuscript. The B-text represents a version with some additional material, and has come down into a series of later manuscripts.[5]

We do not know when Adomnán wrote his *Life* of the saint: it was sometime after 688, but beyond this it is difficult to say. The most recent translator, Richard Sharpe, suggests that one incident, where Adomnán describes himself returning from 'the Irish Synod' probably refers to the Synod of Birr in 697.[6] If Sharpe is right, then the writing of the *Life* would date to between 697 and Adomnán's death in 704. A very rough date of 690x700 will do for the moment. There may be indications in the text that the *Life* had, in fact, a fairly long gestation period, and was written over a number of years. The fact that the B-text manuscripts contain additions apparently made by Adomnán after the A-text was copied might support this.[7] I will return to the unlikelihood of securely dating the *Life* further on.

The *Life* is non-biographical, being in essence a catalogue of Columba's miracles. Structured in three books, it is formed on the model of Sulpicius Severus's *Life of Martin*, as is the double preface; and these are drawn ultimately from Evagrius's Latin version of Athanasius's *Life of Antony*. Adomnán was acquainted with both texts, as well as the works of many other church fathers. This is not the place to consider textual influence in detail, except to say that Adomnán uses other books intelligently: there are quotes, but he has sewn them into the fabric as a whole, and made subtle allusions to Columba's connections with other saints like Martin and Anthony by means of them.[8]

The *Life* was certainly composed in Iona, and has then claims to being the earliest surviving piece of extended Scottish prose writing.[9] The author was an Irishman, as was the subject. Adomnán was the ninth abbot of Iona, and author of other works: most famously *De Locis Sanctis*, a work on the Holy Land.[10] He was also promulgator in 697 of *Lex Innocentium*, an impressive piece of legislation and diplomacy aimed at protecting women, clerics and children from violence.[11] He may have been involved in other types of more ecclesiastical legislation too: the 'Canons of Adomnán' may be his, and he may have had a hand in the beginnings of the great church-law project brought to fruition by another Iona monk, Cú Chuimne, and a southern Irish monk, the work now known as *Collectio Canonum Hibernensis*.[12] Adomnán was also a relative of the saint himself, and it is with this personal side of the connection between author and saint in the *Life* we should begin to focus on the text.

Personal

Of the first importance is the fact that both author and subject were from the same family. Iona was in essence a family project of the Cenél Conaill, the branch of the powerful Uí Néill dynasty, rulers of much of the northern half of Ireland, from which Columba was born, and from which, sporadically, overkings of the Uí Néill continued to be drawn.[13] Columba's near relatives ruled the Uí Néill for most of his career, though during Adomnán's abbacy only from 695 did that family control the overkingship. Most of the successors of Columba were his kinsmen, though some were only distantly related, and in the centuries after Adomnán this continued by and large to be the case. We know that some of the companions who began Columba's exile with him were also his relatives: his uncle Ernán, prior of the monastery on the unidentified isle of Hinba; and his cousin Baíthéne, who was at varying points in his career prior of Hinba, the Tiree monastery of Mag Luinge, and ultimately Columba's successor.[14] Lest this be thought a peculiarly Gaelic or Celtic emphasis on kinship within the church, it should be pointed out that none of this is out of keeping with family religious projects elsewhere. For instance, Columba's contemporary, Gregory of Tours, had a pedigree containing several saints and bishops as well as men in secular positions of authority in the local area.[15] Some of his hagiography is also directed towards the promotion of 'family projects' of an ecclesiastical nature.

The importance of kinship ties may not always be obvious in the *Life*. Nonetheless, given the fact that the poetry on Columba stresses his descent very heavily,[16] we may be entitled to ask where family interests sit in Adomnán's list of priorities. A poem attributed to Adomnán, and possibly by him, refers to Columba as 'the name of Níall's famous descendant, not small its protection'.[17]

There are numerous miracles in *Vita Columbae* which suggest the family background, the partisanship of Adomnán. Donald Meek has recently pointed out – how has it been missed before? – that the famous incident in the *Life* where Columba commands a stray heron or crane to be taken in and fed as a pilgrim guest for three days depends not on Columba's love of animals, but on family connections: the heron is from his homeland.[18] The saint himself stresses this, saying,

> Look after it and feed it there as a guest for three days and nights. Afterwards, when the heron is revived, it will no longer want to stay as a pilgrim with us, but when its strength is recovered it will return to the sweet district of Ireland from which it came. This is the reason I am so solicitous you should do this, for the heron comes from my own homeland (*VC* I.48).

So too it is a relative who calls on Columba's name in childbirth for help, and his assistance of her in this miracle seems to be at least partly motivated by her kinship with the saint. Columba points out that 'her father belonged to my mother's kindred' (*VC* II.40).

It should not be forgotten that Adomnán was no mere hagiographer: he was Columba's successor, his heir. The term *comarba*, which at a later date was used for the head of a monastic *familia*, meant originally 'heir to property'.[19] Though it is not in evidence in the seventh century, it is possible that the thinking behind this term, in which the monastic federation is an extended kindred and its possessions an inheritance, would have been evolving in Adomnán's time.[20] Certainly it is likely that his status as Columba's successor was more than simply a job: symbolically, he was Columba, his heir in spiritual power, as well as heir to the administration of the temporalities of the Columban federation. Adomnán writing about Columba is, to an extent, Adomnán writing autobiographically, in the sense that the role he creates for Columba is one which he will have to live up to. This is not to imply that he would have to perform miracles himself, but he would need to draw Columba's mantle judiciously over his shoulders.[21] In other examples of Gaelic hagiography, it is clear that the power of the saint was meant to imply the current power of the saint's successor: in daily life, that power would be understood through his inheritance and his possession of relics, but within the hagiographical tradition relics are not emphasised. Rather, the saint who originally possessed the power and the relics is centre-stage. Does Adomnán turn this idea to his own ends? We shall see when we turn to look at the political side of Adomnán's agenda.

Adomnán is also involved in the *Life* as investigator. Máire Herbert has convincingly demonstrated many of the sources which combine in *Vita Columbae*, and these consist partially of testimonies of companions and contemporaries of Columba and beneficiaries of his miracles.[22] Some of these testimonies appear to have been given formally before earlier abbots, particularly abbot Ségéne. Herbert has argued that these are part of a period of collecting activity in the first half of the seventh century, and that this collecting activity may have been linked with the production by the later abbot Cumméne Find of a *Book of the Miraculous Powers of Columba*.[23] But Adomnán also appears in the *Life* as a collector: he frequently gives his sources or notes the witnesses to miracles. This gives the impression of Adomnán as a very busy central character in the text itself, gathering and verifying material, working to assure us of the veracity of what is described.

Two examples should suffice: this is an avenue also explored well by Richard Sharpe.[24] First, the story of King Oswald of Northumbria's vision of Columba before his battle is given an explicit pedigree: 'My predecessor, our Abbot Failbe, related all this to me, Adomnán, without question. He swore that he had heard the story of the vision from the lips of King Oswald himself as he was relating it to Abbot Segene' (*VC* I.1). In a somewhat different vein, Adomnán tells us the origins of a tale of a vision of miraculous light:

> So it was that only after the blessed man had passed away Fergnae told the story of this praiseworthy and marvellous event to many people. I, Adomnán, who have written this account, heard it in testimony from the worthy priest Commán, who was the son of Fergnae's sister. He had heard it firsthand from his uncle Fergnae, who had himself seen the event inasmuch as his strength permitted (*VC* III.19).

Partly then, this form of internal verification gives the *Life* an air of a testimonial; legal language often seems to the fore in instances like this.[25] Adomnán is constantly at our side confirming things to be true, well-documented, and trustworthy.

Adomnán is clearly personally involved in the *Vita Columbae* in other ways as well. Without doubt some of Columba's actions, whatever their historicity, mirror Adomnán's own concerns. We will return to more subtle political issues in due course, but some of the material in the *Life* seems clearly directed towards one of Adomnán's own major accomplishments. A number of the miracles relate to the *Law of Innocents*, in that (whether we consider the *Life* to have been written before or after 697) these miracles seem directly linked to the idea of Columba as an effective punisher of those who mistreat the innocent. Although in the text of the *Law* as we now have it, Columba never appears, it seems to me most likely that this is a product of the fact that the text was produced at Adomnán's monastery at Raphoe, and was most interested in directing revenue accrued from enforcing the *Law* towards Adomnán's own monasteries, Raphoe specifically. It seems unlikely, given the interest that even the oldest section of the Law shows in saints as enforcers of law, that Adomnán would not have depended strongly on the reputation of Columba for its promulgation.[26] The best, most explicit miracle related to the *Law* is *VC* II.25, where the young Columba curses the killer of a young girl. The scene is perhaps the most propagandistic of all of Adomnán's miracles. Columba's tutor's words to him – 'How long, Columba, my holy son, will God the true judge let this crime and our dishonour go unpunished?' – seem calculated, read in the late 690s, to elicit the response, 'No longer'.

There are also more quirky aspects to the author's interests as revealed in the *Life*. Adomnán seems particularly interested in animals and angels, and I think we are entitled to wonder whether these are part of Columba's legacy, or reflect Adomnán's own priorities. Adomnán is also something of a theorist. In a number of places he – and I feel sure it is he – tries to explain what is going on with some of the more arcane workings of God's universe. Columba's visions are explained by recourse to Columba's quoting Gregory the Great in *VC* I.43, and Adomnán's discussion, almost an exegesis of this explanation, seems to indicate his interest in the question. He also attempts a number of times to explain the workings of angels, for instance at III.16 or in III.15, where he has Columba explain:

> One cannot describe but only wonder at the speed with which an angel flies, for it is as fast as lightning, I think. That heavenly citizen, who flew away from here just now as the man began to fall, came to the rescue in the twinkling of an eye and was there to hold the man before he hit the ground . . . How amazing, I say, is this most speedy and timely help which could be brought so very quickly though so many miles of sea and land lay between.[27]

Finally, and most crucially, some sense of Adomnán's involvement in the text is available in the marked off section in *VC* II.44–46. Here, Adomnán recounts a series of miracles which happened after Columba's death and by which he was personally affected.[28] The first occurs during a time of severe drought. The elders decide to take Columba's relics on a circuit of the island:

We debated what should be done, and decided on this. Some of our elders should walk around the fields that had lately been ploughed and sown, carrying with them Columba's white tunic and books which the saint had himself copied. They should hold aloft the tunic, which was the one he wore at the hour of his departure from the flesh, and shake it three times. They should open his books and read aloud from them at the Hill of Angels, where from time to time the citizens of heaven used to be seen coming down to converse with the saint (*VC* II.44).

This brings rain and fertility back to the land, and Adomnán's coda is instructive: 'In this way the commemoration of St Columba's name, using his tunic and his books, on that occasion, brought help to many districts and peoples in time to save their crops.'

Adomnán invokes himself as witness to three miracles of wind-power in the next chapter. He notes at the start of the chapter: 'The present-day miracles that I have seen myself confirm my faith in such events in the past, which I have not seen. For example, the changing of a contrary wind to a favourable one I have witnessed myself on three occasions' (*VC* II.45). His own involvement in these particular miracles shows the way in which his understanding of the testimonies of others and of traditions concerning Columba has informed his relationship with his patron: his expectations are partly formed by his expert knowledge as a collector of miracle stories.

In one of these miracle stories, Columba's aid is enlisted by rebuking the saint for failing to come to the aid of his monks:

> All the while I complained of this inconvenient change of wind, and began after a fashion to chide our St Columba, saying: 'Is this troublesome delay in our efforts what you wanted, St Columba? To this point, I had hoped that by God's favour you would bring help and comfort in our labours, since I thought you stood in high honour with God' (*VC* II.45).

This technique works, and a favourable wind starts to blow. But the next chapter is the most personal. Adomnán attributes the freedom of Dál Riata and the Picts from the plague to the intercession of Columba, held in honour by many monasteries in those lands. But Adomnán also describes his own experience:

> We often thank God that through the intercession of our holy patron he has preserved us from the onslaughts of plague, not only at home among our islands, but also in England. For I visited my friend King Aldfrith while the plague was at its worst and many whole villages on all sides were stricken. But both on my first visit after Ecgfrith's battle and on my second two years later, though I walked in the midst of this danger of plague, the Lord delivered me, so that not even one of my companions died nor was any of them troubled with the disease (*VC* II.46).

In all these, Adomnán is a participant in experiments with Columba's cult, with the use of relics, and he claims personal experience of his protection. We should note that his reading seems to inform the miracle of the drought, with Gregory the Great's *Dialogues* prompting use of Columba's tunic, but Adomnán, or the elders, introduce innovations personal to the saint, such as reading from his books.[29] I think we are seeing Adomnán the theorist in action, trying to understand and extend his and his community's relationship with the dead saint. This is an extraordinary section of hagiography: we have some posthumous miracles in other Gaelic saints lives but they are few and far between. The closest parallels are in Cogitosus's *Life of Brigit*, but he shows none of the personal emphasis that Adomnán does.[30]

It seems to me that these miracles, taken as a group, provide a good glimpse of Adomnán's sense of structure, because a constant feature of *Vita Columbae* is the movement to and away from the island. Here, the posthumous miracles begin within the monastery itself, with the tender and personal community ceremony, which nonetheless has international consequences. He proceeds on to a series of miracles concerning Columba's care for his own community while away from the island, before going on to a miracle of intense international import, guarding whole regions from the plague, which yet hinges on Columba's protection for the author and his companions while abroad. The balance here, with the stress on the community of Columba's faithful ones, strikes me as characteristic as well.

Adomnán is no mere external observer; his personal involvement in *Vita Columbae* extends to his kinship with the saint, his being protected by the saint, his inheritance of the saint's office: all these, one can imagine fuel his investigation into Columba's powers, and his more narrow agenda, the promotion of his law, and perhaps also of his political and ecclesiastical views.

Political

Reading *Vita Columbae* can be a frustrating experience. Not only does Adomnán not comment on many of the important issues of the day, but the structure of the book is singularly unlinear, amounting sometimes to a mere catalogue. His own sometimes dismissive comments do not help. The best example of this comes after the miracle already described, where Columba curses the slayer of a young girl. Adomnán then switches tone: 'enough about terrible vengeance on opponents. Now we shall say a few things about animals' (*VC* II.25).

But there is a more detailed structure present, even if it is not always terribly obvious. As mentioned above, there is a constant shifting of focus, a desire to point to Columba's involvement in all sorts of people's lives in turn. The opening of the *Life* makes this clear. After two prefaces, there is something of a 'Third Preface', (I.1). In this chapter, two successive posthumous miracles performed by the saint illustrate Columba's continuing activity in people's lives after his death and the way in which he affects both the noblest of laymen (granting victory in battle to king Oswald 'ordained by God as emperor of all Britain') and the worst of criminals (brigands who escape fire and spears by singing Gaelic songs in praise of Columba).

This is followed by what appears to be a random selection of anecdotes, but which close examination, and also consecutive reading, reveals to be a most skillful opening. In outline form, it begins thus:

(I.2): Fintán (the later Fintán Munnu) and Columb Crag are about to set out to visit Columba, when word arrives that he is dead. They decide to continue with their journey, and visit his successor, Baíthéne, who conveys Columba's words to them. Through this opening story, the reader approaches Iona as a pilgrim with these two. The reader knows already that Columba is dead, but holy words continue to be conveyed by his relative and successor. The continuity of Columba's words, wisdom and power are demonstrated through his successors, just as in the previous chapter Columba's continuing ability to help those who call on him was shown. It should be noted that this intial story to some extent also underpins the authority of the author who, like Baíthéne, is Columba's relative and successor, and from whom the reader expects to receive wisom and guidance.[31]

(I.3): Columba visits the midland Irish monastery of Clonmacnoise. Here, we see Columba for the first time. He is treated as if he is already a saint, in scenes reminiscent of the Gospels. Most strikingly, he is paraded through the crowds surrounded by a bower: the term used (*de lignis piramidem*) is used by Adomnán elsewhere to describe the guard-rail around a saint's shrine.[32] Though this is clearly not its literal meaning here, it is unlikely that its use is accidental. Rather, Columba's first appearance is like that of the saint's sacred remains within a reliquary. In this guise, he corrects the monks of Clonmacnoise and stays there to prophesy. The story continues the theme of journeying: here Columba is away from his home monastery, but dispenses wisdom and guidance nonetheless. The two first stories thus form a distinct pair, opposing Columba at home and abroad; dead and alive. In the first, though dead, as a holy man he is still alive in his successors; in the second, though alive, he is already treated with the reverence due the holy dead.

(I.4–5): Two important abbots, Cainnech of Achad Bó and Colmán mac

Beógnae of Lann Elo are envisaged arriving at Iona by Columba. More journeys, then, but now it is the great church leaders of Ireland, come to consult with the saint. Adomnán's radial pattern of movements to and from the island moves into a new category of transit. It should be noted that these two chapters introduce for the first time the theme of the danger of the journey. These two great churchmen are subject, as all are, to the trials of wind, weather and sea. Iona sits surrounded by perils, and Columba resides in calm, seeing these dangers from the centre of his vision.

(I.6): With this vision he follows the careers of his own monks, no matter how far afield they journey. We are introduced to the hapless Cormac Úa Liatháin, and to Columba's concern for properly enforced monasticism.

After this, Adomnán shifts to secular scenes: prayers for kings in battle, including Áedán mac Gabráin (I.7–8); then to prophecies about future kings: Áedán's successor, Domnall mac Áedo, and many others, including the killer of the king of the southern Uí Néill, and the British king of Dumbarton. (I.9–15) Having established Columba's powers of prophecy with regard to the great secular rulers, Adomnán then shifts the focus to humbler layfolk: sons of two local men, a monk's mother, the monastery's gardener. (I.16–18) Finally, Columba has a vision of a great beast of the sea: his mind encompasses also the creatures of the deep, and his prophecies concerning them can help his monks. (I.19)

Although I would not go so far as to say this opening was seamlessly or elegantly constructed, it seems to me that here Adomnán introduces a shifting and balancing of *foci* which he maintains throughout. He introduces Columba through the eyes of other witnesses, and then he proceeds to view the world through Columba's eyes, through his visions of the great and the humble, the human and the wild. If we abandon our notion of chronological structure, Adomnán's own, somewhat grasshopper logic is revealed.

Another example of this structure in action is in II.26–33, the section introduced by Adomnán's suggestion that we hear 'a few things about animals'. Columba first drives off animals in Skye (a boar) and in the Great Glen (a monster); then the scene shifts to Iona, which he frees of danger from serpents. Then we are told of his blessing a knife so that it should not harm anything: this is melted down and spread on other implements, which also refuse to pierce the skin of living creatures. If Columba is capable of dealing with wild animals in the wilder parts of Scotland, then Iona is made by him into a sort of paradise, a place where hurt does not happen. We shift then to healing miracles: he heals his servant Diarmait; then a close companion; then he raises the son of a Pictish layman from the dead. These last two miracles introduce the Pictish court section, which begins with

Columba's confrontation with the Pictish sorcerer Broichan, in which he uses healing as a bargaining tool.[33]

If this does not provide a perfect key to Adomnán's structure in the *Life*, it does at least give a sense of how themes radiate and intersect, and importantly how the context of particular stories can be revealing. It shows also the way in which Adomnán varies the settings of his miracle stories, and these varying settings seem to have different messages. It is with this in mind that we should ask what the specific political settings have to tell us about Adomnán's agenda.

First of all, he is far from transparent. Adomnán is not like the authors of the later *Life of Adomnán*, or the Middle Irish *Life of Columba* in sermon form, who consciously introduce anachronisms and unreal events in order to make potent contemporary political and ecclesiastical points.[34] If he is doing so in *Vita Columbae* it is well-disguised, and must rather consist of his selection, augmentation, and elucidation of events and stories he had assembled for the *Life* from traditions about Columba, set in a relatively conscientiously delineated historical past.

Nevertheless, certain aspects of Adomnán's political agenda are clear. He has certain ideas about kingship, which have been much discussed by scholars.[35] Two kings are singled out for special status: Oswald of Northumbria (I.1) and Diarmait mac Cerbaill of Tara and the southern Uí Néill (I.36). These are desribed in the one case as 'king of all Ireland', in the other as 'emperor of all Britain'; both 'ordained by God'. I do not wish to explore Adomnán's specific agenda with regard to political kingship, but rather simply to notice the people of whom he says this: one a king of Northumbria, the other king of the southern Uí Néill. It is striking that he has less to say of kings of his closer relatives among the northern Uí Néill of whom similar could have been said: Domnall mac Áedo, for instance, about whom Columba prophesies in I.10, describing him only as a 'famous king'. Does this suggest the time of writing of the text? I am not sure. It is possible that his favourable remarks about Diarmait (a king execrated in the general run of tradition), and the fairly large number of stories set within the territory of the southern Uí Néill arise from Adomnán's need or desire to accrue the favour of these midland potentates, who were rulers of Tara for most of Adomnán's career, up to 696. At the very least it makes clear that Adomnán's secular audience is not only his own family, but also the lords of other areas in whose territory Columban monks worked, including the kings of Northumbria.

The episode of the ordination of Áedán mac Gabráin (III.5) is also telling. Although the idea that Adomnán is setting up Columba, and hence the abbots of Iona, as kingmakers, and imposing ecclesiastical authority over that of secular lords, has been rightly refuted by Alan Macquarrie, there is nonetheless a strong message here from Adomnán.[36] His implication is that political rule and succession are accountable to and accounted for by God, and that priests and the church have a role to play in sanctifying and supporting (but sometimes also opposing) kings. This is buttressed by the fact that elsewhere, the sons of Gabrán come in for a certain amount of criticism, as criminals and brigands. Thus, while Columba prays for Áedán's success in battle, subsequent allusions suggest that to Adomnán this springs from his being the properly ordained king (ordained by God, and not by the saint, but through the saint), rather than his lineage.

Does Adomnán use more detailed political events to reflect contemporary reality? This needs further exploration than I can pursue here, though there are some examples ripe for investigation. I put forward here a few observations, which may be worth following up, though there are plenty more such possible connections within the text.

First, the story of Áed Dub's killing of Diarmait mac Cerbaill, the king ordained by God, and his ultimately sticky end in I.36 is suggestive of contemporary resonance. Is there any connection between his discussion of this event and the fact that the most recent king of the southern Uí Néill in Adomnán's time, Fínsnechta Fledach (king for some twenty years), had been murdered by rivals in 695 – incidentally, by someone called Áed? Or that this Áed and his fellows, men of the Fir Cúl, were descended from Diarmait's son Áed Sláine, of whom Columba prophesies elsewhere that he will not profit if he engages in kinslaying? The passage in Adomnán relating to Áed Sláine is worth quoting: 'You should take care, my son, for though God has predestined for you the prerogative of the kingship of all Ireland, you may lose it by the sin of a family murder.'[37] Adomnán goes on to relate Áed Sláine's killing of Suibne mac Colmáin, king of the neighbouring Clann Cholmáin, and Áed's subsequent downfall. It seems quite possible that both the stories, that of the murder of a southern Uí Néill high king, and that of the murder of a relative by one of the Síl nÁedo Sláine, may relate to the internecine killing in 695, and also the fall from power of the southern Uí Néill as a result. If so, this allusion would help to date the *Life* to the years immediately following 695, or perhaps 696, which saw the demise of one of Fínsnechta's murderers, and the elevation of the northern Uí Néill potentate Loingsech mac Óengusso to the kingship of Tara.

A second possible instance of Adomnán engaging in coded commentary on contemporary political events is his story of an exiled Pictish nobleman named Tarain, who is sent by Columba to be harboured and treated well by a rich landowner in Islay. This man, Feradach, treacherously has Tarain killed. One wonders if this story is in any way connected with the Pictish king Tarain son of Ainftech, who was driven from the kingship in 697, and then to Ireland in 699? If the *Life* was written near to 697, it could be that Tarain was already living in exile, and the story told in the *Life*, situated as it is in the midst of a series of stories about the oppression of innocents, could have been meant to send strong signals to any who might intend to harm him. Perhaps he had come under the care of Iona. It is well to note in this context that Tarain's successor, Bruide son of Derile, was signatory to the *Law of Adomnán*.

If it were demonstrable that Adomnán does use his stories as comments on contemporary events, it could in theory help us to date the life more closely. The two events above, taken together, suggest a date certainly not before 697, but perhaps not long after it. On the other hand, it is noticeable that in *Vita Columbae* the kings Adomnán concentrates on belong to the southern Uí Néill, while the *Cáin Adomnáin* guarantor list, if its ordering is any indication of contemporary ideas of importance, is less interested in them. As I have suggested above, however, it may be that the *Life* was being composed over many years, and that its southern Uí Néill bias may belong to its earlier stages, whereas incidents like those discussed above give us more of a date for the completion of the *Life*.

But my overall impression is that this may be an elusive goal, though one worth pursuing further than I have been able to. Adomnán is perhaps not so heavily concerned with the details of power politics as the main point of most of these episodes. His main points are surely not those which might be *ad homines*, but rather the general ones: exiles should not be killed, kings should not be murdered, fratricide and battles between kin groups are a bad thing.

The most strikingly odd aspect of *Vita Columbae* relates not to its specific political agenda but to its lack of a larger, more historically involved political context. Here Adomnán seems strangely detached form his surroundings. For instance, there is a strong contrast between Adomnán's attitude to southern Uí Néill kings and towards Dál Riata. Adomnán provides a mixture of comments on these, from Columba being hosted by Conall mac Comgaill, to his being forced by angelic intervention to ordain Áedán mac Gabráin as king, and praying for Áedán in battle. Contrasted with this is the story of the brigand branch of the Cenél nGabráin who harass Columba and his monks. Here we may be seeing a balance between blessing and hesitancy, a sensible mix of messages for the local landlords. But Adomnán never directly addresses the relationship between Iona and Dál Riata, by recounting the founding of the monastery or another such device. Establishing the relationship between landowner and monastery was common practice in Gaelic hagiography, but there is none here, at least not directly.

So too with the Picts. Adomnán tells us that Columba had many monasteries among the Picts and that Picts, along with the Gaels in Britain, were preserved from the plague because of intervention of Columba (*VC* II.46). Yet his stories about the Picts seem constantly to lead us into a still unchristianised world. The world depicted there is of small isolated groups of Pictish Christians. The portrayal of the Pictish king, recalcitrant, belligerent, unconverted, certainly does not seem to be directed at the Pictish kings contemporary with Adomnán. We are presented neither with a portrait of real friendship, nor, for that matter, a portrait of Columba's dominion. Why? Were the strains between Columba's *familia* in Pictland and the Pictish monarchy, which might have lain behind the expulsion of the *familia* from Pictland in 717, already apparent? Was the Pictish church itching to be its own entity, and Adomnán chose not to ruffle feathers?

Adomnán's depiction of the Picts admits of no ready explanations. However, his failure to engage with political reality as we see it poses some hard questions. Was Adomnán just not interested in the real political world? Is our perception of the political reality of the time wrong? Is Adomnán just not writing for a Pictish audience, and so writes the Pictish episodes not as commentary on the christianising of the Picts but simply as further elaboration of the power of his holy man?

We can ask the same things about ecclesiastical politics. Here too we hear much about certain monks and monasteries, but nothing about others which we know to have been important. Cainnech of Achad Bó, Brendan of Clonfert and Comgall of Bangor are all singled out as among Columba's peers, but still other important contemporaries are not included. Adomnán's picture of the relationship between monks and monasteries as one of fraternal greeting and correction builds up a sense of Iona being part of an extended network, but it also gives us the sense that this was a partly exclusive network, that some monasteries worked well with Adomnán and others perhaps did not. This is nowhere more obvious than in his complete omission of mention of the other monasteries in Dál Riata, with the exception of some rather disparaging remarks. These include the monasteries on Tiree not preserved from a disease because not under Columba's care (III.8), and the strange story of the abbot Findchán in the monastery of Airtchan on Tiree, who ordains the murderer of Diarmait mac Cerbaill, and whose hand subsequently falls off (I 36).

We may note, however, that some of the abbots who seem to play the biggest roles in the *Life* have later traditions of activity in Scotland: Cainnech, to whom numerous churches are dedicated and who may have had an early cult in the east of Scotland; Comgall, founder of the monastery of Bangor, with its connections to Columba's contemporary Mo Luag of Lismore, and a monastery on Tiree, as well as the later Bangor daughter foundation of Applecross under Máel Ruba; and Brendan with his possible foundation at an island called Ailech, and another on Tiree.[38] On the other hand he makes no reference to contemporary local west of Scotland saints whom we know to have been important, for instance Donnan of Eigg, or Mo Luag of Lismore. Here, his silence seems significant, but whether he was simply trying to establish Columba's pre-eminence by not mentioning his peers, or whether he disapproved of these other monastic establishments is far from clear.

One last feature of the political dimension of the *Life* of *Columba*, both secular and ecclesiastical, pertains to its audience. We should remember that the Iona monks and others of the Columban *familia* were participants in the creation of the *Life*, and not a passive audience. The work responds to their needs and demands, incorporating many of their own traditions and tales, and it is too easy to assume that Adomnán's is the only set of values choosing the incidents for inclusion in it. The monks of the Columban *familia*, some of them, had royal backgrounds and well-connected families. They were from diverse places in Ireland and Britain. When approaching the political and genealogical detail of Adomnán's stories, we must bear in mind the network of internal references to the population of Columba's monasteries which might at any time be put into play. We have no hope of recovering these references, but in some cases it could well be that they, and not a wider political agenda, have determined Adomnán's approach to a given incident or episode.

Pastoral

However it is with a more attainable aspect of Adomnán's approach to the monastic setting of the *Life* that I wish to conclude. Columba's care for his own people, especially his monks, is a theme which is shot through the whole of the text.

Without doubt this is the most extraordinary feature of *Vita Columbae* and the one which I think most of all, more than any political allusions, explains the audience and attitudes of the text. Here, with Columba's *familia*, is the real audience, and in some cases the explanation for silences about contemporary political or ecclesiastical events. For instance, if Adomnán largely avoids references to the dispute over Easter dating, we must remember how active and hurtful an issue this would have been in the late 690s in Iona. If he makes only one oblique reference to it (I.3), it is surely through interest in the unity of this family, unity focused around their founder and protector.[39]

Constantly, in and among the doings in the *Vita Columbae*, alongside Columba's meetings with kings and abbots, we find a Columba tenderly solicitous of his flock's well-being. This can be substantiated by a look at two miracles which occur at Durrow, though there are many of a similar sort which occur on Iona.

In I. 29, the saint perceives in a vision, during a cold winter day, that Laisrén, the head of the monastery of Durrow and a cousin of Columba's, is overworking his monks. Columba sees this, and laments the situation. At the same moment, Laisrén's heart changes and he gives the monks a rest, and a special meal, and continues to do this on days when the weather might be bad. Columba rejoices, blessing Laisrén as 'a comforter of monks'. There seems to be an element of commentary on good and bad leadership here, especially given the fact that Laisrén would later become Columba's successor. Columba is shown as an abbot who is more concerned for his monks' well-being than for the projects in which they are involved, or strict application of manual labour regimes. Flexibility and compassion are revealed as the keys to monastic leadership. This is an important theme, given that the author of the work is also a successor of Columba.

In the previous episode, the monks' tiredness was due to work on the 'great house' at Durrow. Its construction must have been a very significant event in the life of the monastery, and seems to have given rise to a small collection of folklore. Another from the same strand is found in III.15. Here Columba sends an angel to save a monk from falling off the big building as he was working on it. Columba comments on the wonderful power and speed of the angel. A story such as this seems to me to be a pastoral story about the care of the head of the Columban family, a care which is capable, through God's help, of being exercised over great distances. These kinds of scenes are Adomnán's masterpieces, and they are liberally sprinkled throughout *Life*. Columba's family is led by kindred priors, and the monasteries within that family are sewn together through time and space by Columba's prayers and care.

It is Columba's successor Baíthéne who voices Columba's care for the monks labouring hard in the field in I.37. Although Columba is clearly still alive in this tale, it is written with him absent, and seems to demonstrate his continuing efficacy even when not bodily present. The story is wedged in a particularly dark section of Book I, in which many of the surrounding tales involve demons carrying off souls and the fates of adulterers. Perhaps this is Adomnán modulating the tone once more, but the tale also seems to

Personal, Political, Pastoral 55

send a note of perseverance to his monks, and a message concerning what their patron's influence feels and smells like (fire, flowers). Baíthéne's words must be intended to buoy up the troubled spirits of the monks of the family:

> You know that our elder, Columba, thinks anxiously about us, and is upset when we return home to him so late, for he knows we are hard at work. And so it is that, since he may not come to meet us in the body, his spirit meets us as we walk and refreshes us in this way so that we are joyful.

One scene more than any other seems oriented towards the local monastic community of Adomnán's own island of Iona. That is the extended chapter which recounts the death of Saint Columba (III.23). Here at the end, Adomnán draws together many of the previous strands of the work. It is a carefully crafted section in which the audience follows Columba through the process of death and is drawn ever deeper into divine mysteries, and made ever more aware of the solidity and continuity of Columba's relationship with his family.

The preceding chapter had revealed how Columba, desiring to die, was suddenly saved by the prayers of many churches for his well-being, and so is forced to delay his journey to the Lord for four years. III.23 brings us to that time of departure – some days before, in May. The chapter begins with him addressing his monks labouring in the fields, recalling for us the joy and lightness of spirit he used to grant them as they were returning from their work (I.37). No doubt that earlier scene heightens the poignancy of his announcement that he is to die soon, and instead of becoming light in spirit they become sad. He then blesses the island, freeing it from the peril of snakes. Adomnán had already mentioned this in a previous chapter (II.28), and so once more, the beginning of Columba's death picks up earlier themes.

Later, on the Sunday, he has a vision of angels. Again we have been prepared for this idea by the entire preceding book. He blesses a barn, giving thanks for the fact that his monks will still have bread for another year. These comments recall the agricultural miracles earlier in the text, including the miracle of Columba helping to relieve the drought stricken island, or the tree in Durrow which bore a miraculous crop (II.44, 2).

He returns to the monastery, resting along the way, and where he rests, a cross is later set up. At this spot the community's milk horse approaches and weeps over him. Much has been made of this bizarre and very sentimental scene, but it seems at once a deft flourish from the hand of Adomnán, with his interest in animals, but also a jolt to the memory. We have seen Columba as master and tender of animals before. We have also had miracles in which he ensured continuing prosperity by blessing milk-skins and pails (II.16, 38).

Columba then proceeds to climb a little hill, recalling other visions he received on that hill (I.30), and he blesses the island for the last time, with a famous quote which again invites us to reflect on some of the miracles Adomnán has revealed to us:

> This place, however small and mean, will have bestowed on it no small but great honour by the kings and peoples of Ireland, and also by the rulers of even barbarous and foreign nations with their subject tribes. And the saints of other churches too will give it great reverence.

He goes to his writing hut and works, copying out the psalms. In the midst of Psalm 34, he stops, leaving it for Baíthéne to complete the rest. We are, as elsewhere in the text, enjoined to listen and respect the words and actions of Columba's successors, but also here we are gently reminded of yet another aspect of the text and the monastic life, the scriptorium in which so much activity happens, and all the various book miracles which also have been revealed to us.[40]

The saint then goes to church for vespers, and then to bed. Through his servant, Columba gives his last command to his *familia*, a highly significant injunction to love one another and live in peace. When the time for midnight office comes, the saint rushes into the church ahead of his monks. The church is observed filled with light, but the light disappears as Diarmait, Columba's servant, reaches the church, and he is forced to grope around to find the saint in the dark. Finding him, Diarmait raises the saint's hand to bless the community, and Columba dies in his servant's arms.

From this intimate family drama, which becomes ever more internal and private, the chapter engages in another reversal, as the vision of Columba's death is broadcast as a great light across the world. Adomnán recounts a series of visions of this light, and in two cases these are people who would later be drawn into the Columban family, and end their days as monks, one on Hinba, the other at Drumhome. To an extent this returns us to the very first chapter (I.2), where monks are drawn to Iona by Columba's reputation, and continue to come even though they know the saint is dead. The imagery of light also returns us to the beginning of book III, where infant Columba's face displays marvellous light, and he is foreseen as a marvellous flower, growing bigger than the earth (III.2, 1).

Finally the scene returns to Iona, for the burial, which lasts three days and three nights. Only the community of monks is present however. Adomnán tells us a last miracle, in which a great storm prevents all visitors from crossing to the island, leaving the community to celebrate the burial undisturbed. Adomnán almost smiles at the irony of the great weather-worker providing this privacy at the end, followed immediately afterwards by a great calm. And this at last is where the *Life* leaves us: the community reflecting during a time of storm and rain on their founder and protector.

I have dwelt at some length on this last chapter because in terms of Adomnán's literary artistry it is his finest achievement, and brings the text to a fitting conclusion in many ways, weaving together a pattern of backward allusions which allow us to see the whole *Life* reflected in Columba's last days. But there is more than this to it. I feel certain that this chapter, so well-crafted, is also partly a map, perhaps even of a traditional pilgrimage round the island prior to the saint's feast. With Columba we journey round the island. We observe the workers in the fields, reflect on the goodness of the full barn, stop to rest by the cross where the horse wept over the saint, visit the scriptorium, observe his last manuscript with his potent and efficacious writing, visit the stone pillow by his grave, which once lay on the bed from which he gave his last injunction of peace, and finally go to the church, where we are blessed (perhaps by an arm relic, recalling Diarmait's gesture with Columba's hand?)[41] . Even if this pilgrimage is not a physical one, it certainly allows the reader a last, consecutive period of inner wandering and prayer, last visits to the special sites of the *Life*: the church, the hill, the fields, the writing hut. Finally, Adomnán makes us aware once again of the communal, the intimate nature of Columba's monasticism. Though the message of his death goes out like a bright light to the world, he reserves his burial for his own.

Adomnán's *Vita Sancti Columbae* is not then simply a book to pilfer for historical detail, nor yet a book which helps us form a view of Scotland's premier saint. It is a conscious, well-crafted literary work. In it, Adomnán pursues many different aims, from the advancement of broad ideas about good governance and right political order, to a strong ideal of the strength of relationships within and between monasteries. Unlike later hagiographers, he does not seem so bent on moulding the *Life* to suit specific political and proprietorial aims and objectives. Rather, this is a true work of hagiography, designed to create wonder, devotion and above all intimate affection. If there is one driving force which stands out in the text, it is Adomnán's own devotion to the man in whose shoes he stood, as a kinsman and a fellow-traveller. In nearly every tale he tells, it is into Adomnán's own circle of devotion that we are invited to join.[42]

Notes

1. The text, cited here as *VC* in the body of the article by book and chapter, may be consulted in *Adomnán's Life of Columba* (eds) A. O. and M. O. Anderson (Edinburgh 1961), revised ed. M.O. Anderson (Oxford 1991). Translations throughout will be from Richard Sharpe, *Adomnán of Iona: Life of St Columba* (London 1995).

2. M. Herbert, *Iona, Kells and Derry:The History and Hagiography of the Monastic Familia of Columba* (2nd ed., Blackrock 1996); J-M. Picard, 'Structural patterns in early Hiberno-Latin hagiography', *Peritia* 4 (1985) 67–82; Clare Stancliffe, 'Irish saints' lives' in *The Seventh Century: Change and Continuity* (eds) J. Fontaine and J.N. Hillgarth (London 1990) 87–115; Gertrud Brüning, 'Adamnans Vita Columbae und ihre Ableitungen', *Zeitschrift für celtische Philologie* 11 (1917) 213–304; Michael J. Enright, 'Royal succession and abbatial prerogative in Adomnán's Vita Columbae', *Peritia* 4 (1985) 83–103; J-M. Picaard, 'The purpose of Adomnán's *Vita Columbae*', *Peritia* 1 (1982) 160–77; A.D.S. Macdonald, 'Adomnán's monastery of Iona', in *Studies in the Cult of Saint Columba*, (ed.) C. Bourke (Dublin 1997) 24–44; 'Aspects of the monastery and monastic life in Adomnán's Life of Columba', *Peritia* 3 (1984) 271–302.

3. Picard, 'The Schaffhausen Adomnán – a unique witness to Hiberno-Latin', *Peritia* 1 (1982) 216–49; 'The metrical prose of Adomnán's *Vita Columbae*' in *Irland und Europa: die Kirche im Frühmittelalter* (eds) P. Ní Chatháin and M. Richter (Stuttgart 1984) 258–71; J. O'Reilly, 'Reading the Scriptures in the Life of Columba', in Bourke, *Studies in the Cult of Saint Columba*, 80–106. See also O'Reilly, 'The wisdom of the scribe and the fear of the Lord in the Life of Columba', in *Spes Scotorum: Hope of Scots: Columba, Iona and Scotland* (eds) D. Broun and T.O. Clancy (Edinburgh 1999) 159–211. Our sense of Adomnán as exegete has also been expanded in recent years through numerous studies by Thomas O'Loughlin: 'The exegetical purpose of Adomnán's *De Locis Sanctis*', *Cambridge Medieval Celtic Studies* 24 (1992) 37–53; 'The library of Iona in the late seventh century: the evidence from Adomnán's *De Locis Sanctis*', *Ériu* 45 (1994) 33–52; Thomas O'Loughlin 'Res, tempus, locus persona: 'Adomnán's exegetical method', *Innes Review* 48 (1997) 95–111; now in Broun and Clancy, *Spes Scotorum*, 139–158.

4. See for instance, the early poems on Columba in T.O. Clancy and G. Márkus, *Iona: the Earliest Poetry of a Celtic Monastery* (Edinburgh 1995); or the twelfth-century Irish Life of the saint, in Herbert, *Iona, Kells and Derry*, 218–69.

5. On this see Anderson, *Adomnán*, liv–lxxii; Sharpe, *Adomnán*, 235–8.

6. Sharpe, *Adomnán*, 55; the account is *VC* II.45.

7. Anderson, *Adomnán*, lviii; Sharpe, *Adomnán*, 237.

8. There are some explicit comparisons as well, such as that with St. Germanus

of Auxerre, *VC* II.34. The whole topic of exegetical reference is treated excellently in O'Reilly, 'Reading the Scriptures'.

9. A number of poems have prior claims on the title of the 'earliest piece of Scottish literature'. For early poetry, see Clancy and Márkus, *Iona* and *The Triumph Tree: Scotland's Earliest Poetry, 550–1350* (ed.) T. O. Clancy (Edinburgh 1998).

10. *De Locis Sanctis*, (ed.) D. Meehan (Dublin 1958).

11. K. Meyer, *Cáin Adomnáin* (Oxford 1905); G. Márkus, tr., *Adomnán's 'Law of the Innocents': Cáin Adomnáin* (Glasgow 1997); Máirín Ní Dhonnchadha, *Cáin Adomnáin* (forthcoming). Commentary in John Ryan, SJ, 'The *Cáin Adomnáin*', in *Studies in Early Irish Law*, by R. Thurneysen, N. Power, *et al.* (Dublin 1936), 269–76; M. Ní Dhonchadha, 'The guarantor list of *Cáin Adomnáin*, 697', *Peritia* 1 (1982), 178–215; 'The *Lex Innocentium*: Adomnán's Law for women, clerics and children, 697 AD', in *Chattel, Servant or Citizen: Women's Status in Church, State and Society*, (eds) Mary O'Dowd and Sabine Wichert (Belfast 1996), 58–69.

12. L. Bieler, *The Irish Penitentials* (Dublin 1975) 176–81; H. Wasserschleben, *Die irische Kanonensammlung* (Leipzig 1885); Clancy and Márkus, *Iona*, 29–30.

13. Herbert, *Iona, Kells and Derry*, charts 310–11; Sharpe, *Adomnán*, 247–8.

14. Herbert, *Iona, Kells and Derry*, 33–5; Sharpe, *Adomnán*, 306, 256–7.

15. See chart in L. Thorpe (tr.), *Gregory of Tours: The History of the Franks* (Harmondsworth 1974) 11.

16. Clancy and Márkus, *Iona*, 117, 154.

17. Clancy and Márkus, *Iona*, 170–1.

18. D. Meek, 'Surveying the saints: reflections on recent writings on "Celtic Christinaity"', *Scottish Bulletin of Evangelical Theology* 15 (1997) 50–60:57.

19. *Royal Irish Academy Dictionary of the Irish Language* (Dublin 1983), s.u. *comarb(b)ae*.

20. John Bannerman, '*Comarba Coluim Chille* and the relics of Columba', *Innes Review* 44 (1993) 14–15.

21. One may note, nonetheless, the tradition in Glen Lyon that Adomnán had turned back the plague from the region. (W. J. Watson, *The Celtic Place-Names of Scotland* (Edinburgh 1926) 271.) This suggests that miracles attributed by Adomnán to Columba (*VC* II.46) might locally be attributed to Adomnán himself.

22. Herbert, *Iona, Kells and Derry*, 13–26.

23. Ibid. 24–5.

24. Sharpe, *Adomnán*, 245–7.

25. Ibid. 371.

26. T.O. Clancy, 'Columba, Adomnán and the cult of saints in Scotland', *Innes Review* 48 (1997) 1–26: 9–10 (revised version in Broun and Clancy, *Spes Scotorum*, 3–33: 10–13).

27. Sharpe, *Adomnán*, 217.

28. On these as relating to the cult of saints, see Clancy, 'Columba, Adomnán and the cult of saints', 10–12.

29. On this see further O'Reilly, 'Reading the Scriptures', 90–4.

30. For further discussion of this section of *VC*, see Clancy, 'Columba, Adomnán and the cult of saints'.

31. For an enlightening and perceptive discussion of Baíthéne in *VC*, see O'Reilly, 'The wisdom of the scribe'.

32. *De Locis Sanctis*, II.4,7; Sharpe, *Adomnán*, 261.

33. For discussion of these scenes, and Adomnán's sense of political and pastoral structure, see Gilbert Márkus, 'Political animals, mental maps: Adomnán's view of ecclesiastical organisation in the *Life of Columba*', in Broun and Clancy, *Spes Scotorum*, 115–38.

34. See Herbert, *Iona, Kells and Derry*, 151–202; M. Herbert and P. Ó Riain, *Betha Adamnáin: The Irish Life of Adamnán* (ITS vol. 54, Dublin 1988), 1–44.

35. M.J. Enright, *Iona, Tara and Soissons: the origins of the royal annointing ritual* (Berlin 1985); M. Meckler, 'Colum Cille's ordination of Áedán mac Gabráin', *Innes Review* 41 (1990) 139–50; but see A. Macquarrie, *The Saints of Scotland: Essays in Scottish Church History, AD 450–1093* (Edinburgh 1997) 76–8, who de-emphasises the political aspects of Adomnán's narratives.

36. See note 35, and also Enright, 'Royal succession and abbatial prerogative in Adomnán's *Vita Columbae*', *Peritia* 4 (1985) 83–103.

37. *VC* I.14; Sharpe, *Adomnán*, 122.

38. W.J. Watson, *A History of the Celtic Place-Names of Scotland* (Edinburgh 1926) 276–7, 274; Sharpe, *Adomnán*, 262, 279–80, 314.

39. The centrality of the community as audience, and the need for unity are stressed in Picard, 'The purpose'.

40. For a superb exegesis of this section, and discussion of the significance of the psalm in question, see O'Reilly, 'The wisdom of the scribe'.

41. I owe this suggestion to Gilbert Márkus. There was apparently an arm-relic of the saint in the later middle ages. See R. Ó Floinn, 'Insignia Columbae I', in Bourke, *Studies in the Cult of St Columba*, 144.

42. As always, this paper has been greatly improved by the conversation and comments of various friends and colleagues, among whom I would like particularly to thank Dauvit Broun, Abigail Burnyeat, Gilbert Márkus, Jennifer O'Reilly and Alex Woolf.

4

Keeping the Customer Satisfied: Barbour's Bruce and a Phantom Division at Bannockburn

Sonja Cameron

The question of interaction between history and literature becomes a sensitive one when the historical event is so far removed in time, and so badly attested otherwise, that a work of literature dealing with it becomes the only, or the main, source for historians. It is no longer allowed to merely function as an individual's processing of history into a work of art, but it is pressed into service as an accurate reflection of the event itself – literature turning into a historical source almost by default, with the borders between faithful chronicling and literary invention obscured. What should be done in such a case is by no means clear. If statements made in the literary treatment are ignored, one runs the risk of discounting evidence that may after all be relevant. If they are accepted as fact, one may end up incorporating a poet's artistic vision into a supposed account of historical fact. It is a field where everyone has to tread with the utmost caution, and this chapter examines a case where it may be possible to show what can happen when a poet's full and persuasive narrative is preferred to the scanty and confused accounts offered by other, more palpably 'historical', sources.

The battle of Bannockburn is probably the most famous battle in Scottish history; it is popularly seen as a landmark, and, fought in 1314, it is the only victory that is annually commemorated even today. Not surprisingly, it has also been extensively scrutinised by historians, so that yet another paper about the battle of Bannockburn would seem to need some justification; one might expect that all relevant questions about the battle have by now been given due attention. But, as a simple enquiry into one protagonist's part in the action will reveal, this is by no means the case. Some questions, far from being answered, are not even being asked – or at least not very loudly. This chapter deals with just one aspect: the 'received' version of the Scottish battle formation and some incidents that are taken to have happened during the battle itself. While this may sound primarily of interest to the military historian, it becomes a fit subject for a discussion of literature and history when the main source for the battle is considered: *The Bruce*, written by John Barbour, archdeacon of Aberdeen.[1] *The Bruce*, called after one of its main heroes, King Robert I, is not a chronicle but a piece of literature – an epic verse romance written around 1375, about sixty years after the battle itself. The poem does not contain the only account of the battle, but it provides the one that has been the most influential.

Barbour's tale of Bannockburn is fascinating, full of detail, and very long. At the start of it, he introduces the leaders of the different Scottish divisions:

> And than in-till a litill thraw
> Thar four bataillis ordanyt thai
> And till the erle Thomas perfay
> Thai gaif the waward in leding . . . (XI.310–13)

'Erle Thomas' who leads the vanguard is the earl of Moray, governor of a vast province of northern Scotland. He is also King Robert's nephew.

> The tother bataill wes gevyn to led
> Till him yat douchty wes of deid
> And prisyt off hey chewalry,
> That wes schyr Eduuard the worthy . . . (XI.321–4)

'Schyr Edward' is Edward Bruce, the king's only surviving brother, earl of Carrick and lord of Galloway.

> And syne ye thrid bataill yai gaff
> Till Walter Stewart for to leid
> And to Douglas douchty of deid,
> Yai war cosyngis in ner degre
> Yarfor till him betaucht wes he
> For he wes young . . . (XI.328–33)

Here we have Walter Stewart and James Douglas. Walter Stewart is the extremely youthful High Steward of Scotland, an hereditary office. Douglas is, at this point, simply lord of Douglas, owner of some estates in southwest Scotland. Later, he will turn into the 'Good Sir James' or the 'Black Douglas', a close friend of Robert I's and designated regent of Scotland.

> Ye ferd bataile ye noble king
> Tuk till his awne gouernyng . . . (XI.337–8)

Finally, in Barbour's account, the king himself leads the fourth division, the reserve.

This outline has been adopted by most modern representations of the battle: line drawings of the Scottish dispositions which accompany accounts of strategy and discussions of location are invariably based on the four-division setup described by Barbour.[2] Scholars may disagree on the actual site of the battle, but not on the general outline of troop movements and events. Post-Barbour accounts are unanimous in their description of the Scottish army's formation at Bannockburn. This is particularly remarkable when we consider the rest of the fourteenth-century sources for the battle, and discover that there is very little agreement on that account at all. At this point, the matter becomes regrettably complicated.

There are three sources besides Barbour's poem, all of them English. The *Vita Edwardi Secundi*[3] was probably written around 1325–6, only 12 years after the battle itself. It is a life of 'Saint' Edward II of England, who led the English army to defeat at Bannockburn. *Scalacronica*[4] was written by the English knight Sir Thomas Gray of Heton while he was held captive in Edinburgh castle between 1355 and 1359. His account of the battle is apparently based on that of his father, who was an active participant. The third source, the *Lanercost Chronicle*,[5] consists of mostly contemporary, diary-type accounts which were entered in the northern English monastery of Lanercost which suffered considerably from Scottish depredations and therefore took a close interest in Scottish affairs.

According to the *Vita Edwardi*, the Scots at Bannockburn were drawn up in three divisions. The author states that Douglas led the first division of the Scots, and that on the second day of the battle he made a ferocious attack on the English division led by the earl of Gloucester.[6] This is the only other fourteenth-century account to mention Douglas at Bannockburn, but the author does not name the leaders of the other two divisions. This is a pity, because it would have been interesting to see which of the higher-ranking nobles – Moray, Carrick or the king – was left without a command. Sir Thomas Gray in his *Scalacronica* also has the Scots drawn up in three divisions. According to him, the first division was led not by Douglas but by Moray, and it attacked not Gloucester but Clifford and Beaumont.[7] However, the English vanguard is in his account, as in the *Vita*, led by Gloucester, so that Moray must be engaging some other part of the English army. Again, we do not learn who led the other two Scottish divisions, although at a guess it could well have been the king and his brother. Douglas, in this account, is not mentioned at all. Finally, the *Lanercost Chronicle* also mentions three divisions on the Scottish side, but only indicates that King Robert led the third which was kept in the rear. The English vanguard is led by Clifford and, interestingly, also contains Gloucester.[8]

Clearly, there is very little agreement between the three English sources. Given the confusion of battle and the fact that not one of the writers was actually present at it, this may not be surprising. Only on two points do we find some consensus: Gloucester was one of the leaders of the English van, and the number of Scottish divisions was three, not four.

At this point we must return to Barbour, who agrees with the three English sources on the matter of Gloucester.[9] The English vanguard according to Barbour also contains Sir Giles d'Argentan, a famous crusader,[10] and this would appear to tally with a statement in *Lanercost*.[11] On the Scottish side, Moray has the vanguard (as in *Scalacronica*), but with it he is said to have attacked Clifford,[12] not Gloucester and therefore the English second division, not the first. Interestingly, however, *Lanercost* places Clifford in the English van alongside Gloucester,[13] which might solve this particular riddle.[14]

In Barbour's account, it is Carrick with his second division who faces the English vanguard commanded by Gloucester and Hereford,[15] while Moray deals with Clifford in the second. To complete the roll-call of persons who are said to have attacked Gloucester at some point, it is necessary to mention the *Vita Edwardi* which ascribes the attack to Douglas.[16] In Barbour's version, Douglas leads the third division (not the van as in the *Vita*) jointly with the young Walter Stewart[17] but there is no indication of him using it to attack Gloucester or indeed anybody else.

It is unfortunate that beyond the role of Gloucester and the number of divisons attributed to the Scottish army, there is so little agreement amongst any of the sources. It is impossible to claim with certainty that any one of them is substantially misinformed, because they harmonise with each other as much as they contradict each other. All sources agree that Gloucester led the English van, but they cannot agree about which division of Scots under which leader attacked it. The *Vita* and Barbour agree that Douglas had a command, but neither indicates which one it was nor what he did with it. Barbour and Gray agree that Moray confronted Clifford, but on very little else. Finally, the *Lanercost Chronicle* both supports and contradicts Barbour, and throws the two most prominent English leaders together in the English vanguard.

Still, if the situation is considered without prejudice in favour of one particular source, one reasonable conclusion would be that the Scots fought in three, not four, divisions. The only account contradicting this is Barbour's, and his version merits closer examination not only on historical, but on literary grounds. There is in fact one division in Barbour's account which arouses a fair amount of suspicion. The king's command is no problem. It is supported by *Lanercost*, but even that is hardly necessary. He is the king, therefore he leads a division, according to good old Scottish tradition. Edward Bruce is the king's brother, he is earl of Carrick, and he has been leading independent campaigns since 1308 at least. Therefore, both the seniority of his rank and his previous experience make it very likely that his leadership of a division is authentic. Thomas Randolph is the king's nephew and earl of Moray – a province which he held 'in regality', that is, with vice-regal powers and responsibilities. Again, it is plausible to assume that he held a command. This leaves James Douglas and Walter the Steward, alleged leaders of the third Scottish division. Stewart is a teenager: Barbour calls him a 'bot a berdless hyne'.[18] While he held the prestigious office of High Steward, this was a heritable position which should not be seen as proof of experience or competence. If Walter Stewart had distinguished himself before the battle, it has completely escaped the notice of contemporary sources. It will also have been noted that not one of the accounts of the battle so much as mentions Stewart.

His youth is, of course, Barbour's excuse for teaming him up with James Douglas. Douglas's most recent biographer, who accepts the four division set-up, praises her hero's generosity for allowing the king to saddle him with this helpless infant:

> Convention precluded the Steward's subordination to a commander of inferior social rank, and the king therefore asked Douglas to accept nominal joint command of a division for whose handling he would of course be responsible in practice. He seems to have accepted this cheerfully enough; the Scots put first things first.[19]

With this comment in mind, it is time for a closer look at James Douglas.

James Douglas was the son and heir of William Douglas, a middle-rank baron who had died in English captivity around 1299. The family held lands in Douglasdale and Carmichael. At this stage, they were neither particularly rich nor particularly important. James Douglas was knighted at Bannockburn – on the first day of the battle according to a French source,[20] on the second according to Barbour.[21] Thus, we are dealing not only with a teenaged High Steward leading this division – the joint leader has barely, if indeed at all, obtained the rank of knight. Douglas's knighting at Bannockburn ties in with the issue of his experience in martial matters, which is a slightly sore point with some writers. The date for his knighting, 1314, has indeed quite often been commented on and indeed disputed, because historians have considered it 'strange that this honour should have been so long delayed, seeing how many deeds of prowess he had accomplished during eight years of warfare.'[22] Douglas's hagiographer refuses to believe that Douglas had not been a knight since at least 1308.[23] But it is surely convincing evidence that before Bannockburn, Douglas was never called a knight in royal charters, whereas the very first surviving charter dated after Bannockburn duly refers to him as *miles*,[24] so that the 1314 date will have to be accepted.

The explanation sometimes put forward by puzzled historians is that knights were customarily created on the field of battle, and that Bruce's eclectic fighting methods and total avoidance of pitched battles resulted in a certain lack of opportunity for this procedure. This is a perfectly valid point, but besides that, it is perhaps advisable to consider the true number of those 'deeds of prowess'. The list of 'deeds committed', upon which statements like the above are based, derives from Barbour's *Bruce*, and it is admittedly long. The list, however, of deeds that can be substantiated is considerably shorter. The number of Douglas's reliably documented activities before 1314 is not particularly impressive. Under Bruce's supervision, he attacked the English garrison in his own castle;[25] he then took part in one or two campaigns in Galloway led by either Robert Bruce or Edward Bruce;[26] he may have participated in a few more attacks on a few more castles, and he took part in Bruce's raids in England. Finally Douglas took Roxburgh castle with a spectacularly successful assault, early in 1314[27] – but at that time, everybody was taking castles. Moray was just about to take Edinburgh, Bruce had taken Perth, and in Barbour's recycling of a well-known folk motif, a peasant with a few cronies and a cart had taken Linlithgow. Apart from the Roxburgh incident, there is no evidence of anything that would have made Douglas's knighting imperative before some conventional opportunity offered itself. We note that even Barbour, who was distinctly partial to Douglas, evinces not the slightest hint of surprise at his 'belated' knighting.

To return to the question of Bannockburn, it could be argued that it is at least unlikely that someone who was on the day before Bannockburn only a squire, and who had not distinguished himself in any major way in the past six years, should a day later be given an entire division of the Scottish army to command in a desperate and vitally important battle. This is the historical side of it. It is now time to consider Barbour's literary rendition of the third division's activities – for a quick review of what Douglas and Stewart, in Barbour's account, do with their command.

Let it be said straight away that Stewart does nothing. Barbour mentions him twice at the start, as the joint leader; then he ignores him until he reaches the climax of the battle on day two, when Stewart is on record as 'being there'.[28] Douglas, in fact, also does nothing, but he does it much more impressively: on day one of the battle, there is a moment when Moray with his division is barely holding off an English advance. Douglas worries about him and suggests that he should go to help:

> He is in perell bot he be
> Sone helpyt for his fayis ar ma
> Yan he and horsyt weill alsua,

Keeping the Customer Satisfied

> And with your leve I will me speid
> To help him for he has ned,
> All wmbeweround with his fayis is he.[29]

The king is unwilling to let him go[30], but Douglas pesters him into submission:

> 'Certis', said Iames, 'I ma na wis
> Se yat his fayis him suppris
> Quhen yat I may set help yar-till,
> With your leve sekyrly I will
> Help him or dey in-to ye payn.'
>
> 'Do yan and speid ye sone agayn,'
> Ye king said, and he held his way.[31]

This is perhaps unlikely, but acceptable so far. When, however, Douglas approaches Moray with his division, he discovers that Moray is, after all, holding his own successfully; this causes Douglas to stop his advance, to deliver sixteen lines of monologue in which he refuses to compromise Moray's glory by bringing unneeded help, and then to relapse into inactivity.[32]

The entire episode is a glowing illustration of Douglas's sense of loyalty and honour. It is also the only action, if such it may be called, of Douglas's division on the first day of battle. On the second day, Douglas's third division charges alongside Moray's first.[33] Douglas's valour is mentioned, but neither with particular emphasis nor as directed towards a particular objective.[34] This sequence of events has for the last six centuries been treated as a perfectly satisfactory account of how Douglas spent his time on those two days in 1314. However, its main elements read like romance rather than reality, literature rather than history. This is a crucial point, because any reopening of the question of what Douglas was really doing during the battle inevitably raises the somewhat more awkward and more far-reaching question of how much trust a historian is entitled to place in John Barbour.

John Barbour has long been considered a fairly reliable source for the history of Bruce's reign. Outstanding historians have called the poet 'a most careful and exact recorder'[35] and his accounts 'strikingly accurate'.[36] Of course, Barbour himself claimed that he was writing a true story, as far as that lay within his intellectual capacity:

> Yarfor I wald fayne set my will,
> Giff my wyt mycht suffice yartill
> To put in writ a suthfast story.[37]

This claim to be writing a true story, however, combined with some kind of modest disclaimer, is something every literary scholar will have encountered. It is a literary topos, and moreover one which was considered indispensable in the middle ages. Even Blind Harry claimed that his *Wallace* was historically accurate, and he was rather more emphatic in his claim than Barbour[38] – but academics have yet to suggest that the *Wallace* is serious history any more than its modern-day Hollywood derivative.

The main reason why so much faith is placed in Barbour is that there is a serious shortage of other evidence. Barbour is often the only writer who presents a coherent story. Charter evidence, or the odd entry in annals or exchequer rolls, are often mere snatches of information without a meaningful context. Barbour provides the context. In ideal circumstances, charter or chronicle information fits in with Barbour's accounts: there are such instances, and they are the foundations of Barbour's reputation for reliability. More often though, Barbour offers a story which is neither substantiated nor contradicted by other sources. The general approach has been to accept these stories as true. Finally, there is a growing number of instances where Barbour can be proven wrong. Individual examples have been pointed out, and continue to be noted, by most academics working with the period. The full extent, however, has not been recognised, and individually, Barbour's errors are regarded with too much indulgence and are not allowed to affect the basic idea of his reliability.

Demonstrably, Barbour errs frequently. Even where his basic narrative is correct, he can rarely resist adding some embellishment. Moreover, it has long been known that he consciously fiddled his facts on several occasions – for instance, his non-account of Bruce's early and less than heroic career. Therefore, historians should know better than to value his evidence over that of more contemporary sources, especially where these other sources support each other. In this particular case, it would appear that Barbour's 'third battle', led by a beardless boy and a newly-made knight[39], is a figment of the poet's powerful imagination. This raises the question of where Douglas really was and what he was doing.

The only person said in the English accounts to be inconvenienced by Douglas is Gloucester. Gloucester was leading the English van, so normally one might have expected his opponent to be Moray, who was leading the Scottish van. The most recent explanation is offered by Matthew McDiarmid in the notes to his edition of Barbour's *Bruce*, a regrettably inconspicuous place for his important observations. McDiarmid points out that in Barbour's account, Douglas only appears in connection with Moray; in the English accounts, both Douglas *and* Moray are mentioned as leaders of the Scottish van. His conclusion is that Douglas may have been subordinate to

Moray in the vanguard; after all, Moray was far more senior in rank. Douglas might have led the spearhead of the division, which could explain why the author of the *Vita* thought that he was commanding it in its entirety.[40]

This argument appears persuasive. Douglas's position in Bruce's entourage was in 1314 by no means as high as Barbour's *Bruce* encourages everybody to believe. In addition, Moray and Douglas were a well-known double-act in later years, with their repeated raids into England. In fact, the idea that Moray and Douglas could have been together is not entirely new. As early as 1577, Raphael Hollinshead assumed that Douglas and his men were part of the division commanded by Moray.[41] In the seventeenth century, Hume of Godscroft argued along similar lines.[42] Why this line of reasoning did not recur in a single one of the later reconstructions of the battle is difficult to comprehend, and this failure must probably be ascribed to a general tendency to place an extraordinary amount of faith in Barbour's *Bruce*. Mr McDiarmid is the only modern academic to raise objections to the 'received', i.e. Barbour's, version.*

The mention of both Douglas and Moray as leaders of the first division makes it appear reasonable to assume, as McDiarmid does, that they were together in that division and that Moray, the senior in rank, commanded it. But how can we reconcile this with the fact that both men with their 'first division' are said to have engaged different opponents? We may have to accept the *Lanercost* account which combines the opponents of Moray and Douglas in one division. Possibly the extreme constraints of space on the English side and the normal chaos of battle are responsible for much of the confusion regarding who attacked whom. Bunched up as they were, it would have been difficult to tell where one English division ended and the next started.

Where does this leave Barbour's account of Douglas's abortive rescue attempt? This writer believes it can be assigned to the realm of chivalric romance. Barbour actually called his work as a 'romanys',[43] a point that is too often ignored by historians. The poet's avowed aim was to praise the heroes of Bruce's time, with particular reference to the king and James Douglas.[44] This clearly makes *The Bruce* a piece of literature, and the rules in literature are quite different from the rules in historiography. It makes sense to expect that the poet will embellish details of the story to achieve his end. Douglas was one of the two main heroes of Barbour's epic. The battle of Bannockburn is the highlight of *The Bruce*, taking up almost 2000

---

* Since this paper was first presented, A.A.M. Duncan has also expressed doubts about the existence of the 4th division and the composition of its leadership (Duncan, *The Bruce*, Edinburgh 1997, p. 445). He suggested that Douglas may have fought under Edward Bruce.

lines. No matter how small Douglas's part in the battle may have been in reality, artistic balance demanded that he should be given a conspicuous role. Barbour's solution is admirable. If in reality Douglas did no spectacular deeds at Bannockburn, a dispassionate look at Barbour's tale still shows Douglas doing no spectacular deeds at Bannockburn. Barbour weaves a tale around reality which does not alter the essence of the facts, but gives his hero an opportunity to shine. Douglas is shown with an honourable command, preparing to do something for wholly admirable reasons, and is then shown deciding not to do it for even more admirable reasons. Actual events remain unaffected. Throughout Barbour's account of the main battle, apart from major attacks involving everyone, Douglas, ultimately, does nothing at all. Barbour succeeds in making his inactivity meaningful and in making Douglas shine in whiter armour than if he had single-handedly taken on the entire English army. It is sheer artistry; no wonder everybody wants to believe that it happened.

Artistic judgement and sensibility are very acceptable reasons why a responsible archdeacon who claims to be telling the truth should do such a thing. But there is another reason which has less to do with art and more with political realities: Barbour wrote his story for consumption at the court of the current king, Robert II, the first monarch of the Stewart dynasty. His father had been Walter Stewart, the 'berdless hyne' and alleged joint commander of the dubious Bannockburn division. Not only was Robert II the son of Walter Stewart – he was also the progenitor of an entire football team, complete with reserve players. Robert II had twenty-one offspring that we know of, and all of the males held wealthy estates or earldoms and powerful positions in the country. They were Walter Stewart's grandchildren, and they were making up half of Barbour's audience.

Douglas's role is explained equally easily. For one thing, after Bannockburn Douglas did become the kind of champion as which he is portrayed as rather prematurely at the battle. His deeds were celebrated and amply rewarded, and by the end of this life he ruled supreme in the Borders. His career laid the foundations of later Douglas power. Only a few years after his death, the head of a collateral branch of the family was created first earl of Douglas, acquired more territory and expanded the power-base. The second earl of Douglas was alive in 1475 and was prominent in campaigning at the side of the king's son against the English in the Borders.[45] He would have been part of Barbour's audience, was the head of the most powerful kin-group besides the Stewarts, and clearly wanted to hear nice things said about his family.

He was not the only one. The audience would have contained another very powerful Douglas who was *not* earl only because he was of illegitimate birth: Archibald Douglas, called the Archibald the Grim. He had a record of unwavering loyalty to the Scottish monarchs; he had been one of the mainstays of first David II's and then Robert II's administration and had refused to join in the antics of the other branch of the family. Amongst his various positions and tasks he was Warden of the West Marches from 1364, and was frequently involved in international diplomacy with France, Rome and England on behalf of both kings. In 1369 he was made lord of Galloway, later also lord of Bothwell. Such was his importance that upon the death of the second earl of Douglas in 1388 he was permitted to inherit the earldom despite his illegitimacy. He was the son of James Douglas, leader of an imaginary division at Bannockburn.

Thus, it all seems to fit together rather uncannily. By claiming that this division existed and was led by Stewart and Douglas, Barbour could count on pleasing the two most powerful kin-groups of his time.

This chapter has attempted to show how a poet can come up with a situation as inherently unlikely as a newly-made knight and a 16-year-old leading a division in a most crucial battle, and something as inherently pointless as Douglas's actions or rather non-actions, and influence perceptions of that battle for centuries, possibly millennia to come. 'Millennia', because ultimately it matters very little what this paper proves or disproves. Nobody cares what Hollinshead said in 1577 and nobody cares what Hume of Godscroft said in the seventeenth century. Despite the rather academic but hopefully convincing exposition at the beginning of this chapter, it is unlikely that doubts about Douglas's role at Bannockburn will ever become part of the canon. Dialogues invented by Barbour *are* part of it, and will remain so. He knew how to capture an audience and how to construct a credible narrative. Literature and myth are stronger than history; eventually, they become accepted as history and it is impossible to do anything about it with mere insistence on fact and evidence. Barbour wins.

It has been suggested to this writer that Barbour's account may be more relevant and influential than modern historical accounts. This statement could be taken further: Barbour's account *is*, for all practical purposes, the modern account. He wrote something that people in 1375 liked to hear, and something that is still popular today. It's a great tale after all, full of chivalry, high ideals, roses falling from chaplets, small folk charging up hillsides to help their betters, and knights leaving the honour of the battlefield to their comrades.

To summarise, there is no overall convincing evidence to suggest that James Douglas commanded a division of the Scottish army at Bannockburn; all sources except one indicate that the Scots fought in only three divisions, and the other named commanders (Moray, Carrick and the king) were far more likely candidates. Douglas's division is suspect from beginning to end. He had been newly knighted, was not part of the king's family, and had not yet performed as many spectacular exploits as Barbour would have us believe. His alleged 'colleague', Walter Stewart, was a teenager and had so far achieved little if anything. Barbour's story seems to be an admirable combination of a fact indicated by other sources (the fact that Douglas played no very conspicuous part at Bannockburn) with a chivalrous, if completely fictitious, tale that accounts for this circumstance to the satisfaction of every Douglas supporter or descendant. The poet's reliability as a chronicler should be regarded as terminally compromised in any case. His competence as an artist can be judged by the number of those who six hundred years later still reserve a little square on their maps of Bannockburn for a division that probably never existed.

Notes

1. References to *Barbour's Bruce* (eds.) M.P. McDiarmid and J.A.C. Stevenson, 3 vols, *Scottish Text Society* (Edinburgh 1980–85). An accessible, very recently published new edition contains a translation of the text. John Barbour *The Bruce* (ed and trans.) A.A.M. Duncan, Canongate Classics (Edinburgh 1997).

2. Cf. the maps which accompany most reconstructions of the battle: Philip Christison, 'Bannockburn – 23rd and 24th June 1314. A Study in Military History', in: *Proceedings of the Society of Antiquaries of Scotland* 90 (1956–1957), facing 173, 174; John E Morris, *Bannockburn*, (Cambridge 1914) appendix; William Mackay Mackenzie, *The Battle of Bannockburn*, (Glasgow 1913), facing 52, 74; W. Seymour, 'The Battle of Bannockburn 1314', *History Today* 23 (1973), 569; Barrie Goedhals, 'John Barbour, "The Bruce", and Bannockburn', *Unisa English Studies* 2 (June 1968), 54. Professor Barrow does not show the divisions on his maps, but accepts that there were four of them, G.W.S. Barrow, *Robert Bruce and the Community of the Realm of Scotland*, 3rd edn., (Edinburgh 1988), 216–17 (hereafter referred to as 'Barrow, *Bruce*').

3. *Vita Edwardi Secundi (Monachi Cuiusdam Malmesberiensis)*, (ed.) N. Denholm-Young, (London 1957).

4. *Scalacronica, by Sir Thomas Gray of Heton, knight. A Chronicle of England and Scotland from AD MLXXI to AD MCCCLXII*, (ed.) Joseph Stevenson, Maitland Club (Edinburgh 1836), (hereafter *Scalacronica*).

5. *Chronicon de Lanercost* (ed.) Joseph Stevenson, Maitland Club (Edinburgh 1839), 225 (hereafter *Chron. Lanercost*).

6. Douglas *prime turme Scotorum preerat* and *aciem comitis Gloucestrie acriter inuasit*. *Vita Edwardi*, 52.

7. *Scalacronica* 141.

8. *Chron. Lanercost* 225, 226.

9. *Bruce* XI 169–71. This otherwise rare unanimity may be due to the fact that Gloucester died spectacularly, which would have left a lasting impression.

10. *Bruce* XIII 309–319. Sir Giles floats about. On the first day he is not in the vanguard but in part of the division commanded by Edward II (possibly the reserve?) *Bruce* XI.179–82.

11. McDiarmid, *Bruce*, 93. However, *Lanercost* also has Clifford in the vanguard, which contradicts Barbour *Chron. Lanercost* 225.

12. *Bruce* XI 312–13, 523–39. Clifford leads the body making for Stirling, the 'best of all ye ost'.

13. *Chron. Lanercost* 225.

14. Barbour has Hereford with Gloucester in the van – we might be dealing with a simple mix-up between the two names.

15. *Bruce* XII 498–501.

16. *Vita Edwardi* 52.

17. *Bruce* XI 328–30.

18. *Bruce* XI 224.

19. I. M. Davis, *The Black Douglas* (London 1974) 69.

20. *Chronographia Regum Francorum*, (ed.) H. Moranvillé (Paris 1891) vol. I, 182.

21. *Bruce* XII 417–18.

22. Sir Herbert Maxwell, *History of the House of Douglas* (Freemantle 1902) 45. Barrow, *Bruce*, 367 n. 42; McDiarmid, *Bruce* I, 92.

23. Davis, *Douglas*, 76n.

24. *The Acts of the Parliament of Scotland*, (eds.) T. Thomson and C. Innes, (Edinburgh 1814–1875) 12 vols. I, 459 and *The Acts of Robert I, Regesta Regum Scottorum* vol. V (ed.) A.A.M. Duncan (Edinburgh 1988) (hereafter referred to as *RRS* V), nos 385, 7, 388, 384, which are all dated before Bannockburn, and compare *RRS* V, no. 42.

25. Public Record Office, Special Collections 8/95 (4730). The episode of the 'Douglas Larder' as narrated by Barbour, *Bruce* V 255–430 is only very tenuously documented in independent sources and may never have taken place.

26. *Calendar of Documents relating to Scotland*, (ed.) Joseph Bain (Edinburgh 1887), vol III, 14, 15; vol. V, (eds.) Grant G. Simpson and James D. Galbraith, (Edinburgh 1986), 655; *Chron. Lanercost* 212.

27. *Johannis de Fordun Chronica Gentis Scotorum* (ed.) W.F. Skene, (Edinburgh 1871), Ann. CXXX; *Chron. Lanercost* 223; *Bruce* X 395–496.

28. *Bruce* XIII 186–187.

29. *Bruce* XI 642–647.
30. *Bruce* XI 648–652.
31. *Bruce* XI 653–662
32. *Bruce* XII 105–29
33. *Bruce* XIII 3–15.
34. *Bruce* XII 186–93.
35. Barrow, *Bruce* 313.
36. Archibald A.M. Duncan, 'The Community of the Realm and Robert Bruce', *Scottish Historical Review* 45 (1966) 199.
37. *Bruce* I 12–14
38. *Harry's Wallace* (ed.) M. P McDiarmid, 2 vols, *Scottish Text Society* (Edinburgh 1968–9) XI 1410, 1438.
39. It should be pointed out that Walter Stewart was also newly knighted *Bruce* XII 417; *Chronographia* 182.
40. McDiarmid, *Bruce* I 89.
41. Raphael Hollinshead, *The Scottish Chronicle* (Arbroath 1805), 441.
42. David Hume of Godscroft, *The History of the Houses of Douglas and Angus*, (Edinburgh 1644), 35. Like Barbour, Hume of Godscroft had an interest in showing Douglas as a principal figure, and he proposed that Douglas and Moray shared the command of the vanguard.
43. *Bruce* I 446.
44. *Bruce* I 21–33.
45. Stephen Boardman, *The Early Stewart Kings: Robert II and Robert III, 1371–1406* (East Linton 1996) 116, 121–22.

5

Aspects of Scotland's Social, Political and Cultural Scene in the Late 17th and Early 18th Centuries, as Mirrored in the Wallace and Bruce Tradition

George M. Brunsden

Scots, wha hae wi' Wallace bled,
Scots, wham Bruce has aften led,
Welcome to your gory bed,
Or to victorie.[1]

Robert Burns, like a number of his near contemporaries, was a devoted admirer of the story of William Wallace, at least insofar as it had been rendered by Hamilton of Gilbertfield in 1722. It was this epic poem – first created by Blind Harry, then re-distilled by William Hamilton – that Burns would claim 'poured a Scottish prejudice in my veins which will boil along there till the flood-gates of life shut in eternal rest'.[2] Thus one extraordinary poem, the *Wallace*, could serve as a catalyst for a good deal of creative genius.

Epics like Blind Harry's *Wallace*, and John Barbour's *Bruce* have stood the test of time not only because of their literary merits, but also because of their inspirational and instructional roles. Perhaps less so today, but certainly in bygone days, poets were never thought to be entertainers alone: they were also teachers, and preservers of communal values and traditions.[3] As such, perhaps one of the initial purposes behind the creation of the *Wallace* was to chastise James III for his 'pro-English drift'.[4] But it is how both the *Bruce* and the *Wallace* served the early modern Scottish community that is the concern of this chapter. Throughout the period, both the Guardian of Scotland and the champion of Bannockburn were called upon many times to serve a higher purpose. Both these legendary figures – distinct from their historical counterparts – survived as symbols of heroism and patriotism, undoubtedly due to the indelible stamp they had made upon the nation at large. Responding to the traditions associated with two universally recognised figures from the Scottish past, several late seventeenth- and early eighteenth-century poets embraced the cults of Wallace and King Robert, with an eye toward promoting their own agendas. As national symbols of heroism, patriotism, and altruism, the legendary Bruce and Wallace could still serve a Scotland, or at least concerned factions within it, grappling with such disruptive eighteenth-century issues as the Union of the Parliaments, Jacobitism, concepts of government and kingship, and even language.

As far as the origin of one half of the myth is concerned, Blind Harry's *Wallace* was seemingly an exceedingly popular subject if its publishing record is anything to go by:

> During the seventeenth and eighteenth centuries at least forty-four editions were printed. The chief presses were those of Edinburgh and Glasgow, although Aberdeen and Belfast helped in the work.[5]

Furthermore, the inventories of books held in stock by a number of seventeenth- to early eighteenth-century printers and booksellers, upon their deaths, reveal a fairly sizeable quota of the *Wallace* on hand. When Henry Charteris died in 1599 his inventory contained 'fyve scoir tua Wallaces'.[6] Upon the settling of her estate in 1717, it was revealed that Mrs Anderson had '662 Wallaces' in her inventory, among numerous other titles.[7] From this and similar evidence we might conclude that although the *Wallace* did not top the best-seller list during this period, it was still a popular item. Though we must concede Carnie's point that 1668–1775 was a 'boom' period for Scottish printing in general,[8] it still seems apparent that the popularity of Wallace grew through the passage of time.

Of the numerous editions of the *Wallace* produced during the eighteenth century, Hamilton's so-called English translation, *A New Edition of the Life and Heroik Actions of . . . Sir William Wallace*, is one of the most familiar for several reasons, not the least being that it was read by Burns.[9] In addition, it is this edition which in the past has been touted as being indicative of the sad state of Scots as a literary language, an idea perhaps partially sustained by the book's own subtitle.[10] Supposedly, Gilbertfield's was *the* singular edition of the *Wallace* that everyone had been eagerly awaiting, an idea that still seems to find favour with modern scholars, including the editor of the most recent reprint of Hamilton's book.[11] The theory goes that the general mass of those (purportedly) dim-witted and 'un-Enlightened' folk of early modern Scotland, just could not possibly cope with Harry's language. It is apparent that the notion of the *Wallace* being a text far beyond the capacity of all save the literary elite, was one long held. As a less than charitable, and certainly patronising, nineteenth-century authority assessed the situation, despite the apparently numerous copies of the *Wallace* in circulation, only the literati possessed the capacity to read such, owing to the difficult language found in the Blind Minstrel's handiwork.[12] In fairness, these opinions may have been influenced by the printing of Dr Jamieson's edition in 1820, a version which claims to have returned to the original manuscript for its authority (as was also the claim made for the 1790 edition). Thus in the 1820 edition, the language of Harry, or a close approximation thereof, had seemingly resurfaced. Such was not the case with previous editions of the *Wallace* (discounting for the moment the special case of Gilbertfield's version). What appears to have occurred with the language of successive editions of the *Wallace* was a sort of gradual, or creeping, anglicisation. The language of Harry's classic was thus transformed into a sort of 'Anglo-Scots'. This last statement, however, requires some explanation, and the nature of the transformation can only be appreciated through an examination of the text of successive editions.

The scholar that virtually all others cite on the demise of literary Scots is David Daiches, who argues that:

> From the late sixteenth century on, this Scottish literary language was increasingly challenged by English. The Reformation, the Union of the Crowns in 1603, the political and religious situation in the seventeenth century, and finally the Union of 1707, all had their effect in helping to make Scottish writers turn to English as their medium, even though they continued to speak Scots.[13]

Daiches adds that the departure of James VI, and the royal court – the nation's 'chief if not only source of patronage of the arts' – for the balmier political climate of the south, resulted in Scotland and the Scots language experiencing something of an artistic drought.[14] Such comments would presumably apply to all forms of poetry, both original, and re-edited. That being so, it is reasonable to assume that the language of an eighteenth-century edition of the *Wallace* would bear little resemblance to Harry's original, which is indeed the case, but the situation is not nearly so 'cut and dried' as some might have thought.

There is no manuscript in Harry's own hand to use as a starting point for a comparison of the language employed in the successive versions of the *Wallace*, the earliest known being John Ramsay's transcription of 1488.[15] An idea of the language Ramsay employed may be obtained from the following episode involving Wallace's (re)conquest of St Johnstoun (modern-day Perth):

> A hundreth men ye kyrk tuk for suc[c]our
> Bot Wallace Wald no grace grant in y*at* hour
> He slay bad all off cruell sotheroun keyn
> And said yai had to Sanct Ihonstoun Enemys beyn
> ffour hundreth men in to ye toun war deid
> Sewyn scor *with* lyff chapyt out off yat steid[16]

The same passage is presented in the second printed edition thus:

> Ane vnndreth men the Kirk tuik for succour,
> Bot Wallace wald na grace grant in that hour.
> He bad slay all of cruell Sutheroun kyn,
> Thame for to slay, he said it was na syn.
> Four hundreth men within the toun was deid,
> Seuin scoir on lyfe, chaipit out of that steid.[17]

There thus are some minor differences in the language and orthography of Charteris' and Lekpreuik's 1570 printed edition, but these are very subtle and far fewer than some commentators have alleged.[18] Generally speaking, Ramsay's manuscript, and the printed edition of the ardent (though at times slightly confused) vernacularist Charteris,[19] are both in Middle Scots. However, Miller is correct when he points to the most obvious, and significant, difference between the two, that 'the manuscript is the work of a . . . Roman Catholic while the printed edition is that of a Protestant'.[20] This mutation is representative of sentiments we would expect to find in a book published only a decade after the Reformation, by a man who would serve as kirk elder for the north-east quarter of Edinburgh during the 1573–74 session,[21] since in the spirit of true Calvinist zeal, Wallace the warrior – whose business it was to waste human life – examines his martial actions for any presence of sin before his God.

In charting the publishing history of Blind Harry's *Wallace* it is noticeable that the language gradually takes on a more English character (see Appendix). However, the change from Scots to English is subtle and protracted, with the most momentous shift occurring around the time of Andrew Hart's 1618 edition, which in itself, still contained some Scots. But after Hart the language of Blind Harry seems to stabilise, so that by the middle of the seventeenth century, it is more or less set. The situation regarding the various efforts at re-editing the *Wallace* during the following century is in partial agreement with Craigie:

> . . . the climax naturally came with the Union of the Crowns. After that date the former equality between the English and Scottish tongues was completely gone, and English was definitely recognised as the standard form for literary work, although the native tongue might persist in colouring it to a greater or lesser degree according to the taste or learning of the writer.[22]

The 'average' reader from the early eighteenth century probably would have experienced little, if any, difficulty in understanding the text. However – somewhat variably between the individual editions themselves – they still contained a notable 'sprinkling' of Scots, roughly on par with some of the early quasi-vernacular efforts of Allan Ramsay. This latter characteristic of the *Wallace*'s text is very evident in Carmichael and Millar's Glasgow printed edition of 1736 (refer to Appendix). It noticeably retains such Scots words as 'bushment' (ambush), 'fra', and 'dang' (strike), words carried over from earlier editions, such as the accompanying examples from Charteris and Hart.[23] In the examples cited here, virtually the only Scots word dropped from 1736 that was present in 1618 is 'syn'.[24] The situation is considerably different when comparing 1736 and 1618 to 1570. The oldest of these three contains much more Scots: 'atouir' (out over), 'quhen' (when), 'quhill' (while), brig (bridge), and 'yet' (gate). The extracts appended, while of necessity brief, serve to underscore the basic point that the text of the *Wallace* was most profoundly affected during the first half of the seventeenth century, with only slight change occurring thereafter.

The reason for these changes to the text of the *Wallace* appears intertwined with the history of Scottish printing, insofar as it was related to the Bible. Though a feeble attempt was made *c.*1520 to produce a Bible in Scots by Murdoch Nisbet,[25] English was the language 'that fostered religious reform in Scotland', while from the reformers' point of view, Scots and English were interchangeable variations of the 'vulgar tongue' of the Lowlanders.[26] Further, the early Presbyterians had a desire to present Scripture to these people in as plain and simple a manner as possible. Certainly in the case of Knox himself, the Almighty's wisdom was pure and direct: 'The word of God is plane . . .'[27] Therefore, it became the reformers' mandate to present God's Word to the people in their own 'vulgar' – English or Scots – language to ensure that His will was commonly understandable, an endeavour in which, in their opinion, the Roman Church had failed.

The reformers thus relied upon English translated Bibles, and it was these which may have had a profound effect upon the language of Scottish literature,[28] including the *Wallace*. But the most significant change, where the *Wallace* was concerned, was not during the Reformation itself, but some fifty years later. The key individual here was Andrew Hart. Though Thomas Bassadyne and Alexander Arbuthnet were producing New Testaments and complete Geneva Bibles during the 1570s, Hart's 1610 Bible was the first produced which seemed to better address the religious character of Scotland, being a more Calvinist (i.e., strongly anti-Catholic) version of the Geneva. It seems reasonable to assume that Hart's mandate was still akin to that of the original reformers, namely to produce a Bible in as straightforward a language as possible.

Hart also printed some of the earliest editions of the *Wallace*, in 1611, 1618, and 1620.[29] Perhaps he viewed the language of Blind Harry in a fashion similar to that of the Bible. Thus, Andrew Hart's *Wallaces* were presented in a language which he thought most literate readers of Lowland Anglo-Scots could understand, even though it still retained traces of Middle Scots in an effort to be faithful to the original. Perhaps Hart's rationale for producing his editions of *Wallace* in this Anglo-Scots had some basis in everyday reality. The tone of the early translated bibles would have been reinforced every Sabbath,[30] and from 1638 (with the introduction of the first pocket-sized bibles[31]) people could experience its language for themselves. This is not to say that this language was, or would become, commonly *spoken*, only that it might have become a universally adopted literary tongue. Nevertheless, if the drive to present the bible in a universally understandable literary language was carried over by Hart into his editions of the *Wallace*, then it is he, and not William Hamilton, who should be credited with producing the first effective, and certainly most authentic, 'modern' version of the Guardian's life.

Most editors of the *Wallace* who followed Hart seemed to follow his lead as to language and orthography, with the aim of producing a book that could be understood by as wide an audience as possible. In fact, they may have actually used his *Wallace* as a model for their own.[32] Some of their own personal predilections obviously were indulged, which were likely guided by such influences as both the printed and spoken versions of God's Word, the original language of Blind Harry as it came to them through previous editions, plus perhaps everyday speech employed by both themselves and those around them. As a result, the text of Harry had metamorphosed to such an extent that it seemingly rendered Hamilton's 'improved' edition largely redundant in its purported aim of creating a more understandable text. What, in effect, is to be discerned in the vast majority of the reprints of Blind Harry produced during the late seventeenth and early eighteenth centuries, and which fall into the rather amorphous category of chap-book literature, is a text related in a palatable form of 'Anglo-Scots.' This may have been the language with which the general reading public was most comfortable, while still being able to appreciate a little of Harry's own diction. And it is apparent that most of these editions were read by numerous readers, since few of the surviving copies fail to have that 'well-thumbed' look about them.

Thus the text of these editions of the *Wallace* were not exactly in Harry's language any longer. This may be the impetus for John Pinkerton's three-volume edition of 1790 which proudly announced that, under the watchful eye of the Earl of Buchan, it had returned to the original manuscript for its authority and was determined to follow 'the ancient and true orthography'.[33] It would appear, then, that Pinkerton, like perhaps Jamieson after him, realised the text of the *Wallace* had mutated over time.

Social, Political and Cultural Scene

One eighteenth-century edition of the *Wallace* seemingly attempted to reverse the long-standing trend of dropping Scots in favour of English words, namely the alleged Freebairn edition, possibly conceived or produced in either 1714 or 1715, but possibly as late as 1730,[34] and certainly only released in 1758. According to Jamieson,[35] and later parroted by Moir,[36] the edition produced by the former King's Printer was held up due to his involvement with the Jacobites in the fateful years of 1714–15. By supporting the Jacobites, Robert Freebairn forfeited the position of King's Printer, and instead turned to printing on behalf of the Pretender. Maybe for this reason the edition in question is curiously in want of a printer's name on the title-page: perhaps in 1758 it was believed that crediting it to a former Jacobite printer might be just too embarrassing, and might possibly hinder sales.

When analysing the preparations taken by Freebairn for the printing of his *Wallace*, McDiarmid's comments seem among the most illuminating. He believes that around 1730, Freebairn employed an individual named Tate to 'transcribe Ramsay's manuscript and collate it with one of Hart's editions'.[37] If McDiarmid's assumptions are correct, then what we have represented in Freebairn's *Wallace* is the first attempt at producing a 'scholarly' edition of the text,[38] but one still in touch with the commonest language standards of the day. Furthermore, Andrew Hart's importance is again brought to the fore, who because of his early work with the *Wallace* and the Bible (not to mention the *Bruce*), may have been regarded later on as something of a textual authority.[39]

Freebairn's version of Blind Harry has one noteworthy feature of language: it contains a slightly stronger dosage of Scots within its text than many other more or less recent editions of the *Wallace*. McDiarmid (in this one instance) is wrong when he chastises 'the modernising policy of Freebairn'.[40] If we are to take this term as referring to the practice of employing English substitutes for Scots words, then Freebairn was in fact somewhat less inclined toward this policy than most of his contemporaries (or near-contemporaries): his Anglo-Scots was ever so slightly more weighted towards the Scots side. With little doubt, his phraseology and style of versification also were still true to Harry. And related to this last point, certainly if the term 'modernisation' is meant to apply to the sort of policy toward modifying Harry adopted by Hamilton, then Freebairn's effort hardly qualifies as a 'modern text'. What then, were Freebairn's motives: why, with his transcription of the *Wallace*, was he interested in producing the first attempt at being more faithful to the Blind Harry tradition?

Perhaps Freebairn's *Wallace* was an expression of its editor's traditionalist-minded ideologies. Another such expression on his part may have been his devotion to the Jacobite cause. In his mind, devotion to the vernacular literary culture of Lowland Scotland could sit comfortably beside empathy for the old lineage – both were causes built upon a framework of centuries of tradition. Both were also thought to have been seriously threatened by recent socio-political events. The former King's Printer was thus quite conservative in his outlook; in addition to hoping that the regal/political clock could be turned back, Freebairn also wished the survival of old literary conventions. Robert Freebairn was not alone in his ideas: others had desired to resuscitate the vernacular while, in varying degrees, holding some loyalty towards the Stewarts. James Watson has been justifiably credited with 'initiating' the so-called vernacular revival and patriotic publishing movement; he too was a likely Jacobite sympathiser, though he would have nothing to do with the 1715 rebellion. Allan Ramsay was another father of the vernacular revival, a patriot, and a nominal Jacobite; wisely he steered clear of the 1715 uprising, and was conveniently out of town when the Jacobites entered Edinburgh during the Autumn of 1745. Watson and Ramsay were cautious about their Jacobitism; not so in the case of Freebairn, whose politics cost him the much coveted title of King's Printer. Nevertheless, the pertinent question that will be addressed below, is how Robert Freebairn's devotion towards the story of a commoner, who had shown people and monarchs alike the path toward freedom, is related to his affinity for a line of monarchs who, ultimately, believed in the supremacy of the ruler.

If the majority of printers involved in replicating the *Wallace* had an agenda of any sort, it was simply to choose those words that were 'closest at hand' to convey a nationally recognised tale of heroism and bravery. There was no attempt to promote a vernacular revival as poets like Ramsay and Robert Fergusson had tried to do; no attempt to promote proper speech and manners through the poetic medium as the Augustan movement was determined to do with its (at times rather lifeless) neo-classic exercises. Rather, the language employed in the seventeenth- and eighteenth-century 'vernacular' versions of the *Wallace* may have been as honest a representation as one could possibly hope of the state of literary Scots at that time.

What then, are we to make of Hamilton of Gilbertfield? To begin with, it might seem a bit perplexing that he would choose to 'translate' an old Scots classic like the *Wallace* into English, given the fact that William Hamilton's first notable attempt at poetry was slanted more toward the vernacular sphere. He contributed, after all, to James Watson's *Choice Collection of . . . Scots Poems*,[41] though how much seems a little unclear. A recent micro-biography claims 'he contributed a number of pieces to the first volume' of the *Collection*,[42] but Watson's most recent editor[43] seems to credit Hamilton with only one piece, a fine example of period Scots poetry, 'The Last Dying Words of Bonny Heck' (1706). Done in imitation of 'Habbie Simson; or, The Life and Death of the Famous Piper from Kilbarchan' – another Scots standard – 'Bonny Heck' was something of a mock elegy relating the final words of a once champion greyhound, who, being now past his prime, is to be rather heartlessly 'put-down' by his penny-counting owners. An innovative application of the 'Standart Habbie' verse form, Hamilton's 'Bonny Heck' represents both a continuation of an old tradition, plus the genesis of new poetic fashion.[44] Nevertheless, the language of 'Bonny Heck' is of a Scots that is neither the medieval language of Harry's *Wallace*, nor as thoroughly anglicised as Hamilton's 1722 reworking of such:

I Wily, Witty was, and Gash,
With my auld felni packy Pash,
Nae man might anes buy me for Cash
    in some respect.
Are they not then confounded Rash,
    that hangs poor *Heck*?[45]

Instead, this is the language of the new Scots vernacular in its most embryonic form. Though a contrivance, it nevertheless represents an amalgam of several Scots dialects, married to certain English words that have been given Scots spellings.[46]

Still later, in their series of poetic exchanges – 'Familiar Epistles' – the former army officer Hamilton and his friend Allan Ramsay maintained both the stanza style and a fair level of the language associated with this same 'Standart Habbie' tradition. Being exercises in mutual admiration, the nature of these 'Epistles' ranges from playful mockery to out-and-out 'back-patting', all done in quasi-Augustan style with an interjection of Scots words, light at times, though fairly hefty at others. Nevertheless, the tone of Hamilton's 'Familiar Epistles' did much to help bolster the fledgling revamped Scots literary language that later poets like Robert Fergusson and Robert Burns would wield with great efficiency.

With works such as 'Bonny Heck' and the 'Familiar Epistles' to his credit, Gilbertfield performs an 'about-face' with his rendering of 'Henry the Minstrel', produced only three years after his 'Epistles'. When considering his anglicised *Wallace* it is important to realise that, as Lindsay points out, Hamilton's version of Harry was not a straight 'translation'; it was, instead, an 'abridged paraphrase'.[47] For example, whereas *all* other versions of Wallace's recapture of St Johnstoun (Book 10) are rendered into 84 lines of text, Hamilton is blissfully content to reduce the same down to 53 lines, though, in fairness, this does not appreciably affect the overall integrity of the general narrative. Purists of the Harry tradition might object to this abridgement; for our purposes, however, the essential point is that the Hamilton edition represents a freer, more interpretative representation of the Minstrel's text, rather than being greatly innovative in terms of language.

As already indicated, the Scots employed in such pieces as the 'Epistles' was somewhat 'artificial' – few people in Scotland actually spoke exactly in that manner. Yet was the language of Hamilton's *Wallace* any less artificial? It would seem that, like some of the Scots poetry both he and (more so) his friend Ramsay produced, Hamilton's anglicised version of the *Wallace*, in addition to being an exercise in patriotism, was also conceived as a profound statement about the nature of literary style, very unlike the more vernacular versions of Blind Harry being produced at the time, which as is hopefully now readily apparent were in themselves very anglicised in language. What was not so 'English' about these *Wallaces* was their verse style. Their versification was still the old courtly style of the ancient makars, not to mention Harry himself. William Hamilton's style of verse, however, is much more akin to the neo-classic type employed by the Scottish (and probably English) Augustans, broadly speaking, those Scottish poets who wrote non-Scots (language) verse.[48] For comparative purposes this short extract from the poetry of Alexander Pennecuik (d. 1730) should provide a basis for comparing the similarities between Scottish Augustan poetry at large, and Hamilton's anglicised *Wallace*:

> By all the Renfrew Shepherds 'tis confess'd
> A glorious Sun arises in the West,
> Thro' spacious Fields, by all the Swains its told
> This Sun hath more adorers than the Old.[49]

Though perhaps not identical, Gilbertfield's new edition of Harry certainly has much more in common with this style, than it does with that of the more traditional *Wallaces*. Augustan poetry was actually 'all-the-rage' within polite circles in both England (largely London), and those places in Scotland which sought to ape polite English society. Though it did draw upon English for its vocabulary, Augustan poetry employed an inflated rhetorical style, which was presumably meant to mimic that of the ancient classical scholars – if not their actual language.

The neo-Augustans' (perhaps chauvinistic) popularity is linked to the desire among a select number of Scots, bent on making their mark within the new state of Great Britain. Crawford, for example, maintains these individuals believed that in order to fully participate in the political and economic entity of Great Britain, all Scotticisms would have to be purged

Social, Political and Cultural Scene

from their speech, an attitude which resulted in the creation of a number of gentlemens' 'improving societies'. These societies sought to foster 'correctness' in speech and manners – in essence, promote English speech and mannerisms – although such associations did show an interest in Scottish culture.[50] However, the desire for certain Scots to express themselves in highly stylised English was not solely an eighteenth-century phenomenon. Some seventeenth-century Scots also chose this literary medium, for example, Patrick Gordon, who will be discussed below. Perhaps this decision on their part was attributable, as Daiches might say, to their desire to mimic the royal court, now that it was based in London. The Union of 1707, therefore, probably only enhanced these beliefs, rather than creating them.

Yet for those determined to make a name for themselves in the new Great Britain, the neo-Augustan could serve as a badge of status, indicating that they had 'made it'. For vernacular poets like Ramsay, Fergusson, and later Burns, adding the neo-Augustan was a way of expanding their repertoire, increasing the range of poetic types they could work within, and giving them even greater appeal. It also marked them as 'proper' poets, thus giving greater impact to their vernacular works, which is probably the medium they preferred.[51] However, the important issue is that anyone working within the neo-Augustan could show themselves to be worthy citizens of Britain. And theoretically at least, any poem – or tale – rendered into this medium was one not only significant for Scotland, but for Britain as a whole. It is in conjunction with this last point that Gilbertfield's *Wallace* found its niche.

It appears that William Hamilton's new edition of Blind Harry was indeed an exercise in relating the old Scots tale using the medium of one of the new 'classic' poetic forms of Scotland and the united Britain. The wrong conclusion should not be drawn, however: the story of the heroic life and deeds of the Guardian did indeed fire the patriotic imagination of Hamilton, every bit as much as the ex-army lieutenant's rendering of that same story would later rouse feelings of national pride within the soul of Robert Burns. But for Hamilton, such a vitally important story deserved to be told in the new 'universal' literary language of the recently united kingdom of Britain. Thus, Hamilton's prime goal was to place the Wallace tradition into a new, united British context.

Others attempted to remould Wallace into a new, universal hero, drawing upon classical traditions filtered through England. In his neo-classical tribute to the land of his birth, James Thomson (1700–48) would speak of the heroic nature of the nation, and of its defender, the scourge of the usurping Edward:

> . . .A manly race,
> Of unsubmitting spirit, wise, and brave;
> Who still through bleeding ages struggled hard,
> (As well unhappy Wallace can attest,
> Great patriot-hero! ill requited chief!)
> To hold a generous, undiminished state.[52]

Slightly later in the century, a little-known poet by the name of John Harvey also treated Scotland's original commoner-patriot in similar fashion. In his *The Life of Robert Bruce King of Scots* (1729), Harvey introduces us to a William Wallace who could have as easily sprung from the works of Homer as from the pages of medieval Scots poetry:

> In glitt'ring Steel, the *Ellerslian* Hero shines.
> Born to chastise the Pride of perjur'd Kings,
> Quick to the Field, the youthful Warrior springs.[53]

A different side to Scotland's Guardian is being portrayed here. Though heavily indebted and even related to the image of the popular hero, this William Wallace is a man who is on the verge of being ennobled through his altruism. In a sense then, the Wallace who is portrayed by Harvey and even Hamilton is no longer a 'simple' commoner. This slightly different defender of Scotland's liberty is thus removed from the realm of populist legend to become part of polite eighteenth-century society, and the language employed tended to help ensure this.[54] True enough, even Harry related a notable background for his hero:

> We reide of ane rycht famouss of renowne,
> Of worthi blude that ryngis in this regioune:
> And hensfurth I will my process hald
> Of Wilyham Wallas yhe haf hard beyne tald.
> His forbearis likis till wnderstand,
> Of hale lynage, and trew lyne of Scotland.[55]

Here, the Minstrel is appropriating an ancestry for the Guardian created by earlier chroniclers, such as Fordun, who had been concerned with reversing 'slanders' told by the English that Wallace had been the most base of the base, not only in status, but in actions also. Despite this, and even the fact that he makes his hero king for a day, Harry is not overly consumed with pressing the issue of Wallace's ancestry. What Wallace did, rather than what he was, concerned Harry most.

But as we move into the eighteenth century, Wallace's status seems to become slightly more of an issue. Perhaps, in a post-Union Scotland, concerned with its own status within that union, this is what we should expect. Certain historians of the time seemed determined to build (or build upon) an image of an ennobled version of Scotland's premier patriot. Heading the list is George Mackenzie MD, who in his derivative history, based upon the work of previous individuals, including Harry, proclaims that Wallace's father 'was Laird of Ellerslie'[56] – a statement which appears to be based upon a creative reading of Harry's 'Malcom Wallas hir gat in marriage, / That Elrislé than had in heretage'.[57] Mackenzie, in fact, expends a fair bit of energy in his attempts to shed light upon the Wallace lineage, real or imagined.

Another historian was Matthew Duncan: by virtue of the title of his work, *The History of the Kings of Scotland*, it would seem obvious that the author had only limited interest in the lives of the 'lowly'. Sixteen or seventeen pages of Duncan's work were devoted to the career of the victor of Bannockburn.[58] Nevertheless, Elderslie's finest receives much more than just an honourable mention within the section dealing with the Bruce. But even more significantly, Duncan includes 'An Appendix Containing the Lives of several Persons of Quality, who were concern'd in the Government, Civil or Military;' the persons contained within such, could be described as being extraordinary commoners. Gracing this appendix is the Guardian, and Duncan's treatment of him is unreserved: 'William Wallace was of this Humour: He was incredibly Strong, and his Aversion to the English could not be equalled but by the Love he had for his Country . . . '[59]. Then after having related a toned-down version of the horrific ending to Wallace's life Duncan attempts to put the Guardian of Scotland on the same footing as the ancient Classical hero:

> This fate had Sir William Wallace the famousest Man of his Time, and comparable to the greatest Heroes of Antiquity, both for his Courage in undertaking Dangers, and Wisdom and Valour in overcoming them.[60]

However for Duncan, it seems that the deeds performed by a quasi-classical Wallace – the rescue of his nation from a more potent foreign power – can only be those undertaken by one of higher birth. As such, he takes great pains to set the record straight; despite the slanders of past chroniclers from the south, 'Sir William Wallace . . . was a Gentleman of very low Fortune, but Noble Birth . . . English authors will not allow him to have been born of a Gentleman, but this is a Falsehood even demonstrable in our Days . . .'[61]. Duncan's 'proof' for this claim spans the bridge of nearly two pages, folio sized.

Such statements regarding the 'noble' lineage of William Wallace perhaps underpin a sense of insecurity. Certainly there were Scots who believed themselves, as a nation, to be the inferior partner in the newly united

Greater Britain. Matthew Duncan's concern over the 'disparaging' comments offered by certain English sources concerning Wallace seem to reflect, to a degree, this insecurity. Pride in his own nation, by itself, was not enough for Duncan; he was compelled to define his patriotism in relation to the traditions of the southern partner in the Union. A freedom-fighter like a Wallace hailing from relative obscurity – though his deeds and bravery truly were beyond compare – still was not quite of the same status as, for example, an Alfred, who not only defeated the Danish menace, but was also of royal blood. This is not to say that all individuals concerned with retelling and propagating the tale of William Wallace were insecure about the status of Scotland's original patriot. Undoubtedly, some would find great comfort in the notion that even the ordinary could rise to the call of national pride. And even when it comes to a person like Duncan, it is not difficult to envision his chest swelling with patriotic fervour as his pen frantically scribbled away; but in the back of his mind we can imagine also a voice telling him that the opinions of the English must be heeded. Status was thus an important issue for Duncan: the status of Scotland when compared to England, and the status of the smaller nation's hero when viewed by the larger neighbour.

On a different level, however, this attempt at ennobling the legendary figure of Wallace could have the drawback of effectively diminishing the Guardian's achievements. The actions of Wallace the commoner were uncommon: defending the liberty of his nation; leading it in its struggle against a potentially more powerful foreign adversary; few commoners could lay claim to having achieved so much. Among the general populace, the deeds of Wallace were inspirational.

Conversely, by raising Wallace to the status of nobility, the impact of his deeds was reduced. The Guardian never actually freed his homeland, as he would have been expected to do, and as the Bruce did. The actions of the ennobled Wallace pale by comparison with those of true kingly or noble birth. Wallace as noble was ineffectual, at least as far as his achievements were concerned. Perhaps this is why the image of him as objectified by Harry's (extra-)ordinary man who confronts the situation at hand, still retained its popularity, alongside the legend of Robert Bruce.

To start at the same point where the discussion on Wallace began, it is noteworthy that John Barbour's *Bruce* also found favour with early modern Scottish printers up to the end of the eighteenth century,[62] although the number of printings of the *Bruce* was less than that of the *Wallace*. Thirty-seven editions of the *Wallace* (excluding Gilbertfield's version) from the sixteenth, seventeenth and eighteenth centuries can be accounted for, as opposed to 12 printings of John Barbour's epic. During the period 1700–

50, only one edition of the *Bruce* appears to have been printed, whereas there were about 11 of Blind Harry's *Wallace*. The vast majority of the individual printings of both the *Bruce* and *Wallace* produced during the late seventeenth to early eighteenth centuries could be described as 'popular editions'. Addressing as broad an audience as possible, these printers may have sensed that the general public had a greater affinity with Wallace as compared to Bruce, and were therefore more compelled to relate the story about a commoner who did uncommon things, rather than one which told of a king who performed kingly deeds. This is not meant to say that the *Bruce* was unpopular; quite the opposite in fact, yet as popular as Barbour's tale was, Harry's was even more so.

Turning to the language of the various editions of the *Bruce* it is important to emphasise at the outset that Barbour's original language, although closely related to that of Harry, was nevertheless not precisely on the same level. Since the Lowland Scots tongue of Barbour's days was one that had yet to fully establish itself as distinct from the dialects of Northern England, it might be somewhat redundant to look for any changes from Scots to English within the text of the *Bruce*; rather it would be more useful to look for a shift toward more modern English. Still, one importance of the *Bruce* as Barbour had originally created it, was that it performed a similar function for Scots as Chaucer's *Canterbury Tales* performed for English. The *Bruce* seems to have paved the way for the codification of literary Scots.

Two manuscripts of the *Bruce* are known to exist: the Cambridge Manuscript, incomplete and written in 1487; and the so-called Edinburgh Manuscript, written by John Ramsay in 1489.[63] The first known printed version of Barbour's epic is that of Lekpreuik and Charteris in 1571. As noted above, the previous year saw the printing of this duo's version of the *Wallace*. It appears that the language and orthography of their *Bruce* is slightly more inclined towards an early modern English tone than their *Wallace*, even though the differences between the two are extremely subtle.

During the period 1600–1800 the majority of editions of the *Bruce* continue to adopt more modern English words and spelling conventions. This is much the same as was the case for similar editions of the *Wallace*. And once again, the trend toward providing a more modern English tone to the *Bruce* seems most fully realised first in Andrew Hart's versions, while an attempt to reverse this can be noted in the Freebairn 1758 edition. However, overall, there seems to be slightly less emphasis given toward providing an up-to-date English tone to Barbour's text, when compared to the *Wallace*.[64] The differences that are being referred to are, admittedly, extremely subtle, and can only be seen superficially in the necessarily brief examples appended. Nevertheless, the reasons for these slight differences are puzzling. It may be that because there were fewer editions of the *Bruce*, there was less opportunity for 'editorial tampering'. Since it was a story very concerned with the ancient nobility of the land, it may be that Barbour's book was meant to appeal to a *slightly* more exclusive (and more literate) audience. This does not explain the fractionally greater trend for more up-to-date anglicisation in 1571 (when compared to the *Wallace* of the previous year). Perhaps the initial idea was to make Barbour as accessible as Harry.[65] But because the *Wallace* eventually garnered more attention from both printers and (probably) the populace, perhaps its language gradually conformed more with general tastes. However, for the most part, the same general trends concerning language and orthography in successive editions of the *Bruce* broadly mimic those of the *Wallace*.

Though there were sufficient reprints of Barbour's original in fairly regular circulation, he also had his imitators. The figure of Robert Bruce as a neo-classical figure perhaps first emerges in Patrick Gordon's *The Famous History of . . . Robert, sirnamed The Bruce, King of Scotland*.[66] Originally published in 1613, Gordon's effort was reprinted twice, in 1718 and 1753, but then disappeared.[67] Significantly, the 1718 edition was published by the pro-Jacobite, anti-Union James Watson of Edinburgh for reasons that will shortly become clear.

Gordon's book, or more likely the 1718 reprint, may have inspired John Harvey's later work. Like Harvey after him, Gordon melds classical iconography with established Scottish tradition. For example, and in the spirit of martial glorification taken to almost unreasonable extremes, Sir Patrick Graham is referred to as 'that brave *Mars* of men'.[68] Also, melded into his treatment of the hapless John Baliol, Gordon resurrects that age-old concept of the 'pure' Scottish kingdom of antiquity, hitherto unconquered by any foe, and in itself representing a number of traditions coming to fruition:

> But little knew the Princes of the Land
> That he [Baliol] to *England's* King should Homage Pay;
> The Crown that sixteen Hundred Years did stand
> 'Gainst endless War and cruel Arms Eflay;
> Nor *Romans*, *Danes*, nor *Saxons* could command,
> Unconquer'd still, nor conquer'd would obey,
> Was now betray'd by him, whose hapless Name
> Because his Country's Scorn, and Kingdom's Shame.[69]

Playing upon the concept of the indomitable martial nature of the Scottish kingdom and people (a belief to which it is easy to imagine Barbour and Harry subscribing), the above quote actually reveals a lot about the personage and political slant of Gordon, a political slant which appeared in at least one of his imitators.

There seems good reason to identify Gordon as the same Patrick Gordon who wrote *Britain's Distemper*.[70] Gordon was a contemporary and devoted admirer of James Graham, the first Marquis of Montrose. It might be suspected that a devotee of the premier covenanter turned royalist, might hold some pretty strong pro-Stewart beliefs, and such suspicions are indeed justified given the way Gordon bemoans the execution of Charles I in *Britain's Distemper*.[71] In like vein, Gordon devotes almost as much space in the *Famous History of Bruce* toward praising the Stewarts as he does in relating the deeds of Robert the Bruce, who he stresses was the progenitor of the entire line. Momentous was the day, says Patrick Gordon, when 'The South and North Crowns [were] joined by that great King', and better yet the day when that same monarch, James VI, produced two promising sons!'[72] Related to this train of thought, the 1718 reprint of Gordon's *Famous History of Bruce* acquires enhanced significance due to it being the handiwork of James Watson. It is no surprise, given Watson's own Jacobite and episcopalian leanings, that he would find himself compelled to reprint a work such as Gordon's. Yet as far as nostalgia for the old lineage was concerned, there certainly was a growing trend for such to become interwoven with respect for the mystique surrounding the Bruce. Certainly this appears to be the case for the man who produced the most thorough neo-classical tribute (as far as the genre went) to King Robert I, namely John Harvey.

As William Hamilton was to Blind Harry, so John Harvey was to Barbour. A somewhat obscure individual,[73] it nevertheless seems certain that Harvey was an inhabitant of Edinburgh for at least part of his life, since he endeavoured to take subscriptions for his *The Life of Robert Bruce King of Scots* at a residence in Scotland's capital city.[74] Not only sold, but also printed in Edinburgh, Harvey's effort appears to have had some admirers initially, even though later in the century its popularity seemed to greatly fade. As far as content is concerned *The Life of Robert Bruce* is an amalgam of different literary strains brought together. It is very much grounded in the classical mould; and while quite obviously inspired by John Barbour's *Bruce*, it is not simply a re-editing of the earlier work. Harvey in fact states that it was never his intention to 'present the Reader with an Epic Poem' – in essence, to reproduce Barbour's poem. Instead, he admits that his is an 'imitation' of an epic, a fact of which the reader will become aware in working through the poem's pages. Harvey betrays his literary slant when he is critical of those who create epic based upon fable, underscoring his own knowledge of, and belief in, the classics:

> The Patrons of absolute Necessity of Fable have the whole Current of Antiquity against them ... unluckily, the *Iliad* and *Æneid* stand in the way, built upon certain Fact, upon true and undeniable History.[75]

Despite having created a classically-patterned work, Harvey's *Bruce* is a sincere testimonial to established Scottish literary traditions, given the nature of its subject matter: the 'fact' which his effort is at least partially based upon is Barbour's *Bruce*. Furthermore, it seems that since Harvey also introduced William Wallace into his 'epic', he was obviously familiar with Harry's work, since the subject of the minstrel's poem is nowhere to be found in Barbour's original. This underscores the point that Harvey's *Bruce* was not a simple 'updating' and re-editing of Barbour's classic. In this sense, Harvey's poem differed from Hamilton's *Wallace*, which retained the general narrative of Harry's original. Thus, Wallace does make a limited (albeit important) appearance in Harvey's *Bruce*. By his own admission, Harvey is only interested in Wallace in those major instances when his career intersects with that of Bruce.[76] The Guardian therefore only appears for the Battle of Falkirk, after which he has his pivotal conversation with Bruce, the father of the later Robert I, chastising him for his insincere and factious attitude toward Scotland.[77] After this, the Guardian of the realm performs his disappearing act and leaves for France, never to be seen again, at least in Harvey's version of events.

Though Harvey did no great service to the Scots tongue he nevertheless displayed respect for both Barbour, and certain traditions drawn from Scottish history and legend. His treatment of William Wallace has already been noted; Harvey's treatment of the Bruce is such that any god of Olympus would find himself flattered, and Scotland itself is raised to the status of being the home of the gods:

> Thence to Imperial *Scoon* they bend their Way,
> The far fam'd Seat of *Albion's* ancient Sway.
> Arriv'd, they enter; Guards surrounding wait,
> Whilst *Bruce* is seated on a Throne of State.
> Then from the Altar of hallow'd Fame,
> The sacred Officers the Rites began.
> The Regal Oyl first, plac'd by pious Hands,
> In holy Vases on ther Altar stands.[78]

So like Hamilton slightly before him, Harvey's main claim to fame was the conversion (some would say bastardisation) of an already famous, and successful, Scots classic into a neo-classical tribute to a popular hero from Scotland's past. That Harvey's *Bruce* and Hamilton's *Wallace* were indeed two works that were on the same stylistic (and linguistic) wavelength is perhaps best attested by the fact that the two were, by century's end, often edited together into one volume. The first time this momentous event in the annals of Scottish literature occurred was in 1770, thanks to the initiative of H. Galbraith from Dundee.[79] The original purchasers of this volume probably were as much impressed by its neo-classic style, as they were with the actual narrative of events. However the sad fact is that probably the best way to sell Harvey's poem towards the end of the eighteenth century, was to append it to Hamilton's work, which in all honesty did seem to perform well enough on its own.

Part of the motivation on the part of Harvey for composing his panegyric in honour of King Robert I may have been political. There appears to be a strong possibility that John Harvey, perhaps like others involved in the promotion of the Bruce cult, held sentiments for the Jacobite cause.[80] Furthermore, it seems certain that Harvey held strong anti-Union sentiments. We can catch glimpses of both these aspects of Harvey's politics within his *Bruce*, especially in the concluding couplets:

> While circling Spheres their endless Rounds shall run
> And feel the genial Influence of the Sun:
> While Earth shall daily on her Axle roll,
> And the slow Wain attend the freezing Pole;
> While Monthly Moons their Revolutions keep,
> By Turns shall raise, and sink by Turns the Deep;
> While Fortha, spacious, rolls her winding Waves,
> And Tay's rich Stream Æneian Borders laves;
> Still dear to Albion be her Bruce's Fame,
> Sacred his Merit, and rever'd his name.
>
> So may just heav'n maintain her ancient Crown,
> And Banquho's Race for ever fill her Throne.
> May both, ye Gods! one final Period know,
> That cease to rule, and Fortha cease to flow.[81]

More explicit evidence of Harvey's political leanings is suggested through a new introduction written for an edition of his *Bruce*, published in London, 1769, and given the rather pretentious-sounding name of *The Bruciad*. The anonymous editor is quite willing to praise Harvey's poetic skills, referring to him as 'perhaps one of the best classical scholars of the age he lived in'.[82] It was a different matter, however, when it came to his politics and nationality: according to his new (in the greatest likelihood English) editor, Harvey had excessively 'confined his observations to the narrow boundaries and prejudices of the land of his nativity, which made it unsuitable for a more general audience'. We may rightly assume that the 'general audience' in question is one which has just tentatively breathed a sigh of relief, hopeful that no new rumours of an intended Jacobite invasion would surface.[83] Still, according to his editor, the sort of politics Harvey had held when he first created his version of the *Bruce*, had since that time 'embarrassed both England and Scotland'. Thus the editors took it upon themselves to modify Harvey's effort, and expel the allegedly offending lines representative of the original author's anti-Union and pro-Jacobite sentiments. As part of this agenda *The Bruciad* features a totally reworked conclusion, bearing only a superficial resemblance to that in Harvey's original ode to King Robert I:

> Whilst circling Spheres their endless rounds shall run
> And feel the genial influence of the sun:
> Whilst earth shall daily on her axle roll,
> And flow, the wain attend the freezing pole;
> While monthly, moons, their revolutions keep,
> By turns to raise, by turns to sink the deep;
> While Fortha, spacious, flows in curling waves,
> And Tay's rich stream, Æneian borders laves;
> Be Albion's sons and Bruce's name still fir'd,
> And distant times, with Brucian worth inspir'd.
>
> From him – till heav'n propitions to our pray'r
> May bliss Great Britain with one sov'reign care!
> A sov'reign! glorying in Britain's name!
> A royal pattern, to perpetuate fame!
> May Union! ever decorate his crown,
> And may his race, for ever fill the throne:
> May both, ye gods! one final period know,
> That cease to rule, – the Thames and Forth to flow.[84]

In this version 'Bruce's Fame' and name are less to be thought of as 'Still [being] dear to Albion' but rather to be revered for their significance in 'distant times'. Scotland no longer retains 'her ancient Crown' perpetually ruled by a representative of 'Banquho's Race'; rather, one sovereign (of an unspecified lineage, but we might expect not that of the Stewarts) should 'for ever fill the throne' of a United Kingdom of Britain. It seems fair to suggest, therefore, that the new editor of Harvey's *Bruce* is pushing a pro-Union, pro-Hanoverian platform.

Returning to the links between eighteenth-century Jacobitism and the cult of the Bruce, it is not too difficult to see how this relationship could be arrived at. Without stretching reality excessively, it was possible to make the claim (as did Gordon and Harvey) that Robert I was the ultimate progenitor of the Stewart lineage. But the cult of Wallace was not totally immune from being intertwined with Jacobite politics either. This might seem a little hard to grasp, since at the centre of the Wallace cult was a (relatively) ordinary man who rose to become his country's defender, and even led aristocrats into battle. Also at the centre of this cult was the embodiment of the free man making a conscious decision as to how he will be governed, and by whom. However, Jacobitism in its 'purest' form embodied a devout following of the later Stewarts, a line that believed themselves worthy of rule by divine right, an authoritarian concept seemingly in opposition to some of the principles Wallace stood for. How then could the mythos of Harry's hero find itself in the middle of the Jacobite controversy?

Wallace's career spanned part of the period when Scotland had fought for her independence from a foreign power. His 'successor' of sorts was Robert Bruce. Both these historical figures had been absorbed into the common consciousness as the original liberators of Scotland. But in the minds of some people, Wallace had 'paved the way' for Bruce. A person who shared such a view may have been the already mentioned Robert Freebairn.

Opinion has it that as a companion to his edition of the *Wallace*, Freebairn also produced a volume devoted to the subject of John Barbour's book.[85] A close examination of the alleged Freebairn editions of the *Bruce* and the *Wallace* reveals many striking similarities between the two volumes: both are in quarto format and are in black-letter type; the title-pages of both profess a publishing date of 1758, though the actual date of composition of this edition of the *Bruce* is as fraught with controversy as is the companion volume dealing with Blind Harry's subject; the title-page of the 1758 edition of the *Bruce* claims to have been 'carefully corrected from the edition printed by Andro Hart in 1620', which, it will be remembered, is similar to the claim made by McDiarmid for the *Wallace* of that same year – although no mention of consultation with the original manuscripts is made in either work. If, however, the mysterious Mr Tate did copy the manuscript of the *Wallace* on Freebairn's behalf, it makes sense that he could have done likewise with the manuscript of the *Bruce*, as both were at one time bound together in the Faculty of Advocates' collection.

If all the above suppositions are correct, then it appears that like a number of others both before and after him, Freebairn seemed bent on creating two parallel volumes, each respectively devoted to one half of the William Wallace/Robert the Bruce tandem. Having said this, it should not be assumed that because Freebairn was a Jacobite who happened to transcribe an edition of the *Wallace* and one of the *Bruce*, that all such individuals who similarly produced parallel volumes were also Jacobites. Nor was it a natural progression for an editor of the *Wallace* to also attempt an edition of John Barbour's classic, though many did. However, even for most printers who produced both poems, the story of Wallace was deemed worth retelling more often; Blind Harry was published almost three times as often as the *Bruce* during much of the period of inquiry. Rather it would seem that some individuals who produced both volumes probably believed that the stories of the Guardian of Scotland and the Victor at Bannockburn deserved to be told simultaneously; that one epic complemented the other. And again, just because a printer happened to believe one story complemented the other, did not automatically make him a supporter of the Stewart cause.

Naturally of course, in terms of relating the historical account of the Wars of Independence, Bruce and Wallace are two of the most significant figures. But something far more significant may have been going on in the mind of a person like Freebairn at least: no King Robert I without a Wallace; or, no protective monarchy without the support of the commoner. This latter point is indeed related to recently made remarks by Cowan, regarding the Wallace myth, 'that true patriotism resided in the ranks of the lowly'; although those who sought to idolise both Harry's hero and the Bruce probably did not believe that 'those who shared the blood royal were [in fact] quislings'[86] but were instead the people's champions, who still needed to be spurred-on by the commons in order to find the correct path toward righteousness.

This last point would appear to allow for a little too much dependence upon the common-folk on the part of a line of monarchs that still counted themselves the Almighty's chosen to rule on earth. However, it was increasingly becoming the case, that, despite any pretensions about being God's chosen they may have made, few of the Stewarts found widespread acceptance among their followers because of any claim they may have had for Divine Right.[87] Possibly the events connected with the Revolution of 1688 played a role in watering-down this final concept. Yet to this end, even a staunch supporter of the cause like Freebairn, who went as far as to forfeit his post as King's Printer and became instead a devotee of the Earl of Mar's cause,[88] seemed to play down the concept of Divine Right in one of his own pro-Jacobite tracts:

> He [James Francis Edward Stewart] is our Lawful Right Sovereign: And we all know that He is the Undoubted Lineal Heir by Blood and Descendent of the Ancient Race of our Scottish Kings . . . a Prince upon who the Crown is entail'd by the Fundamental Laws of our Country, and to whom, even before he was born; we have often sworn Allegiance and Fealty, by those Oaths given to former Kings, by which we bound our selves not only to them, but to their Lawful Heirs and Successors.[89]

Certainly some of this has the ring to it of being designed to deflect any rumours concerning the Pretender's alleged illegitimacy. But on the other hand, it also seems to make clear the point that it was more the traditions of the nation, than the laws of God, that stood in support of James Stewart's right to govern.[90] Freebairn's tract goes on to say that the alternative to James is a German Prince who 'knows not one Tittle of our Constitution'[91] – probably meaning he understands nothing of the ancient traditions of Scotland concerned with the relationship between ruler and ruled.

Perhaps, then, we have an explanation for the Jacobite Robert Freebairn's fascination with the figure of William Wallace. Possibly he rationalised the situation by recounting that it was the Guardian who first responded to his own apprehensions about a Scots nation that had been forced to bow to an alien prince bent on breaking tradition. And had Wallace not responded as he did, the way would not have been cleared for the Bruce, the progenitor of the Stewarts. It was those same Stewarts – Freebairn might have thought – that now seemed most committed to expelling yet another power originating from outside of Scotland.

Certainly none of this is to say, for even the briefest moment, that devotion for the Blind Minstrel's epic should be equated with devotion for the Jacobite cause, though in the instance of the alleged Freebairn edition of the *Wallace*, the equation might be possible. But another example of possible connections between Jacobitism, perhaps on a much more intimate level, and the entire Wallace (literary) tradition, is evident in the anonymous 'A Curious Poem to the Memory of Sir William Wallace'. A work which retold selected aspects of the Lord Protector's deeds (and eventual execution) in the neo-classic mould, the said piece was part of a larger collection devoted toward commemorating Charles Edward Stewart's arrival in Edinburgh in 1745. Needless to say, by virtue of the collection's title, the affinity with the cause of the Stewarts is quite clear. Nevertheless, the ideology of the supporters of Bonnie Prince Charlie seems clearly spelled-out in lines which could as easily refer to a Scotland caught-up in the 1745–46 Jacobite uprisings, as to her struggle for freedom during the Wars of Independence:

> Oppress'd with Woes, ill fated *Scotia* lay,
> To Edward's Power a sunk defenceless Prey;
> Her drooping Friends beheld with mournful Eyes,
> Their Lord in Exile, and his Right a Prize.[92]

The sentiments expressed in the highlighted last line are typical of any group of people deprived of their perceived leadership. Jacobitism aside the nation in general had suffered considerably in this sense. In 1603, Scotland's king had left for England, to return only once, while in 1707, its parliamentarians departed for the southern land. The same Act of Union appeared to threaten their kirk, to which many had turned for guidance in lieu of an absentee monarch. The idea of the absentee monarch was one of the most telling. In Harvey's *Bruce*, the future King Robert I had been exiled in France before finally returning to rescue his people from perceived unjust rule; and during the period of the Jacobite uprisings, those Scots who, perhaps very conservatively, clung to older concepts of monarchical rule for security, hailed the arrival of this latest Pretender as the first step in the process toward returning the old lineage (comprising the rightful rulers, so these folk would have maintained) to its rightful place. These are the sorts of ideas that appear embedded in the above quotation.

One final work devoted to replicating (or distorting) the Wallace tradition while tending to display Jacobite leanings was Nisbet's drama *Caledon's Tears: or, Wallace. A Tragedy*. What this amounted to was a fairly brief five-act play, dedicated to Sir Thomas Wallace who, according to the play's creator, not only was a descendant of the elder Wallace, but bore 'all the beautiful Resemblences' to William!*[93]* However, the speech attributed by the play to Wallace, upon hearing of his sentence of death from Edward, embodies not only some pro-Jacobite sentiments, but also an anti-Englishness that equally could have originated in a post-Union, or for that matter, a Wars of Independence era Scotland:

> *Wal.* Think not, inhumane Tyrant, that your Threats
> Or cruel Treatment, can deter the Fates
> From doing so far Justice to my Name,
> As, when I'm falling, to defend my Fame
> And know, you Savage, That these shackled Hands
> Have shed the Blood of your beloved Friends,
> Your Brother *Hugh*, Six Nephews, second Son,
> Dropt from Gardies to my Girdle down.
> Know I am he who have your Hopes deforc'd
> And dares the *Saxons* still to do their Worst.
> For all my Wishes are, That *Albion's* King
> May finish what I have referr'd to him;
> So a red *Finis* shall receive Empire,
> And *English Edward* in its Arms expire.[94]

Edward's immediate reply to Wallace, 'Treason, Treason – Guards remove the Scots, /For so aught all such Rebels to be treat',[95] undoubtedly would be sufficient to incite any anglophobic Scot to immediately jump on the anti-Union bandwagon, although at the time of the writing of *Caledon's*

Tears (1733) that same wagon may not have been quite as swiftly rolling as it had been earlier.

As it happens, the dual traditions of the *Wallace* and the *Bruce* played a significant role in anti-Union propaganda. Knowledge of the whole struggle for Scottish independence from its neighbour to the south was sustained during the Union era through popular editions of both works.[96] The Union was extremely unpopular throughout many sections of the new Kingdom of Great Britain, and most areas of Scotland were hardly the exception to this. Reasons for opposition to the Union ran the gamut from overt hostility toward the English, through concerns for the maintenance of the Scottish Kirk, to the question of monarchical succession and economic concerns regarding taxation and trade. The fact that the union was to be wholly incorporating, may have helped foster ideas that concerns for Scotland's welfare would be drowned out in a wave of English parliamentarian strength, since the southern partner would have greater representation.

Symbolic gestures against this union were enacted throughout Scotland: in Dumfries dissatisfaction was expressed by burning the Articles of Union in great public spectacles. And as part of the war in print, waged by both sides in the union debate, the account of events in Dumfries was issued as a broadside. This same account hints at a potentially bigger concern – that Scotland's representatives in the union debate had put concerns other than the welfare of their nation at the forefront when negotiating union: ' . . . the Commissioners for this Nation, have been either Simple, Ignorant, or Treacherous, if not all three'.[97] The modern analysis of the sincerity of the nobility when it came to negotiating for union, has been varied indeed. However, the analysis of (in particular) Whatley's recent study,[98] and also that of Whyte,[99] might cause us to doubt that Scotland's negotiators in the Union debate were beyond criticism. It seems that more than a few members of the Scottish nobility received perks for supporting union.

Even before the actual signing of the Treaty of Union, segments of the Scottish population did seem to believe that they had been 'sold-out' or betrayed by those members of Scotland's nobility who were in favour of such. This idea of the Scottish nation being betrayed by grasping nobles – who had been bribed into handing over their homeland's freedom to the old enemy, failed to escape the notice of the printer:

> the degenerate Cowardice of too many of my [Scotland's] Sons, of sordid Mercenary Spirit. It is a foul brand (but a most unjust one) upon your Predecessors, that they Sold their King. Pray man not the dishonourable Imputation of Selling your Country . . .[100]

The idea that the nobles of eighteenth-century Scotland were once an illustrious lot, but now were as low as the original Fallen Angel, continued for a while at least. With the imposition of such taxes as the linen duty in 1711, and the Malt tax in 1712 (contrary to the terms of the Treaty), calls to dissolve the Union were issued. In the wake of these events, the war of words once again started, and the events of the Wars of Independence were recalled. One pamphleteer reminds his readers that though outnumbered ten-to-one, the nation's stout forefathers had defeated '300,000 of our treacherous Enemies' at the Battle of Bannockburn[101] – an obvious acknowledgement of the Bruce tradition, initiated by John Barbour. But gone are such heroes who will fight for the sake of national pride, he maintains, for the sons of the nation ('her born Magistrates') have done their best to undo the nation, and the people's slothfulness has only contributed to this distress:

> Since the Union of the Crowns, which commenc'd our Misery, God for Chastisement of our Sins, hath given up the Nobility to a reprobate sense; they have taken as indefatigable Pains to pull down their own Houses, as their gallant Ancestors did to build up.[102]

According to the petitioner, the Scots peers were responsible for such calamities as the Darien disaster,[103] and for turning their backs on their country, were rewarded with perks from the English: it was 'Knavery, Bribery, Equivalent' that caused the death of 'old Scotia' and she is buried 'In the Grave of great Britain'.[104]

The sentiments expressed through a conspicuous portion of anti-(incorporating) union literature concerns the potential turn-coat nature of the aristocracy, particularly in recent times. At one time, so certain people believed, the majority of the nobles were a respectable group – had not many fought alongside Wallace and Bruce? Yet, especially in recent times, greed and avarice had set in, and in the rush for personal gain, no price was too high to pay, not even turning over their own country to the 'old enemy'. Selling one's own country for personal aggrandisement was the worst form of treason, and for many people it certainly appeared that their own present parliamentarians were culpable in that respect. But the tradition of the past and its glories still remained, and one way in which it was sustained was through the iconography surrounding Wallace and the Bruce. It was also in these that an antecedent could be found for the current situation.

Particularly in the *Wallace* the theme of the self-serving aristocrat finds a precedent. The theme of betrayal by grasping nobles plays a crucial role in the building of the Wallace saga. It is the hero's undoing when those in his confidence deal behind his back, selling Elderslie's finest, and their nation, to the highest bidder. Unfortunately for Wallace, the highest bidder is his sworn enemy, Edward Longshanks, and the betrayer is Monteith. In Harry's own work, Monteith – though at one point uncertain about placing Wallace into Longshank's clutches – is beguiled by the sweet words of Vallance. Thus, in exchange for 'Thre thowsand punys of fyn gold', and title to the lordship of Lennox – held in fief of Edward – Monteith agrees to turn Wallace over to the English.[105] Though it may be argued that Monteith is presented as a reluctant Judas, Harry makes it abundantly clear that he has no sympathy for the turncoat Scot, who allowed covetousness to be his guide rather than any sense of loyalty.

The treacherous alliance of Sir John Monteith, Sir Vallance and his king, Edward, rarely escaped the notice of those committed to retelling the Wallace story, all in their own unique fashion, during the eighteenth century; witness Hamilton of Gilbertfield's treatment:

> Vallange the Knight, to Scotland did repair,
> The false Montieth Sir John did meet him there.
> Sir John the Lennox greatly did desire,
> To whom Sir Aymer promised it in Hire.
> To hold in Fee, and other Lands moe,
> Of Edward; if to London he would go.
> Thus they accepted and to London went,
> Which pleas'd King Edward to his Hearts content.
> Montieth on sight was bound to the fierce King,
> In Scotland to assist him, in each Thing
> Then both return'd no longer did wait
> Pox on their nasty Snouts for Villians great.
> For Montieth told Edward every Thing,
> And that the Scots designed Bruce for King.[106]

Thus Hamilton follows the minstrel's lead and relates how a grasping, greedy noble conspired to sell Wallace, and Scots autonomy, for personal gain. But not to be outdone, other authors give Scotland's nobles a rough ride by portraying certain of them as a treacherous, untrustworthy group; according to Patrick Gordon the chief Judas of the crowd was, once again, Monteith – 'When him [Wallace] betray'd by that accursed Thought / Of false Montieth'.[107] Similarly, in Nisbet's *Caledon's Tears*, after portents allude to the Guardian's downfall, the unholy trinity plot against Wallace. Once again it is Vallance who goads the traitors into action:

> I verily believe the Victor will,
> One Day or other, undermine us all,

> If Care and Cunning be not quickly us'd,
> And all his Projects presently oppos'd;

while remaining true to the tradition started by Harry, Nisbet reminds his readership of the lucre Monteith received for handing over Wallace: 'You shall have Gold, and whate'er else / You ask in Honour . . .'.[108]

The name of Wallace, therefore, becomes synonymous with the nation of Scotland at large: he was betrayed by those he trusted; Alba was betrayed by those entrusted with its care. Wallace became a rallying point for those wishing to rouse the nation to action, just as he allegedly did back in the late thirteenth century. One Union-era broadside sums up this sentiment:

> Remember *William Wallace* Wight:
>   and his Accomplices,
> *Scotland* they [ ] [t]ook to free,
>   when it was in Distress.[109]

Though Wallace was the more visible of the two, the name of Bruce will always be remembered in association with one of Scotland's most resounding statements of its independence – the victory at Bannockburn. Perhaps recent political events in Scotland (another resounding statement?) will give renewed impetus to the traditions associated with both the Guardian, and the would-be Robert I. Only time will tell.

During the early modern period, neither the subject of Blind Harry's poem, nor that of John Barbour, were forgotten entities. For those individuals supportive of certain ideologies, Wallace and Bruce were two readily accessible figures noted for facing the difficulties of their own times head-on, thus making them ideal for championing a variety of causes in early modern Scotland. The strength of the images of Bruce and Wallace lay in their accessibility, allowing them to fully permeate the common consciousness. Perhaps Wallace was the more successful of the two in the latter regard. Readily identifiable traditions are thus more easily exploitable by those seeking to 'prove a point'. But though they might have had a personal agenda for exploiting Wallace and Bruce, those that retold the tales of the two heroes were first drawn to such because of their attractiveness as living stories. As such, the *Wallace* and the *Bruce* were primarily two genuine extensions of the voice of Scotland. It is this same voice that would find new, and varied, listeners throughout time.

Social, Political and Cultural Scene

Appendix

The Acts and Deeds of Sir William Wallace
'How Wallace won St Johnstoun by a Jeopardy'

Blind Harry's 'Wallace'
(John Ramsay's MS, 1488)[110]

Schyr Ihon Ramsay baid w*ith* a buschement still
Quhen myster war to help yaim with gud will
yir trew cartaris past w*ith* outyn let
A tour the bryg and entryt throu ye [y]et
quhen yai war in yar clokis kest yaim fra
gud Wallace yan the mays*ter* portar can ta
wpon the hed quhill dede he has him left
Syn oy*ir* twa the lyff fra yaim has reft
Guthre be yat did rycht weyll in ye toun
And ruwan als dang off y*ar* famen doun.

Charteris and Lekpreuik
Printed Edition, 1570

Schir John Ramsay, baid iu (sic) the buschem[en]t still,
Quhen myster war, to help yame with gude will.
Thir trew Carteris past on withouttin let,
Atouir the brig, and enterit at the [y]et.
Quehen thay war in, thair cloikis kest thame fra,
Gude Wallace than the cheif portat couth ta.
Upon the heid, quhill deid he hes him left,
Syne other twa the lyfe fra thame he reft.
Guthrie, Bissat, did richt weill in the toun,
And Rothuen als, dang of thair fey men doun.

Andrew Hart's
Printed Edition, 1618

Syr Iohn Ramsay, bade in the Bushment still,
When mister were to help them with good will.
These true Carters past out withouttin let,
Out over the Bridge, and entred at the Gate.
When they were in their Cloaks they cuist them fra:
Good Wallace then the chief Porter could ta
Upon the heid, whill deid hée hes him left:
Syn other two the life from them hée reft.
Guthrie and Bisset did right well in the Town,
And Ruthuen als dang of thir fey men down

Alex. Carmichael and Alex. Millar
Printed Edition, 1736

Sir John Ramsay bode in the bushment still,
When mister were to helg (sic) them with good will.
These true carters past withoutten let,
Out over the bridge, and entred at the gate,
When they were in their clocks they cast them fra
Good Wallace then the chief porters could ta
Upon the head, while dead he hath left,
The other two the life from the reft.
Guthrie and Bisset did right well in the town.
And Ruthven als dang of their fey man down,

William Hamilton's
'New' Printed Edition, 1722

Good Sir John Ramsay, lay in Ambush till,
He warning got then marched with good will.
Over the Bridge, the Carters quickly past,
Enter'd the Gate, and then thair Cloakes do cast,
WALLACE with three good Strokes, which he got,
The Porter kill'd and Two more on the Spot.
Guthrie and Bisset, Ruthven of Renoun,
Most manfully did cut the Suthron down.

Robert Freebairn
Printed Edition, 1758

Sir John Ramsay bode with a bushment still,
When mister were to help them with good will.
Thir true Carters then past withoutten let,
Attour the bridge, and entred through the yate.
When they were in, their clokes they cast them fra,
Good Wallace can the master-porter ta,
Upon the head, while dead he has him left,
Syne other two the life from them reft.
Guthrie, by that, did right well in the town,
And Ruthven als dang of their foe-men down.

The Acts and Life of Robert Bruce King of Scotland
'How Sir Edward Bruce made war in Ireland'

Master John Barbour's Life of
Robert Bruce, King of Scotland[111]

Social, Political and Cultural Scene

And quhen yai assemblit war
Yar war wele ner [tuenty] thousand.
Quhen yai wyst yat in-till yar land
Sic a men[y]e aryvyt war
With all ye folk yat yai had yar
Yai went towart yaim in gret hi,
And fra schyr Eduuard wist suthly
Yat ner till him cummand war yai

>Charteris and Lekpreuik
>*Printed Edition, 1571*

And quhen thay all assemblit wair,
Thay war weill neir twentie thousand.
Quhen yat thay wist, that in thair land
Sic an Men[y]e arryuit wair,
With all the folk that yai had thair,
Thay went towart thame in hy.
And quhen Schir Eduuard wist surely,
That till him neir cümand war thay.

>Andrew Hart's
>*Printed Edition, 1616*

And when they all assembled were,
They were well-néere tweentie thousand.
When that they wist, that in their land,
Sik a Menyie arríued were,
With all the folke that they had there,
They toward them in hy.
And when Sir Edward wist surely,
That to him néere comming were théy

>Alex. Carmichael and Alex. Millar
>*Printed Edition, 1737*

And when they all assembled were
They were well near twenty thousand,
When that they wist that in their land,
Sik a menze arrived were,
With all the folk that they had there:
They went toward them in hy.
And when sir Edward wist surely,
That to him near coming were they,

Robert Freebairn
Printed Edition, 1758

And when that they assembled were
They were well near twenty thousand,
When that they wist that in their land,
Sik a men[y]ie arrived were,
With all the folk that they had there:
They went toward them in great hy.
And fra Sir Edward went soothly,
That near to him coming were they.

Notes

1. Robert Burns, 'Robert Bruce's March to Bannockburn' in *The Poems and Songs of Robert Burns*, (ed.) J. Kinsley, 3 vols (Oxford 1968) ii, 707.

2. Robert Burns to Dr John Moore, 2 Aug. 1787, in *The Letters of Robert Burns*, (ed.) J. De Lancy Ferguson, (rev.)G.R. Roy, 2 vols (Oxford 1985) i, 136.

3. M.W. Bloomfield and C. W. Dunn, *The Role of the Poet in Early Societies* (Cambridge 1989) 1–4.

4. M. Lynch, *Scotland. A New History* (London 1991) 113.

5. J.F. Miller, *Blind Harry's 'Wallace'* (Glasgow 1914) 9–10. However, only (!) 36–37 of the 44 editions Miller refers to could be accounted for. However, his figure may be correct (if not an understatement) if the printings of Gilbertfield's version of the *Wallace* were to be included.

6. *The Bannatyne Miscellany*, 3 vols (Edinburgh 1836) ii, 224.

7. *Bannatyne Miscellany*, ii, 184.

8. R.H. Carnie, 'Scottish Printers and Booksellers, 1668–1775: A Study of Source Material', in *The Bibliotheck – A Scottish Journal of Bibliography and Allied Topics*, 4 (1963–66) 213.

9. Burns was also a subscriber to the 1790 Perth edition of the *Wallace*, which attempted to replicate Harry's medieval Scots. In a letter to Mrs Dunlop (who never tired of telling people that William Wallace was a distant ancestor of her's) Burns praises the book for being 'the most elegant piece of work that ever came from any Printing-Press in Great Britain'. (Robert Burns to Mrs Dunlop, 6 Dec. 1790, in *The Letters of Robert Burns*, ii, 64).

10. See *A New Edition of the Life and Heroik Actions of the Renoun'd Sir William Wallace General and Governour of Scotland. Wherein the Old obsolete Words are rendered more Intelligible; and adapted to the understanding of such who have not the leisure to study the Meaning, and Import of such, Phrases without the help of a Glossary* (Glasgow 1722).

11. William Hamilton, *Blind Harry's Wallace*, (ed.) E. King (Edinburgh 1998) xvi.

12. *Traditions, &c. Respecting Sir William Wallace, collected chiefly from Publications of recent Date*, by a Former Subscriber for a Wallace Monument (Edinburgh 1856) 21.

13. D. Daiches, *The Paradox of Scottish Culture: The Eighteenth-Century Experience* (London 1964) 19–20.

14. D. Daiches, *Literature and Gentility in Scotland* (Edinburgh 1982) 1–2.

15. Formerly the only *Wallace* MS was bound together with one of the two surviving MSS of Barbour's *Bruce*. They have now been separated.

16. National Library of Scotland, Adv. MS. 19.2.2 (ii) folio 83b.

17. *The Actis and Deides of Schir William Wallace* (1570) (Facsimile reprint for STS, Edinburgh 1940) book 10, chap. 1.

18. Miller, *'Wallace'*, 7, whose comments on such are largely based around the assessment of Moir. See *Actis and Deidis of the Illustere and Vailyeand Campioun, Schir William Wallace Knicht of Ellerslie by Henry the Minstrel, Commonly Known as Blind Harry*, (ed.) J. Moir (STS, Edinburgh 1889).

19. M.A. Bald, 'The Pioneers of Anglicised Speech in Scotland', in *SHR*, 24 (1927) 181–82. According to Bald, the occasional English word that may have crept into any of Charteris's works is the result of him not even realising that it was such.

20. Miller, *'Wallace'*, 7; M. Lyndsay, *History of Scottish Literature* (London 1977) 23.

21. M. Lynch, *Edinburgh and the Reformation* (Edinburgh 1981) Appendix iii, 267.

22. W.A. Craigie, 'The Present State of the Scottish Tongue', in *The Scottish Tongue* (London 1924) 5.

23. M.A. Bald, 'The Anglicisation of Scottish Printing', in *SHR*, 23 (1926) 114, claims that the copy of this edition of the *Wallace* (as well as the 1611) held by the Advocates' Library (NLS) had vanished, yet one is there today.

24. 1618 also retains several English words given a 'quasi-Scots' spelling, such as 'heid' and 'deid'.

25. His Bible, largely still in the (English) language of Purvey's revised Wycliffe Bible, was not published until the early twentieth century. See *The New Testament in Scots . . . by Murdoch Nisbet c. 1520*, (ed.) T.G. Law, 3 vols (STS, Edinburgh 1901–1905).

26. D.F. Wright, '"The Commoun Buke of the Kirke": The Bible in the Scottish Reformation', in *The Bible in Scottish Life and Literature*, (ed.) D.F. Wright (Edinburgh 1988) 160.

27. *The Works of John Knox*, (ed.) D. Laing, 6 vols (Edinburgh 1846–95) ii, 284.

28. B. Galloway, *The Union of England and Scotland 1603–1608* (Edinburgh 1986) 7.

29. He also printed John Barbour's *Bruce* three times: in 1616, 1618, and 1620.

30. Of course some 'translating' of Biblical language into common speech may have occurred. Wright, 'The Common Buke' 170, believes that Knox utilised 'the spoken word, and oral techniques' in his writings. Similarly, printers like Hart could have introduced some elements of everyday speech into the *Wallace* text .

31. Wright, 'The Common Buke', 155.

32. The 1758 edition of the *Bruce* makes the claim that it was 'Carefully corrected from the edition printed by Andro Hart in 1620'. See *The Life and Acts of the most victorious Conqueror Robert Bruce, King of Scotland by John Barbour* . . . (Edinburgh 1758).

33. However, neither the publishers, nor Pinkerton, worked from the original MS. This is clearly stated by the printers in their address to David Stewart, the Earl of Buchan, when they thank him '. . . for the trouble Your Lordship has taken, in procuring for us a Copy of the valuable Manuscript of Henry's Life of Wallace . . . in comparing the Copy with the Original; in suggesting to us Directions concerning its Publication . . . '; see *The Metrical History of Sir William Wallace, Knight of Ellerslie, by . . . Blind Harry* . . . (Perth, R. Morison and Son, 1790) printer's introduction.

34. Miller, '*Wallace*', 11; *Hary's Wallace. Vita Nobilissimi Defensoris Scotie Wilelmi Wallace Militis*, (ed.) M.P. McDiarmid, 2 vols (STS, Edinburgh 1968–69) i, xii.

35. *The Bruce and Wallace; published from two ancient manuscripts preserved in the Library of the Faculty of Advocates*, (ed.) J. Jamieson, 2 vols (Published 1820, this 2nd edition reprinted with some additional notes appended, Glasgow 1869) ii x.

36. *Actis and Deidis*, (ed.) J. Moir, xviii.

37. *Hary's Wallace*, (ed.) McDiarmid, i, xii.

38. However, even Freebairn exercised a fair deal of creative license with the text. This is especially apparent with his choice in dividing the book up into books and chapters. He, like most of his contemporaries, divided up the *Wallace* into 12 books, whereas the MS is divided into 11. Most of the so-called scholarly editions of Harry, starting with 1790, employ 11 books of text – McDiarmid's most recent one being the notable exception, which reverts to 12. Freebairn was also (overly) creative when he went about dividing these 12 books into chapters, especially in the twelfth. There is no extant MS authority for dividing the various books into chapters of any sort.

39. Bald (1926) 113, believed that Hart was the most prolific printer of his time. She appears to have been correct, and a perusal of works printed by him indicates that he turned out bibles, and other liturgical works; vernacular

Social, Political and Cultural Scene

works like Barbour, Harry, and Henryson; classical works of all sorts; not to mention works on moral philosophy, etc.; see H.G. Aldis, *A List of Books Printed in Scotland Before 1700* (printed 1904; reprinted with continuum for 1700, Edinburgh 1970).

40. *Hary's Wallace*, (ed.) McDiarmid, i, xii.
41. Which contained a multitude of poems written in more or less standard contemporary poetic English.
42. T. Royle, *The Mainstream Companion to Scottish Literature* (Edinburgh 1993) 142.
43. *James Watson's Choice Collection of Comic and Serious Scots Poems*, (ed.) H.H. Wood, 2 vols (STS, Edinburgh 1977–91).
44. *Four Scottish Poets of Cambuslang & Dechmont Hill: Patrick Hamilton, Lieutenant William Hamilton, John Struthers, and Duncan Glen*, (ed.) D. Glen (Edinburgh 1996) 9.
45. 'The Last Dying Words of Bonny Heck, A Famous Grey-Hound in the Shire of Fife' (ll. 43–54) in *Watson's Choice Collection*, (ed.) Wood, i, 68–69.
46. *The Works of Allan Ramsay*, (eds.) B. Martin and J.W. Oliver, vols 1–2, and (eds.) A.M. Kinghorn and A. Law, vols 3–6, 6 vols (STS, Edinburgh 1945–74) iv, 200.
47. Lindsay, *History*, 169; Wittig, *Scottish Tradition*, 161.
48. For a description of 'Scottish Augustan', see A.M. Oliver, 'The Scottish Augustans', in *Scottish Poetry: A Critical Survey*, (ed.) J. Kinsley (London 1955).
49. [Alexander Pennecuik] *Croydeon and Cochrania, A Pastoral on The Nuptials of . . . His Grace James Duke of Hamilton . . . with the Lady Anne Cochran . . . Solemnized February 14, 1723* (Edinburgh 1723) 7.
50. R. Crawford, *Devolving English Literature* (Oxford 1992) 18 and 20.
51. This clearly appeared to be the case with Fergusson (1750–74) who after producing works solely in English initially, turned, in 1772, to writing in Scots. Certainly Fergusson's Scots poems were more noteworthy than his English; see *The Christis Kirk Tradition. Scots Poems of Folk Festivity*, (ed.) A.H. Maclaine (Glasgow 1996) x–xi.
52. James Thomson, 'Autumn', in *The Poetical Works of James Thomson*, 2 vols (London 1860) i, 131.
53. John Harvey, *The Life of Robert Bruce King of Scots* (John Catanach, Edinburgh 1729) 8.
54. Though Scotland's accomplished poet of common tradition, Robert Burns, would find inspiration through this more elite version of the Knight of Ellerslie. It is interesting to see how Burns reacted to the language of Hamilton's *Wallace*. In yet another letter to Mrs Dunlop (Robert Burns to

Mrs Dunlop 15 Nov. 1786, *The Letters of Robert Burns*, i 62) Burns renders Book II, chap. I, lines 11–12 of Hamilton's *Wallace* thus:

> Syne to the Leglen wood when it was late
> To make a silent and a safe retreat

which is not *exactly* identical to the original:

> Then to the Laigland-Wood when it grew late,
> To make a silent and a soft retreat.

In addition to making the narrative a little more understandable, Burns slightly 'Scotticises' this passage, including substituting the Scots 'syne' for the English 'then'. Though undoubtedly – at least in part – attempting to 'show-off' his abilities as a vernacularist, Burns seems to be attempting to 'retranslate' a 'translation'. However, we might ask if he actually conceptualised certain English words in Hamilton's *Wallace* as their Scots equivalents. Though we will never know the certain answer, his treatment of the above passage hints that though he read in English, perhaps Burns more readily understood in Scots.

55. *The Bruce and Wallace*, (ed.) Jamieson, ii, 1–2 (book 1, ll. 17–22).

56. George Mackenzie MD, *The Lives and Characters of the Most Eminent Writers of the Scots Nation . . .* 3 vols (Edinburgh, 1708) 'The Life of John Blair', i, 248.

57. *The Bruce and Wallace*, (ed.) Jamieson, ii, 2 (book 1, ll. 27–28).

58. [Matthew Duncan] *The History of the Kings of Scotland From Fergus I to the End of Q. Ann's Reign . . .* (William Duncan, Glasgow 1722) 108–24.

59. Duncan, *Kings of Scotland* 387.

60. Duncan, *Kings of Scotland* 393.

61. Duncan, *Kings of Scotland* 385–86.

62. And at least one English printer, that being the London-based one who produced the 1790 edition on behalf of James Pinkerton.

63. John Barbour, *The Bruce*, (ed.) A.A.M. Duncan (Edinburgh 1997) 32.

64. Bald (1926) 114, noted this of Hart's respective editions of the *Wallace*, and the *Bruce*. She did not offer a fully satisfactory explanation for this characteristic of the two books, but observing that his 1621 versions of Henryson's *Fables*, and the *Gude and Godly Ballates* contained more Scots than either his *Bruce* or his *Wallace*, Bald believed that Andrew Hart had waited until he had established 'his reputation as an anglicised printer' before releasing these works in Scots, which were solely meant to be antiquarian curiosities. If this was the case, why then is Hart's 1620 edition of the *Bruce* still mainly in modern English, perhaps – *very marginally* – even more so than that of 1616? And even if Hart's later efforts were meant to appeal to a narrow readership, it still does not detract from the idea that efforts like the *Bruce* and the *Wallace* were intended for a more general audience.

Social, Political and Cultural Scene

65. It is only after Andrew Hart's final editions of the *Wallace* and the *Bruce* (both from 1620) that the printing of Harry began to massively outpace that of Barbour.

66. *The Famous History of . . . Robert, sir named The Bruce, King of Scotland . . . with . . . the Scottish Kings lineally descended from Him to Charles now Prince . . . Set forth . . . in Heroic Verse* (John Hall, Glasgow 1753).

67. R. McKinlay, 'Barbour's *Bruce*' in *Records of the Glasgow Bibliographical Society*, 6 (Glasgow 1920) 34–38.

68. Gordon, *Famous History of Bruce*, 23. This appears to be the same Graham who apparently conspired against King Robert I after Bannockburn, et al. See, *The Bruce*, (ed.) Duncan, 698n.

69. Gordon, *Famous History of Bruce* , 14.

70. Patrick Gordon, *A Short Abridgement of Britain's Distemper From the Yeare of God M.CD.XXXIX. to M.DC.XLIX*, (Spalding Club, Aberdeen, 1844). That Gordon the poet and Gordon the historian were possibly one and the same might be obvious on stylistic grounds, since there is much poetry interspersed throughout the history. The existing politically-based similarities will be discussed below. Also, a recent biographical sketch of Gordon asserts that poet and historian may be one; see D. Stevenson, *King or Covenant? Voices from the Civil War* (East Linton 1997). The shortcoming to this poet turned historian theory is that, as Stevenson says, 'the two . . . are separated by a silence of thirty years' (175).

71. Gordon, *Britain's Distemper*, 219.

72. An obvious allusion to Henry and Charles; see Gordon, *Famous History of Bruce* 47.

73. Almost the only biographical information on Harvey uncovered so far comes from McKinlay, 'Barbour's *Bruce*':

    He is said to have been a school-master in Edinburgh and to have died there. It has been conjectured that he was a graduate of Aberdeen University and perhaps an Aberdonian, because he works into his poem a glowing eulogy upon the city, as if no one but an Aberdonian could have a good word to say about it. Harvey and his *Bruce* have received scant attention from literary historians. Even those who devote a sentence or two to castigate Hamilton for his ill-executed Wallace, do not apparently consider Harvey worth their lash. (33)

74. This conjecture is based upon the contents of an advertisement for selling Harvey's *Bruce* from his home, inserted into a copy of the poem. See National Library of Scotland, LC 286; *Proposals For Printing by Subscription, The Life and Acts of Robert Bruce King of Scots Done in Modern Verse By Jo. Harvey M.A.*

75. Harvey, *Bruce*, preface page.

76. Harvey, *Bruce*, 6n.

77. Repeatedly throughout his *Bruce*, Harvey bemoans the damage that faction has done to divide loyalties within Scotland.

78. Harvey, *Bruce*, 70.

79. *A new Edition of the Life . . . of . . . Sir William Wallace . . . to which is annexed, The Life and Martial Achievements of . . . Robert Bruce . . . By John Harvey* (H. Galbraith, Dundee 1770).

80. The possibility of a link between the cult of Bruce during the eighteenth century and Jacobitism, was first brought to my attention by Prof. E.J. Cowan during a personal communication. Tradition held that Robert I was the progenitor of the Royal Stewarts, an idea not too fanciful when the actual lineage of the Bruce's descendants is considered.

81. Harvey, *Bruce*, 231–32.

82. *The Bruciad, an Epic Poem, In Six Books* (London 1769) preface.

83. On the various (unsuccessful) Jacobite plots of the 1750s, see C. Erickson, *Bonnie Prince Charlie* (London 1989) 252–268.

84. *The Bruciad*, 237.

85. This claim has been made before; see *The Bruce or The Book of the Most Excellent and Noble Prince Robert De Broyss, King of Scots Compiled by Master John Barbour*, (ed.) W.W. Skeat, 2 vols (STS, Edinburgh 1894) i, lxxxii; [John Pinkerton] *Ancient Scottish Poems Never Before In Print But now Published From the MS Collections of Sir Richard Maitland . . .*, 2 vols (London 1786) i, xci. Pinkerton's remarks are faithfully quoted in full by Miller, 'Wallace', 10.

86. E.J. Cowan, 'The Wallace Factor in Scottish History' in *Images of Scotland*, (eds.) R. Jackson and S. Wood, *The Journal of Scottish Education Occasional Papers*, no. 1 (Dundee 1997) 15.

87. *The Jacobite Threat – England, Scotland, Ireland, France: A Source Book*, (eds.) B.P. Lenman & J.S. Gibson (Edinburgh 1990) xvi–xvii.

88. The 1715 Uprising was in no small way indebted to the aspirations of John Erskine, the Earl of Mar. For more on this see B. Lenman, *The Jacobite Risings in Britain* (London, 1980) 126; and by the same author, *The Jacobite Cause* (Glasgow 1986) 46.

89. *To All True-hearted Scotsmen, Wether (sic) Soldiers Or others* (Perth, Robert Freebairn, 1715) 4.

90. Of course most concepts of 'the law of the land' were thought to be ultimately handed down by God. However, the tone of the tract is such that we might conclude that people like Freebairn conceived of the ancient law of succession as being intrinsically linked to the land itself. On this last

Social, Political and Cultural Scene 113

point, the pamphlet chastises the Hanoverians because they 'are fighting against [their] Lawful and Rightful King, born of our own Island . . . ' (*To All True-hearted Scotsmen*, 6.) The idea here seems to be that land and the royal line are linked.

91. *To All True-hearted Scotsmen*, 9.
92. 'A Curious Poem to the Memory of Sir William Wallace', in *A Full Collection of all Poems upon Charles, Prince of Wales . . . Published since His Arrival in Edinburgh the 17th Day of September, till the 1st of November, 1745* (Edinburgh 1745) 20; italics mine.
93. G. Nisbet, *Caledon's Tears: or, Wallace. A Tragedy. Containing the Calamities of Scotland from the Death of King Alexander III to the betraying and butchering of that faithful Father of his Country, Sir William Wallace of Elderslie* (P. Matthie, Edinburgh 1733) iii.
94. *Caledon's Tears*, 59.
95. *Caledon's Tears*, 59.
96. I.S. Ross and S.A.C. Scobie, 'Patriotic Publishing as a Response to the Union', in *The Union of 1707 – Its Impact on Scotland*, (ed.) T.I. Rae (Glasgow 1974) 94–95.
97. *An Account of the Burning of the Articles of the Union at Dumfries* (n.p., 1706?).
98. C.A. Whatley, *'Bought and Sold for English Gold'? Explaining the Union of 1707* (Glasgow 1994) passim.
99. I.D. Whyte, *Scotland Before the Industrial Revolution* (Harlow 1995) 291–309.
100. *Scotland's speech to her Sons (against union)* (1706).
101. *A Proper Project for Scotland, In a humble Address to the Peers, for Using their utmost Application in the ensuing Parliament, for having the Union dissolv'd* (Glasgow 1722) 4.
102. *A Proper Project*, 6.
103. *A Proper Project*, 7.
104. *A Proper Project*, 14.
105. *The Bruce and Wallace*, (ed.) Jamieson, ii, 341 (book 11, ll. 821–30).
106. *A New Edition of the Life and Heroik Actions of the Renown'd Sir William Wallace . . .*, 298.
107. Gordon, *Famous History of Bruce*, 24.
108. *Caledon's Tears*, 46–47.
109. *The true Scots Mens Lament for the Loss of the Rights of their Ancient Kingdom*.
110. My own reading of MS.
111. M.P. MacDiarmid's reading of MSS.

6

'Surely one of the greatest poems ever made in Britain': The Lament for Griogair Ruadh MacGregor of Glen Strae and its Historical Background[1]

Martin MacGregor

I

For George Buchanan, part of the *raison d' être* of the historian was, 'to restore us to our own ancestors, and our own ancestors to us'.[2] My purpose is to bring back a woman who was almost lost to us, whose life and art compel our attention, who deserves to be recognised as a highly gifted Scottish poetess. I wish to do so through the exploration of three landscapes of experience – external, internal and artistic – in which she moved.

II

A valuable source for the history of the central and western Highlands in the late medieval period is the *Chronicle of Fortingall*.[3] Under 7 April 1570, the chronicle has the following entry:

Gregor MacGregor of Glenstrae heddyt at Belloch.

Balloch (Gaelic *Bealach*, or *Bealach nan laogh*),[4] at the east end of Loch Tay, was by this time the site of the principal fortress of the dominant kindred in Breadalbane, the Campbells of Glen Orchy.[5] A history of the kindred compiled in the late sixteenth and earlier seventeenth centuries, the *Black Book of Taymouth*,[6] gives more details of the execution in its treatment of Cailean Liath,[7] chief of the Glen Orchy Campbells from 1550 until 1583. He is described as:

> ane great justiciar all his tyme, throch the quhilk he sustenit thee deidlie feid of the Clangregour ane lang space. And, besydis that he caused execute to the

death mony notable lymmaris, he beheiddit the laird off McGregour himselff at Kandmoir [hard by Balloch] in presens of the Erle of Atholl, the justice clerk, and sundrie vther nobillmen.[8]

The same source also states that the executed chief, Gregor Roy or Griogair Ruadh, 'mariet the laird of Glenlyouns dochter', but does not give her first name.[9] The lairds of Glen Lyon were Campbells, a branch of the Glen Orchy kindred.[10]

From 1570 we advance to 1813, and the publication at Edinburgh of Paruig Mac an Tuairneir's *Comhchruinneacha do dh'orain taghta Ghaidhealach*. He includes a song to which he gives the following rubric:

> Cumha le nighean do Dhonncha dubh, Moir-fhear Bhraigh-dealbunn, an uair a thug a h-athair, agus a brathair an ceann dheth a fear, Griogair Mac Griogair, agus a ciad leanabh air a glun.

> [an elegy composed by the daughter of Donnchadh Dubh, lord of Breadalbane, when her father and her brother beheaded her husband, Gregor MacGregor, while her first child was but an infant][11]

We shall examine in due course the flaws in this statement. For now let us note simply that if the elegy in question were the work of the wife of Griogair Ruadh, and were composed not long after 7 April 1570, then it would have experienced some eight generations of oral transmission before being printed in 1813.

In fact the song is still current within the oral tradition of Gaelic Scotland, being generally known as *Griogal Cridhe*. Since 1813 many other versions have been recorded both in Scotland, especially the Western Isles, and in Cape Breton.[12] *Griogal Cridhe* has also received a measure of recognition outwith the Gaelic world: witness its inclusion in a recently published *Anthology of Scottish Women Poets*.[13] One of its greatest advocates was the late Sorley MacLean, who has described it as:

> surely one of the greatest poems ever made in Britain. In it there is almost everything that there could be in such a poem: pride, remembrance of past happiness, desire for revenge but realisation of what that revenge would mean to other women, tenderness and anxiety for the infant son, fear that he will never avenge his father, and piercing lonely sorrow.[14]

Appreciation of the qualities of *Griogal Cridhe* has been undiminished by nagging uncertainties over its authenticity and authorship. These exist over and above the understandable doubts which hardbitten record historians might harbour about the trustworthiness of a text which has apparently survived for nearly 250 years in a purely oral milieu. Gaelic scholars familiar with the remarkable tenacity of that milieu have nevertheless had to address the problem of reconciling 1 August, the date of Griogair Ruadh's capture given in the first line of *Griogal Cridhe*, with 7 April 1570, the known date of his execution. This led W.J. Watson to doubt the contemporaneity of the song, and thus its ascription to Griogair Ruadh's wife.[15]

To date, however, the debate as to the authenticity of *Griogal Cridhe* has been conducted in something of a vacuum, since the historical background to the song has not been properly investigated. Discussion has been based on little more than the bald snippets from the *Chronicle of Fortingall* and the *Black Book of Taymouth* already cited.[16] Furthermore, insufficient attention has been paid to the relationship between *Griogal Cridhe* and a second, more obscure song, *Rìgh gur mór mo Chuid Mhulaid*, apparently no longer current in tradition, but which was committed to paper in the later eighteenth and again in the early nineteenth centuries.[17] This song was edited by the late Alasdair Duncan, who believed that it and *Griogal Cridhe* were the work of one person, and the product of one historical process;[18] but it was not his task to investigate that process more fully.

In this chapter I wish to provide a fuller account of the historical process of which these songs purport to be a part, culminating in the execution of Griogair Ruadh on 7 April 1570. In so doing I hope to resolve the questions of authenticity and authorship, thereby allowing us to reunite with her artistic legacy the woman to whom I referred at the outset. From an historian's viewpoint, acceptance of the legitimacy of her texts means that we can reincorporate them into history; and their testimony is all the more precious since it is at points unique. From the literary standpoint, a theme which I shall not address directly is whether a deeper understanding of the circumstances which gave birth to the songs enhances our appreciation of them as art. As already noted, to date *Griogal Cridhe* has required no such assistance to establish its reputation.

III

At the outset I propose to examine the internal evidence of these songs, with a view to establishing nothing more than their content and potential coherence.[19] *Griogal Cridhe* is the song of a woman whose lover was captured on 1 August, before midday, turning the joy of their love-play into despair (v. 1). They have a child (refrain, v. 2). The lover was captured by aristocrats, kinsmen of hers, by surprise and through deceit (v. 3). His name is Griogair, and he is apparently head of his kindred (v. 4). He has been beheaded (v. 5). She seeks vengeance in verse 5 on her father and

'Cailean', in verse 6 on Cailean Liath and Donnchadh Dubh; there is perhaps a temptation to assume both that these are the people she cursed in verse 3, and that 'Cailean' and Cailean Liath are one and the same, and hence that her father is Donnchadh Dubh. There is mention of a woman, *nighean an Ruadhanaich*, who is closely connected to these men. There is also an implication that these men are Campbells, which would make the authoress herself a Campbell. In verses 8, 9 and 10, Balloch, also mentioned in verse 7, is linked to her grief; presumably this is the site of the castle which (v. 9) she wishes to destroy, a wish reiterated in verse 10. Verses 11 and 12 set her loss against the contentment of other women; verse 12 seems to imply that she and Griogair had been husband and wife. Verses 13 to 15 set life with Griogair – lived out of doors, on the move, in material hardship but happiness – against a life of domestication, comfort but sterility with the mysterious *baran crìon na dalach*. Perhaps we wonder whether the experiences described in these verses are real, or imagined, or a combination of the two: is this baron a past or present suitor, or even her present partner or husband, and provider of the comparative luxury which she is actually 'enduring'; or is he simply a rhetorical foil for her late husband? Rhetoric or reality also applies to verse 16. Finally, verse 17 tells us that her child is very young. Since the father is dead, clearly the song is set, and was presumably composed, not very long after his death.

Rìgh gur mór mo Chuid Mhulaid is the song of a woman who begins by recollecting the origins of her relationship with her beloved (vv. 1–2). She has been unable to marry him because of opposition, primarily from her father (vv. 2–4, 28). Her beloved is a MacGregor, who is involved in armed conflict; there is specific reference to *cumasg Beinn Lòchaidh*, 'the skirmish of Ben Lochy' (vv. 5–8). His antagonists are Campbells, and they are her kin; thus she is a Campbell (vv. 7, 9). She failed to keep a tryst with her beloved, whose continued success means suffering for her (vv. 10–12). At present she is being held against her will within a fortress, under lock and key (vv. 13–14). She imagines escape, going to meet her beloved, journeying with him, and their physical union (vv. 15–22). She would rather him than wealth in any form (vv. 23–25). With remarkable vehemence she wishes destruction on those who keep her from him (vv. 26–28). She sees death as the only solution to her predicament (vv. 29–31).

Even at this bald level of analysis, if we regard *Rìgh gur mór mo Chuid Mhulaid* as the earlier song, then we can suggest a chain of events which plausibly incorporates both songs, and makes them the work of one authoress. Here we have a Campbell woman, in love with a MacGregor chief, named as Griogair. On her side there is parental and clan opposition to contact, far less marriage, between them, presumably linked to the active hostilities between their kindreds. She has turned against her own people and wishes destruction upon them. *Griogal Cridhe* implies that at some point a change took place which allowed them to marry, with issue. But then comes Griogair's capture and execution, apparently at the hands of her father and other named kinsmen; the same grouping, perhaps, whom she previously held responsible for preventing the marriage. Now she may be an unwilling participant in a relationship, even a marriage, with *baran crion na dalach*. Beyond conjunction of circumstance, there is also a strong sense of the one emotional and artistic sensibility shaping both songs, and manifesting itself in specific points of contact: the 'journeying' sequences; the rejection of material things for love; the almost shocking violence of her feelings towards those who have opposed her; the identification with nature, and creatures such as gull, lark and squirrel.

IV

We turn now to the historical background. I have dealt at length elsewhere with the early history of the MacGregors, and their relationship with the Campbells, down to the immediate aftermath of the execution of Griogair Ruadh in 1570. Here I extract from that history only the information we need to help us understand these songs.[20] Our point of departure must be the common assumption, based on the role played by the Campbells in helping to implement government policies against the MacGregors following the latter's proscription in 1603, that the relationship between these kindreds was confrontational from the first; that the Campbells, indeed, pursued a deliberate policy of displacing the MacGregors from their lands. The reality was very different.

The MacGregors came into being as a clan in the later fourteenth century, within the lordship of Glen Orchy, specifically the lands of Glen Strae. They were the dominant lineage within this lordship for a time, but lost their position to the Campbells, who were expanding rapidly eastwards in the period, and whose chief in 1432 granted his property lands within the lordship to his son, Cailean, progenitor of the Campbells of Glen Orchy. This, however, did not entail displacement of the MacGregors. An accommodation was reached whereby the MacGregors continued to hold their Glen Strae lands as vassals of the Campbell chiefs (earls of Argyll from c.1457), and became a client kindred of the Campbells.

The key to that clientship was military service, expressed most significantly in the joint expansion of the MacGregors and the Campbells of Glen Orchy eastwards into Perthshire, particularly Breadalbane, after

1432, ultimately resulting in the creation of a very extensive Campbell sphere of influence. By 1513, when Donnchadh, second head of the Glen Orchy Campbells, died with his chief Gilleasbuig earl of Argyll at Flodden, his kindred was already dominant within Breadalbane. MacGregor military power was fundamental to this process.

Between 1513 and 1550 the Campbells of Glen Orchy experienced stagnation and decline. They made virtually no fresh territorial acquisitions, ceased to have direct influence in central government, and effectively lost their position within the Campbell firmament to the new rising star, Iain Campbell of Cawdor. Symptomatic of the change in status of the Campbells of Glen Orchy was their loss of the service of the MacGregors, transferred by the earl of Argyll to Iain of Cawdor, perhaps as early as 1513 itself. Clearly the MacGregors played a role in the establishment of this new Campbell branch in the eastern and western highlands. This was one indication that they were not subject to the same process of decline as the Campbells of Glen Orchy between 1513 and 1550. Another was their continuing expansion, notably into Rannoch. The contrasting fortunes of the two kindreds may mean that by 1550, and the accession of Cailean Liath, sixth chief of the Glen Orchy Campbells, the MacGregors – numerous, militarily powerful, still expanding; Campbell clients but, as events in Rannoch seem to prove, capable of independent action – had come to represent a threat to the continued predominance of their erstwhile immediate masters in Breadalbane.

The year 1550 proved far more decisive a turning point than 1513. Cailean Liath, then around 50 years old, and the third son of the third chief, became head of his kindred through dynastic accident. Between 1550 and the death of his son and successor, Donnchadh Dubh, in 1631, these two men transformed the lordship of the Campbells of Glen Orchy, presiding over a phase of phenomenal expansion. Within the Breadalbane heartlands, the existing pattern of power was obliterated and replaced by the single hegemony of Cailean Liath and Donnchadh Dubh. Their influence was inescapable, cutting across tenurial patterns, and embracing all levels of society. Central to the ethos of their lordship was the use of a range of devices, including feudal superiorities, bonds of manrent and adoption, and rights of jurisdiction, in order to make others subject to them in precisely defined ways. They were absolutists, intolerant of opposition. Within a hegemony of this nature, there could be no place for a kindred as powerful as the MacGregors, possessing a capacity for independent action, or for action at the behest of another, such as Campbell of Cawdor.

Cailean Liath acceded on 5 July 1550. At some point between 1548 and 1554, and arguably close to the date of Cailean Liath's accession, the

MacGregor chief Iain Ruadh died, 'of the hurt of ane arrow going betuix Glenlyoun and Rannoch'.[21] His nearest male heir, his brother Griogair Ruadh, was legally a minor until late 1562. Cailean Liath took full advantage, by resecuring the grant of the service of the MacGregors from the earl of Argyll, and using this as the launchpad for a series of further measures which sought to reduce the role of MacGregor chief to that of a nominal figurehead, or indeed to bypass him altogether, leaving Cailean Liath as the effective head of the kindred. These measures included the eviction of an important MacGregor from Balloch in June 1552. Balloch was the site of one of the strongholds of the MacGregor chiefs; before 21 November 1559 Cailean Liath had completed the building of his principal fortress here. Between July and December 1552, a series of MacGregor kingroups gave bonds of manrent to Cailean Liath, in each case taking him as their chief and renouncing their own. Most importantly, in 1554 Cailean Liath purchased the superiority of Glen Strae, and the ward and marriage of Griogair Ruadh, from the earl and master of Argyll – the feudal corollary of the kin-based attack on the MacGregor ruling family represented by the bonds of manrent of 1552.

The next key developments came in late 1562. Griogair Ruadh's minority had apparently ended by 24 November. As his feudal superior, Cailean Liath promised to give him possession of Glen Strae on two conditions: that he accept certain unspecified legal restrictions, and that before 1 January 1563 he surrender to Cailean Liath two men for whom he was deemed to be responsible, and who had recently slain a servant of Cailean Liath.

For Griogair Ruadh, early in his chiefship, the dilemma could not have been more acute nor the conflicting pressures more intense. If he wished to retain Glen Strae, the *dùthaich* of his clan, it would be at the price of accepting conditions which would reduce him to a degree of vassalage unknown to any of his predecessors, and manifestly compromise his authority as chief. This would particularly apply to the surrender of the two dependants. Protection of his people was an indispensable duty of a chief, dereliction of which could lead to his deposition.

The stark choice was submisssion or defiance, and it had to be made by 1 January. The choice was made on the night of 7 December. At the head of an estimated 120 men of his kindred, Griogair Ruadh attacked first an inn near Killiecrankie, where nine men, five of them Campbells, en route to Glen Lyon after attending a fair at Perth, were lodging for the night. The inn was set ablaze, and eight of these men slain. The warband then passed to Kincraigie in Strath Tay, where Pàdraig, brother of Donnchadh Ruadh Campbell of Glen Lyon, and several others, mainly MacCormicks, who were probably also returning to Glen Lyon from Perth, were asleep in a barn. The barn was fired and the occupants taken prisoner, although one of them was subsequently slain.

These attacks were tantamount to a declaration of war on the Campbells, and were understood as such. They marked the beginning of a feud which lasted until 1570. It was exceptionally bitter, bringing violence, suffering and destruction to much of western Perthshire. Its course was profoundly shaped by national politics during the personal reign of Mary (1560–67), and the subsequent civil war (1567–73). I recapitulate only the essential points here. The feud fell into two distinct phases, the first from 7 December 1562 until late 1565, the second from the summer of 1567 until late 1570.

Throughout most of the first phase, the Campbells enjoyed strong central support from Mary in pursuing the MacGregors. But the pursuit proved ineffective, partly because of the high degree of resetting and assistance which the MacGregors received over a wide area and from across the social spectrum, and partly because of internal Campbell dissensions. By spring 1565 there was stalemate. At this point the relationship between crown and Campbells began to break down, and that summer and autumn the Campbells participated in the rebellion against Mary known as the Chaseabout Raid. Threatened by external dangers, the Campbells closed ranks. It became imperative to reach a settlement with the MacGregors, not only to end a damaging source of internal dissension – Cailean Liath and Gilleasbuig fifth earl of Argyll had come to differ greatly in their attitudes to the feud – but also to restore the MacGregors to their traditional role of Campbell military clients who could lend support to the rebellion. For her part, Mary firstly fomented the feud, and then competed with the Campbells in bidding for the MacGregors' services, using the earl of Atholl as her local agent. The MacGregors found themselves courted by the very elements which had previously acted in tandem against them. Despite all that had happened since 1550, most of the MacGregors took the Campbells' part, which says much for the strength of that hereditary bond. Thus it was that, when Argyll was finally reconciled to Mary in March 1566 because of fresh political developments which flowed from the Riccio murder, the MacGregors were included in his remission, and the revolution in their political fortunes completed.

After March 1566 the feud was held in check as Mary steered conciliatory courses at the national and local levels. But with the queen's fall in 1567, civil war began and, that summer, the feud resumed. The key to this second phase was the reconciliation at the local level of Cailean Liath and Atholl. In May 1568 they made a defensive alliance specifically directed against Griogair Ruadh and his associates; as the violence escalated, on 6 May 1569 they made a much more aggressive offensive alliance against the MacGregors. From then to early August 1569, the pursuit of the MacGregors was very intense.

It is now that we must turn to *Griogal Cridhe* and the reference in its first line to *latha Lùnast'*, 1 August. W.J. Watson, assuming that the first line referred to the point of Griogair Ruadh's death, regarded *latha Lùnast'* as an 'error', which was 'seriously against the poem having been composed by his wife, or, indeed, till some time after his execution'.[22] Derick Thomson, starting from the basis that the song itself gave the strong impression of being contemporary and authentic, proposed either emending *latha Lùnast'* to *latha Tùrnais* (Palm Sunday, which in 1570 fell on 19 March), or regarding the first verse as a later accretion. He also considered, but rejected, the possibility of Griogair Ruadh having been captured on 1 August 1569, and remaining unexecuted until 7 April 1570.[23] More recently, Alasdair Duncan accepted 1 August 1569 as the date of capture on the grounds that political factors may have dictated that Griogair Ruadh remain imprisoned and unexecuted for eight months.[24]

We can now confirm the accuracy of the last interpretation, and remove any doubts about the contemporaneity or authorship of *Griogal Cridhe*. The crucial evidence is a precept from Regent Moray, charging Cailean Liath to surrender Griogair Ruadh, who *iam apprehensus et captus est* ('was recently captured and imprisoned'), to be tried before a justiciary court for various crimes committed within the bounds of Glen Orchy, Breadalbane, Balquhidder and Menteith. The precept is dated at St Andrews on 6 August 1569.[25] On 20 November Cailean Liath was again charged to present Griogair Ruadh, 'presentlie being in his handes and keping', before Moray by the 28th of that month at the latest, under pain of treason.[26]

Moray was clearly anxious to prevent Cailean Liath executing Griogair Ruadh himself, probably for two reasons. Since Griogair Ruadh had been fully pardoned by Mary, he would need to be tried and his guilt established before any action could be taken against him. Secondly, the most likely outcome of Griogair Ruadh's execution at the hands of Cailean Liath would surely be an intensification of the feud, and of local disorder, rather than its resolution.

Cailean Liath refused to relinquish his prize. His motive, simply, was the desire for personal vengeance, but various hurdles stood between him and his objective: the opposition of the Regent; the possible legal consequences; the threat of a MacGregor backlash. He would also require the sanction of the earl of Argyll, for whom the feud had never been the personal crusade it had become for Cailean Liath. While Cailean Liath and Atholl had now sunk their differences, various local antagonisms remained between Argyll and Atholl, which seem to have been responsible for the opposing stances the earls had adopted with regard to national politics since 1567. Atholl had become increasingly involved in the pursuit of the MacGregors during the second phase of the feud, and this almost certainly explains Argyll's lack of involvement; the least that can be said is that Argyll did nothing to prevent the difficulties the MacGregors were causing his eastern neighbour.

The murder of Regent Moray on 23 January 1570 meant the end of central opposition to Cailean Liath, and created the circumstances which led inexorably to Griogair Ruadh's death. For the next five months the Regency was vacant, 'the *de facto* government was without a focus', and the queen's party, including Argyll, in the ascendant.[27] A faction which wanted Mary restored became evident within the king's party. That faction included Atholl, and, nationally and locally, he and Argyll now came into close alignment. Full reconciliation between the earls took place on 24 March, and that contract reveals that Argyll was now minded to take a more positive attitude to the cause of MacGregor repression in which Atholl was engaged. In fact, he shifted his position sufficiently to remove any scruples he held about the execution of Griogair Ruadh. At Balloch, on 29 March, in his capacity as Justice General of Scotland, Argyll gave Cailean Liath licence to carry out the execution, and promised to assist him in the event of MacGregor reprisals.[28]

The fear of reprisals was now all that stood between Cailean Liath and his goal, and helps to explain a document he issued the same day. This is the second known document in which our poetess appears, here called *Marie* Campbell. It reveals that by now, she and Griogair Ruadh had a son. His name is here left blank, but we know from later sources that it was Alasdair Ruadh. In the document, Cailean Liath bound himself that, should he execute Griogair Ruadh, within forty days thereafter he would give the ward and non-entry of most of the MacGregor Glen Strae lands to Alasdair Ruadh and his mother. Her share was contingent upon her not remarrying without Cailean Liath's advice,[29] which could confirm the statement in *Rìgh gur mór mo Chuid Mhulaid* that her relationship with Griogair Ruadh had initially been opposed. Secondly, Cailean Liath would in due course give Alasdair Ruadh heritable legal possession of Glen Strae, to be held, 'with all securitie neidful as sall pleis my Lord of Ergyle to deviss'.[30]

In other words, Cailean Liath was now prepared to concede an issue central to the feud – MacGregor possession of Glen Strae – but only at the price of Griogair Ruadh's life. Griogair Ruadh had become a talisman of resistance for whom there could be no forgiveness. At Balloch nine days later, Cailean Liath took the unusual step, as the *Black Book of Taymouth* takes due care to emphasise, of assuming personal responsibility for the execution.[31] By now he was nearly 70 years old.

V

Let us now return to our songs, bearing with us the knowledge that the key stumbling block to the acceptance of the authenticity of *Griogal Cridhe* as a contemporary witness has been removed. We have one documentary reference to their creator prior to 29 March 1570. At Carnban Castle in Glen Lyon, on 10 September 1568, as *Marioun* Campbell, spouse of Gregor MacGregor and daughter of Duncan Campbell of Glen Lyon, she granted her father letters of reversion to certain lands in Glen Lyon which he had granted them in joint fee.[32] This accords both with the statement in the *Black Book of Taymouth*, and with the songs' internal evidence that she was a Campbell. We can reject the assertion by Paruig Mac an Tuairneir that she was a daughter of Donnchadh Dubh.

Five further documentary references to this woman have so far been discovered. On 26 October 1570 she is referred to as *Marioun*;[33] on 7 December 1575 and 19 June 1599 as *Mariota*;[34] on 13 December 1597 as *Meriorie*;[35] and on 25 July 1601 as *Marjorie*.[36] The interchangeability of most of these names in the contemporary Latin and Scots record is well known,[37] and we can be certain that they refer to the same person, although, regrettably, we cannot say for sure what her true, Gaelic name was.[38] I shall call her Marion.

Let us now attempt to synthesise the historical landscape as we have reconstructed it, with the evidence of our songs, and in particular with the emotional landscape of Marion Campbell's experience, as she reveals it to us in them. Even if we possessed no evidence beyond that of the texts themselves, we might conclude that in its elemental, wilful power, *Rìgh gur mór mo Chuid Mhulaid* bears the stamp of a younger authoress than *Griogal Cridhe*, in which vehemence, although still present, is only one of a number of ways in which emotion finds expression, resulting in different shades of mood and tone.[39] In fact, *Rìgh gur mór mo Chuid Mhulaid* must be the earlier song, composed when Marion was as yet unmarried. The most likely point for that marriage to have taken place was in the interval between the two phases of the feud, that is between late 1565 and *c*. 30 July 1567, as a concrete manifestation of the *rapprochement* between the MacGregors and Campbells; doubtless it was at the same time that Donnchadh Ruadh granted to his daughter and her husband the lands in Glen Lyon which presumably sustained them thereafter, given Griogair Ruadh's continued exclusion from Glen Strae. *Rìgh gur mór mo Chuid Mhulaid* was therefore probably composed during the first phase of the feud, between 7 December 1562 and late 1565. Its content makes it clear that the feud was now well established and ongoing,[40] and that Marion and Griogair Ruadh were still unmarried, largely because of the opposition of Donnchadh Ruadh, who was keeping his daughter separated from Griogair Ruadh against her will.

It is difficult to judge when the relationship came into being. Through his mother Griogair Ruadh was related to the Campbells of Ardkinglass and the MacNaughtons of Dunderave, and there is evidence to suggest that he may have spent some or all of the years of his minority among these kinsfolk in the neighbourhood of the head of Loch Fyne, and at a remove from the territories of his own kindred.[41] Marion says that her first sighting of Griogair Ruadh took place at a point where marriage was already an impossibility for her, which might seem to fit the scenario of active hostilities which existed after 7 December 1562. Yet for first contact between them to have taken place between then and late 1565 seems inherently unlikely, given Griogair Ruadh's status as outlaw and fugitive in these years.

Relations between the Campbells and the MacGregors were deteriorating before the outbreak of war on 7 December 1562, and particularly in May and June of that year.[42] Perhaps more significantly, at a point apparently falling between 25 March 1561 and 25 March 1562, the MacGregors had laid waste the lands of Kilmorich in Strath Tay, which were held by Donnchadh Ruadh of Glen Lyon.[43] To this we may link the fact that the Campbells of Glen Lyon seem to have borne the main brunt of the attacks of 7 December 1562. Those slain by Killiecrankie were *en route* to Glen Lyon from Perth, and included five Campbells. True, two of these Campbells did not belong to Glen Lyon, but nevertheless it was Donnchadh Ruadh, along with the families and dependers of the victims, who initiated legal action against the MacGregors responsible.[44] We do not know the onward destination of the group attacked at Kincraigie, but they were headed by Pàdraig, brother of Donnchadh Ruadh. *Rìgh gur mór mo Chuid Mhulaid* provides further support, since Marion makes it clear in verse 9 that it is her close kinsfolk who have suffered at the hands of Griogair Ruadh; this would strengthen the case for seeing verses 6 to 9 as referring to the events of the night of 7 December 1562. It is possible then, though hardly proveable, that the relationship was already in being prior to that point, and that its suppression, whether or not it was an extra factor in precipitating the feud, helps to explain both the devastation of Kilmorich, and why it was by means of attacks on the Campbells of Glen Lyon that the MacGregors chose to declare war on the Campbells.

The commencement of her relationship with Griogair Ruadh, and of the feud, left Marion caught between her own kindred and that of her lover. *Rìgh gur mór mo Chuid Mhulaid* reveals her response (vv. 3, 7, 26–28) as an emphatic, violent rejection of her own family and people. Yet verses 9 and 12 suggest that her decisiveness did not preclude the payment of a psychological price.

In seeking to reconcile this song with the historical process insofar as we can recreate it, verses 6 to 9 are particularly tantalising. Could these refer to the events of the night of 7 December 1562? If so, it would presumably need to be to the confrontation by Killiecrankie rather than that at Kincraigie, for in the latter case Pàdraig Campbell of Glen Lyon and his companions were taken prisoner, and although the MacGregors subsequently slew a Lachlann Campbell, 'eftir he was takin, breakand thair promis maid to him of assurance and salftie of his lyiff',[45] there is no evidence that the others were killed.[46] We have already noted an obvious point of contact, in that Marion refers to the victims as Campbells and relations of hers. Note also the macabre, almost exclusive emphasis she places upon the stripping of the clothing – boots, silk shirts and coats, clearly of a high quality – from the bodies of the slain. Indeed, Ronald Black has suggested that in the line, *Dhan ghearr thu 'mhuineal mu 'chotan*, 'the use of the preposition *mu* – around, about – seems also to imply that the throat was targeted in order to avoid spoiling the coat', and translates, 'Whose throat you cut for his coat'.[47] Now, the contemporary documentary evidence provides two references to the clothing of those slain by Killiecrankie on 7 December 1562. It is stated that these men 'wer preparand thame to pas to thair beddis, thair claythis beand lowis [loose]', when Griogair Ruadh's warband arrived, implying that they were still dressed, and thus capable of being stripped once slain as envisioned in the song. Secondly, a list of those suspected of providing reset and assistance to the MacGregors in 1562 and 1563 includes the name of:

> Andro mcglassane [in *Desert*, Glen Errochty] quhay wes spy to the glengregor[sic] quhone thai slew Alexander Campbell the lard of barbraikson[48] and his servandis in to the saidis androw mcglaschanis barne and to weryfe this he is posest as yit with part of the saidis Alexander Campbellis claithyng as his nychtboris knawis.[49]

As we have seen, it was by Killiecrankie that Alasdair Campbell of Barbreck was lodging on the night of 7 December 1562. The building in question, identified here as a barn, is identified in another document issued less than a week after the slayings as an 'oistler hous',[50] but these descriptions need not be mutually exclusive. Of greater moment for our present purposes is the indication that the body of one victim at least was stripped of its clothing. Whatever other motives may have existed for doing so, one was straightforwardly economic: to Griogair Ruadh and his allies, fugitives before the law after 7 December 1562, clothing could function as a form of currency. Such is the conclusion we can draw from the case of another individual cited in this same list of MacGregor resetters, who:

> resettit and cost the spuilze and claithing That wes tane of the saidis Lardis [Cailean Liath] servandis quhone thai wor slane at the burning of the kyll and barnis of Balloch and this his nychtboris knawis.[51]

Marion's use of the term *cumasg*, a skirmish, might also seem appropriate to what happened by Killiecrankie, which, although significant because of the status of those who died, and in its consequences, was hardly a full-blown confrontation. But with the reference to *Beinn Lòchaidh*, we encounter problems. There seems to be no Beinn Lòchaidh known in Scotland. There is of course Gleann Lòchaidh on Loch Tayside, an area of MacGregor settlement, where there were at least two incidents during the first phase of the feud, but hardly of the sort described by Marion.[52] It may well be then, that our text is corrupt here, but I can offer no convincing emendation based on the known place-names in the immediate vicinity of Killiecrankie.[53]

Other specific details in *Rìgh gur mór mo Chuid Mhulaid* need not long detain us. Marion's reference in verse 10 to a tryst she failed to keep may indicate that she had planned to elope with Griogair Ruadh, perhaps at the very point at which the feud broke out. In *cladhaire gòrach* (v. 11) there may be an allusion to the vassalage and loss of status which would have been Griogair Ruadh's lot had he accepted the conditions imposed by Cailean Liath; compare *fear taighe* (v. 4), where Marion may be underlining her loss of a husband who was also in her eyes a man of property.

In describing her imprisonment, Marion refers to 'the castles'. The plural may simply be poetic, but it is worth noting that the 'fyrst stayn vas layd in the voltis of the new castell of Duninglas in Glenlyon', on 4 July 1564.[54] Presumably its construction was a direct response to the state of war in Breadalbane in the early 1560s. The Campbells of Glen Lyon probably had an existing fortress at Meggernie, higher up the glen, by this time.[55]

Finally, towards the end of the song, in Marion's anticipation of her coming together with Griogair Ruadh, of travelling with him, and of living a life of poverty as opposed to one of material comfort, there surfaces a dimension which, in the light of her subsequent experience as revealed by *Griogal Cridhe*, seems almost prophetic.

Of the period between late 1565 and 30 July 1567, we can say nothing of Marion's personal experience beyond the likely fact of her marriage. Following the resumption of hostilities from the summer of 1567, the personal testimony of *Griogal Cridhe* now becomes significant. We can suggest immediately that a rhetorical interpretation of verses 13 to 16 should be rejected: this is surely reminiscence based on Marion's real experiences, living rough with her husband during the feud's second phase.[56]

Before midday on 1 August 1569, in the company of his wife at a place unknown, Griogair Ruadh was captured. Those responsible apparently included Marion's father, and some form of treachery or deceit was involved. This is the testimony of Marion, obviously an eye-witness. In its specifics it may be unique, but the case for accepting it is, I believe, compelling. We now appreciate that she has correctly identified for us the date of capture, while there is circumstantial evidence to support her implication of close kinsmen in the act. Marion's father, Donnchadh Ruadh, was Cailean Liath's uncle, and his closest ally throughout the 1550s and 1560s.[57] During the six months of concentrated violence which followed Griogair Ruadh's execution, the pattern of MacGregor attacks was focused upon Cailean Liath and Marion's father Donnchadh Ruadh, from which we can conclude that these were the men held chiefly responsible by the MacGregors for the death of their chief, and that vengeance was the chief motive of their campaign. Donnchadh Ruadh was fortunate to survive an attempt on his life between 30 May and 10 June, 1570, and it was believed that the MacGregors harboured similar designs towards Cailean Liath.[58]

Verse 1 of *Griogal Cridhe* defines the abruptness and completeness of the transformation of Marion's emotional world on the morning of 1 August 1569. From then until her husband's execution on 7 April 1570, we would naturally assume that Griogair Ruadh's imprisonment, almost certainly in Balloch Castle, meant that they were separated. These eight months of mental uncertainty and agony, as her husband's life hung in the balance, subject to fluctuating political forces far beyond her control, must have formed one of the imperatives for the creation of *Griogal Cridhe*.

Yet *Griogal Cridhe* is not only elegy but also lullaby, rooted in birth as well as death. We know that Marion bore Griogair Ruadh two sons, Alasdair Ruadh and Iain Dubh. It must be Alasdair Ruadh, the elder son, who is mentioned although unnamed in the document of 29 March 1570 already discussed, effectively as his father's heir. The existence of a second son is first attested on 26 October 1570.[59] On the assumption that Griogair Ruadh and Marion remained separated from his capture until his death, then the latest point at which the second child could have been conceived would be the morning of 1 August 1569 itself, giving a *terminus ante quem* for his birth of mid-May, 1570. It is a possibility, then, that for part or even all of the duration of her husband's imprisonment, Marion was pregnant. It is not clear to which son *Griogal Cridhe* is addressed.[60]

We turn to other specific aspects of the text of *Griogal Cridhe*, beginning with two details which bear out the song's status as an authentic product of the later sixteenth century. The reference to *dà fhear dheug d'a chinneadh* has many parallels, which collectively confirm this to have been the standard size of the *luchd-taighe* or immediate retinue of a chief.[61] Marion's expressed wish to drink the blood of her husband is likewise to be taken literally. Many other allusions in Gaelic literature suggest that we have here a genuine ancient survival, an integral part of the keening process carried out by women, whether lamenting husband, brother or foster-son.[62] For us the most important parallel comes from Edmund Spenser in his *A View of the Present State of Ireland*, composed between 1580 and 1599, and hence nearly contemporary with *Griogal Cridhe*:

> So I have seen some of the Irish [drink] not their enemies' but friends' blood, as namely at the execution of a notable traitor at Limerick called Murrough O' Brien, I saw an old woman which was his foster mother took up his head whilst he was quartered and sucked up all the blood running there out, saying that the earth was not worthy to drink it, and therewith also steeped her face and breast, and tore her hair, crying and shrieking out most terribly.[63]

Spenser's description also confirms Marion's reference to the tearing of her hair as another authentic detail.[64]

In verses 6 and 7 we need to address the issue of textual manipulation by the first editor of *Griogal Cridhe*, Paruig Mac an Tuairneir. Independent testimony to this effect comes from Donnchadh Campbell, who was born in 1828, and whose *Reminiscences and Reflections of an Octogenarian Highlander* vividly recreates for us the Gaelic-speaking society of his native Glen Lyon, whose oral traditions stretched back to the Middle Ages and beyond; a milieu, in fact, within which the accurate oral preservation of the text of a poem composed *c*. 1570, and intimately connected with Glen Lyon, seems hardly a matter for surprise.[65] According to Campbell:

> Turner, in taking down the lament for Gregor, fell into a blunder, because he thought the lamenting widow was the daughter of Sir Duncan Campbell [Donnchadh Dubh], or his father, Sir Colin Campbell of Glenorchy [Cailean Liath], when in reality she was the daughter of their near kinsman, Duncan Campbell of Glenlyon [Donnchadh Ruadh]. To my grand-aunt's annoyance, he muddled two verses to suit his theory.[66]

In fact, Campbell's statement does not precisely represent Mac an Tuairneir's position as revealed in his rubric to *Griogal Cridhe*, which make no mention of Cailean Liath. But Mac an Tuairneir does say that our authoress was a daughter of Donnchadh Dubh, and that he, along with her brother, was responsible for beheading her husband.[67] Through a footnote he further asserts that *nighean an Ruadhanaich* was the mother of our authoress, and hence wife of Donnchadh Dubh.[68]

Mac an Tuairneir seems to have assumed – possibly on the basis of nothing more than his own erroneous interpretation of the text's internal evidence – that the *Cailean* of verse 6 must correspond to the *Cailean Liath* of verse 7, and that by the same rationale, the *Donnchadh Dubh* of verse 7 must correspond to *m'athair* – 'my father' – of verse 6. Judging by his rubric, he would have us understand the Cailean/Cailean Liath figure as a son of Donnchadh Dubh,[69] and thus, by his way of thinking, a brother of the authoress; this implies that he was, perhaps surprisingly, completely unaware of the existence of the historical Cailean Liath of Glen Orchy. As our nineteenth-century evidence suggests, Mac an Tuairneir seems to have gone one step further, by transposing the second couplets of verses 6 and 7. The motive was apparently to bring the reference to *nighean an Ruadhanaich* into the same verse as the reference to *m'athair*, 'my father', thereby creating a stronger impression that these two were man and wife.

Of course, we now know that *m'athair*, 'my father', in verse 6 must refer to Donnchadh Ruadh of Glen Lyon. It is also generally known that *nighean an Ruadhanaich* must be Katherine, daughter of William Lord Ruthven, whom Cailean Liath married as his second wife in 1551.[70] This leaves as the only unresolved problem the identity of the Cailean/Cailean Liath figure; is this one person or two? Donnchadh Ruadh of Glen Lyon did in fact have a son called Cailean.[71] To equate him with the Cailean of verse 6 would be natural,[72] but at first sight not unproblematic. *Chron. Fortingall* tells us that Cailean son of Donnchadh Ruadh was born at midnight on 5 August 1557. He would thus have been not quite 12 years old on 1 August 1569, which surely renders his active involvement in the capture of Griogair Ruadh highly doubtful.

I believe this leaves us with two possible interpretations, the key being whether we assume that Marion's sole purpose in verses 6 and 7 is to single out the *maithibh is càirdean* she curses in verse 3 as responsible for the treacherous capture of Griogair Ruadh. If so, then they are probably three: her father, Donnchadh Ruadh, of Glen Lyon, and Cailean Liath and his son, Donnchadh Dubh, of Glen Orchy, with Cailean Liath being mentioned twice. The repetition would accord an understandable emphasis to the capturer, gaoler and executioner of her husband. But what if Marion's rationale, flowing from the death of her husband and the plight of her son, is to be avenged, not merely upon the prime movers in Griogair

Ruadh's capture – Donnchadh Ruadh and Cailean Liath[73] – but also upon their sons and heirs, irrespective of the latter's actual involvement? *A plague on both your houses.* This brings clarity and sense to the parallelism Marion obviously intends between the first couplets of these verses (a parallelism recognised but interpreted wrongly by Mac an Tuairneir), and makes the emendation suggested by Donnchadh Campbell's grand-aunt a matter of necessity.[74] Furthermore, the restored text is artistically and emotionally far more satisfying, reuniting in the one verse Cailean Liath, Donnchadh Dubh and *nighean an Ruadhanaich*, Katherine Ruthven, wife of the former and mother of the latter.[75] Clearly, Marion's loss of her husband and concern for her child makes her acutely sensitive to what Katherine Ruthven would suffer were harm to befall *her* husband and son. Harm to these men may be what Marion desires, yet instinctively she identifies with the woman who would be affected thereby. The empathy is underlined by the reference to Katherine, *suathadh bas is làmh*, and Marion's allusions to her own hands in verses 8 and 12.

There may be an additional factor underlying Marion's attitude to Katherine Ruthven. There survive three letters written to Katherine during the course of the feud, one (probably dating to late 1564) in the name of Griogair Ruadh himself.[76] Their tenor suggests that she was regarded as potentially more sympathetic to the MacGregors than her husband, and thus a means of prevailing upon him to reach a negotiated and lasting settlement. After Cailean Liath and the MacGregors finally came to terms in late 1570, a brother of Katherine's wrote asking her:

> to be the instrument to labour at the Lairdis hand to accept [the MacGregors] efter ther gud mening, and to be ane patrone and defender of tham in tymes cuming in ther guid caussis.[77]

Griogair Ruadh was executed at Balloch, at the east end of Loch Tay. In the late 1550s it had been chosen by Cailean Liath as the site of his chief fortress, built as an appropriate centre and symbol of the new form of lordship he was engaged in creating. These might seem to be reasons enough for the emphasis Marion places upon Balloch, in verses 7 (*recte* 6), 8, 9 and 10, and for the destruction she wishes upon the castle there. Yet we can now offer another, for the likelihood is that it was here that Griogair Ruadh was imprisoned from August 1569 until 7 April 1570, eight months in which it must have been the epicentre of his wife's emotional world. Her choice of imprisonment and handcuffs as an appropriate form of punishment for certain of her enemies likewise leaps into focus, given both Griogair Ruadh's incarceration, and her own period under house-arrest in the early 1560s.

In verses 13 to 15 we face the most intractable problem still presented by the text of *Griogal Cridhe,* the identity of *baran crìon na dalach*. Since I have already argued that these verses are as rooted in real experience as is the rest of the song, it follows that we have here a real person, irrespective of how we envisage his relationship to Marion. The genitive form *na dalach* suggests nominative *an dail*, and although Mac an Tuairneir printed the word in lower case, subsequent editorial practice has been to capitalise it, on the assumption that it refers to a particular place.[78] The root – *dol, dul,* later *dal* – means 'meadow', 'dale', 'valley'. It is noticeable that in the sense of 'meadow', *dail* often seems to mean specifically a discrete area of level ground, close to a river or water and hence probably alluvial in origin. In this sense, *dail* corresponds to Lowland Scots *haugh*.[79] Historically, the combination of flatness and fertility has made such places natural settlement sites, doubtless usually possessed by important people.

The element is common in Perthshire placenames.[80] Probably the best-known instance is *Dul* (angl. *Dull*) by Aberfeldy, but since in Gaelic this was used 'without the article and not declined',[81] it cannot be the place Marion means. The candidate which tradition seems to favour is *An Dail* (angl. *Dall*), which formed a part of Ardeonaig on south Loch Tayside.[82] Throughout the sixteenth century the lands of Ardeonaig were divided equally between the heads of two families, the Napiers of Merchiston and the Haldanes of Gleneagles, as crown tenants-in-chief. In the charters of 1509 confirming this arrangement, their half-shares of Ardeonaig formed only a part of the lands granted separately to Archibald Napier and Sir John Haldane, and both grants were made *in liberam baroniam*.[83] These charters each describe one of the component parts of Ardeonaig as *le Halch* (Haugh), which must translate *An Dail*. Part of *An Dail*, presumably, was the farm named in later record as Mains of Ardeonaig, and here in the later eighteenth century there still stood a two-storied house of unknown antiquity known in English as Mains Castle.[84] It has been suggested that Mains Castle went with the part of Ardeonaig held by the Napiers of Merchiston.[85]

There is no hard evidence for the active or continuous presence of the Napiers or Haldanes at Ardeonaig in the sixteenth century. For them it was peripheral country, and we might surmise that their interest in it would not extend beyond the economic. In local and kin-based terms, Ardeonaig was very much part of the Campbell nexus. For most of the sixteenth century the most important people on the ground there were a Campbell kin-group called *Sliochd Theàrlaich Duibh*, who seem to have held seven merklands in tack, presumaby from either the Napiers or Haldanes, but whose presence in reality depended upon the support of the earls of Argyll, who regarded them with particular affection: Gilleasbuig, the fifth earl,

The Lament for Griogair Ruadh MacGregor

referred to them as his 'tender freindis'.[86] The Napiers and the Haldanes doubtless depended upon the Campbells to exert local control, and this may have its corollary in the marriages made between the Campbells of Glenorchy and the Napiers in the first half of the sixteenth century.[87]

Can a case be made for identifying *baran crìon na dalach* with the contemporary head of either the Haldane or Napier family *c.*1570? These men could perhaps have been described as barons of *An Dail*, since the latter was the likely site of the *caput* of Ardeonaig, whose lands were split between baronies held by them. What evidence we have (the apparent though unproven location of Mains Castle – assuming its existence in the sixteenth century[88] – on their land, and the earlier marriage ties) favours the Napiers rather than the Haldanes. However, the contemporary head of the Napiers, Sir Archibald, whose first wife had died in 1563, is said to have married Elizabeth Moubray 'about 1570'.[89] The case for a link with Ardeonaig, and the Napiers or Haldanes, is weak.

Marion did remarry after 1570, although we do not hear of this until 1597. In that year her husband was Raibeart Menzies of Comrie.[90] This is Comrie on the south bank of the Lyon, at and immediately above its junction with the Tay. It had been a Menzies possession since at least the later fourteenth century,[91] and we can trace a distinct Menzies lineage here from the first half of the fifteenth century.[92] By the sixteenth century, it is clear that the head of this lineage could be styled *Am Baran*, 'the Baron'. Raibeart's predecessor Iain is referred to as *Barron de Commere Menzheis* on his death in 1548,[93] while Raibeart himself is called 'the baron Comrie' in 1595.[94] Within the bounds of Comrie there seems to be no actual place now known as *An Dail*, but there are at least eight places which contain *dail* as a generic element, two of them within a subdivision whose name has only survived as the Mains of Comrie.[95] As this suggests, much of Comrie is a low-lying, relatively fertile alluvial plain. It may be that part or even all of this plain bore the name *An Dail*, which has now been lost. Alternatively, if in verses 13 to 15 of *Griogal Cridhe* we read with Mac an Tuairneir not *na Dalach*, referring to a place specifically called *An Dail*, but *na dalach*, a descriptive term, then *baran na dalach*, 'the baron of the river-meadow', would seem to be a legitimate way of identifying Menzies of Comrie.[96] The remains of the Menzies tower-house can still be seen there, and it is clearly marked on Timothy Pont's manuscript map of the upper Tay from Balloch to Dunkeld drawn up between *c.* 1583 and 1596.[97] In 1601 it is referred to as a *manerium*.[98] Doubtless it could fairly be described as *taigh cloiche 's aoil*, sustaining in its heyday a lifestyle of modest grandeur along the lines of that evoked by Marion. Indeed, her choice of *na Dalach/dalach* as an epithet could have been inspired by the connotations of

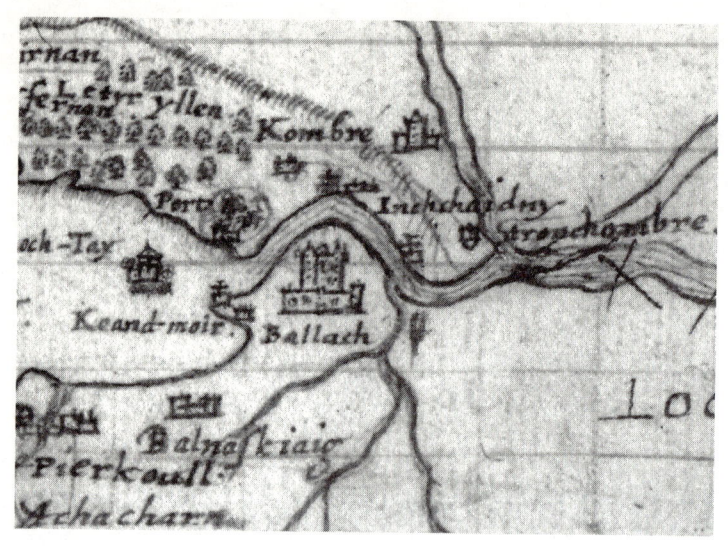

'An taigh cloiche 's aoil' (In a house of stone and lime)? The Menzies tower-house at Comrie near the east end of Loch Tay as depicted by Timothy Pont in the late sixteenth century. (National Library of Scotland, *Adv. MS. 70. 2. 9. Pont Manuscript 18.* Reproduced by permission of the Trustees of the National Library of Scotland.)

cultivation, prosperity and comfort it bears, and which it transmits to *am Baran*. Thus it stands in pointed opposition to *coille, fraoch, gleann* and *cragan*, the habitats she associates with her life with Griogair Ruadh.

The case for the identification is strengthened by the fact that at certain periods Raibeart Menzies of Comrie was clearly a member of the retinue of Cailean Liath and of his son Donnchadh Dubh after him. He first figures in the witness list of a document involving Cailean Liath in 1555, and recurs sporadically thereafter down to 1563. Most strikingly, at Perth on 11 December and again on 29 December 1558, he witnessed two deeds by which Cailean Liath was sold lands by his two nieces, the only other common witness to both deeds being Donnchadh Ruadh of Glen Lyon; and in early 1563, as the first phase of the feud gathered momentum, he witnessed two vital contracts by which Cailean Liath enlisted the support of the MacDonalds of Keppoch and of Glen Coe against the MacGregors.[99] He fades from view thereafter, probably because of the developing tensions between Cailean Liath and the earl of Atholl, who was on close terms with the head of the Menzies kindred throughout the 1560s,[100] but reappears in the retinue of Donnchadh Dubh from 1585 to 1588.[101] In 1599, Raibeart gave his bond of manrent to Donnchadh Dubh, on behalf not only of himself, but also, interestingly, of his wife and children.[102]

The Lament for Griogair Ruadh MacGregor

The date of the marriage of Marion to Raibeart Menzies is difficult to pin down precisely. It is clear that Raibeart had been married before.[103] Likely sons of this marriage were Pàdraig, described in May 1585 as 'apparent of Comrie', and Uilleam, first on record in 1591; both were servitors of Donnchadh Dubh.[104] The earliest certain reference to a child of Marion and Raibeart comes on 19 June 1599, when their son Iain and his spouse-to-be were given possession of an annual rent out of the Comrie lands, as part of the settlement for their marriage which was clearly imminent.[105] There may have been at least one other son, for a document of 1601 calls Iain, 'eldest son of Robert Menzies procreat between him and Marjorie Campbell his spouse.'[106]

We have already argued that *Griogal Cridhe* must have been composed in the early 1570s, and noted its portrayal of *baran na Dalach/dalach* as Marion's husband or suitor.[107] For Raibeart and Marion's marriage to have taken place in that same period would not be inconsistent with their having a son who was himself of marrying age in 1599. If we remember also the potential role held by Cailean Liath in selecting Marion's future partner, then from his point of view Raibeart Menzies of Comrie would seem a safe enough choice, notwithstanding any distance between them which the political climate between 1563 and 1571 may have created.

I believe, then, that *baran na Dalach/dalach* was Raibeart Menzies of Comrie, and I suggest that he and Marion were married in the early 1570s, shortly after Griogair Ruadh's execution. Approaching *Griogal Cridhe* afresh with this hypothesis in mind, we find potential support, and, perhaps, hitherto obscured nuance. In verses 13 to 15, the preposition *aig* surely demands to be translated as, 'married to', while the parallelism of *aig Griogair . . . aig baran crìon na dalach*, allows the possibility that Marion and Raibeart were in fact married by the time she composed *Griogal Cridhe*, and that the final couplets of these verses describe her present reality. Likewise, in verse 12, *mnathan chàich*, 'other men's wives', could imply that Marion is also a wife: the contrast which she is evoking is not between 'other men's wives' and herself, *a widow*, but between 'other men's wives' and herself, *likewise married*, but to a husband whose presence, far from bringing solace, serves only to accentuate her sense of the loss of her true partner.[108] Marion's isolation, the predominant emotion conveyed by the old reading of this verse, is still there in its second couplet, but is all the more poignant and insidious if, physically, she is not in fact alone.

I come to the final verse of *Griogal Cridhe*. Reference has already been made to the prophetic quality of *Rìgh gur mór mo Chuid Mhulaid*,[109] and in her expression of her final fear in her later song, there is again a hint of the uncanny, of Marion Campbell as seer. Both her sons by her first husband died young and violently, Iain Dubh – 'a very brave and expert man'[110] – at the battle of Glen Fruin in February 1603, and Alasdair Ruadh on the gallows at Edinburgh in January 1604 in circumstances eerily reminiscent of the death of his father, after being betrayed and captured through the machinations of Gilleasbuig seventh earl of Argyll.[111] This was not the only point of contact between the lives of father and elder son, for despite Cailean Liath's obligation of 29 March 1570, Alasdair Ruadh was never granted legal possession of Glen Strae, and this issue continued to dominate relations between the MacGregors and the Campbells of Glen Orchy before and after 1604.[112] The latest mention of Marion Campbell alive known to me is on 25 July 1601,[113] which means we cannot at present say for certain whether she lived to see the early deaths of the two sons she bore to Griogair Ruadh of Glen Strae.

VI

I turn finally from the worlds of Marion Campbell's external and internal experience to consider the artistic landscape within which she moved. To explore this landscape is to try to understand why Marion's response to what she experienced took the particular form of *Rìgh gur mór mo Chuid Mhulaid* and *Griogal Cridhe*.

The sixteenth-century Breadalbane to which Marion belonged was culturally very rich, a ferment of creation and collection. It was here, at Fortingall at the mouth of Glen Lyon itself, that that priceless miscellany of Gaelic poetry and other material, the *Book of the Dean of Lismore*, was compiled between *c.*1512 and *c.*1542.[114] Poets of Breadalbane provenance are well represented therein, both professionals and lay aristocrats such as Fionnlagh, chief of the Macnabs of Glen Dochart. The poem by Fionnlagh which seems to anticipate the making of the collection refers to *sracairean*, *pacairean* (packmen), and *lorganaich* – the last equated by Watson with the *Cliar Sheanchain* or itinerant minstrel bands – as fruitful sources to be tapped, and such individuals and groups, however importunate their demands upon their hosts, were well placed to perform a key role as literary receptors and disseminators, operating between the spheres of high and popular culture, and across social classes.[115]

Professional poetic activity in the area is represented at the highest level by the MacEwen lineage which served the Campbells of Glen Orchy as well as the MacDougalls and the earls of Argyll to the west,[116] and perhaps also by another Lorne-based kindred, the MacLachlans of Kilbride;[117] and at lower levels by 'The Bard McAlester', on record in 1582 in the Balloch area.[118] His domicile may have been at *Ruigh a' Bhaird*, 'the Bard's Slope', on Drummond Hill,[119] while *Druim a' Bhaird*, 'the Bard's Ridge', is at Carie further along the north side of Loch Tay.[120] It is natural to find the Campbells so prominent in providing the patronage which was the prerequisite of such activity, and indeed the *Book of the Dean of Lismore* can be interpreted as a *duanaire* or songbook formally dedicated to them.[121] But the same source provides striking evidence of the extent to which members of Campbell ruling lineages were both patrons and practitioners of Gaelic poetry. Sir Donnchadh Campbell, second head of the Glen Orchy kindred, is the best represented of any Scottish poet in the *Book of the Dean of Lismore*, while there are also contributions by at least one earl of Argyll, the wife of the first earl, and the daughter of either the first or second earl.[122]

These Campbell poets and poetesses bring us back to Marion, and the fact that metrically *Griogal Cridhe* has a syllabic basis which indicates that she too had access to the classical tradition.[123] This could have come about through formal tutelage, for the education of the sons and daughters of the Gaelic elite was one of the functions of the learned orders, and perhaps particularly the poets. This remained the case into the seventeenth century, when, for example, Cathal MacMhuirich was tutor to Catrìona, daughter of Domhnall Gorm Óg, chief of the MacDonalds of Sleat.[124] In Marion's case, the MacEwens would be likely candidates for the role, given their links to the Campbells of Glen Orchy. But an awareness and appreciation of classical poetry would have been virtually impossible for a woman of Marion's status to avoid, especially in the Breadalbane of her time, and, let it also be said, given the reputation of her father. To her and to us it seems clear that Donnchadh Ruadh of Glen Lyon sacrificed his daughter's happiness to his loyalties to kindred and Cailean Liath (although initially at least he may have believed he was acting in her best interests), but in temperament he had little in common with the latter. Glen Lyon tradition remembered him positively and affectionately as *Donnchadh Ruadh na Féile*, 'Red Duncan of the Generosity',[125] and there is contemporary confirmation in the record of his death in 1579.[126] The court of such a man would of course have been a magnet for poets, and indeed we know that it was one of the many throughout the Highlands visited by the notorious lampooner Aonghas nan Aoir, who seems to have come specifically to test Donnchadh's reputation for hospitality beyond the average, and did not find it wanting.[127]

Griogal Cridhe reveals Marion as marked by the classical tradition, but not bound by it. The influence of vernacular folksong is strong and clear,[128] and in the case of *Rìgh gur mór mo Chuid Mhulaid* this is emphatically so.

The social and artistic exclusivity and esotericism of classical poetry can, we know, be exaggerated, for it proved capable of spawning various types of hybrid which have been referred to collectively as 'semi bardic' verse, a description for which the dual affinities of *Griogal Cridhe* make it well-suited.[129] Lay aristocrats were a grouping particularly well placed to adapt classical forms to their own artistic needs. In this respect, *Griogal Cridhe* bears comparison with the work of two earlier poetesses to be found in the *Book of the Dean of Lismore*. First, there is *A phaidrín do dhúisg mo dhéar*, 'O rosary that has awakened my tear', the elegy by *Aithbhreac inghean Coirceadail* for her 'loved yokefellow', Niall Óg, chief of the MacNeills of Gigha from *c*. 1455 until his early death *c*. 1463 or *c*. 1472:

> O rosary that has awakened my tear, dear the finger that was wont to be on thee; dear the heart, hospitable and generous, which owned thee ever until tonight . . .
>
> For want of one man alone, all lonely am I after him, without sport, without kindly talk, without mirth, without cheer to show . . .
>
> My heart is broken within my body, and will be so until my death, left behind him of the dark, fresh eyelash, o rosary that has awakened my tear . . .[130]

Second, though more speculatively, there are two poems by *Iseabal Ní Mhic Cailein* – *Is mairg dá ngalar an grádh*, 'Alas for him whose sickness is love', and *Atá fleasgach ar mo thí*, 'There is a youth intent upon me'. The extent to which these poems are rooted in immediate reality may be questionable, since the first at least has been taken as a specimen of the *dánta grádha* or courtly love genre in Gaelic.[131] But if their composer were the Iseabal who was daughter of the first earl of Argyll, and wife of the famous Aonghas Óg who died in 1490, then there might just be grounds for identifying him with the male persona of whom she speaks, given the turbulent political background to that relationship:

> There is a youth intent upon me; King of kings, may he come to fortune! Would that he were stretched by my body, his breast to my breast! . . .
>
> But it is not easy unless his ship come, a tale most grievous to us both; he is east and I am west, so that our mutual desire comes not to pass again.[132]

In these three women we glimpse a lineage of aristocratic poetesses of the late medieval Scottish Highlands for whom the classical tradition became a means to personal utterance. For them, and the women who followed them in the seventeenth and eighteenth centuries, although working exclusively within the vernacular tradition, that utterance was sometimes a response to the dilemmas confronting them *as women* within the upper echelons of a kin-based society for which marriage assumed an even greater political significance than it did in other societies. A woman placed in a very similar predicament to Marion in the mid-seventeenth century, for which she also found an outlet in song, and which tradition asserts ultimately drove her to madness, was Fionnaghal Campbell of Auchinbreck. Trapped in a loveless marriage to Iain Garbh, chief of the MacLeans of Coll, her song on the Battle of Inverlochy in 1645 reveals that she made the opposite choice to Marion, lamenting the decimation of the Campbells and in particular the death of her brother Donnchadh, and rejecting the kindred of her husband, and their son, Eachann Ruadh.[133]

Here we stand on the edge of a fourth landscape, that of the experience of women in the late medieval and early modern Scottish Highlands. Within this world which as yet we hardly know,[134] perhaps we may say even now that, although Marion Campbell of Glen Lyon was not alone in the extremity of her experience, yet for none was the extremity greater, and none gave more lasting utterance to it than she.

Acknowledgements

I am deeply indebted to J.W.M. Bannerman, R. Black, E.J. Cowan, and the late D.A. MacDonald for their very helpful comments on a draft version of this chapter.

Postscript

At a late stage in the production of this chapter I came across another song, apparently hitherto unnoticed, and apparently relating to the same historical process which gave rise to the two songs discussed above. I hope to discuss this song in a supplementary article in the near future.

Appendix: Texts and Translations[135]

Rìgh Gur Mór Mo Chuid Mhulaid

1.	Rìgh gur mór mo chuid mhulaid On chiad là thrumaich do bhròn orm,	Lord, how great is my sorrow, From the first day your grief oppressed me,
2.	On a ghlac mi 'n ciad iùl ort 'S nach do dhùraig mi pòsadh.	Since I caught the first sight of you And I did not dare (? to contemplate) marriage.
3.	Gur diombach mi air m' athair, S caol a sgath e o m' fheòil mi:	How I resent my father, Who has almost torn me in two:
4.	Chum e uamsa fear taighe Nach robh adhannt' no gòrach –	He kept from me a husband Who was not bashful or foolish –
5.	Sàr Ghriogarach gasta Nach bu tais air an tòrachd.	A fine MacGregor hero Who was not faint-hearted in the pursuit.
6.	Bhuidhinn do làmh dhuit urram O Là cumasg Beinn Lòchaidh.	Your hand won you honour From the day of the skirmish of Ben Lochy.
7.	S iomad Guinneach[136] mór prìseil Dhen tug thu 'shiòda 's a bhòtan	From many an important, wealthy Campbell You removed his silk shirt and his boots.
8.	Agus ògan deas innealt' Dhan gheàrr thu 'mhuineal mu 'chòtan.	And many an elegant, fashionable youth Whose throat you cut along the line of his coat.
9.	Gum meal thu 'n cuid aodaich Ged as dìleas iad dhomhsa!	May you have the profit of their garments Though they are closely related to me!
10.	Na biodh ortsa bonn mìghein Ged a dhìobair mi 'chomhdhail,	Do not let yourself be displeased Although I failed to keep the tryst,
11.	Rach thusa air adhart 'S na b'ann 'nad chladhaire gòrach,	You go forward And not as a witless coward,
12.	'S na bu mhisde do phiseach Ged tha mise dheth brònach	And may your success not diminish Although it saddens me.
13.	Mur bhith daingneach nan caisteal 'S nan geatacha móra	If only it were not for the strength of the castles And of the great gates,
14.	Agus cuingead nan glasan Nach fhaigh mi asta gun òrdaibh!	And the restraint of the locks Which I cannot escape without hammers!
15.	Truagh nach eil mi mar fhaoilinn No cho caol ris an fheòraig –	It is a pity that I am not like a gull Or as slender as a squirrel –
16.	Gun leumainn an uinneag 'S cha chumadh an tòir mi;	Or I would leap from the window And the pursuers would not restrain me;

The Lament for Griogair Ruadh MacGregor

17. Gun snàmhainn am buinne
 Gun aon fhuireach ri òrdugh;

I would swim the stream
Without once stopping when commanded;

18. S dearbh gun siubhlainn ri gaillinn
 Mìle fearann gun bhrògaibh,

Indeed I would travel through the storm
A thousand lands without shoes,

19. Dol an coinnimh an òig laghaich –
 Ceist 's roghainn bhan òg' e!

Going to meet the kind youth –
The darling and choice of young women!

20. Shiubhlainn leis an fhleasgach
 'Na bhreacan caol bòidheach;

I would journey with the young man
In his fine, close-fitting tartan;

21. S beag do dh'fheartaibh Dhé fhathast
 Ar cur a laigh' a dh'aon sheòmra:

It wouldn't be asking too much of God yet
To let us lie in the one chamber:

22. Bhithinn 'n-sin 'na do ghlacaibh
 'S gheibhinn blas air do phògaibh.

I would be there in your embrace
And I would taste your kisses.

23. Ged bhiodh agams' deich mìle
 De ghìnidhean òirdhearg,

Though I had ten thousand
Of red-gold guineas,

24. Urdal eile de dh'fhearann,
 De dh'earras 's de stòras,

As much again of land.
Of treasure and of wealth,

25. S dearbh gun lùiginn mi fhéin ort,
 A lùb threubhach dheas bhòidheach.

Indeed I would wish myself on you,
Handsome, valorous, fine young man.

26. Sgrios nàmhad gun iarr mi
 A ghearradh 'n gialla 's an sgòrnain.

For an enemy I wish a destruction
Which would cut jaws and throats.

27. Sgrios eil' a theachd a-nìos orr'
 Gun aon trian theachd ás beò
 dhiubh –

May another destruction come upon them
Which would leave not even a third of them alive –

28. Gach aon neach a chuir seach orm
 Do phearsa ri phòsadh.

Every single one who put beyond my reach
Marriage to you.

29. Ach! Och! Dèantar mo leabaidh:
 Cha chadal tha sheòl orm,

Ach! Och! Let my bed be made:
But not with sleep in mind,

30. Chan iarr mi den t-saoghal
 Ach léine chaol 's ceithir bòrdain,

I ask of this world
Only a close-fitting shroud and four narrow planks,

31. Mo chur an ciste nan tarrag
 An déis a sparradh le h-òrdaibh.

And to be placed in a coffin
Nailed shut with hammers.

Cumha Ghriogair MhicGhriogair Ghlinn Sréith (Griogal Cridhe)

1. Moch madainn air latha Lùnast'
   Bha mi sùgradh mar ri m' ghràdh,
   Ach mun tàinig meadhan latha
   Bha mo chridhe air a chràdh.

   Early on Lammas morning
   I was in love-play with my darling:
   But before midday came
   My heart was tormented.

2. Ochain, ochain, ochain uiridh
   S goirt mo chridhe, a laoigh,
   Ochain, ochain, ochain uiridh
   Cha chluinn t' athair ar caoidh.

   Ochain, ochain, ochain uiridh
   Sore is my heart, my baby.
   Ochain, ochain, ochain uiridh
   Your father hears not our cry.

3. Mallachd aig maithibh 's aig càirdean
   Rinn mo chràdh air andòigh,

   Thàinig gun fhios air mo ghràdh-sa
   'S a thug fo smachd e le foill.

   A curse on nobles and kinsfolk
   Who have brought anguish upon me unjustly,
   Who came without warning upon my love
   And made him captive by treachery.

4. Nam biodh dà fhear dheug d'a chinneadh
   Is mo Ghriogair air an ceann,
   Cha bhiodh mo shùil a' sileadh dheur,
   No mo leanabh fhéin gun dàimh.

   Were there twelve men of his clan
   With my Gregor at their head,
   My eyes would not be weeping tears
   Nor my child without kin.

5. Chuir iad a cheann air ploc daraich,
   'S dhòirt iad 'fhuil mu làr:
   Nam biodh agamsa an-sin cupan,
   Dh'òlainn dith mo shàth.

   They placed his head on a block of oak,
   And spilt his blood on the ground;
   Had I but had a cup there
   I'd have drunk of it my fill.

6. S truagh nach robh m' athair an galar,
   Agus Cailean am plàigh,
   Ged bhiodh nighean an Ruadhanaich
   Suathadh bas 's làmh.

   Would that my father were stricken by disease
   And Cailean by the plague,
   Although Ruthven's daughter
   Would be wringing her palms and hands.

7. Chuirinn Cailean Liath fo ghlasaibh,
   'S Donnchadh Dubh an làimh;
   'S gach Caimbeulach th' ann am Bealach
   Gu giùlan nan glas-làmh.[137]

   I would put Cailean Liath under lock,
   And imprison Donnchadh Dubh;
   And each Cambell in Balloch
   Put under handcuffs.

8. Ràinig mise réidhlean Bhealaich,
   'S cha d'fhuair mi ann tàmh:
   Cha d'fhàg mi ròin de m' fhalt gun tarraing
   No craiceann air mo làimh.

   I came to the meadow of Balloch
   And found there no peace;
   I left no hair of my head unpulled,
   Nor skin on my hands.

9. S truagh nach robh mi 'n riochd
  na h-uiseig,
 Spionnadh Ghriogair ann mo làimh:
 Si a' chlach a b' àirde anns a' chaisteal
 A' chlach a b' fhaisge don bhlàr.

If I were in the lark's shape,
Gregor's strength in my hand,
The highest stone of the castle (would be)
The stone nearest the ground.

10. S truagh nach robh Fionnlairg na lasair
  'S Bealach mór na smàl,
  'S Griogair bàn[138] nam basa geala
  Bhith eadar mo dhà làimh.

Would that Finlarig were aflame,
And great Balloch ablaze,
And fair Gregor of the white palms
Between my two hands.

11. 'S ged tha mi gun ùbhlan agam
  'S ùbhlan uil' aig càch,
  Sann tha m' ubhal cùbhraidh grinn
  'S cùl a chinn ri làr.

Though I am without apples
And all the rest have apples
My apple, fragrant and shapely,
Has the back of his head to the ground.

12. Ged tha mnathan chàich
  aig baile
  'Nan laighe 's 'nan cadal sèimh,
  Sann bhios mis' aig bruaich mo leapa
  A' bualadh mo dhà làimh.

Although the wives of other men are at
home
Lying and peacefully sleeping,
I shall be at the edge of my bed
Beating my two hands.

13. S mór a b' annsa bhith aig Griogair
  Air feadh coille 's fraoich,
  Na bhith aig baran crìon[139]
  na dalach[140]
  An taigh cloiche 's aoil.

Far better to be married to Gregor
Roaming wood and heather,
Than married to the little baron of the
river-meadow
In a house of stone and lime.

14. S mór a b' annsa bhith aig Griogair
  Cur a' chruidh don ghleann,
  Na bhith aig baran crìon
  na dalach
  Ag òl air fion 's air leann.

Far better to be married to Gregor
Driving the cattle to the glen,
Than married to the little baron of the
river-meadow
Drinking wine and ale.

15. S mór a b' annsa bhith aig Griogair
  Fo bhrata ruibeach ròin,
  Na bhith aig baran crìon
  na dalach
  A' giùlan sìoda 's sròil.

Far better to be married to Gregor
Under a tattered hair mantle,
Than married to the little baron of the
river-meadow
Stifled by silk and satin.

16. Ged a bhiodh ann cur 's
  cathadh
  'S latha nan seachd sìon,
  Gheibheadh Griogair dhomhsa cragan
  San caidlimid fo dhìon.

Though there would be snowfall
and snowdrift
And a day of the seven elements,
Gregor would find for me a rocky place
Where we would find sleep and shelter.

17. Ba hu, ba hu, àsrain bhig,
  Chan eil thu fhathast ach tlàth;
  S eagal leam nach tig an latha
  Gun dìol thu t' athair gu bràth.

Ba hu, ba hu, forlorn little one,
You are but innocent yet:
It is my fear that the day will never come
When you avenge your father.

Notes

1. Mar chuimhneachan air Somhairle MacGill-Eain (1911–1996).
2. James Aikman, *The History of Scotland, translated from the Latin of George Buchanan; with Notes, and a Continuation to the Union in the reign of Queen Anne* (Glasgow 1827), i, 116.
3. Edited by Cosmo Innes as 'The Chronicle of Fortingall' [hereafter *Chron. Fortingall*] in *The Black Book of Taymouth*, Bannatyne Club (Edinburgh 1855) [hereafter *Taymouth Bk.*], 109–48. For a brief discussion of *Chron. Fortingall*, see MDW MacGregor, 'A Political History of the MacGregors before 1571', unpublished Ph.D dissertation (University of Edinburgh 1989) [hereafter MacGregor, 'Political History'], 15–18.
4. MacGregor, 'Political History', 156; W.J. Watson, *The History of the Celtic Place-names of Scotland* (Edinburgh and London 1926), 483; W.J. Watson, 'The Place-names of Breadalbane', *Transactions of the Gaelic Society of Inverness* xxxiv (1927–28) [hereafter *TGSI*], 266.
5. See below.
6. MacGregor, 'Political History', 255.
7. For the epithet, see W.J. Watson, 'Marbhnadh Dhonnchaidh Duibh', reprinted from *An Deò-Gréine* (Glasgow 1917), 6.
8. *Taymouth Bk.*, 22–3.
9. *Ibid.* 65.
10. MacGregor, 'Political History', 145–8.
11. Paruig mac-an-tuairneir, *Comhchruinneacha do dh' orain taghta Ghaidhealach* (Edinburgh 1813) [hereafter Mac-an-tuairneir, *Comhchruinneacha*], 286.
12. For a list of the extant printed, manuscript and oral versions of *Griogal Cridhe*, see A Duncan, 'Some MacGregor Songs', unpublished M.Litt dissertation (University of Edinburgh 1979) [hereafter Duncan, 'Some MacGregor Songs'], 48–52. The evolution of the song is a subject worthy of investigation in its own right.
13. *An Anthology of Scottish Women Poets* (ed.) C. Kerrigan, (Edinburgh 1991), 56–9.
14. *Ris a' Bhruthaich: The Criticism and Prose Writings of Sorley MacLean* (ed.) W. Gillies (Stornoway 1985), 77.
15. *Bàrdachd Ghàidhlig* (ed.) W.J. Watson (Inverness 1976) [hereafter Watson, *Bàrdachd Ghàidhlig*], 334.
16. The fine local history by Revd W.A. Gillies, *In Famed Breadalbane* (Perth 1938) [hereafter Gillies, *In Famed Breadalbane*], 128–31, contains an account flawed in some particulars but accurate in others, notably the crucial question of the date of Griogair Ruadh's capture. He names Griogair Ruadh's wife as *Marion* Campbell, daughter of Donnchadh Ruadh of Glen

The Lament for Griogair Ruadh MacGregor

Lyon, but it is not clear whether he is drawing upon oral or written testimony here. See also D. Campbell, *The Lairds of Glenlyon* (2nd edition, Perth 1984) [hereafter Campbell, *Lairds of Glenlyon*], 183–8, esp. 185.

17. Versions of this song survive among the manuscripts of Perthshire-born James MacLagan (1728–1805), minister at Blair Atholl from 1781 (Glasgow University Library, *MS Gen 1042, MacLagan MS 91*), and of the historian Donald Gregory, who died in 1836 (National Library of Scotland, *MS 2135*, vol.7, 303). W. Gillies, 'Some Aspects of Campbell History', *TGSI* l (1976–8) [hereafter Gillies, 'Campbell History'], 288, n.14, notes another version printed in A. and A. MacDonald, *The MacDonald Collection of Gaelic Poetry* (Inverness 1911), xxxi–xxxii, and 179; and, at 265, discusses an excerpt from the 'Gregory' text, but suggests the poetess is a MacGregor married to a Campbell rather than vice versa.

18. Duncan, 'Some MacGregor Songs', 22–5 [text], 81–5 [notes].

19. For the texts and translations, see the Appendix.

20. Most of the statements made in this section depend upon discussion in MacGregor, 'Political History', esp. ch VI, and specific references may be found there.

21. *Taymouth Bk.*, 64–5.

22. See n. 15 above.

23. D.S. Thomson, 'Scottish Gaelic Folk-Poetry ante 1650', *Scottish Gaelic Studies* 8 (1955) [hereafter *SGS*], 13; DS Thomson, 'A Disputed Reading in Cumha Ghriogoir Mhic Ghriogoir', *SGS* 10 (1963–5), 68–70.

24. Duncan, 'Some MacGregor Songs', 69.

25. Scottish Record Office [hereafter SRO], *The John MacGregor Collection (MacGregor Transcripts)*, GD 50/187/1, at date.

26. SRO, *Breadalbane Muniments*, GD 112/1/3/180.

27. G. Donaldson, *All the Queen's Men: Power and Politics in Mary Stewart's Scotland* (London 1983), 118.

28. SRO, *Breadalbane Muniments*, GD 112/1/3/182.

29. For the right of veto which, at a lower social level, Cailean Liath and Donnchadh Dubh exercised over whom their widowed women tenants might marry or take in concubinage, see MacGregor, 'Political History', 244.

30. SRO, *Breadalbane Muniments*, GD 112/1/3/182a.

31. *Taymouth Bk.*, 22–3. For the probable precise location, see J. Christie, *The Lairds and Lands of Loch Tayside* (Aberfeldy 1892), 21; for the 'heading axe' which may have been used, see *Taymouth Bk.*, xxvii, 344. There is one other definite instance of Cailean Liath carrying out an execution himself. Under 7 April 1574, four years to the day from the death of Griogair Ruadh, *Chron. Fortingall* has, 'Donald Dow McCouil VcQuhewin heddyt at the Kenmor

be Collyn Campbell of Glenwrquhay'. For *McCouil* we should probably read *McConil*. For brief discussion of the kin-group to which this individual belonged, see MacGregor, 'Political History', 238–9, 296; Gillies, *In Famed Breadalbane*, 139, 364. I have been unable to substantiate Gillies' claim that these people were MacGregors.

32. *Argyll Transcripts* made by 10th Duke of Argyll, in Glasgow University Scottish History Department, at date.

33. SRO, *Breadalbane Muniments*, GD112/1/3/191.

34. *Argyll Transcripts*, 7 December 1575; SRO, *Breadalbane Muniments*, GD112/5/10, 233.

35. SRO, *The John MacGregor Collection (MacGregor Transcripts)*, GD50/187/2, at date.

36. *Ibid.* GD50/187/2B, at date.

37. K.A. Steeer and J.W.M. Bannerman, *Late Medieval Monumental Sculpture in the West Highlands* (HMSO, Edinburgh 1977) [hereafter Steer and Bannerman, *Monumental Sculpture*], 149, n.2; *Highland Papers*, (ed.) J.R.N. MacPhail, Scottish History Society (Edinburgh 1934), iv, 65, n.3. *Chron. Fortingall* calls Mary Queen of Scots *Mare* or *Marion/Maryon* (1558, 128; 1560, 129; 9 February 1566) and Gilleasbuig Campbell of Glen Lyon's wife *Mariota* or *Margareta*: 12 August 1537. Cf. also *The Exchequer Rolls of Scotland* (Edinburgh 1878–1908), xx (1568–79), 533: *Margareta vulgo Mawis*.

38. *Marion* was one of the names usually equated with Gaelic *Mór*: *Scottish Historical Review* xxxv (1956), 184. For the existence of *Máire*, *Mairghréad*, and *Màiri* in late medieval Gaelic Scotland, see the 'Index of Persons, Etc.', in *Scottish Verse from the Book of the Dean of Lismore* (ed.) W.J. Watson, Scottish Gaelic Texts Society (Edinburgh 1937) [hereafter Watson, *Scottish Verse*], 324. The (Lowland) wife of Seumas Campbell of Lawers is referred to as *Mairghréad* in a Gaelic source (ibid., 120), and as *Mariota* by *Chron. Fortingall* on her death on 31 October 1527.

39. See also D.S. Thomson, *An Introduction to Gaelic Poetry* (2nd edition, Edinburgh 1989) [hereafter Thomson, *Gaelic Poetry*], 108.

40. See esp. verses 11, 12.

41. MacGregor, 'Political History', 310–11.

42. *Ibid.* 306–9.

43. *Accounts of the Collectors of Thirds of Benefices 1561–1572* (ed.) G. Donaldson, Scottish History Society (Edinburgh 1949), 114. The connection of the Campbells of Glen Lyon with Kilmorich, which they feued from the Bishop of Dunkeld, probably began with Donnchadh Ruadh's father Gilleasbuig, who died there in 1552; *Chron. Fortingall*, 29 April. See also *Registrum Magni Sigilli Regum Scotorum* (eds.) J.M. Thomson and others (Edinburgh 1882–1914) [hereafter *RMS*] v (1583–96), no. 1930.

44. SRO, *Breadalbane Muniments*, GD112/1/3/124 *verso*.

45. SRO, *Breadalbane Muniments*, GD112/1/3/142.
46. There is no doubt concerning Pàdraig's survival; *Taymouth Bk.*, 410, 223.
47. Ronald I.M. Black, 'Some Poems from W.J. Watson's *Bàrdachd Ghàidhlig*' (University of Edinburgh, Department of Celtic 1996), 53.
48. According to SRO, *Breadalbane Muniments*, GD112/1/3/142, on the night itself Alasdair was wounded 'in his wamb' by an arrow. It would appear that the wound proved fatal.
49. SRO, *Breadalbane Muniments*, GD112/1/3/127. Cf. GD112/1/3/157a, where Anndra is described as, 'the cause of thair deid and . . . possessit yit wyth thair gyr'.
50. SRO, *Breadalbane Muniments*, GD112/1/3/142.
51. SRO, *Breadalbane Muniments*, GD112/1/3/127.
52. SRO, *The John MacGregor Collection (MacGregor Transcripts)*, GD50/187/1, 31 March 1564, 1 December 1564.
53. The site of the first confrontation of the night of 7 December 1562 is identified specifically as 'Aldgerenaig within the boundis of Faschalze' (SRO, *Breadalbane Muniments*, GD112/1/3/142). Allt Girnaig flows down Glen Girnaig to join the Garry at Killiecrankie. If one continues north-east beyond the head of Glen Girnaig by way of Allt Coire Lagain, one reaches another Gleann Lòchaidh, and Loch Lòch(a); but these are surely too removed from Glen Girnaig itself to be able to refer to the scene of the events of 7 December 1562.
54. *Chron. Fortingall*. This is claimed to be the castle better known as Carnban; D. Campbell, *The Book of Garth and Fortingall* (Inverness 1888), 314, n. 2. We do not hear of it being occupied before 10 Sept 1568, but the much larger fortress at Balloch, on which work apparently commenced in the summer of 1557, was already in use by 21 Nov 1559; MacGregor, 'Political History', 232.
55. *RMS* vi (1593–1608), no. 1420, 4 March 1603; '. . . turrim vocatam Meggirney in glenlyoun ad ripam aque de Glenlyoun, nuncupand. castellum de Glenlyoun, principale fore messuagium . . . '. I have been unable to establish with certainty the order in which these fortresses were built. See also *Geographical Collections relating to Scotland made by Walter Macfarlane* Scottish History Society (Edinburgh 1906–8), ii, 562, and Campbell, *Lairds of Glenlyon*, 18.
56. This phase of the feud was at its most intense between 31 July 1568 and 1 August 1569, and especially after 6 May 1569. The broad coalition of anti-MacGregor forces included not only the house of Glen Orchy with its Glen Lyon and Lawers branches, but also the earl of Atholl, the earl of Mar, Murray of Tullibardin, Stewart of Grandtully, Menzies of Weem, Stewart of Appin, MacDougall of Dunollie, and Campbell of Duntrone. See MacGregor, 'Political History', 363–370, esp. 368.
57. *Chron. Fortingall*, 16 June 1552, and 17 January 1579, the latter being the

record of Donnchadh Ruadh's death at Balloch, his nephew's main fortress; *RMS* iv (1546–80), no. 944, and below.

58. MacGregor, 'Political History', 377–80.

59. SRO, *Breadalbane Muniments*, GD112/1/3/191.

60. If Iain Dubh were already born when the song was composed, as seems more than likely, then its references to the tender age of the child (*leanabh, tlàth*) might seem to suit the younger son better. But would it not be more natural to refer to the elder child as a potential avenger of his father?

    Thus far I have been unable to use later record to determine the dates of birth of Griogair Ruadh's sons with satisfactory precision. The earliest reference I have to Alasdair Ruadh as an adult is on 18 December 1585 (*Miscellany of the Spalding Club* (Aberdeen 1849) iv, 233–4). Here he acts with the advice and consent of his tutor, Eòghan, brother of his father. His marriage contract is dated 25 December 1586 (SRO, *Court of Session Papers*, CS7/250, f. 253). He acts alone for the first time on 7 April 1587 (SRO, *The John MacGregor Collection (Menzies Writs)*, GD50/186/7/36), but on 12 February 1588, Eòghan was still his tutor and curator (SRO, *The John MacGregor Collection (MacGregor Transcripts)*, GD50/187/2, at date). Alasdair Ruadh was clearly chief of his kindred by September 1589 (*The Register of the Privy Council of Scotland* (eds.) J.H. Burton et al (Edinburgh 1877–) [hereafter *RPC*] iv (1585–92), 453–4, and *Taymouth Bk.*, 244–6. Iain Dubh is first on record as an adult on 4 February 1590; *RPC* iv (1585–92), 454.

61. Duncan, 'Some MacGregor Songs', 74. A retinue of 12 men in the service of Domhnall mac Iain 'ic Sheumais is one of the most persistent features of the numerous oral and written accounts we possess relating to *Blàr Chàirinis*, the Battle of Carinish, in 1601. See R. Gordon, *A Genealogical History of the Earldom of Sutherland* (Edinburgh 1813), 244; 'Iain', 'Blar Chairinnis', *An Gàidheal*, Treas Mìos an Fhoghair (1876), 310; F.W.L. Thomas, 'Notices of Three Churches in North Uist, Benbecula and Grimsay, said to have been Built in the Fourteenth Century', *Archaeologica Scotica* v (1890), 232; School of Scottish Studies (University of Edinburgh) Sound Archive 1968/68/A2, 1968/223/B1, 1968/273/A4. For the term *luchd-taighe* see Martin Martin, *A Description of the Western Islands of Scotland circa 1695* (Edinburgh 1994), 167; *Orain Iain Luim* (ed.) A.M. MacKenzie Scottish Gaelic Texts Society (Edinburgh 1964), line 1334.

62. Duncan, 'Some MacGregor Songs', 75–6; Martin, *A Description of the Western Islands*, 171, in his treatment of *The Ancient and Modern Customs of the Inhabitants of the Western Islands of Scotland*: 'Their ancient leagues of friendship were ratified by drinking a drop of each other's blood'; E. Dwelly, *The Illustrated Gaelic–English Dictionary* (Glasgow 1911), 462: '*is milis fuil nàmhaid, ach is milse fuil caraid*' – sweet is the blood of an enemy, but sweeter still the blood of a friend.

63. Edmund Spenser, *A View of the Present State of Ireland* (ed.) W.L. Renwick (Oxford 1970), 62.

64. Cf. R. Bromwich, 'The Keen for Art O' Leary, its Background and its Place in the Tradition of Gaelic Keening', *Eigse* 5 (1945–7), 249.
65. Cf. J. MacInnes, 'Gaelic Poetry and Historical Tradition', in The Inverness Field Club, *The Middle Ages in the Highlands* (Inverness 1981), 145.
66. D. Campbell, *Reminiscences and Reflections of an Octogenarian Highlander* (Inverness 1910), 201–2.
67. See above.
68. Mac-an-tuairneir, *Comhchruinneacha*, 287.
69. In fact Donnchadh Dubh's eldest son, who succeeded him, was called Cailean, but this could be coincidence rather than a reflection of genuine knowledge on Mac an Tuairneir's part; *The Scots Peerage* J. Balfour Paul (ed.), 9 vols (Edinburgh 1904–14) [hereafter *SP*] ii, 185, 188–9.
70. *Ibid.* iv, 260; MacGregor, 'Political History', 256–7.
71. SRO, *Breadalbane Muniments*, GD 112/1/4/225; *The John MacGregor Collection (MacGregor Transcripts)*, GD 50/187/2, 5 September 1590; *RMS* v (1580–93), no. 1930; *RMS* vi (1593–1608), no. 1420; *SP* v, 504. This son is known to tradition as *Cailean Gòrach*, 'Colin the Fool'; see Campbell, *Lairds of Glenlyon*, 15–20, 327–33; *TGSI* xxxv (1929–30), 293.
72. This suggestion is made in Duncan, 'Some MacGregor Songs', 77, following Campbell, *Reminiscences and Reflections of an Octogenarian Highlander*, 202.
73. For evidence already reviewed which is consistent with this assertion, see above, and n. 57.
74. This emendation could still be made if we wished to argue for three rather than four protagonists, but the logic for doing so would be weaker. It is ironic indeed that responsibility for one of the major problems presented by the text of *Griogal Cridhe* can be laid at the door of the song's first editor, not oral tradition, and that oral tradition then helps us to resolve the problem.
75. *Taymouth Bk.*, 20, confirms that Donnchadh Dubh was the eldest child of Cailean Liath's second marriage to Katherine Ruthven.
76. SRO, *The John MacGregor Collection (MacGregor Transcripts)*, GD 50/187/1, Griogair Ruadh to Katherine Ruthven, filed under 1 February 1565; Eòghan MacGregor [tutor of Glen Strae] to Katherine Ruthven, late 1570; 'Ruthven' to Katherine Ruthven, 7 January 1571.
77. *Ibid.*, GD 50/187/1, 'Ruthven' to Katherine Ruthven, 7 January 1571.
78. Watson, *Bàrdachd Ghàidhlig*, 245–6, 407, and see also below, n. 84.
79. W. J. Watson, *The History of the Celtic Place-names of Scotland*, 414–9.
80. *Ibid.* 414.
81. *Ibid.* 415.
82. Watson, *Bàrdachd Ghàidhlig*, 334; H. MacMillan, *The Highland Tay* (London 1901), 58.

83. MacGregor, 'Political History', 139.
84. *Survey of Lochtayside 1769* (ed.) M.M. McArthur Scottish History Society (Edinburgh 1936) [hereafter *Survey of Lochtayside*], xxviii; 89–123, esp. 89, 112–3 (*Margnadallich*).
85. J. Christie, *The Lairds and Lands of Loch Tayside*, 77–8.
86. MacGregor, 'Political History', 92, 308
87. *SP* ii, 177, 180; vi, 410, 413.
88. See below, n. 97.
89. *SP* vi, 413–5.
90. SRO, *The John MacGregor Collection (MacGregor Transcripts)*, GD 50/187/2, 13 December.
91. *Sixth Report of the Royal Commission on Historical Manuscripts* (London 1877), pt. i, Menzies MSS, 691, no. 10.
92. *RMS* ii (1424–1513), no. 492. Cf. SRO, *The John MacGregor Collection (Menzies Writs)*, GD 50/186/ii/10; *Chron. Fortingall*, 13 May 1508.
93. *Chron. Fortingall*.
94. *Taymouth Bk.*, 252. Whatever the meaning or nuances of *baran* within the Gaelic context, the lands of Comrie did form a barony: *Survey of Lochtayside*, 66–7; Gillies, *In Famed Breadalbane*, 410.
95. *Survey of Lochtayside*, 63–8.
96. For a possible parallel see the song by Màiri Cameron in which she addresses her dead husband, Pàdraig Campbell of Inverawe, as *Eudail a dh'fhearaibh na Dalach [?dalach]*, 'treasure of the men of the river-meadow'; *TGSI* xxvi (1904–7), 240. Here the 'river-meadow' is that formed where the Awe flows into Loch Etive.
97. National Library of Scotland, *Adv. MS. 70. 2. 9, Pont manuscript 23*. It should be noted that *Pont manuscript 18*, of Loch Tay, does not suggest the existence of Mains Castle at Ardeonaig at this point in time, although this cannot be taken as conclusive evidence for its absence. I wish to thank Mr Chris Fleet of the National Library for his very kind assistance with the Pont manuscript maps, now available for consultation in digital image form under the auspices of *Project Pont*.
98. SRO, *Breadalbane Muniments*, GD 112/5/10, 271–2.
99. *RMS* iv (1546–80), no. 1526; *Taymouth Bk.*, 200, 204, 205, 206–8. For appearances of Raibeart's brothers Iain and Seumas as witnesses see ibid., 202, 204, 208.
100. MacGregor, 'Political History', 331, 365–6, 370, 393. The head of the kindred, Menzies of Weem, was a member of the coalition pursuing Griogair Ruadh by 1569. Comrie was one of the locations at which the peace terms between Atholl and the MacGregors were drawn up in 1571; ibid., 391.

101. *Taymouth Bk.*, 231, 234–5, 237–9, 241; SRO, *Breadalbane Muniments*, GD112/1/4/261, 263, 276, 278, 279, 287; GD112/5/10, 59–60, 71–2, 101–3. For Raibeart as a witness to a series of documents of significance to Campbell/MacGregor relations in 1584, see GD112/2/117/57/1/4, and SRO, *The John MacGregor Collection (MacGregor Transcripts)*, GD50/187/2, 12 May and 13 June, 1584.

102. *Taymouth Bk.*, 256.

103. SRO, *Breadalbane Muniments*, GD112/5/10, 233, where Marion is called Raibeart's present (*moderna*) spouse.

104. *Ibid.* 57–8, 271–2 (Pàdraig), 115–7, 151–3 (Uilleam); See also *Taymouth Bk.*, 233 (Pàdraig), 252, 418–9 (Uilleam); SRO, *The John MacGregor Collection (MacGregor Transcripts)*, GD50/187/2, 1/2 February, 1591 (Uilleam). Both are on occasion referred to as the lawful or legitimate sons of Raibeart.

105. SRO, *Breadalbane Muniments*, GD112/5/10, 233.

106. SRO, *The John MacGregor Collection (MacGregor Transcripts)*, GD50/187/2B, 25 July.

107. See above.

108. On 7 December 1575, Marion renounced to her father some of the lands he had granted her and Griogair Ruadh in joint fee (*Argyll Transcripts*, at date), perhaps a pointer to her having remarried by this point.

109. See above.

110. *Calendar of the State Papers relating to Scotland and Mary, Queen of Scots, 1547–1603* (eds.) J. Bain and others (Edinburgh 1898–) xiii pt. 2 (1597–1603), 896. I believe Alasdair Duncan to be correct in identifying Iain Dubh as the subject of the well-known MacGregor song beginning *A Mhic an Fhir Ruaidh*, commonly called *Saighdean Ghlinn Lìobhann*; 'Some MacGregor Songs', 87–8.

111. For an account of his career see D. Gregory, *Inquiry into the Early History of the Clan Gregor, with a view to ascertain the causes which led to their Proscription in 1603* (Edinburgh 1831), 22–33.

112. MacGregor, 'Political History', 267–273.

113. SRO, *The John MacGregor Collection (MacGregor Transcripts)*, GD50/187/2B, at date.

114. R. Black, *Catalogue of the classical Gaelic MSS. in the National Library of Scotland* (forthcoming); MacGregor, 'Political History', 13–14, 75–77.

115. Watson, *Scottish Verse*, xvi, 2–5. For *pacairean* or chapmen in the Breadalbane area, cf. SRO, *Breadalbane Muniments*, GD112/1/4/224a, GilleFaoláin *mcchepman* buidhe, parishioner of Inchadin, 1580, probably one and the same as ibid., GD112/5/10, 134–5, Faolán (*phillan*) *mcchepman* in Inchadin, 1593.

116. *The Companion to Gaelic Scotland* (ed.) D.S. Thomson (Oxford 1983), 170–1; MacGregor, 'Political History', 252; A. Matheson, 'Bishop Carswell', *TGSI* xlii (1953–59), 203.

117. J.W.M. Bannerman, 'The MacLachlans of Kilbride and their Manuscripts', *Scottish Studies* 21 (1977), 13.

118. MacGregor, 'Political History', 253.

119. *Ibid.*; *Survey of Lochtayside*, 60–1; W J Watson, 'Place-Names of Perthshire: The Lyon Basin', *TGSI* xxxv (1929–30), 278.

120. *Survey of Lochtayside*, 31; Gillies, *In Famed Breadalbane*, 400.

121. MacGregor, 'Political History', 75–77; Gillies, 'Campbell History', 259.

122. MacGregor, 'Political History', 77, and nn. 32 and 34; cf. Gillies, 'Campbell History', 259 and n.3. The poems by the earl(s) of Argyll bear the rubrics, *Autor Mccallein erle of ergyle*, and *Mccallein moir id est callein mat(h)*. The second at least must be by either the first or third earls, both called Cailean, who died in 1493 and 1529 respectively. For the identity of the first earl's wife, see Watson, *Scottish Verse*, 307, and see also W. Gillies, 'Courtly and Satiric Poems in the Book of the Dean of Lismore', *Scottish Studies* 21 (1977), 42. On the daughter of the first or second earl, see below, and n. 132. I see no good reason to doubt these attributions of authorship.

123. Watson, *Bàrdachd Ghàidhlig*, xliii–xliv; Duncan, 'Some MacGregor Songs', 71–2; Thomson, *Gaelic Poetry*, 107–8.

124. J.W.M. Bannerman, 'Literacy in the Highlands', in *The Renaissance and Reformation in Scotland* (eds.) I.B. Cowan and D. Shaw (Edinburgh 1983), 218.

125. Campbell, *Lairds of Glenlyon*, 12–15.

126. *Chron. Fortingall*, 17 January: *Non fuit avarus. Hilarem datorem diligit Deus*. For the use of the epithet in Donnchadh Ruadh's lifetime, see n. 127. It is attested in an early seventeenth century poetic source (Gillies, 'Campbell History', 263). This may have been a trait Donnchadh Ruadh inherited through his mother, of whom it is said in her obituary in *Chron. Fortingall*, 12 August 1537, *hilaris et larga fuit*.

127. G. Henderson, 'Aonghus nan Aoir, or an Irish Bard in the Highlands', *TGSI* xxvi (1904–7), 460. Cf. W. Matheson, 'Aonghus nan Aoir: A Case of Mistaken Identity', *Scottish Studies* 21 (1977), 105–8.

128. Thomson, *Gaelic Poetry*, 107–8.

129. *Ibid.* 106–9; *The Companion to Gaelic Scotland*, 301.

130. Watson, *Scottish Verse*, 60–65, 271; Steer and Bannerman, *Monumental Sculpture*, 147.

131. W. Gillies, 'Courtly and Satiric Poems in the Book of the Dean of Lismore', *Scottish Studies* 21 (1977), 36–7; T.F. O Rahilly, *Dánta Grádha* (2nd edition, Cork 1926), 74.

132. Watson, *Scottish Verse*, 234–5, 307–8; Steer and Bannerman, *Monumental Sculpture*, 211. The authoress cannot be one and the same as Iseabal Countess of Argyll, as asserted (by James Carmichael Watson) at Watson, *Scottish Verse*,

The Lament for Griogair Ruadh MacGregor

307; see J.M. Bannerman and R. Black, 'A Sixteenth Century Gaelic Letter', *Scottish Gaelic Studies* xiii (1978), 64, n. 10.

133. A. Maclean Sinclair, 'A Collection of Gaelic Poems', *TGSI* xxvi (1904–7), 238–40; Sorley MacLean, 'Obscure and Anonymous Gaelic Poetry', in the Inverness Field Club, *The Seventeenth Century in the Highlands* (Inverness 1986), 97. For another parallel, see the song by Màiri Cameron, a contemporary of Fionnaghal Campbell, whose husband died of wounds received at Inverlochy, and whose father is said to have forced her to remarry against her will; *TGSI* xxvi (1904–7), 240.

134. For welcome pioneering work in this field, see now the Highland contributions in *Women in Scotland c. 1100–c. 1750* (eds.) E. Ewan and M.M. Meikle (Tuckwell Press, forthcoming).

135. The text of *Griogal Cridhe* is essentially that of Mac-an-tuairneir, *Comhchruinneacha*, 286–9, with modernisations of spelling and syntax. The text of *Rìgh gur mór mo Chuid Mhulaid*, which is essentially that of Glasgow University Library, *MacLagan MS 91*, has been taken from Duncan, 'Some MacGregor Songs', 22–5, as emended and printed by Ronald I.M. Black, 'Some Poems from W.J. Watson's *Bàrdachd Ghàidhlig*' (University of Edinburgh, Department of Celtic 1996), 51–3. Mr Black hopes in due course to bring out a fourth edition of *Bàrdachd Ghàidhlig*, now regrettably out of print. I am very grateful to him, and to Mr Colin Arthur, for permission to use this text. The translations are my own, but owe much to previous commentators, notably Black, op. cit., D.S. Thomson, 'Scottish Gaelic Folk-Poetry ante 1650', *SGS* 8 (1955), 12–13, and Thomson, *Gaelic Poetry*, 108–9.

136. A variant of *Duibneach*, which derives from the Campbells' original kindred name, *Clann Duibhne*.

137. The italicised couplets should be transposed; see above.

138. The epithet may appear at odds with Griogair's known cognomen, *ruadh*, but *bàn* here may mean 'fair-skinned' rather than 'fair-haired', thereby complementing the reference to his 'white palms'. The implication, of course, is of high social rank. Alternatively, the fact that *ruadh* was also the cognomen of Griogair's elder brother (Iain Ruadh) and his own elder son (Alasdair Ruadh) might just suggest that it had become hereditary within their lineage, and divorced from actual physical reality. But against this is the fact that *ruadh* is nowhere used with reference to Griogair's father.

139. The primary meaning of *crìon* is 'small'. Watson (*Bàrdachd Ghàidhlig*, 334) has 'petty', taking it to refer to the baron's social status, but this seems rather to undermine the contrast between wealth and the lack of it evoked in verses 13 to 15. Thomson (*Gaelic Poetry*, 109) has 'wrinkled', presumably referring to the baron's age, but what we know of Raibeart Menzies of Comrie (see above) need not suggest he was markedly older than Marion.

140. Or *na Dalach*: see above.

7

A Taste of Scotland: Historical Fictions of Sawney Bean and his Family

Fiona Black

The limbs o' men, women, an' weans on the wa's,
Like beef that is dried were hung up in grim raws,
An' some laid in pickle fu' sune tae be ta'en,
By that horde in the Hades o' aul Sawney Bean.[1]

The Manyuema are the most bloody, callous savages I know . . . Their cannibalism is doubtful, but my observations raise great suspicions. A Scotch jury would say 'Not proven'. The women are not guilty.[2]

The version of the story of Sawney Bean and his cannibal family which is the best known today is taken from John Nicholson's *Historical and Traditionary Tales connected with the South of Scotland* of 1843.

The young Sawney, born in East Lothian of an honest and industrious father, at the time of King James I of Scotland was, as Nicholson has it, 'very prone to idleness'. He disliked honest labour and ran off with 'a woman as viciously inclined as himself'.[3] This pair took as their abode a cave in Galloway where they lived for over twenty-five years, during which time they produced numerous children and grandchildren. The whole gang were robbers and murderers. Nicholson adds that murder was not the most horrific of their crimes. He tells how:

> As soon as they had robbed any man, woman, or child, they used to carry off the carcass to the den, where cutting it into quarters they would pickle the mangled limbs, and afterwards eat it; this being their only sustenance; and notwithstanding they were at last so numerous, they commonly had superfluity of this their abominable food, so that in the night-time they frequently threw legs and arms of the unhappy wretches they had murdered into the sea, at a great distance from their bloody habitation; the limbs were often cast up by the tide in several parts of the country, to the astonishment and terror of all beholders, and others who heard of it.[4]

Historical Fictions of Sawney Bean and his Family   155

It seems that the cannibal family were a strange mix of the purely bestial and the careful cunning human: the idle youth and vicious woman grew up to live in a 'den', they took to eating human flesh, but human flesh which was carefully prepared before consumption. It is notable that they threw the surplus limbs in to the sea 'at a great distance' from their abode. Such cunning resulted in their avoiding detection and capture while the countryside around them grew increasingly fearful, and many innocent men, including innkeepers, were wrongfully hanged for the crimes of this monstrous family. Unsurprisingly many innkeepers left their trade and 'the whole country was almost depopulated'. The infamy of this wild region of Galloway spread, 'so that it became the admiration of the whole kingdom how such villainies could be carried on and the perpetrators not discovered'.[5] The people put their trust in Providence. But the cannibals continued their savage and cunning attacks, ambushing travellers with almost military precision.

Their cave was as impenetrable as any fortress:

> The place which they inhabited was quite solitary and lonesome, and, when the tide came up, the water went near two hundred yards into their subterranean habitation, which reached almost a mile underground; so that when people, who have been sent armed to search all the places about have passed by the mouth of the cave, they have never taken any notice of it, never supposing that any human being would reside in such a place of perpetual horror and darkness.[6]

Nicholson says that the tally of the victims of Sawney and his family was commonly acknowledged to be around one thousand, and that it was by the aid of both Providence and the king himself that the vicious crew were captured before this total could become any greater. One night the cannibals attacked a man and woman on horseback. The woman fell from the horse and was savagely murdered but the man was saved by the providential arrival on the scene of twenty or thirty people travelling from a market. This man, the only witness of the family's monstrous acts, told his tale to the magistrates in Glasgow who informed the king of the existence of this hideous band of cannibals. His majesty, with four hundred men and bloodhounds, set off to find and apprehend them. The bloodhounds sniffed out the entrance to Sawney's cave. This is how Nicholson describes what the royal party discovered:

> Now the whole body, or as many of them as could went in, and were all so shocked at what they beheld that they were almost ready to sink into the earth. Legs, arms, thighs, hands and feet of men, women and children, were hung up in rows, like dried beef; a great many limbs laid in pickle, and a great mass of money, both gold and silver, with watches, rings, swords, pistols and a large

quantity of cloaths, both linen and woolen, and an infinite number of other things which they had taken from those that they had murdered, were thrown together in heaps or hung up against the sides of the den.[7]

The cannibals were then taken to the tolbooth in Edinburgh before being executed at Leith. Sawney's wife, daughters and grandchildren watched while their male relatives had their hands and legs cut off. After the men had bled to death the women and children were burned on three fires.

This is the standard version of the Sawney Bean legend as we have it today. 'Legend' because, despite Nicholson's assertions of historical fact, all evidence, or lack of it, seems to suggest that Sawney and his 'monstrous' and incestuous family never existed. Nicholson's tale is an attractive and attention-grabbing one, with its mixture of meticulous detail, its descriptions of Sawney and his family (they are vicious/savage/hideous/hellish), its racy plot and its resolution which ties up all loose ends.

That said, the story of Sawney and his family is more traditionary than historical. There is no mention of Sawney by name in any history of Scotland nor is there any record to be found of the cannibal family's execution. Ronald Holmes in his investigation, *The Legend of Sawney Bean*,[8] suggests that Sawney first appeared in print in the first half of the eighteenth century in broadsheets containing lurid accounts of his supposedly 'true' story. These were all printed, and therefore probably written, in England. These broadsheet accounts of Sawney are all similar in content and largely concur with Nicholson's later version. Unfortunately none of them are dated. The first time that we can specifically date Sawney in the history of print is with Captain Charles Johnson's collection of 1734, which was printed in London and entitled:

> *A General and True History of the Lives and Actions of the most famous Highwaymen, Murderers, Street-Robbers etc. To which is added a genuine Account of the Voyages and Plunders of the most Noted Pirates, Interspersed with Several Remarkable Tryals of the Most Notorious Malefactors, at the Sessions-House in the Old Baily, London. Adorn'd with the Effigies, and other material Transactions of the Most remarkable Offenders, engraved on copper-plates.*

Johnson obtained much of the material for this 'true crime' or 'pulp fiction' collection from an earlier work of 1719 (again printed in London) by one Captain Alexander Smith which was also colourfully titled:

> *A Compleat History of the most Notorious Highway-men, Foot-pads, Shop-lifters and Cheats of both Sexes, in and about London and Westminster and all parts of Great Britain for above an hundred years past, continued to the present time.*

Both Smith and Johnson's works are largely composed of collected broadsheets, and, as Sawney does not appear in Smith's collection of 1719, Holmes argues that it is probable that these broadsheets emerged at some point between the 1720s and 1734, some twenty years after the Union. A research paper by Sandy Hobbs and David Cornwell[9] points out that of the four broadsheet versions only one could possibly have been produced at this time, the others almost certainly dating from the late-eighteenth or early-nineteenth centuries. Hobbs and Cornwell use this evidence to suggest that the legend of Sawney Bean was an English invention of the eighteenth century.

The monstrous figure of Sawney, as written history, was probably an English invention. Cannibalism has a long history as a means of political propaganda used by a dominant culture against those they want to colonise; as an English invention Sawney may be considered as a colonial fiction written to demonstrate the savagery and uncivilised nature of the Scots in contrast to the superior qualities of the English nation.

An end note to Alasdair Gray's novel, *Poor Things*, says that the story of Sawney Bean was 'a fiction based on *English* folk tales: tales told by the English about the Scots during centuries when these peoples were at war with each other, or on the verge of it'.[10] Gray's suggestion that Sawney's family symbolized the Scottish people alludes to the pattern of cannibalism as xenophobically generated propaganda.

This view of tales of cannibalism as cultural constructs designed to demonstrate the barbarity of those who are different to those telling the story (the authors or storytellers being, of course, decent members of a civilised society) does not, however, preclude Sawney as a Scottish invention. Native Scots and indeed Galwegians have been happy enough to perpetuate the historical fiction of Sawney and his family. Nicholson's *Tales* were written and published in Galloway and S. R. Crockett's novel of 1896, *The Grey Man*, telling of the bitter feuding in sixteenth-century Galloway between the rival Kennedy clans of Culzean and of Bargany, during the reign of King James VI, is the first Scottish novel in which Sawney and his 'hideous crew' appear. The young hero of *The Grey Man*, Launcelot Kennedy of Culzean, enters into the cave of death accompanied by the dominie and the two young ladies, Nell and Marjorie Kennedy. They have escaped from the clutch of the evil Grey Man of the title, who is John Mure of Auchendrayne, a leader of the Bargany Kennedys, but Launcelot soon has misgivings that they have walked into an even more chilling situation. He remembers the stories he was told as a child of the 'unknown being' who lived in a cave on the shore of Benane and the 'fireside tales of travellers who had lost their way in that fastness, and who falling into the power of his savage tribe returned no more to kindlier places'.[11]

Sawney and his family are here presented as characters from Scottish oral tales. Evidence of the reality of their cannibalism is soon found and grotesquely detailed by Launcelot:

> . . . amid the smoke were certain vague shapes, as if it had been of the limbs of human beings, shrunk and blackened, which hung in rows on either side of the cave. At first it seemed that my eyes must certainly deceive me, for the reek drifted hither and thither, and made the rheum flow from them with its bitterness. But after a little study of these wall adornments, I could make nothing else of it, than that these poor relics, which hung in rows from the roof of the cave like hams and black puddings set to dry in the smoke, were indeed no other than the parched arms and legs of men and women who had once walked the upper earth but who by misfortune had fallen into the power of this hideous, inconceivable gang of monstrous man-eaters. Then the true interpretation of all the tales that went floating about the countryside, and which I had hitherto deemed wholly vain and fantastical, burst upon me.[12]

Crockett here gives narrative flesh to the pickled limbs of Nicholson's tale, allowing his narrator and hero to enter the deadly cave, and minutely describe the evidence of his own eyes. Unsurprisingly, since this is after all a historical romance, Launcelot and his friends escape the cave unharmed, and it is Launcelot who leads the King and his bloodhounds to the cannibal's den in Crockett's reworking of Nicholson. The encounter with Sawney Bean is used by Crockett to add an extra element of adventure, intrigue and horror to his entertaining novel of Galloway feuding.

These cannibals are as Scottish as Launcelot himself. W. Arens in his study, *The Man-Eating Myth*[13], shows that the history of cannibalism in the Americas of the sixteenth and seventeenth centuries, in the Africa of the eighteenth and nineteenth, and in twentieth-century New Guinea is littered with the accounts of missionaries, explorers, and anthropologists who have encountered tribes who themselves do not commit cannibalistic acts but who have neighbours who are bitter enemies, less civilised than themselves and who eat other human beings. Accusations of cannibalism can be inter-tribal as well as between nations. The history of internal division within sixteenth-century Galloway proved ripe ground for Crockett's Scottish production of the historical fiction of cannibalism.

A story concerning the eldest son of James Douglas, second Duke of Queensberry at the time of the 1707 Union, shows how cannibalism can also be used as popular propaganda against an individual figure. The son, also called James, was apparently an idiot who was kept confined in a room, under guard, in the Edinburgh household of Queensberry. As Robert Chambers narrates in 1825 a 'tale of mystery and horror is preserved by

Historical Fictions of Sawney Bean and his Family 159

tradition respecting this monstrous and unfortunate being'.[14] On the day the Union was passed the whole family was at the Canongate:

> Two members of the family alone were left behind, the madman himself and a little kitchen boy who turned the spit. The insane being, hearing everything unusually still around, the house being completely deserted and the Canongate like a city of the dead, and observing his keeper to be absent, broke loose from his confinement, and roamed wildly through the house. It is supposed that the smell of preparations for dinner led him to the kitchen, where he found the little turnspit seated by the fire. He seized the boy, killed him, took the meat from the fire, and spitted the body of his victim, which he half roasted, and was found devouring, when the Duke, with his domestics, returned from his triumph.[15]

The story goes that the Duke had his son smothered but could not avoid the damage to his own reputation, the general populace seeing the affair as a judgement set upon him for the part he played in bringing about the Union. The facts of this tale are almost certainly blatantly untrue but the currency of it among the 'common people' as oral propaganda is easier to believe as having some historical veracity.

Passing reference to Sawney Bean and family is made in Elspeth Barker's novel *O Caledonia*. In this novel, however, Sawney and his clan were not Galwegian but lived in the North East at some unspecified date:

> They hid in these caves and kept themselves diverted and alive by making man-traps on the high road to Aberdeen and consuming their prey. When the law finally tracked them down they found a pullulating tribe of Beans, mainly the issue of incestuous unions, but still guided by the patriarchal Sawney. Smoked black flitches and plump haunches of human flesh were suspended from the cavern walls drying in the salt breeze; the babies cut their teeth on finger bones. They were all burned in Aberdeen market square, the last cannibals in Europe. Or so it was said.[16]

This account has no drastic differences from that of Nicholson, except for location and the fact that Sawney and wife are given past lives as servants in a big house. In Barker's novel the cannibals are very much the product of oral tradition, acting as little more than local colour and diversion for a tedious car journey.

The following extracts from historical writings about Scotland demonstrate that Sawney and his family may well have had their origins in the oral tales of Scotland, interestingly they also tend to place the cannibals in the north east. Hollinshead's *Chronicle* briefly details how in 1341,

> there was such a miserable dearth, both through England and Scotland, that the people were driuen to eat the flesh of horses, dogs, cats, and such like vnused

kinds of meats, to susteine their languishing liues withall, yea, insomuch that (as is said) there was a Scotish man, an vplandish felow named Tristicloke, spared not to steale children, and to kill women, on whose flesh he fed, as if he had been a woolfe.[17]

According to Hollinshead, an English historian, even though both the Scots and the English were suffering the effects of famine it was a Scot who resorted to cannibalism; note also that Hollinshead's source for this example of Scottish cannibalism is an oral one – 'as is said'.

Robert Lindsay of Pitscottie's *History and Chronicles of Scotland* (1570s), contains the following narrative, set in the year 1460:

About this tyme thair was appriehendit and tain for ane abominable and cruell abuse ane breigand quho hanted and dualt witht his haill famelie and houshald out of all mens companie in ane place of Angus callit Feindes den. This mischevous man haid ane excreabille fassone to tak all zoung men and childerin that ether he could steill quyitlie or tak away be ony moyen witht out the knawledge of the peopill and bring thame and eit them and the moir zoung thai war he held thame the more tender and greatter deliecat. For the quhilk damptnabill and cursit abuse he witht his wyffe bairnes and familie were all brunt except ane zoung lase of ane zeir auld quhilk was sawit and brocht to Dundie quhair scho was fosterit and brocht wpe. Bot quhen scho come to the age of ane womans zeiris scho was condemnit and brunt quick for the samin cryme [hir father was conuik]. It is said that quhen this zoung womane was command fourtht to the place of execution that thair gaderit ane wnnumerabill mulltitud of pepill about hir and spetiall of wemen curssand and warieand that scho was sa wnhappie to committ sa dampnabill deidis, to quhome scho turnit about witht ane wode and furieous contienance, sayand, 'quhairfoir cheide ze witht me as I had committit ane wnworthie act. Gif me credit and trow me, gif ze had experience of eittin of women and mens flesche ze wald think the same sa delicious that ze wald never forbeir it againe' and sa witht ane obstinat mynd this wnhappie creature but signe or outward taikin of repentance dieit in the sight of the haill pepill for hir misdeidis that scho was adiugit to.[18]

Commenting on sixteenth- and seventeenth-century prose after Knox, David Reid claims that 'the best story tellers are the best historians, with an eye for the telling fact, an ear for pithy dialogue and a feeling for strongly marked character'.[19] Pitscottie's so-called historical account, written over one hundred years after the supposed events it describes so vividly, is typical of this historian's method of 'retelling tales that have been told him'.[20]

If the historical veracity of these accounts can be doubted they are however evidence that Sawney and his family have a long history in the oral culture of Scotland.[21] The similarities between the Pitscottie and Nicholson accounts are telling; we have the cannibal and his cannibalistic

Historical Fictions of Sawney Bean and his Family 161

family, the savouring of the taste of flesh, the abduction and murder of the victims, the death by burning. What is perhaps most interesting is the leading role the female plays in Pitscottie's account, which is comparable with Nicholson's avowal that Sawney's wife was as 'viciously inclined as himself'. The idea of the female as central to the Sawney Bean legend is taken up and developed in Harry Tait's historical novel of 1990, *The Ballad of Sawney Bain*, where the wife is given a name, Agnes Douglas, and is accused of witchcraft as well as cannibalism. Tait's novel will be discussed later.

Returning to Nicholson's version of the legend we can note some small but interesting changes from the historical extracts relating to Scottish savagery and from the English horror stories about Sawney and his family. While Pitscottie's story of the cannibal of Angus emphasises the fact that the whole family indulge in the consumption of human flesh, and asserts that the female cannibal is as vicious as the male, there is no mention of incest. Nicholson explicitly details the savagery of the females of the Bean family. A female passer-by falls from her husband's horse and immediately becomes the victim of the bloodthirsty Beans:

> the female cannibals cut her throat and fell to sucking her blood with as great a gust as if it had been wine: this done they ript up her belly, and pulled out all her entrails.[22]

Nicholson also points out the incestuous nature of the cave-living family: the careful numbering of the clan comprising Sawney, his wife, eight sons, six daughters, eighteen grand-sons and fourteen grand-daughters all conceived and born in twenty-five years points to the horrendous pleasure that these savages, including the women, took in other delights of the flesh as well as those of eating. Of course Nicholson, writing for a wide public in the mid-nineteenth century, does not dwell on this sexual aspect and Ronald Holmes points out that he also edits some of the more racy passages from Johnson's English version of the history of the cannibal clan. One example is the first sentence of the last paragraph, which reads in Johnson's version:

> the men had first their privy members cut off and thrown into the fire before their faces, and their hands and legs were severed from their bodies; by which amputations they bled to death in some hours.[23]

From a story of entrails, pickled limbs and amputations, Nicholson has removed all mention of genitals.

If such prudery can be explained by the time of Nicholson's writing then so can the major change he made to the story be explained by the fact that he was writing after Walter Scott had written his world-famous historical fictions of Scotland. This change which Nicholson made to the legend of Sawney Bean lies in the different historical location of the story. Johnson's 1734 tale of Sawney states that the cannibal was born during the reign of Queen Elizabeth while James VI governed Scotland. This becomes in Nicholson's version 'sometime during the reign of James I of Scotland'. Ronald Holmes succinctly sums up some of the implications of this change. Sawney has transmogrified from,

> a depraved criminal who had been executed less than one hundred years before the first printing, to a legendary figure who was said to have existed about four hundred years before the Nicholson version.[24]

In other words Sawney has been removed to a time in Scotland's past which is both far away and long ago. Of course Nicholson claims that Sawney is a figure from history and not an ogre from legend, but I suggest that Nicholson was aware that Sawney's credentials as a real historical person were at best dubious. By removing him from the recent past Nicholson was following the ideals of the late eighteenth and early nineteenth centuries as they saw the historical process. He was also following the example set by Walter Scott in his novels about Scotland's past, in which less civilised cultures and characters are shown as having to evolve in order to take their place as parts of a modern Scotland which was itself an integral part of Britain.

Sawney is not and was not the first figure in Scottish culture to be fictionally constructed as historically real. In the eighteenth century James Macpherson introduced the ancient, highland figures of the Gaelic bard Ossian to the Scottish reading public. The impact of these fictional figures on the European imagination, and the consequences for the development of literary and historical scholarship was massive, not least on the minds of the Scottish philosophers and historians of the Enlightenment. In his *Critical Dissertation on the Poems of Ossian* of 1763 the Edinburgh Professor of Rhetoric, Hugh Blair, compared the Ossianic Highlanders with native Americans, both being peoples in a primitive stage of historical evolution.[25] Macpherson's ancient heroes, while primitive, were neither so bestial nor so savage as Sawney and his clan. Scott admired the elegant primitiveness of Macpherson's creations; *Waverley*, set in the eighteenth century and not in the ancient past of Ossian, owes much to Macpherson and his Noble Savages and their contribution to the development of the Enlightenment's evolutionary view of the history of society. Fergus MacIvor inhabits a stage of societal evolution which is more developed than that of Ossian or of Sawney, but he understands how a yet more civilised society and its written history will 'one day or other – when there are no longer any wild Highlanders – blot it from their records, as levelling them with a nation of cannibals.'[26]

In the historical world of Scott's fiction and in terms of the Enlightenment MacIvor's understanding is accurate. The reason that he knows of the existence of cannibal nations is because of the tales brought back to Europe by travellers, traders and colonisers from the fifteenth century onwards. Scotland, and especially the wild Highlands, had occupied a shared space in the minds of many in England with these newly discovered lands and peoples on the margins of the known world. The idea of Scotland as a colony is not a new one. The convergence of the availability of documents about primitive contemporary nations with that of texts such as Ossian detailing how we ourselves used to inhabit primitive and savage societies allowed the western mind, and especially the minds of the Scottish enlightenment, to draw strong comparisons between the two, hence Blair and his Ossianic Highlanders and American Indians.

This view of human nature as a constant resulted in the birth of the social science of anthropology which had as its teleos the objective, scientific understanding of man. In the twentieth century anthropology has been the main purveyor of narratives of cannibals.[27] Conclusions such as those of Blair and Scott are questioned in the fictions of Harry Tait and Alasdair Gray as well as by some modern-day anthropologists such as Arens but at the beginning of the nineteenth century historian and novelist alike shared the view of history as progress.

Scott's short story 'The Two Drovers' has a Carlisle judge link the Highland drover, Robin Oig, with the natives of America, a conclusion with which Scott, as nineteenth-century anthropologist, concurs. Sympathetically summing up the actions of Robin, who stabbed his one-time friend, the English drover, Harry Wakefield, as vengeance for being called a coward after Robin's poor show in a wrestling contest the saddened judge concludes:

> His case is a very peculiar one. The country which he inhabits was, in the days of many now alive, inaccessible to the laws, not only of England, which have not even yet penetrated hither, but to those to which our neighbours in Scotland are subjected, and which must be supposed to be, and no doubt actually are, founded upon the general principles of justice and equity which pervade every civilised country. Amongst their mountains, as among the North American Indians, the various tribes were wont to make war upon each other, so that each man was obliged to go armed for his protection. These men, from the ideas which they entertained of their own descent and of their own consequence, regarded themselves as so many cavaliers or men-at-arms, rather

than as the peasantry of a peaceful country. Those laws of the ring, as my brother terms them, were unknown to the race of warlike mountaineers; that decision of quarrels by no other weapons than those which nature has given every man, must to them have seemed as vulgar and as preposterous as to the noblesse of France. Revenge, on the other hand, must have been as familiar to their habits of society as to those of the Cherokees or Mohawks. It is indeed, as described by Bacon, at bottom a kind of wild untutored justice; for the fear of retaliation must withhold the hands of the oppressor where there is no regular law to check daring violence'.[28]

Such comparisons between the Highlanders and the native Americans, fictional or so-called historically true, were partly made possible by the encounters with native Americans made by Scots who had set up home in the New World. While emphasising the primitiveness of both, these comparisons also allow each a kind of exotic honour and nobility. We need to look in a different area of colonisation to find the foreign cousins of the wholly uncivilised Sawney and family.

Arens includes in his study the tale of one Hans Staden, a common seaman, who apparently witnessed cannibalism on the South American coast in the sixteenth century. Staden's work, published in Germany after his return from the New World, is entitled:

Hans Staden: The True History and Description of a Country of Savages, A Naked and Terrible People, Eater's of Men's Flesh, who Dwell in the New World Called America. Being wholly Unknown in Hesse Both Before and After Christ's Birth Until Two Years Ago, When Hans Staden of Hamberg in Hesse Took Personal Knowledge of Them and Now Presents His Story in Print.[29]

Staden's account, printed nine years after his return to Germany, claims that this is a 'True History'; Arens doubts this. Staden was a common seaman who could not communicate with his Portuguese shipmates but who found no difficulty in understanding and quoting verbatim the conversations of his captors, the Tupinamba Indians. He also demonstrated the typical good luck of westerners captured by cannibals, escaping with limbs intact to tell their tales of these bloodthirsty and vicious savages. Arens further points out the ways in which Staden's 'true' account bears remarkable similarities with descriptions contained in other accounts contemporary to Staden and with studies of so-called cannibal tribes right up to the present day. It also shows a close resemblance to elements of Nicholson's cannibal account. The Indians are all nearly naked, they are decorated with bones and feathers, they indulge in free love, having no taboos on adultery or incest, and the females are as cannibalistic as the males. Arens points out that such depictions of the female as more savage than the male are typical of many colonial accounts of cannibalism — as they are in the historical account of Pitscottie and in Nicholson. It seems that when propaganda and entertainment are being used to demonstrate the barbarity of less civilised peoples then it is an easy enough task to throw a little misogyny into the cooking pot too.

Alasdair Gray's novel *Lanark,* which explores cannibalism as a metaphor for the self-destructive impulses of modern Scotland, utilises and explores this tradition of the female being more cannibalistic than her male counterpart. Lanark, trapped in the Institute, a nightmare parallel of modern Glasgow, where all the inhabitants are either patients, nurses, or doctors has discovered that the only food available is that which has been processed from patients who have died. He refuses to eat but wants his girlfriend, Rima, a patient, to continue eating as she needs nourishment to recover. Rima notices that he is not eating and forces him to tell her why. He explains:

> 'You know that the institute gets light and heat from people with our kind of sickness. Well, the food is made from people with a different sickness.'
> 'These people aren't deliberately killed are they?'
> 'No, but the staff don't cure people as often as they pretend.'
> 'But without the staff they would go bad anyway.'
> 'Perhaps. I suppose so.'
> 'Anyway, if I stop eating I'll die, and nobody extra is going to be cured. Why shouldn't I eat?'
> 'I want you to eat. I made you promise to eat!'
> 'Why won't you eat?'
> 'No logical reason. I have instincts, prejudices, that stop me.'[30]

It is the female, Rima, who thinks logically in a fantastic world where the human body has become a basic unit of economic necessity and self-preservation is the highest ideal; Lanark, it is implied, is more primitive in his emotive reaction to the idea of consuming human flesh. Gray uses and complicates the traditional images of cannibalism and female savagery in his fantasy world, which unlike the cave in Galloway or the South American coast of the sixteenth century is, apparently, at the high point of human society's evolution. Gray uses cannibalism to explore questions of gender and of enlightenment anthropology.

Harry Tait's historical novel *The Ballad of Sawney Bain* is structured by numerous narratives, including the tales and journals of various ministers of the covenanted kirk and Agnes Douglas's 'Black Book'. Sawney's own voice is however notably absent. We know of his life in the Galloway cave and his previous actions through the account written by Agnes in her 'Black Book' and through the interrogation of the frightened Dugald Bain who replaces the young female of Pitscottie's history. Sawney, an enigmatic figure throughout, is silent about his cannibalism and incestuous lifestyle; it is Agnes who delights in shocking the mind of the minister who reads her book, ultimately driving him into a madness and confusion which mirrors the Scotland of the seventeenth century. Agnes is a double outcast from society and the kirk, being both witch and cannibal. Unlike those who hold authority in Gray's novel – practising cannibalism as part of an efficient economy – the ministers of Scotland's glorious reformed kirk of the late seventeenth century are shown by Tait to view cannibalism and witchcraft as evidence of palpable evil, especially in the figure of Agnes. Arens states that witchcraft and cannibalism are linked in the minds of many cultures and he draws comparisons between colonial Africa in the late nineteenth and early twentieth centuries and the European Middle Ages – both cultures using witch trials to suppress opposition and questioning of the ruling order and both utilising the accusation of evil as the basis of their charges. Agnes is accused of witchcraft largely because her mother refuses to respect the local minister, the Revd Munro or the laird, John Doig. She describes the actions of her righteous tormentors:

> In sic fashion they took us, and dragged us throught the toun and stripped us naked, and stuck a needle intae awe parts o us sparing nane, looking for what they caed Satan's mark. Awe this Munro wad watch, his red face glowering and his een triumphant.
> When did you last see the Deil Agnes? When did ye last tak him to yer bed? He canna help ye now Agnes and sae ye maun confess.
> On and on his voice ranted and I could see the blude running ower my flesh, and he could see it, and it may be that made his ain blude boil the faster, and I could hear mither's banes cracking under their instroments, and her screaming and cursing at them, and they left nae part unmolested sae sure were they that the Deil had not.[31]

Female nakedness, the female body and blood, all linked with the narratives of cannibalism considered above, are used by civilised and godly men to extract Agnes's confession to witchcraft. Tait, in different ways from Gray, is also asking whether the idea of evolution and improvement can help make much sense out of historical actions carried out by a seemingly more civilised society to eradicate difference which is viewed as primitive. Tait seems to suggest that civilization needs to invent savagery to maintain its certainty of its own more highly developed humanity, and to indulge its repressed desires. The minister who reads Agnes's 'Black Book' in the 1690s is shocked by the barbarity of the witch trial which took place half a century earlier but is obsessed by what he sees as the real evil of the cannibal cave:

The cave, he thought, had become almost a clearly imagined thing in his mind. In good weather they went naked, father, mother, brother and sister. They were locked like animals from the earliest age in incestuous fornication. They left off only to emerge like wolves from holes in the ground. They attacked, violated and murdered the world of men, dragging their corpses below ground where she-wolves dismembered them and salted down their flesh, singing psalms as they worked, with knives held in their intelligent hands.[32]

Nicholson's version is added to here by the singing of psalms, and the reader is also told that Sawney the cannibal patriarch spends his days reading his old bible. This feature, the religious nature of the cannibals, is what shocks the minister most. The fact that they share some of the cultural orthodoxies with the dominant culture of the religious seventeenth century confounds the enlightened mind which would see the civilised and the wholly savage as always being separated by thousands of miles or hundreds of years. The minister sees himself as more civilised and humane than Munro but he also has to resort to superstition to explain the actions of Sawney and Agnes. For him the angels who visit Sawney in the cave (seen by Agnes as evidence of Sawney's mental breakdown) are demons sent from the Devil – cannibalism and fornication with family members have simply replaced witchcraft and sex with the Deil himself, a flawed sort of improvement, where the one constant is opposition between the civilised (in the form of the two ministers) and the female figure of Agnes.

Tait's novel and *Lanark* both share as one of their chief concerns the corruption of so-called civilised societies; where they differ is that for Gray cannibalism as metaphor is evidence of this corruption at the heart of the civilised today, while Tait offers literal cannibalism as an escape from the chaos and corruption of the kirk-dominated seventeenth century. Gray's novel is set in a much more secular age, but men of the church still play an important part. It is the presbyterian minister whom the adolescent Duncan Thaw (Lanark's real-world alter ego) meets on a highland holiday who puts the idea of Glasgow as hell into Duncan's mind leading to the Institute sections of the novel. Within the Institute it is a very different religious figure who provides Lanark and Rima with food which is not derived from the human body. For once the church defeats cannibalism by kindness rather than oppression. This figure also provides a clue as to how Gray's urban and fantastic novel is concerned with Scotland's cultural history. Monsignor Noakes brings the real food and explains some of the history of the Institute and of cannibalism to Lanark and Rima:

> I was director of this Institute once, though not called that, for in those days the titles were different. Never mind. The only relic of my ancient status is the privilege of attending ecclesiastical conferences in continents where the

connection between feeding and killing folk is less obvious. This has enabled me to stock a small larder of delicacies which you may find useful . . .

Cannibalism has always been the main human problem. When the Church was a power we tried to discourage the voracious classes by feeding everyone regularly on the blood and body of God. I won't pretend the clergy were never gluttons, but many of us did, for a while, eat only what was willingly given. Since the institute joined with the council it seems that half the continents are feeding on the other half. Man is the pie that bakes and eats himself and the recipe is separation.[33]

This Catholic priest's words show how the institute acts in Gray's novel as a metaphor for Scotland, past and present. When the titles were different Noakes was not director of the Institute but the figurehead of Calvinism, the father of the Calvinist church in Scotland. Staunch Presbyterianism has transformed into high Catholicism and the John Knox of history with his mythic misogyny has become the one to save both male and female from cannibalistic acts with kindness. Now the Church, of whichever denomination, is no longer a power in Scotland, Noakes can condemn cannibalism as a human problem caused by greed and economic gluttony rather than supernatural evil. His words, which echo throughout the novel, 'Man is the pie that bakes and eats himself and the recipe is separation' are in agreement with the so-called primitive Agnes Douglas's thoughts on man in the seventeenth century, where separation is caused by religious, political, national and ideological differences and the assumptions of a higher authority and civilization by all of the fighting factions. Her cannibalism is an escape from the propaganda and oppression of such a world, where the literal replaces the symbolic devouring of humanity. It is, however, doomed to fail because the cannibals within the cave are also human, and the democracy of a closed-off society with no king and no minister is dissolved when Patrick Bain attempts to overthrow the patriarchal position of Sawney. In Sawney and Agnes's cave the improving impulse comes from within. The idyll of the cave which mocked the Enlightenment ideal of an evolved society where the institutes of religion, law and learning hold sway over a prosperous and civilised society is shown itself to be an unsustainable one; the primitive and the cannibalistic, in whatever form they take, as Gray and Tait both suggest, are parts of human nature which evolutionary views of the history of society and of humankind, along with those who hold them, cannot suppress and which they themselves promulgate.

Sawney and his family (or a family very like them) existed in print in Pitscottie's sixteenth-century narrative and they are still thriving today in the fictional histories of Scottish writers such as Barker, Tait and Gray. Scott and Enlightenment figures such as Blair may have led Nicholson to push Sawney further back in time, but paradoxically they are ultimately just as responsible as Nicholson for the healthy state the primitive cannibal and his family are to be found in today in the Scottish imagination.

The case for the existence of Scottish cannibals as real historical figures is one which cannot be proven beyond reasonable doubt; the evidence for the continuing fascination of Scottish writers with Sawney Bean and his not-so-innocent wife is, however, compelling.

Notes

1. John Wilson of Gatehouse, fom *Strains of Galloway* (1914), in Innes MacLeod, *Discovering Galloway* (Edinburgh 1986), 262.
2. *The Last Journals of David Livingstone in Central Africa, from 1865 to his Death* (ed.) Horace Waller, 2 vols. (London 1874), 2, 98.
3. John Nicholson, *Historical and Traditionary Tales Connected with the South of Scotland* (Kirkcudbright 1843), 73.
4. Ibid. 73–4.
5. Ibid. 75.
6. Ibid. 76.
7. Ibid. 79.
8. Ronald Holmes, *The Legend of Sawney Bean* (London 1975), 18.
9. Sandy Hobbs and David Cornwell, 'Sawney Bean, the Scottish Cannibal' in *Folklore* 108 (1997) 49–54.
10. Alasdair Gray, *Poor Things* (London 1992) 301.
11. S. R. Crockett, *The Grey Man* (London 1896; Ayr 1980) 242.
12. Ibid. 246.
13. W. Arens, *The Man-Eating Myth: Anthropology and Anthropophagy* (New York 1979).
14. Robert Chambers, *Traditions of Edinburgh* 2 vols. (Edinburgh 1825) 2, 286.
15. Ibid. 286–7.
16. Elspeth Barker, *O Caledonia* (Harmondsworth 1992) 55–6.
17. Raphael Hollinshead, *Chronicles of England, Scotland and Ireland* 6 vols. (London 1808) 5, 380.
18. Robert Lindsay of Pitscottie, *The Historie and Chronicles of Scotland*, 3 vols. (Edinburgh and London 1899–1911) 1, 146–7.

19. David Reid, 'Prose after Knox' in *The History of Scottish Literature* (ed.) Cairns Craig, 4 vols. (Aberdeen 1987–8) 1, 187

20. *Ibid.* 188.

21. References to cannibalism by Scots can also be found in E. G. Cody, *The Historie of Scotland: written first in Latin by the most reverend and worthy Jhone Leslie Bishop of Rosse; and translated in Scottish by Father James Dalrymple* 2 vols. (Edinburgh 1888) i, 99; and *The History and Chronicles of Scotland; written in Latin by Hector Boece Canon of Aberdeen; and translated by John Bellenden* 2 vols. (Edinburgh 1821) i, xxvii.

22. Nicholson, *Historical and Traditionary Tales* 77.

23. Quoted in Holmes, *The Legend of Sawney Bean* 20.

24. *Ibid.* 21.

25. Hugh Blair, *A Critical Dissertation on the Poems of Ossian, the Son of Fingal* (Edinburgh 1763) 23.

26. Sir Walter Scott, *Waverley,* (ed.) Andrew Hook (Harmondsworth 1972) 474.

27. See Robert Crawford, *Devolving English Literature* (Oxford 1992) 16–20 for a more detailed examination of the links between Enlightenment historians and the development of anthropology.

28. Walter Scott, 'The Two Drovers' in *Scottish Short Stories 1800–1900* (ed.) Douglas Gifford (London 1981) 44–5.

29. Arens, *The Man-Eating Myth.* 63.

30. Alasdair Gray, *Lanark* (New York 1985) 98.

31. Harry Tait, *The Ballad of Sawney Bain* (Edinburgh 1990) 55–6.

32. *Ibid.* 86–7.

33. Gray, *Lanark,* 100–101.

8

Among Sublime Prospects: Travel Writers and the Highlands

E. Mairi MacArthur

Travel literature is by definition concerned with place. The genre is about much more, however, than the accumulation of facts and figures, as in timetables or gazetteers. At its heart lies the relationship of the travel writer with that place.

The eye of the wayfarer may be focused on a natural landscape, on a built environment or on the life and mores of a people. He or she may be among the first to venture into a particular location or may be following a well-trodden path. What is set on record by the end of the journey, however, is an interpretation of what that traveller has experienced. In the course of creating his or her own individual sense of a place, the writer also becomes aware that its physical, social and cultural characteristics have all been shaped by events – in short, that every place has a history. And Scotland is most certainly no exception.

Are travellers' tales a legitimate historical source then, or should they be viewed primarily as a literary form? How have the two disciplines interacted? The first problem in wrestling with such questions is the vast body of material to consider. Scotland has been a much-visited place. Over 250 years, at least, very many of those visitors have been inspired, or provoked, to put pen to paper. Mitchell and Cash's classic source-book *A Contribution to the Bibliography of Scottish Topography* includes a dozen pages of 'General Descriptions and Guides' and two dozen of 'Tours', each page averaging twenty items. On the very first page, it is true, the eye lights upon a letter written in 1701 to a young gentleman: 'Scotland characterised . . . to dissuade him from an intended journey thither'. It is reasonable to assume, however, that the motives of most writers were positive and that their intentions were to instruct or amaze and, perhaps, to persuade the reader to follow in their steps. There was indeed a veritable snowball effect, the most famous and enduring example probably being the journey made by Dr Samuel Johnson and James Boswell in 1773. The good doctor's record of the tour was published two years later, swiftly became a best seller and has regularly inspired re-enactments, in print and on film, down to our own day.

The extensive bibliography begun by Sir Arthur Mitchell and brought to fruition by C.G. Cash in 1917 admits in its very title that the task was far from complete even then. Extra lists were published by Mitchell in the *Proceedings of the Society of Antiquaries for Scotland* in 1902, 1905 and 1910 but it was noted that, under 'foreign tours', only those translated into English were included. Visitors from abroad may indeed remain an underestimated category. For example, Dr Alison Hiley found a great deal of neglected but very interesting material, some of it from archives in the former East Germany, in her literary study of German travellers to Scotland in the first half of the nineteenth century. A phrase quoted by one of these – 'Scotland's name is poetry to our ears'[1] – gives some inkling of the strong attraction felt for the land of Schiller's *Maria Stuart* and Mendelssohn's *Hebrides Overture*.

The sheer amount of post-Mitchell & Cash material is also dauntingly large. The local topography or local history shelves of any Scottish library testify to the proliferation of a particular kind of travel writing through the first few decades of the twentieth century, where authors strayed and daydreamed amid the quiet backwaters of the countryside. Even the titles of their books evoke a romantic, old-world charm, as a few examples demonstrate: T. Ratcliffe Barnett, *The Road to Rannoch and the Summer Isles* (Edinburgh 1924), *The Land of Lorne and the Isles of Rest* (London & Edinburgh 1933); M.E.M. Donaldson, *Wanderings in the Western Highlands and Islands* (Paisley 1921); Alistair Alpin MacGregor, *Behold the Hebrides! Or Wayfaring in the Western Isles* (London & Edinburgh 1925), *The Haunted Isles* (London 1933); Thomas Nicol, *By Mountain, Moor and Loch to the Dream Isles of the West* (Stirling 1931); Halliday Sutherland, *Hebridean Journey* (Edinburgh 1939). While this genre has been criticised for presenting a quaint and over-idealised version of Scotland, several of these volumes are considered classics of their kind and remain staples of the second-hand book market.

Since 1950 travelogues have become more varied in approach and glossier in presentation, although no less abundant. With each summer season has come the rustle of notebooks and, increasingly, the click of cameras as tour coaches rumble north up the A9 and ferry ramps clank on to island piers. People have found ever more idiosyncratic pretexts for going from A to B, on ever more ingenious forms of transport, and a bigger range of specialist interests, such as mountaineering, sailing or wildlife, are now the target of travel writing. Photography frequently plays as significant a part as the written word. It is all grist to the tourist industry mill and each batch of new visitors harbours within it the potential roving reporters of the future.

This brief overview of travel literature about Scotland cannot claim to be exhaustive and it reflects the limits of the author's own interests and expertise. This chapter will look primarily at descriptions of the Highlands and Islands which, rightly or wrongly, have long provided the outsider with identifiable national images for Scotland as a whole. Almost since the start, the travel industry has been fed by the public's ready consumption of these images and, in turn, has itself helped feed that appetite. The material presents a rich and varied seam but two periods or categories in particular merit closer attention: the late eighteenth century, the Age of Enlightenment; and the nineteenth century, when the guidebook as we know it today came into its own.

Fresh Fields for Inquiry

A brief phrase from the biographical sketch of Richard Pococke, a clergyman born in Southampton in 1704, evokes neatly and elegantly one significant aspect of that age: 'He desired pastures new, fresh fields for inquiry'.[2] As a young man in the 1730s, Pococke had travelled widely in Europe as was the custom. He became Archdeacon of Dublin in 1745 and, a thirst for travel clearly undiminished, made a couple of forays across to Scotland followed by a major six-month tour in 1760, which he recorded in the form of descriptive letters.

He was not alone in regarding the lands north of the Tweed as fresh fields. In the late eighteenth century a spirit of inquiry was abroad when the natural environment and the human condition became objects of active quest. Men of science and letters wished to journey, intellectually and literally, into new territory. Scotland and, in particular, the Highlands – geographically remote and culturally distinct – formed an obvious challenge. There may have been an added frisson for some in the lingering notion that to go there was to venture boldly among barbarians. Dr John Leyden, a friend of Sir Walter Scott who took two young foreign students on a Highland exploration in the summer of 1800, wrote upon reaching back to Perth: 'I may now congratulate myself on a safe escape from the Indians of Scotland, as our friend Ramsay denominates the Highlanders.'[3]

It may be argued that a number of the most useful accounts from late eighteenth century visitors had their origins in the zeal to acquire knowledge rather than directly in the lust to wander. The Revd John Walker, who was also a botanist and geologist, combined in his Hebridean tours of 1764 two reports commissioned specially from him: one on the state of religion and education for the General Assembly of the Church of Scotland, the other a survey of agriculture, fishing and industry for the Commissioners of the Annexed Estates.[4] Thomas Garnett, a professor of natural philosophy and chemistry, suggested that it was perhaps highly presumptuous of him 'to intrude on the world another tour through the Highlands after the number that have already been published'. But he went on to state that the aim of his journey, undertaken in 1798, was 'to give as perfect an account as possible of every place and every thing' and that only the journal of his contemporary, Thomas Pennant, was as extensive.[5] Pennant, whose published tour of 1772 ran to three editions in his lifetime and was translated into German, was indeed enormously influential. References to his work by later travellers come a close second to those echoing the opinions and sentiments of Dr Johnson. It was a desire that work in his own field, zoology, reflect an understanding of the whole country which spurred Pennant: ' . . . struck therefore with the reflection of having never seen Scotland, I instantly ordered my baggage to be got ready, and in a reasonable time found myself on the banks of the Tweed'.[6]

Despite this disarming impression that one could fly effortlessly north on a magic carpet, none of these learned gentlemen will have escaped the rigours of long and arduous journeys. These were no armchair scholars. The Age of Enlightenment visitors did go and see for themselves and the range of issues to which they were alert was very wide indeed. Their accounts have handed down to subsequent historians much illuminating detail about the social and economic life of the people, their customs and dress, their material circumstances and religious attitudes. The observers were aware too of the major transformation in land patterns underway on some Highland estates and commented on attempts to introduce or revive industries such as sheep-farming, kelping or fisheries. A number of touring parties included an artist, thus also bequeathing a clutch of visual interpretations from the days before the camera lens. In Pennant's volumes the sketches of conical shellings on Jura and of women on Skye turning a quernstone and waulking tweed with their feet are particularly memorable.

What the people being so assiduously documented felt themselves about their own condition and prospects is less clear. In 1688, as William Sacheverell, Governor of Man, crossed the island of Mull, he had reflected:

> Men, manners, habits, buildings, everything different from our own; and if we thought them rude and barbarous no doubt the people had the same opinion of what belonged to us and the wonder was mutual.[7]

This degree of perception seems to be rare among those visitors from a century later, who tended either to pity the people they encountered for their state of apparent misery or chide them on account of their apparent idleness. In Islay Pennant wrote of '... a set of people worn down by poverty ... my picture is not of this island only'.[8] An overall impression of penury and backwardness pervades these accounts – only to be expected, perhaps, from those whose perspectives were steeped in the improvement ethic of the times.

Now and again the clash of two different worlds was resounding. In the summer of 1797 Edward Clarke, Professor of Mineralogy at Cambridge, set out on a sailing tour of the Scottish west coast. As the party landed on Iona, three of them began to recite with reverence the words of Dr Johnson before them:

> We were now treading that illustrious island which was once the luminary of the Caledonian regions, whence savage clans and roving barbarians derived the benefits of knowledge, and the blessings of religion. ... That man is little to be envied whose patriotism would not gain force upon the plain of Marathon, or whose piety would not grow warmer among the ruins of Iona.[9]

They were by no means the first nor the last to take up this famous refrain. On this occasion, however, the spell was rudely broken when some of the local people approached:

> We found ourselves surrounded by a crowd of the most importunate and disgusting objects I ever beheld. Bedlam disgorged of all its inhabitants could hardly have presented a more dismaying spectacle ... a miserable idiot grinned horribly in my face; ... here a wretched cripple exposed his naked sores; there a blind and aged beggar besought pity on his infirmities.[10]

Clarke raved on in this near-hysterical tone for a lengthy paragraph but the key to his distress is exposed about halfway through: 'All the warm feelings excited by the ruins of Iona or the retrospect of its former glory were in one moment obliterated'.[11] The expectation, undoubtedly bolstered by the accounts of earlier travellers, that this holy and historic spot would surely be enshrouded in an atmosphere of peace and piety for its pilgrims had been shattered. Real life had intruded upon the visitor experience.

The hapless professor's evident shock may have led him to exaggerate somewhat. His reaction was not unique but neither was it widely replicated. If things were in fact fully as bad as that on the Sacred Isle, then this would have been a fairly damning portrayal of the real condition of people's lives. One is also tempted to wonder, wrily, if the locals themselves did not begin to respond in the manner expected of them by these visitors from such a totally different milieu, although to what degree this was conscious role-playing is impossible now to judge. As many travellers also reported, Iona's children were early practitioners of the souvenir business. For William

Wordsworth, this was 'How sad a welcome!' when he saw that, for each new arrival, 'some ragged child holds up for sale a store of wave-worn pebbles...'[12] For the people it was a way of turning pebbles and shells into a few useful pennies each short summer season.

A contributory factor to this gulf between expectation and reality may have lain in a strand of thought that ran counter to the Enlightenment's search for rational analysis and scientific observation and one that held tremendous sway in the late eighteenth and early nineteenth centuries.[13] A trawl through the titles or opening lines of dozens of literary offerings from early travellers reveals that these were peppered with a particular kind of vocabulary, designed to stir the soul and uplift the feelings: antiquity, natural curiosity, scenic splendour, the picturesque, the wild, the romantic. The manifestation in Scotland of this wider romantic movement owed much to literary sources. In the 1760s, James Macpherson's purported translations of the poems of the Fingalian bard Ossian dwelt on the grandeur and gloom of nature, on the passion of an heroic and mythical past. With the publication of his poem *The Lady of the Lake* in 1810, and in the string of *Waverley* novels soon to follow, Sir Walter Scott took up the Ossianic baton and invested his literary creations with a heady mix of Highland history, legend and landscape. Both Macpherson and Scott became immediately and hugely popular, their work appealing to an enthusiastic audience not only throughout Scotland and England but across Europe and beyond. Their influence continued long after their deaths and, as is argued regularly by some commentators on the evolution of Scottish tourism, the images they fostered remain with us still.[14] Their names are inextricably linked to the travel literature of Scotland.

Fellow Pedestrian Tourists

In 1800 a George Douglas set out from Edinburgh on a tour which ended up in Braemar. Stopping overnight in Oban he noted in his journal:

> Every apartment of the small inn is occupied by tourists... the Hon Mr. Ward is here with a large party and the Hon Mrs. Murray is exercising her graphic talents in an adjoining lodging... my friend Auchterlony with his fellow pedestrian tourists were here two days ago and seem much delighted with their excursion.[15]

Routes north and west were clearly becoming ever busier and more popular. Indeed, one of the few women from this period about whose travels we know something, Mrs Sarah Murray of Kensington, felt impelled to give an array of practical advice to readers about the hire of horses and carriages and the state of the inns.[16] She was doubtless making notes on that very subject as George Douglas was making his in the hostelry next door.

By 1811 *The Travellers Guide through Scotland and its Islands* was already in its fifth edition and claimed to have sold 5000 copies of earlier editions. The stakes grew higher as Henry Bell's *Comet* sailed from Glasgow to Fort William in 1819, heralding the opening of the steamship era. Within a decade west coast waters became a thriving commercial highway and when Mendelssohn's party arrived at the River Clyde in 1829 they found seventy steamboats lying at the ready. James Johnson vividly captured the scene in Oban in 1832, comparing it to a modern, western Ormuz with caravans approaching from all points of the compass in the form of three steamers and a stagecoach:

> The whole of Oban is instantly roused from torpor to activity . . . The innkeepers are on the alert while the scouts, videttes and purveyors of the rival hotels are on active service . . . meanwhile, the contents of the steamers – men, women, children, sheep, poultry, pigs, dogs, salmon, herrings, cakes, trunks, bags, baskets, hampers, books, portfolios, maps, guns, fishing tackle and thousands of other articles are in rapid transit from vessel to vessel, from steamer to coach, under such a conclatteration of tongues . . . as was never heard round the Tower of Babel . . . [they then] diverge like radii from the centre in quest of new scenes and fresh sources of excitement.[17]

As the nineteenth century progressed, the new excursionists continued to pour in from far and wide and from all walks of life. Many of them kept a diary or later recalled their memories, snapping for posterity a lively wordpicture of their fellow passengers. John Phillips, for example, left York in July 1826 with three friends, headed for Mull and Iona and, after a night spent in Tobermory:

> Awakened at five by the music/noise? [sic] of the parading bagpiper, we soon entered the ready packet and set off at 5.30 with four Frenchmen, a gentleman who attached himself to us at Oban, two Cantabs, a blackguard Scotch writer, good hopes and bad weather.[18]

And the Revd C.H. Townshend, on board the Oban-Iona boat in 1840, found himself in the company of a motley crew: a French marquis, three sketchers, a young woman 'eccentrically' dressed who wore a man's hat and green veil, a portly dame enveloped in gold jewellery who was drinking a tumbler of foaming ale with great satisfaction and a young man with long yellow locks who turned out to be a keen geologist.[19]

The swelling tourist numbers were met by an equal growth in the numbers of printed guides and companions, many of them published by the steamboat owners and, towards the end of the century, by the railway companies. They thus included factual information in the form of timetables and advertisements but these were usually accompanied by introductions and descriptions, to fire the imagination of the prospective traveller. Here the images and language of the romantic era continued to come through loud and strong. 'Nothing can appear more awful or more interesting to a stranger', proclaimed the 1811 *Travellers Guide,* 'than the general scenery of the Highlands'. *Lumsden & Sons Steam-Boat Companion* came out in 1820, was to run to several editions and confidently stated its case in the introduction: 'There is certainly no country whose ancient history, magnificent scenery and national peculiarities are more replete with interest than those of Scotland'. The title of this chapter is culled from farther down the same page: 'To the devotee of beauteous Nature, there are endless subjects for contemplation among the sublime prospects of the Highlands . . . '.[20] The *Scottish Tourist and Itinerary,* first published in 1825, was dedicated to Sir Walter Scott and its preface credited him, along with James Macpherson and Robert Burns, with helping attract attention to 'the romantic and sublime scenery' of Scotland.[21] 'To the admirer of Nature,' it goes on, in confident tone, 'no part of Europe affords more varied landscape than its Lowland dells and Highland wilds'.

These texts, and the many which followed, are profusely studded with lines or stanzas of poetry, even entire sonnets, and with literary allusions. One example issued for the 1883 season by Caledonian and London & North Western Railways, *Summer Tours in Scotland,* opens with the voice of William Wordsworth and then, within the first few lines, aims to capture the book-loving tourist's attention:

> Not only are there special attractions in the landscape, but it is so rich in legendary lore, identified with so much that is of historical interest, and has been so vividly conjured up before the mind's eye by the inimitably descriptive pen of the author of the Waverley Novels, that it becomes invested with a peculiar charm for the traveller.[22]

In the views that unfold thereafter, as from the window of a railway carriage, places associated with historical figures and events are strung seamlessly together with – to pick out but a few examples – the spot beyond Loch Voie '. . . where Sir Walter laid the scene of the escape of Rob Roy', or Ardforuish Castle, where 'he had the sound of minstrels open the story of *The Lord of the Isles*', or the Falls of Bora, where 'Ossian sang of the roar of thy climbing waves'.[23]

It must have been quite clear that popular literature, in modern advertising terms, simply made good copy. The alacrity with which the reading public swarmed to the Trossachs or to the West Highlands, in search of their favourite fictional backdrop, ensured that tour operators at least would try to blend the poetic and the prosaic for as long as they could. And this attitude seemed to prevail despite a cautionary note sounded relatively early by John MacCulloch who was, moreover, a good friend of Sir Walter Scott. He made several visits to the Highlands, on foot, between the years 1811 and 1821 and his reports were thorough and practical rather than impressionistic or sentimental. He did appreciate the great beauty of the landscape but expressed concern that too many romantic notions about the past would raise unreasonable hopes:

> Visitors will be disappointed . . . if they expect to meet a Helen MacGregor, a Dugald or a Captain Knockdunder at every corner, to be greeted in Iona or Skye by a gifted seer or to find every cottage and every stream and hill surrounded with the songs of Ossian or the heroic deeds of Fingal. The day is now some time past since these delusions should have subsided.[24]

We Merely State What We Saw . . .

More than sixty years after John MacCulloch's warning, travel writers Joseph and Elizabeth Pennell, from London, confessed to an uncannily similar set of preconceptions about Scotland:

> Our knowledge was made up of confused impressions of Hearts of Midlothian and Painters' Camps in the Highlands, Macbeths and Kidnappers, Skye terriers and Shetland shawls, blasted heaths and hills of mist, Rob Roys and Covenanters; and added to these positive convictions of an unbroken Scottish silence and of endless breakfasts of oatmeal, dinners of haggis and suppers of whisky.[25]

Despite these misgivings the couple set out on a walking tour, which was to include part of the Hebrides, in 1883. The Pennells' work is interesting, and unusual, on account of its relationship with contemporary events in the places through which they passed. The historical detail in much travel literature, in particular in the commercial guide books, tended to look to the past, to ancient glories preserved in ruined castles or overgrown churchyards. Historic sites were generally the main focus, and although there might also be comment on the current health, welfare or numbers of any local population, attempts were seldom made to probe beneath the surface or to seek a wider context.

A Revd Thomas Grierson, who visited Iona in 1848, did comment on the divisive effects among the islanders of the Disruption in the Church of

Scotland a few years earlier, and the formation of a new Free Church congregation. It may well have been an issue close to his own heart. He also complained about 'scores of famished-looking children' trying to sell souvenir pebbles,[26] yet he betrayed no awareness that the disastrous potato famine of 1846-47 still haunted many parts of the West Highlands. As the Pennells crossed from Mull to Iona their ferryman told them that there had been trouble in the area and that the commission was coming in a week. He had only a house and a boat and paid five shillings and sixpence rent:' . . . it was not much but it was about the land there was trouble and he had no land'.[27] This was history in the making for the anticipated body was the Napier Commission, set up to enquire into crofters' conditions and grievances and which led ultimately to security of tenure under the Crofters' Act of 1886. The Pennells had several other such encounters, made it their business to delve more fully into the background of the problems and declared themselves strongly in support of the people's cause.

For this they were severely criticised. *The Scotsman* dismissed their articles as 'sentimental nonsense' and 'amazing impertinence'. The couple's stout rebuttal revolved around the claim that 'We merely state what we saw, what it was impossible to avoid seeing, wherever we went'. They had eschewed what had been made 'the fashion' to discover in Scotland, along with the 'second hand descriptions which are the stock in trade of Scottish guidebooks, whether romantic or real'. Recalling the island of Ulva, they summed up their stance:

> The Highlands and the Hebrides are lands of romance. There is a legend for almost every step you take. But the cruellest of these are not so cruel as, and have none of the pathos of, the tales of their own and their father's wrongs and wretchedness which the people tell today.[28]

The Pennells, certainly, held on to no illusions that they were visiting a land peopled only by characters from a romantic past. It is hard to know, however, if this bold intrusion by outsiders into a live political debate made any impact at all on those affected by it on a day-to-day level. No other travel memoirs, to the author's knowledge, emulated their approach nor did the general run of tour brochure significantly modify the purple prose of their texts.

William Carson, visiting Skye and Uist in 1897, stumbled upon living history too and, in fact, photographed a crowd at the auction of household goods following an eviction. His diary recorded that the landlord, Sir John Orde of Lochmaddy, was believed to have put tenants out of their homes for being in arrears of rent.[29] However, the sympathies of Carson's companion, a Dr Harmsworth, seemed little affected by what they had witnessed. There is a whiff of that late eighteenth century yearning for solititude and a noble, primitive past in the doctor's initial words, anticipating the trip: 'We shall see the wild Highlander on his native heath. We shall get right away from the civilised world'. Later, he appeared keener to 'civilise' the same natives by bringing in 'a legion of sturdy lowland Scots' to build better houses, work the land properly and generally bring the islanders up to scratch.[30] They might, he continued, 'give an appearance of prosperity even to South Uist'.

Old Legends . . . and Similar Spurious Things

The Norwegian scholar P.A. Munch visited Iona in 1849, at the suggestion of noted antiquarian David Laing of the Signet Library in Edinburgh. Munch's special interest lay in any evidence of Norse influence in the buildings, inscriptions and placenames of the islands. He expressed concern at popular confusion between the designations 'Danes' and 'Norwegians' when his Viking ancestors were under discussion. And he was certain where the blame lay:

> Incidentally, it cannot be denied that travel accounts, antiquarian writings and so on studied by schoolmasters and cicerone, have done much damage by mixing the old legends with all sorts of later conjectures and similar spurious things, so that one must be on guard against taking everything one hears of that kind for old and genuine.[31]

A visit to Iona was a highly apposite context for an observation of this kind. Still alive then was the longest-serving of the island's local guides, Alan Maclean, who had been appointed schoolmaster in 1796. From the many references by travellers who used his services, it is clear he had a lively interest in the historic sites in his care. A native of Mull, he was familiar with traditions transmitted orally among the locals; indeed, he told Thomas Garnett that he himself knew, from his grandfather, a poem by Ossian on the death of Oscar. He was undoubtedly open to the written word also and it is no surprise that tourist Robert Carruthers found him, in 1835, with a staff in one hand and a little book, *The Historical Account of Iona,* in the other. Alan informed the new arrivals that he was not the author himself, but added, 'I am of the same clan and I have some copies to sell'.[32]

Alan's little book, which was to enjoy a brisk trade, was the first to be devoted entirely to Iona itself. The title-page quoted a Gaelic couplet by Ossian and revealed the author, Lachlan Maclean, to be an honorary member of the Glasgow Ossianic Society. Maclean was an enthusiast for all things antiquarian and the book was essentially a compilation. It quoted at length, for example, from Pennant's account of Iona. Overall it was a mixture of the straightforward and factual, such as extracts from charters and the Great Seal, and the decidedly spurious, on topics such as druidic religion on Iona or conjectured royal burials in the fifth century.

Maclean's booklet points up the main danger in relying upon travelogues for historical information, namely their tendency to reiterate previously published 'facts' without ever subjecting the original source to fresh scrutiny. Repeated like a litany through guides and articles about Iona, for instance, are the precise numbers of kings whose graves are said to be there: 48 Scottish, 8 Norwegian, 4 Irish. Maclean in fact reprinted the passage from Dean Monro to whose visit in 1549 these figures may be traced. Monro did record material evidence of what had appeared once to be separate royal burial chapels. But the actual number of burials was, he wrote, 'according to our Scottes and Erishce cronikles'.[33] Reliable interpretation of those same Scottish and Irish chronicles, moreover, is highly problematic and current scholarship takes the line that the numbers, and most of the names, of any early kings buried on Iona are impossible to verify.[34] Once in print often enough, however, even the least well-founded facts have a way of entering orthodoxy. One of the most common questions asked by tourists to Iona today is where are the graves of Duncan and Macbeth. The Stratford bard bears no little responsibility for this, of course, having put into MacDuff's mouth the words that King Duncan's body had been carried to Iona, 'The sacred storehouse of his predecessors, And guardian of their bones'.

Shrines of History and Shrines of Literature

Few writers about place can have made their aim as crystal clear as did William Winter, when he published *Old Shrines and Ivy* in 1892. He wanted to bring together literary tributes to William Shakespeare and an evocation of scenes associated with the great playwright's work and life. His homage was constructed from 'shrines of history and shrines of literature'.[35] This very single-minded travel memoir included a trip from Edinburgh to Forres – 'the land of *Macbeth*' – a meditative wander on Culloden field and a few days on Iona where, in addition, Winter noted a great deal of useful factual information about the life of the inhabitants.

For writer and photographer M.E.M. Donaldson in 1920, the focus was more avowedly an historical one. In the preface to the first edition of *Wanderings in the Western Highlands and Islands,* she cited a couplet from Ossian, whom she called 'true Scotland's national poet': 'It is the voice of the years that are gone. They roll before me with all their deeds'. It was the voices and deeds of the past which had prompted her, ' . . . to strengthen an intimacy with some of the most fascinating of characters and of events in Scottish history by becoming familiar with scenes from which their memory is inseparable'.[36] In the revised edition, Donaldson apologised for earlier errors of fact and, while welcoming criticism, robustly defended the stance she had chosen to take on the history of the Scottish Episcopal Church. Clearly she intended her books not merely to be travelogues but to enter the fray of historical debate.[37]

In the copious travel literature about Scotland, and about the Highlands and Islands in particular, the shrines of history and of literature come together. The desire to visit in the first instance was very frequently kindled by the written word. Much of that writing drew on aspects of the past, reclothing selected elements in romantic or legendary garb. The journals and memoirs that resulted from the visits alluded back to their literary inspiration, while creating their own interpretation of a place's story. Similarly, the guidebooks proper, although proactive rather than reactive, peopled the Highland landscape with characters and events from both a real and an imagined past. It was a continuous cycle.

The books themselves are certainly a respected form of literature. The old pocket guides, in particular, are also attractive items in themselves; delicate illustrations, artistically lettered advertisements and handsome bindings make them fascinating to browse through and a delight to handle. A number of travel diaries are now in print though many others remain in manuscript form. Never meant for publication, perhaps, these were presumably written for personal satisfaction rather than to meet the needs of a publisher or readership. They are often refreshing and irreverent, full of surprising detail and great fun to read.

As a historical source, travel writing has to be treated with some care and the particular approach or subjective bias of the author must be borne in mind. Yet it can yield much of considerable interest and can help greatly to fill out the picture of a place or period when set alongside other documentary material, oral testimony and archaeological evidence.

From the very beginnings of outside interest in the land of the mountain and the flood over two centuries ago, the lure of certain types of image has been strong. A glance through brochures from much more recent times confirms that, where it can still gain a hold, that grip remains firm. A Macbraynes' timetable from 1961 classified the entire area its steamers served as 'The Isles of Youth', a place which lay, enchanted, 'on the chord of the setting sun' and where 'the warriors, heroes and heroines step out of their ancient days'. In 1992 an area tourist board sold the attractions of the west coast, from Lochaber south to Colonsay, under the title 'Experience the Dream', asking visitors if they could imagine a land of 'Celtic legend, history and wildlife; a rural, wild scene of quaint villages and friendly folk?' The text was crammed with magic, spectacle, tranquillity, mystique and sublime wilderness. Ossian's cave received the obligatory mention. And in the spring of 1998, on the wall of the ticket-office in Inverness bus station, in gilt lettering and flanked by two paintings of Urquhart and Cawdor castles, there reads the legend:

> The story of the Highlands is one of kings and clans, serpents and salmon, warriors and witches, castles and kilts, whisky and freedom.

Now the freedom of the Highlands can be yours, it invites the traveller, with the Tourist Trail Day Rover Ticket…

The circle keeps on turning.

Notes

1. Title of paper given by Dr Hiley at a conference entitled 'Scottish Tourists and Tourism', organised by the Scottish Records Association in Glasgow, 5 November 1994. Her doctoral thesis was undertaken at Edinburgh University.
2. 'Pococke's tours in Scotland' in *Scottish History Society* (ed.) D.W. Kemp (Edinburgh 1887) xl.
3. J. Leyden, *Journal of a Tour in the Highlands and Western Islands in 1800* (Edinburgh 1903), 252, letter to Dr R. Anderson. The mutual friend referred to will have been John Ramsay of Ochtertyre, a noted literary patron and also a friend of Scott, whom Leyden had visited on the way north.
4. See John Walker *Report on the Hebrides of 1764 and 1771* (ed.) M.M. Mackay (Edinburgh 1980).
5. T. Garnett, *Observations on a Tour through the Highlands and part of the Western Isles of Scotland* (London 1910) preface iii.
6. T. Pennant, *A Tour in Scotland 1769* (London 1776) iii.
7. W. Sacheverell, *An Account of the Isle of Man… with a Voyage to I-Columb-Kill* (London 1702) 128.
8. T. Pennant, *A Tour in Scotland and Voyage to the Hebrides 1772* (London 1776) 261–2.
9. Dr S. Johnson, *A Journey to the Western Islands of Scotland*, (London 1925) 205–6.
10. W. Otter, *The Life and Remains of Edward Daniel Clarke* 2 vols (London 1825) i, 313.

11. *Ibid.* 313.
12. Opening line of *Iona (upon landing)*, one of four sonnets composed by Wordsworth after his visit in 1835. *William Wordsworth Poetical Works,* (ed.) T. Hutchinson (Oxford 1936) 372.
13. For further discussion see T.C. Smout 'Tours in the Scottish Highlands from the Eighteenth to the Twentieth Centuries' in *Northern Scotland* vol.V (1982–2) 99–121.
14. For further discussion, see *Scotland – the Brand. The Making of Scottish Heritage* (ed.) D. McCrone (Edinburgh 1995) 4–5, 51–61.
15. G. Douglas, 'Tour in Hebrides AD 1800' (National Library of Scotland, ms 213).
16. The Hon. Mrs Sarah Murray of Kensington, *A Companion and Useful Guide to the Beauties in the West Highlands of Scotland and in the Hebrides* (London 1803).
17. J. Johnson, *Recess in the Highlands and Islands* (London 1834).
18. J. Phillips, 'Tour in Scotland' (Mitchell Library, ms 240800).
19. C.H. Townshend, *A Descriptive Tour in Scotland* (Brussels 1840, London 1846) 99.
20. *Lumsden & Son's Steam-boat Companion* (Glasgow 1820) 1.
21. *The Scottish Tourist and Itinerary* (2nd edn, Edinburgh 1827) preface vi.
22. *Summer Tours in Scotland* (Caledonian and London & North Western Railways 1883) 6.
23. *Ibid,* 9, 44, 18.
24. Dr J. MacCulloch, *The Highlands and Western Isles of Scotland containing descriptions of their scenery and antiquity* 4 vols., (London 1824) i, Introduction.
25. J. and E. Pennell, *Our Journey to the Hebrides* (London 1890) 3-4. The material in the book had first come out as a series of articles in *Harpers Magazine.*
26. T. Grierson, *Autumnal Rambles among the Scottish Mountains* (Edinburgh 1850) 38.
27. Pennell, *op. cit.,* 84.
28. *Ibid* 58.
29. W.E. Carson, 'Through the Hebrides. The Journal of a Tour to the Western Isles of Scotland in 1897' (Aberdeen University, ms 987–8) p.98. Orde had bought the N. Uist estate from the trustees of Lord MacDonald in 1855 but, following the Crofters' Act of 1886, was on several occasions in dispute with tenants over their applications for fair rents. See also E. Richards, *A History of the Highland Clearances* (London & Canberra 1982) 498–9.
30. Carson 'Journal' *op. cit.*

31. *Laerde Brev*, letters of Peter Andreas Munch, vol. 3, translated by E. Uldall; extract courtesy of I. Fisher.

32. R. Carruthers, *The Highland Note-Book or Sketches and Anecdotes* (Edinburgh 1843) 244.

33. Sir Donald Monro, *Description of the Western Islands of Scotland called Hybrides* (Glasgow 1884) 32.

34. For example, see the Royal Commission on the Ancient and Historical Monuments of Scotland, *Argyll. An Inventory of the Monuments,* vol. 4 (Edinburgh 1982); also J.G. Dunbar and I. Fisher, *Iona A Guide to the Monuments* (HMSO 1995) 14.

35. W. Winter, *Old Shrines and Ivy* (Edinburgh 1892) 7.

36. M.E.M. Donaldson, *Wanderings in the Western Highlands and Islands* (2nd edn, Paisley 1923), Preface to First Edition 1.

37. *Ibid,* Preface to Second Edition 7–11.

9

'Intent upon my own race and place I wrote': Robert Louis Stevenson and Scottish History

Edward J. Cowan

> I saw rain falling and the rainbow drawn
> On Lammermuir. Hearkening I heard again
> In my precipitous city beaten bells
> Winnow the keen sea wind. And here afar,
> Intent on my own race and place, I wrote.[1]

In June 1881 Robert Louis Stevenson learned that Professor Aeneas Mackay was retiring from his chair of History and Constitutional Law at Edinburgh University. Since the job paid £250 and involved lecturing only in the summer months Louis wrote to Mackay, signifying his intention of applying for the position. Within days the professor had responded, putting the 31-year-old aspirant firmly in his place while recalling his unimpressive performance as an undergraduate. Displaying his famous lack of tact Stevenson riposted, 'You are not the only one who has regretted my absence from your lectures; but you were to me then, only part of a mangle through which I was being slowly and unwillingly dragged – part of a course which I had not chosen: part, in a word, of an organised boredom'.[2] The mangle might be an appropriate metaphor for History, or at least History teaching, but Stevenson was not destined, at this point in his career, to caw the handle. He knew himself that his qualifications were virtually non-existent but he requested references from anyone he could think of, including his close friend Sydney Colvin who was asked to use his best art to circumvent 'the difficulty of my never having done anything in History, strictly speaking'.[3] The chair episode illustrates Stevenson's arrogance and brashness as well his desire to establish a modicum of financial independence since his income was totally reliant upon the generosity of his father. Yet Louis was possessed of a consuming interest in the Scottish past inspired initially by the traditional tales of his nurse, the much adored Alison Cunningham or 'Cummy', and nurtured by a fascination for place, landscape and his own family origins. As a writer Stevenson embarked upon a lengthy quest to come to terms with what he distinguished as Scottish History but the historical grail eluded his grasp until the last years of his life in distant Vailima.

The previous September, while discovering the delights of Strathpeffer – 'no country, no place, was ever so delightful to my soul . . . I have been a Scotchman all my life, and denied my native land!' – he informed the historian, John Hill Burton, of his intention to write a 'circumstantial history' of the Union of 1707, 'an attempt to posit Scotland as she was at the epoch, socially, economically, religiously' and packing the text with colourful characters.[4] Writing from Davos in Switzerland, in December, he asked his father to despatch a wide range of books on the Highlands. In a characteristic flush of enthusiasm he was now planning three volumes – *Scotland and the Union*, *A Historical Description of the Highlands from 1700 the the Present Day*, and 'last and probably to be written when I am seventy', *The Stuarts in Exile*. But it was the second project, to be entitled *The Transformation of the Highlands* which truly seized his imagination, 'a real, fresh, lively and modern subject, full of romance and scientific interest'. In several days he drafted as many outlines but the fullest was communicated to his father.

> I begin the book immediately after the '15, as then began the attempt to suppress the Highlands.
>
> I. THIRTY YEARS' INTERVAL
> 1 Rob Roy.
> 2 The Independent Companies: the Watches.
> 3 Story of Lady Grange.
> 4 The Military Roads, and Disarmament: Wade and
> 5 Burt.
>
> II. THE HEROIC AGE
> 1 Duncan Forbes of Culloden.
> 2 Flora Macdonald.
> 3 The Forfeited Estates; including Hereditary Jurisdictions; and the admirable conduct of the tenants.
>
> III. LITERATURE HERE INTERVENES
> 1 The Ossianic Controversy.
> 2 Boswell and Johnson.
> 3 Mrs Grant of Laggan.
>
> IV. ECONOMY
> 1 Highland Economics.

2 The Reinstatement of the Proprietors.
3 The Evictions.
4 Emigration.
5 Present State.

V. Religion
1 The Catholics, Episcopals, and Kirk, and Society for the Propagation of Christian Knowledge.
2 The Men.
3 The Disruption.

Here was RLS's projected 'noble work' which was intent upon, as he curiously put it, 'touching the privates of the old mystery of race'. He initially intended to learn Gaelic but within a few weeks he had convinced himself that he could complete the project without it[5] – 'few things are written in that language or ever were' – and he, in company with numerous writers who have published on the topic since, was wrong. As one Gael observed in 1882, 'almost as much to be dreaded as Butcher Cumberland were the writers who commented on the Highlands without knowing anything about them',[6] and a knowledge of the language of the Garden of Eden was clearly essential.

It was characteristic of Stevenson that his project should commence with Rob Roy, an individual who, despite his fame, is not at all well documented[7] though he would doubtless have served as some kind of metaphor. The inclusion of Lady Grange (exiled to St Kilda by a husband as callous as she was demented), Flora Macdonald, Boswell and Johnson, and Anne Grant of Laggan's *Superstitions of the Highlands* (1811) is also unsurprising though the author protested that this was just 'a bird's-eye glance' and that all would change. Many of his other ideas were sound, and potentially pioneering, for at that point no history of the modern Highlands was available. The inclusion of the military material in Section 1 made perfect sense and he was already devouring Burt's *Letters*[8]. The striking absentee in Section II is Bonnie Prince Charlie. Louis planned a discussion of Ossian and 'the growth of the taste for Highland scenery'; a sampling of J&B was pretty well mandatory, though it is to be hoped that his own blend would have included the highly critical remarks of the terrible twosome made by Donald M'Nicol[9], who deserves to be much better known. But it is in his fourth and fifth sections that he demonstrated greatest originality. He would have been among the first to treat 'the odd inhuman problem of the great evictions' as part of the fabric of Scottish history and few in his day would have integrated the religious factor, 'wild, unknown and very surprising'[10], including 'The Men' or *Na Duine*, the evangelical lay preachers who in the nineteenth century had such an impact on Gaelic-speaking Scotland, in quite such an all-encompassing fashion. Although none of the planned historical works was ever to appear the frenzy of reading in which he indulged upon the subject was to inform much of his later literary production. In a very real and important sense it could be said that throughout his career Stevenson's Literature fed off his History.[11]

It must be significant that during the summer of '81 when he was so preoccupied with historical matters he produced, while at Pitlochry 'Thrawn Janet', 'The Body Snatchers' and 'The Merry Men'. At Braemar he worked on *Treasure Island* and from Davos in October he told his father that he was about to write an article on 'Burt, Boswell, Mrs Grant and Scott'. Shortly thereafter he confided that he might improve his chances of the chair by writing 'The Murder of Red Colin. A Story of the Forfeited Estates' which would no doubt incorporate what he distinguished as 'the beautiful story of the tenants', beautiful because while paying rents to the government they also paid them to their exiled chiefs. Clearly some of the material from the putative Highland history was to be diverted for literary purposes.

> I am just about . . . to write an odd little historical bypath of a tragedy: very picturesque in the circumstances; a story of an Agrarian murder, complicated with fidelity to chiefs, clan hatreds, an unjust trial, an attempted abduction in which Rob Roy's son figures as the foiled abductor – and you will note, it was a murderer whom he was to kidnap, which thickens the broth – all happening so late as 1752.

He had already picked out sites for illustrations, including a couple in Inveraray which he had never visited. The prototype of *Kidnapped*, which was not in fact published until 1886, was also to draw upon a book which his father had recently purchased for him in Inverness and which he later said should be bound in velvet and gold.[12]

As usual the long-suffering, if ever-obliging *pater*, Thomas, was requested to ship various publications for the project, including material on the trials of Rob Roy's sons, which, interestingly and significantly, were derived from references in the introduction to Sir Walter Scott's great novel. In some sense Louis was self-consciously continuing the work of Scott from both a literary and historical point of view. It has been suggested that RLS may have first acquired his interest in Rob Roy during boyhood visits to Bridge of Allan and Stirling. A native of the latter burgh, George Robert Gleig, published a novel, *Alan Breck*, in 1834, though it cannot be proved that Stevenson actually read it. What is certain is that in the autumn of 1881 a series of letters on Rob and his family appeared in the *Stirling Observer*.

Louis challenged one contributor, 'N. A.', whose letter essentially focused on the differing and incompatible reports about Rob's son, Robin Oig, to be found in the pages of the *Caledonian Mercury* as opposed to oral tradition. It was a debate which greatly exercised nineteenth-century people and which marked something of an acrimonious divide between academic and popular opinion. As an aspirant for the Edinburgh chair Stevenson adopted a rather high tone as he attempted to display his academic credentials and his skill at dialectic. 'N. A.' was unimpressed, dismissing his critic as an 'inexperienced student', unsympathetic to the vivid traditions 'still floating about in the minds of aged people'.[13] Meanwhile the coveted chair had followed the same route as the history, the electors choosing 'mediocre drones in preference to men of genius',[14] thus sparing a drone of genius a life of mediocrity.

Stevenson later claimed that *Kidnapped*, 'infinitely my best, and indeed my only good, story', was put together in five months at Bournemouth during 1885–6, but the plot had obviously been feeding upon his imagination for considerably longer. He announced to his American publisher, Scribner's, in January 1886 that the book was forthcoming – 'it is laid in 1749 and deals with kidnappers and Jacobites and wild Highlanders all about Scotland; the Scotch is kept as low as possible'.[15] In writing the novel he drew upon John L. Buchanan's *Travels in the Western Hebrides from 1782 to 1790* (Edinburgh 1793), as well as on his own experience, for example of the Isle of Earraid in 1870, which was also the setting for 'The Merry Men'. The story's progress was reflected in his correspondence – 'I have just murdered James Stewart semi-historically'; period and place had never been used before, 'why Scott let it escape him I do not know'; was Gregory's Mixture, a ghastly-tasting powder designed to cure children of imaginary illness long after Stevenson's time, a 'clan secret of the MacGregors' and the source of Rob's 'remarkable activity'? A letter signed 'Alan Breck Stewart' related that 'Colin Campbell is shot; and we are now lying on the top of a boulder within sight of the redcoats, the famous flight well begun'. By February 1886 he could announce to Charles Baxter, his friend and lawyer, that he was minded to dedicate *Kidnapped* to him. Baxter was delighted; the 'beautiful practice (of) putting a friend's name on a book (was) like a handgrasp that lives for ever'. His difficulties in finishing the book were resolved by the neat device of deciding upon a sequel.[16]

David Balfour as the author affectionately dubbed the novel and its sequel (titles were not a Stevensonian forte) is so well known as to require little comment. It is a romance in which History seldom intrudes yet is ever present, a novel of landscape – 'it seemed a hard country, this of Appin, for people to care as much about as Alan did' (*cap.* 17), and a novel of heart-pounding exhaustion all the way from the House of Shaws to the crossing of the Forth after hundreds of adventurous miles traversed through sea spray and wet heather. A story for boys (serialised as it originally was in the magazine *Young Folks*) was not the obvious medium for an in-depth analysis of Scottish history, but with much subtlety the author also contrived to send Davie on a journey of historical transition from the ford of Essendean – whence he was despatched by the lowland minister with the highland name, who added to his benediction the comfort of a bible and a folk panacea – to his ultimate destination of the British Linen Company's Bank in Edinburgh, founded in 1746 after the last Jacobite rising. Nowhere in literature is there a more colourful, more adventurous or more scenic transition from Calvinism to capitalism, with Davie's 'gallivantings' in an anachronistic wilderness framed, at beginning and end by the beacons of progress – Edinburgh 'smoking like a kiln' (*cap.* 2) and the well-tended fields of West Lothian, 'the comfortable, green, cultivated hills and the busy people of the field and sea' (*cap.* 26). History overtly impacts only occasionally as when Davie encounters the emigrant ship at Lochaline, the sound of mourning from the occupants piercing the heart. The Red Fox, Colin Campbell of Glenure, was an historical personage whose killer is still the subject of oral tradition and who met his end at the wood of Lettervore, a location at which, one suspects, just such an event might have been expected. The author's historical sympathies are not in doubt when, only two pages apart, David Balfour is told by by Cluny Macpherson that he is 'too nice and covenanting' (*cap.* 23), while Alan Breck is described as 'a treacherous child' (*cap.* 24).

And so the grand scheme for *The Transformation of the Highlands* metamorphosed into a novel centred on the assassination of a government rent collector, and literary fame triumphed over scholarly oblivion, since novelists who deal with insignificant historical themes have a much longer shelf-life than historians intent upon the bigger picture. It was, perhaps above all, a fortunate development, since, although *Kidnapped* is not great history, his *Transformation* would not necessarily have turned out to be memorable literature. Indeed, from what is known of RLS, plagued by illhealth and distracted by his flashing mind, a person who self-confessedly possessed 'a poetic character with no poetic talent' and who was 'constipated in the brains', it is inconceivable that he could ever have mustered the discipline to complete his ambitious historical project, for the absence of which David Balfour and Alan Breck provide some compensation.

Jenni Calder reminds us, quite forcefully, that Stevenson was not Scott,[17] and nor was he, but his attitude towards Sir Walter was highly ambiguous.

He was very conscious of his grandfather having accompanied Scott on the Northern Lights cruise, a tour of lighthouse inspection, in 1814. *The Pirate* was inspired by that voyage and it shadowed Louis's visit to Orkney and Shetland in 1869. He, like his father and most of their close associates, had a thorough knowledge of Scott and his works. He found *Waverley* 'poor and dull' while *The Fortunes of Nigel* was 'very strong and mature'. *Guy Mannering*, *Rob Roy* and *The Antiquary* were each three times better than *Waverley* though he thought the latter one of the best crafted of the novels. 'It is understandable that the love of the slap-dash and shoddy grew upon Scott with success'. He counselled his father against reading Lockhart's *Life of Scott*; no Waverley novel could match 'in power, blackness, bitterness and moral elevation ... Lockhart's narrative of the end', though he admitted that the novels were to be preferred for everyday reading – 'you may take a tonic daily but not a phlebotomy'. He could be highly critical of Scott but he nonetheless regarded him as one of the 'really great masters of narrative' who was possessed of 'the real creative brush'.[18] Yet Stevenson, like many Scottish writers, could not escape from Scott even though he spent much of his professional career trying to avoid the latter's obsession with detail. It is highly significant that *Kidnapped* was conceived as a kind of sequel to *Rob Roy*. He perhaps paid Scott the greatest compliment of all once he reached Samoa for Vailima was surely intended as an Abbotsford in the South Pacific.

Louis was, in fact, quite widely read in Scottish History before 1881 though, remarkably for one who was supposedly embarking upon a study of the Jacobite risings and their impact upon Highland history, the bulk of his reading had been on the subject of the covenanters, an antisyzygical approach to the Scottish past if ever there was one. It is well known that his first publication in 1866 was on the Pentland Rising (1666). For that project he had clearly plundered most of the main extant primary printed sources and he continued to trawl through covenanting literature as he was to do for the rest of his life. At the age of 18 he found Aikman preferable to the dense detail of Wodrow and he had already become acquainted with the latter's 'frightful' manuscripts in the Advocates' Library,[19] though it may be doubted whether he made much of them. Three years later he displayed true historical insight when a reading of Clarendon's *History* prompted the observation that 'one gets more real truth out of one avowed partisan than out of a dozen of your sham impartialists – wolves in sheep's clothing – simpering honestly as they suppress documents ... one wants to know not what people did, but why they did it – or rather why they thought they did it; and to know that, you should go to the men themselves. Their very falsehood is often more than another man's truth'.[20] Too many historians, and not only of the Scottish variety, have still failed to heed Stevenson's words.

In Germany and England he cultivated his nationalistic prejudices in the usual Scottish fashion. A perusal of George Sand prompted the thought that 'even the most wholesome food palleth after many days banquetting and History's little dishful of herbs (seems) at last preferable to the stalled ox of pampered fiction'.[21] By 1874, having put together, in manuscript form, a collection of covenanting stories, he was planning a book on *Four Great Scotsmen* – Knox, Hume, Burns and Scott. Burns and Knox had interested him for some time; two years earlier he had asked his mother to obtain the multi-volume *Works of John Knox* and Thomas McCrie's biography which afforded him much hilarity though he greatly admired its scholarship. Each of those individuals was to illustrate one of four great themes in Scottish history. The events of Knox's career, for example, were 'romantic and rapid, the character very strong, salient and worthy', offering much of interest 'to the future of Scotland.' David Hume the philosopher would represent (he thought) 'the urbane, cheerful, gentlemanly, letter-writing eighteenth century, full of niceness'. Burns would exemplify

> the sentimental side that there is in most Scotchmen, his poor troubled existence, how far his poems were his personally, and how far national, the question of the framework of Society in Scotland and its fatal effect upon the finest natures. Scott again, the ever delightful man, sane, courageous, admirable; the birth of Romance, in a dawn that was a sunset; snobbery, conservatism, the wrong thread in History and notably in that of his own land.[22]

As with so many Stevensonian historical enterprises the grand plan was never fulfilled. He expressed interest in the works of the sixteenth-century playwright, Sir David Lindsay, and in those of his contemporary, the great humanist, George Buchanan, and he flirted with a project linking the poets Alan Ramsay, Robert Fergusson and, once again, Burns, but he preferred to console himself with the spicier offerings of James Boswell.[23] Clearly Louis's approach to the Scottish past was as literary as it was historical and even the covenanting works intrigued him equally for their potential as literature as for their historical content.

The published essay on John Knox, and that on Burns which attracted so much critical flak at the time, are still worth reading, displaying as they do, flashes of alpha-minus in the Honours class. The man obviously wanted to be an historian just as many historians yearn to be writers.[24] What is noteworthy in Stevenson's voluminous correspondence, however, is his absence of interest in contemporary Scottish, or for that matter world, affairs. He could never have been a great authority on the past because he had virtually no interest in the present. While applauding Chris Harvie's valiant efforts to argue the relevance of *Prince Otto* and *Treasure Island* to the current political scene one can agree with J. C. Furnas that it is difficult to regard Stevenson 'as a significant political animal until he reached the South Seas'.[25]

The view that Stevenson only achieved full reconciliation with Scotland once he reached Samoa has become very fashionable with recent critics. Jenni Calder makes a convincing case for his need to 'come to terms with the Scottish past and his own background'.[26] Douglas Gifford, in a highly stimulating essay on Stevenson's first great unfinished novel, *The Master of Ballantrae* (1889) addresses the same point – 'he avoided the full task of evaluating his Scottish background'.[27] Frank McLynn regards the book as its author's 'greatest complete full-length work' and reiterates the obvious point that 'the struggle for the national soul between the contending traditions of Jacobitism and Calvinism' is common to all of Stevenson's Scottish novels.[28] Louis's vision, however, was not as narrow as this would suggest. Not all Lowlanders were Calvinists and not all Highlanders were of the Jacobite persuasion. As he had tantalisingly indicated in *Kidnapped* there were other traditions to take into account such as capitalism and commerce, the military, emigration, religion, the supernatural, and the folk tradition, not to mention Gaelic, Norse and the whole complex question of language. He had also long been aware of another, and this time a lowland, dualism – 'to pass a true judgement upon Knox and Burns implies a grasp upon the very deepest strain of Scottish thought ... for, in a sense, the first re-created Scotland, and the second is its most essentially national production'.[29]

The Master is notable as a study in ambiguity though it is perhaps more interesting as a documentation of Stevenson's inability to come to terms with the past (both his own and his country's) than it is as a satisfying work of fiction. Innovative techniques of narrative and plot do little to resolve the apparently unresolvable, with the consequence that the novel totally lacks historical conviction. As with *Kidnapped* the story begins at the end of a process; the author is interested in exploring the consequences of historical events yet, as his literary imagination takes over to investigate the nature of evil, credible history seems to be pushed to one side. Edward Purcell had noted that Stevenson's 'puzzling, enigmatic ethics' had hindered his desire to produce 'a great romance worthy of his genius'. Louis responded with a confession that such remarks were,

> all too true. It is where I fall, and fall almost consciously. I have the old Scotch presbyterian preoccupation about these problems; itself morbid; I have alongside of that a second, perhaps more – possibly less – morbid element – the dazzled

incapacity to choose, of an age of transition. The categorical imperative is ever with me but utters dark oracles. This is a ground almost of pity ... Ethics are my veiled mistress; I love them, but I know not what they are. Is this my fault? Partly, of course, it is; because I love my sins like other people. Partly my merit, because I do not take, and rest contented in, the first subterfuge.[30]

Although this admission was written in 1886 a similar ethical confusion survived to inform, or confuse, the tale of Ballantrae. If *Jekyll and Hyde* is a Scottish story which takes place in London *The Master* is a psychological tale which is set nowhere in particular. This was deliberate for, paradoxically, one essential way for the novelist to deal with History is to manipulate time and space. He would later rejoice that since Weir of Hermiston never existed the author was 'set free from any little irksome question of date'. He once observed, on a voyage at sea, that History was a godsend because he could 'put in time getting events coordinated and the narrative distributed, when my much-heaving numskull (*sic*) would be incapable of finish or fine style', thus subordinating the mechanical craft of History to the sophisticated creativity of Literature.[31] He told Bob Stevenson that before embarking on an historical novel a writer would often consult memoirs but that these do not teach 'the selective criterion'. The writer learns about selection through the practice of his art, 'in the crystallisation of day dreams, in changing not in copying fact, in the pursuit of the ideal, not in the study of nature'. Artistic insight is governed by 'a kind of ardour of the blood', which under the influence of knowledge and craft permits clear expression so that 'significance and charm, like a moon rising, are born above the barren juggle of mere symbols'.[32] One book which possibly influenced *The Master* is James Hogg's *Confessions of a Justified Sinner* (Edinburgh 1824) which Stevenson believed may have, in turn, owed something to the hand of John Gibson Lockhart, son-in-law and biographer of Scott. He claimed that he read Hogg's masterpiece in the early 1880s though he sensed that he had some previous knowledge of it, 'the common ground ... supplied by a common devotion to Covenanting literature'. Louis, however, 'never read a book that went on the same road with the *Sinner*'.[33] The same could be said of his own *Master of Ballantrae*.

RLS clearly had the greatest difficulty in satisfactorily concluding the latter novel. It was originally to be set near Kirkcudbright which is geographically at some remove from Ballantrae in Ayrshire. He admitted that the second part of the book was giving him problems. A year later he was still troubled by 'that damned ending' which hung over him 'like the arm of the gallows', the 'hardest job I ever had to do'. As late as 1894 he felt compelled to apologise for rushing its completion, under the twin pressures of his publisher and his cruising schedule.[34] David Daiches noticeably takes an almost purely historical approach in writing on 'Stevenson and Scotland'[35] wherein he correctly describes our writer as the genius of place, although place is strangely absent in *The Master*. Andrew Lang noted that the novel should have been entitled *The Master of Durrisdeer*,[36] but why on earth did the author use the name Durrisdeer at all when there was a perfectly good and historic place of the same name in Dumfriesshire? Why is there barely one convincing historical statement in the whole book? One possible answer, to be more fully developed below, is that in his experimental manipulation, or distortion, of time and space Stevenson anticipated what would be his ultimate resolution of the relationship between History and Literature from the safe haven of Samoa.

Kenneth Gelder has argued the supreme importance of the covenanting myth for the development of Stevenson's literary and historical imagination[37]. This point was anticipated by none other than S.R. Crockett in a *Bookman* article of 1893:

> In 'The Pentland Rising' Stevenson writes of a flame that would often rise from the grave, in a moss near Carnwath, of some of the poorer rebels; of how it crept along the ground, of how it covered the house of the murderer ... and scared him with its lurid glare ... This idea long haunted the imagination of the boy – the picture of the flame-wrapped house and the persecutor within, clammy terror sitting in the innards of his soul – an idea which came out of the same basket as the spiritual terrors of Dr Jekyll, Gordon Darnaway and Uncle Ebenezer ... shows Stevenson, even as a schoolboy, continually wandering round the confines of the other world and companying with the men of the time to whom such things were the sternest of realities...[38]

It may be suspected that Douglas Gifford had such matters in mind when he wrote of how, in *The Master*, Stevenson 'objectifies ... the relations of any creative and troubled mind with Scotland as a whole, and a kind of spiritual fragmentation which is universal'.[39] It is important to realise that Stevenson is not to be condemned for failing to confront his own past; one hundred years later Scottish historians have failed to come to terms, historiographically, with the mythos of the Covenant or of Jacobitism and certainly no-one has attempted the unenviable, and probably impossible, task of reconciling the two.[40]

When Stevenson honoured the (to him) slightly irritating S.R. Crockett with the evocative lines,

> Grey recumbent tombs of the dead in desert places,
> Standing-stones on the vacant wine-red moor,
> Hills of sheep, and the howes of the silent vanished races,
> And winds, austere and pure,[41]

he was imbued with the same mood which inspired his 'To My Wife' with its vision of rain on Lammermuir and the sound of Edinburgh's bells on 'the keen sea wind', while half a world away he wrote about his 'own race and place'.

J.C. Furnas is guilty of causing some damage, in an otherwise excellent book, when he remarks that Louis was greatly taken with the theories of Francis Galton on eugenics.[42] If he encountered such ideas, – as he surely did, universal as they were, – they may have been reinforced through his Californian experience since that state eagerly embraced the theory and it continued to sterilise people in the name of eugenics until only a few years ago. While the current fad for trying to make people of the past as politically correct as we fondly imagine ourselves to be is plainly ludicrous, it can safely be argued that Stevenson was not a serious eugenicist. 'I deny that there exists such a thing as a pure Saxon, and I think it more questionable if there be such a thing as a pure Celt'. Furthermore while he noted that Britain had become more 'pigmented' in his lifetime he denied that colour was 'an essential part of a man or a race'. In a memorable passage he told Adelaide Boodle who was about to go into mission work, 'you cannot change ancestral feelings of right and wrong without what is practically soul murder . . . remember that all you can do is to civilise the man in the line of his own civilisation, such as it is. And never expect, never believe in, thaumaturgic conversion'.[43] At Vailima he attempted to teach young Austin Strong some history. He found corroboration for his own views in E.A. Freeman's *Old English History for Children* (1869) but he had to admit that

> Scottish is the only history I know . . . it is a very good one for my purpose, owing to two civilisations having been face to face throughout, or rather Roman civilisation having been face to face with our ancient barbaric life and government, down to yesterday, to 1750 anyway;

and he proceeded to make some unflattering remarks about Scott's *Tales of a Grandfather*, which had all his 'damned defects' and all of his 'hopeless merit'. Scott, he claimed 'never knew, never saw, the Highlands; he was always a Borderer. He has missed that whole, long, strange pathetic story of our savages'.

Any interest in eugenics was tempered by his contact with the South Sea Islanders. Stevenson advised Sydney Colvin that in dealing with the Tahitians it was a good idea to invoke 'our Middle Ages, Highland clans etc.' in order to put them at their ease, a point which he reiterated in *In the South Seas*, an appeal to shared experience in which the barbarisms and superstitions of the Gaelic past met those of the contemporary South

Pacific. Louis knew that he had 'some historic sense, I feel that in my bones',[44] and he had high hopes of his *Footnote to History*,

> the history of a handful of men, where all know each other in the eyes, and live close in a few acres, narrated at length and with the seriousness of history. Talk of a modern novel; here is modern history. And if I had the misfortune to found a school, the legitimate historian might lie down and die, for he could never overtake his material.

The first chapter of the book, 'a history of nowhere in a corner', is brilliant. His anthropological approach would not disgrace the modern school of new historicism, but unfortunately, after his optimistic expectations, the book was a failure; as he said himself, 'it is not literature, only journalism and pedantic journalism'. As might have been predicted he was defeated by 'history extending to the present week . . . and where almost all the actors upon all sides are of my personal acquaintance'. Furthermore he did not believe that people were attracted to History for the purpose of reading, but rather for 'education and display' and he feared that few would be interested in Samoa 'with no population, no past, no future'. He had a similar problem with his story 'Rahero', 'a perfect folk tale . . . ancient as the granite rocks' but unappealing to those raised in the classical tradition. He had travelled far since his questioning of 'N. A.' in Stirling.[45]

So far as can be discerned Louis used 'race' in the sense of 'people' and especially with reference to his own people, the Stevensons, 'decent, reputable folk, following honest trades – millers, maltsters, and doctors, playing the character parts in the Waverley Novels with propriety, if without distinction'.[46] He showed some interest in his family history, as opposed to simply that of his father and grandfather, from early in 1888, expressing excitement when a correspondent told him that his surname was one of those used by the proscribed MacGregors; like many Scots he apparently wanted to be a Highlander. In researching his family history he recruited some pretty distinguished assistance – J.H. Stevenson the documentary historian, J.R.N. MacPhail the future sheriff and historian of the Highlands and Sir Herbert Maxwell, medievalist and placename scholar.[47] He missed out, though, on one of the greatest historians that Scotland produced in the nineteenth century – William Forbes Skene, author of the three-volume *Celtic Scotland*. Louis had apprenticed to Skene and Edwards but he did not at that time realise who Skene was.[48] He traced an ancestor to 1665 in the parish of Neilston, Renfrewshire – 'Can I really have found the tap-root of my illustrious ancestry at last? Souls of my fathers! What a giggle giggle-orious moment!' He eventually delighted in telling Bob Stevenson, his cousin, that their family came from Cunningham or

Clydesdale and were hence British folk, Cymry and Pict. 'We may have fought with King Arthur and known Merlin'. He continued, almost echoing or supplementing the oft-quoted passage in *Weir of Hermiston* that in the Scot 'there burns alive a sense of identity with the dead even to the twentieth generation':

> So much is certain of that strange Celtic descent that the past has an interest for it, apparently gratuitous, but fiercely strong. I wish to trace my ancestors a thousand years if I traced them by gallowses. It is not love, not pride, not admiration; it is an expansion of the identity, intimately pleasing and wholly uncritical. I suppose perhaps it is more to me who am childless and refrain with a certain shock from looking forwards.[49]

Such genealogical matters were something of a preoccupation with Stevenson during what would prove to be the last years of his life. When he wrote of his reluctance to face the future he had only six months to live. At the same time he was working on *Catriona* and *Weir of Hermiston* in which, as several critics have pointed out, he attempted to resolve the difficulties with his own immediate family. His response to his father's death, in May 1887, is difficult to chart. He later wrote that Thomas never accepted the condition 'of man's life or his own character and his inmost thoughts were ever tinged with Celtic melancholy'. It would hardly be surprising if there were difficulties between the two, since RLS was a free spirit dependent upon parental income, a situation grievously aggravated by his marriage to Fanny Osbourne in 1880. Thomas's religious devotion which stimulated the painful and well-documented personal disruption of 1873, his well-intentioned yet irritating criticisms of his son's literary output, and his creeping dementia which led to his 'changeling' status, generated further tensions, thus contributing, in no small measure, to the classically difficult conundrum of the father-son relationship, a perennial theme which has attracted a number of Scottish writers apart from Stevenson. Yet by the end of the month RLS was working on a version of his grandfather's report on the building of the Bell Rock lighthouse, initially using the late Thomas's copy. The account was later incorporated into the posthumously published *Records of a Family of Engineers*, the exercise possibly representing an act of filial pietas and contrition. As with so much else in his life Louis's relationship with his father was ambiguous. A moving letter of 1878 told his parents how much he loved them though it was apparently never sent. A year before Thomas's death Louis proudly and emphatically told his publisher that the 'sea-lights in Scotland are signed with our name'. His father enjoyed great distinction in that particular field. 'I might write books till 1900 and not serve humanity so well'. It filled him with impatience 'to see the little, frothy bubble that attends the author his son, and compare it with the obscurity in which the better man finds his reward'.[50]

Unable to attend the funeral Louis worked on 'Ticonderoga', 'a ballad in a genteel muddle of Lord Macaulay and the old ones'. One critic[51] complained that he made the whole ballad turn on the mystery of a name:

> It sang in his humming ears
> It hummed in his waking head
> The name Ticonderoga
> The utterance of the dead.[52]

But that, of course, is precisely the point. The mystery of a name was more than enough for Stevenson; he was utterly entranced by place, a point well made in his essay on Fife:

> History broods over that part of the world like the easterly haar. Even on the map, its long row of Gaelic place-names bear testimony to an old and settled race. Of these little towns, posted along the shore as close as sedges, each with its bit of harbour, its old weather-beaten church or public building, its flavour of decaying prosperity and decaying fish, not one but has its legend, quaint or tragic: Dunfermline in whose royal towers the king may be still observed (in the ballad) drinking the blood-red wine; somnolent Inverkeithing, once the quarantine of Leith; Aberdour, hard by the monastic isle of Inchcolm, hard by Donibristle where the 'bonny face was spoiled'; Burntisland where, when Paul Jones was off the coast, the Reverend Mr. Shirra had a table carried between tidemarks, and publicly prayed against the rover at the pitch of his voice and his broad lowland dialect; Kinghorn where Alexander 'brak's neckbane' and left Scotland to the English wars; Kirkcaldy, where the witches once prevailed extremely and sank tall ships and honest mariners in the North Sea...[53]

Herein RLS presents the perfect evocation of history, literature and tradition which make up the Scottish past. Dunfermline and Donibristle are both associated with ballads, respectively 'Sir Patrick Spens' and 'The Bonnie Earl o Moray'. Burntisland's lengthy history is reduced to an anecdote about prayer against the American privateer, Paul Jones. Notice of Alexander III's fatal accident at the cliffs of Kinghorn in 1286, an event which led to the Scottish Wars of Independence, contains a clever allusion to Burns' 'Tam o Shanter'. Kirkcaldy was more famous as centre of witches than it was as the birthplace of Adam Smith.

It is still the case that Scottish places – and perhaps the same is true for locations worldwide – are more famous for their literary than for their historical associations. Stevenson was well aware of this point and he also knew who was largely responsible:

The character of a place is often most perfectly expressed in its associations. An event strikes root and grows into a legend when it has happened amongst congenial surroundings ... To a man like Scott, the different appearances of nature seemed each to contain its own legend readymade which it was his to call forth.[54]

In 'A Gossip on Romance' he remarked that 'The Lady of the Lake' is 'just such a story as a man would make up for himself, walking, in the best health and temper, through just such scenes as it is laid in'. Hence long after the book, with its 'slovenly verses', has been cast aside 'the scenery and adventures remain present to the mind'. Louis was intrigued by the idea that 'there is a fitness in events and places', that the right kind of thing should fall out in the right kind of place. He was particularly attracted by 'the genius of place and moment', by certain locations where 'something must have happened ... and perhaps ages back, to members of my race'. To such places he was tempted to fit a story, an idea which he had long possessed; a visit to Orkney when he was 18 prompted the reflection that he 'knew nothing so suggestive of legend, so full of superstition, so stimulating to a weird imagination, as the nooks and corners and bye-ways of such a church as St Magnus, in Kirkwall'. Five years later he could observe that 'there are names that stir in us strange chords, awaken fanciful representations of the places'. Americans were already visiting one of his favourite hostelries, the Hawes Inn, at Queensferry because it had been mentioned in *The Antiquary*, but he was convinced that the place held some other appeal – 'there is some story unrecorded or not yet complete, which must express the meaning of that inn more fully'.[55] RLS of course was happy to supply the want; it was a place to meet one's kidnapper.

The years 1891–4 were the most productive of Stevenson's literary career, apart from the *annus mirabilis* of 1881, and that of 1886 according to McLynn, and once again he had the twin steeds of History and Literature harnessed to a careering chariot. At Vailima he completed *Catriona*, 'nearer what I mean by fiction' than anything so far accomplished. He also worked on *Weir of Hermiston*, *The Young Chevalier*, a story about the Forty-five rebellion, and *Heathercat*. At the same time he produced many of his South Sea tales, notably the near-perfect *The Beach of Falesa* and his non-fictional *Footnote to History*, a follow-up to the disappointing *In the South Seas*, a book of which Fanny disapproved because he actually carried out research for the project instead of relying upon his imagination. During those years he was also heavily involved in the politics of the islands, firing off broadsides to the London *Times*, meeting with activists on all sides, Samoans, diplomats and government officials while, for a time, he was highly exhilarated to be caught in the midst of tribal warfare.

In pursuit of his various literary projects projects he read furiously in the works and state papers of the later covenanting era as well as devouring materials from the late eighteenth and early nineteenth centuries for *Weir*. He had always self-confessedly been 'a purchaser and a student of covenanting books' to many of which he now returned. In August 1893 he confided to Henry James that he was impatient with fiction and was rapturously reading Fountainhall's *Decisions*, formless and 'inexpressibly dreary' though it was – 'it's like walking in a mine underground, and with a damned bad lantern, and picking out pieces of ore'. Such a volume suited his mood.

> And Fountainhall is prime, two big folio volumes, and all dreary, and all true, and all as terse as an obituary; and about one interesting fact on an average in twenty pages, and ten of them unintelligible from technicalities. There's literature, if you like! It feeds; it falls about you genuine like rain. Rain: nobody has done justice to rain in literature yet: surely a subject for a Scot. But then you can't do rain in that ledger-book style that I am trying for – or between a ledger-book and an old ballad. How to get over, how to escape from, the besotting *particularity* of fiction.

In the course of his researches he discovered that the covenanting classics, which he had consumed as a youth in the Advocates' Library, were the true source of his literary inspiration.[56]

He also renewed his acquaintance with the Icelandic sagas in the translations of William Morris and Eirikr Magnusson.[57] Just when he first encountered the medieval vernacular prose narratives is uncertain but in 1881 he fulsomely praised Morris's rather odd verse translation of *Volsunga Saga* and he later made passing reference to George Dasent's *The Story of Burnt Njal*.[58] Stevenson and the sagas (the supreme blend of history and literature) were made for each other; the saga style perfectly suited one who had declared war on the adjective and the optic nerve.[59] Louis personally thanked Morris for his *Saga Library* achievement though he criticised the artifice employed in his rather contrived and deliberately archaic translations. A gift from Rider Haggard of his *Eric Brighteyes* (London 1891), 'a romance founded on the Icelandic saga', elicited the admission that RLS had been planning to try his hand at a similar project. His enthusiasm did not diminish – 'I cannot get enough of sagas; I wish there were nine thousand: talk about realism!' He did, however, experiment with a saga fragment in 'The Waif Woman. A Cue from a Saga' which due to his wife's misgivings was not published until after his death. Fanny objected that Louis had lifted the piece directly from Morris and Magnusson's translation of *Eyrbyggja Saga*, 'and the few changes made, to my mind, do not improve the thing'. In fact RLS considerably altered the translated text, not least in changing the names of some of the original characters, and he succeeded in producing quite a satisfying short story, albeit one that was written in saga-ese. It may be that Fanny feared that the acquisitive, grasping central character, Aud, might be identified with herself![60] The value of the sagas for Scottish history had been recognised in the eighteenth century and subsequently developed by a number of scholarly commentators, including Scott who published a long abstract of *Eyrbyggja Saga* in Weber and Jamieson's *Illustrations of Northern Antiquities* (Edinburgh 1814), so that once again RLS was following in the footsteps of the master. By Stevenson's time a central figure in saga publishing was David Douglas who was a friend of the family.[61]

Long before his years of exile proper RLS was often to be found teetering on the Kailyard dyke, and he occasionally tumbled off as in 'An Old Scots Gardener' (1871), 'Pastoral' (1887) and 'The Manse' (1887) while his habit of reprinting early pieces in later collections tended to suggest that such attachments never entirely left him. The burns and mountains around Pitlochry were with ease transposed to Saranac. Certain correspondents, notably Alison Cunningham and S. R. Crockett could prompt a stream of sentimentality. 'The clearest burn in the world' was 'that which drums and pours in cunning wimples in that glen behind Glencorse old kirk'. At sea, in the Paumotu, he brilliantly and powerfully evoked the aspirations of youth in his vision of Rutherford's Bar. Yet the indescribable longing of exile is a reality which cannot be dismissed by critics who have seldom ventured north of Potters Bar or of Loch Lomond. It comes through in hundreds of emigrant letters of the period. Once established at Vailima it must have seemed entirely natural to him to promote his own personal cult of exile. He responded to an invitation to attend the bicentennial Burns Exhibition with a reluctant refusal –

> I have said my last farewell to the hills and the heather and the lynns ... I have gone into far lands to die, not stayed like Burns to mingle in the end with Scottish soil. I shall not ever return like Scott for the last scene. Burns Exhibitions are over. 'Tis a far cry to Lochawe from tropical Vailima.[62]

He happily confessed to being homesick. He thought that he and J.M. Barrie were rather 'Scotty Scots'; 'my own Scotchness' he wrote 'tends to intermittency, but is at times erisypelitous – if that be rightly spelt', which it was not, but which nonetheless communicated the idea that love of country was a disease. 'It is a singular thing that I should live here in the South Seas under conditions so new and striking, and yet my imagination so continually inhabit that cold old huddle of gray hills from which we come'.[63] And yet he could have predicted that such sentiments would overwhelm him. They were present in both 'The Foreigner at Home' (1882) and in 'The Scot Abroad' (1883). He described himself as a man 'infatuated with the interests of the great Anglo-Saxon Commonwealth' but crucially he was also a Scot, 'one of a people imperially one; domestically different: in a back-kitchen way still managing its own affairs; and in every point, by law, faith, habit and tradition clinging to its not very beautiful ancestral pattern'.[64] He believed that 'all races are better away from their own country' but he could not, nor did he have any wish to, break the ties that bind.

In 1881 he produced one of his greatest creations in 'Thrawn Janet'. He returned to Janet's parish of Balwearie for *Weir of Hermiston*.[65] Louis mischievously mentioned that the story was 'set about Hermiston in the Lammermuirs'. Sydney Colvin appended a laborious note to the effect that, in his view, Hermiston was located in Upper Tweeddale but that it borrowed elements from Glencorse and the Pentlands. As the book unfolds it becomes apparent that Balwearie is in the presbytery of Ayr, so placing it to the west of the southern upland watershed; in other words it is many places and nowhere. The author invents, or borrows, placenames to render his fictitious parish more real – Deil's Hag, Francie's Cairn, Cauldstaneslap. But there is another story that, curiously, also returns to Balwearie, and that is *Heathercat*, a name with which Alan Breck was once dignified (*cap.* 16). Unfortunately it contains only three short chapters and is thus the poor wee sister of the unfinished *Weir of Hermiston*. In the opening passage there are echoes of Louis's genealogical and antiquarian interests. The landscape is clearly one in which important historical events have taken place and will do so again.

> It is a land of many rain-clouds; a land of much mute history, written there in prehistoric symbols. Strange green raths are to be seen commonly in the country, above all by the kirkyards; barrows of the dead, standing stones; beside these, the faint, durable footprints and handmarks of the Roman; and an antiquity older perhaps than any, and still living and active – a complete Celtic nomenclature and a scarce-mingled Celtic population. These rugged and grey hills were once included in the boundaries of the Caledonian Forest. Merlin sat here below his apprentice and lamented Gwendolen; here spoke with Kentigern; here fell into his enchanted trance. And the legend of his slumber seems to body forth the story of that Celtic race, deprived for so many centuries of their authentic speech, surviving with their ancestral inheritance of melancholy perversity and patient, unfortunate courage.[66]

Here is a place with a past, precisely in the sense in which it is absent in some of Stevenson's other novels. Here surely is a place moulded by the centuries and waiting for stirring events to happen, such as those which, according to Wodrow's *Select Biographies*, had impacted upon RLS's colourful collateral ancestor, John the land-labourer who suffered deprivation and delusion in the name of the covenant.[67] Here is a place where covenanting conventicles are held beside standing stones of the prehistoric era. The third chapter, 'The Hill-end of Drumlowe' is a wonderful piece of writing. Louis once confessed, 'I am a child of the Covenanters – whom I do not love, but they are mine after all, my father's and my mother's – and they had their merits too, and their ugly beauties, and grotesque heroisms, that I love them for, the while I laugh at them'.[68] And laugh at them he does.

> They were the last of the faithful; God, who had averted His face from all the other countries in the world still leaned from Heaven to observe, with swelling sympathy, the doings of his moorland remnant ... And over against them was the army of the hierarchies, from the men Charles and James Stuart, on to King Lewie and the Emperor; and the scarlet Pope, and the muckle black devil himself, peering out the red mouth of hell in an ecstasy of hate and hope. 'One pull more!' he seemed to cry; 'one pull more and it's done. There's only Clydesdale and the Stewartry, and the three Bailieries of Ayr, left for God'.[69]

More placenames enliven the parish topography. A younger (and sexier) Thrawn Janet is introduced, her skirt 'kilted very high', drinking, daffing and laughing with Hell Haddo on a mound of heather. The story was to be set in the Killing Times, taking its characters to Darien and Carolina. To speculate on how *Heathercat* would have turned out is futile but what is present in these three fragments is a veritable kingdom of the mind, an imagined place inhabited by believable people who are about to be exposed to the forces of History. There is no doubt whatsoever that Stevenson was writing about his own ancestors. He told cousin Bob that this was an attempt at a real historical novel, 'to present the whole field of time; the race – our own race – the west land and Clydesdale blue bonnets, under the influence of their last trial, when they got to a pitch of organisation in madness that no other peasantry has ever made an offer at'. His aim was to harness all the 'weary reading' of his youth, supplemented by a mass of more recently available material.[70] Fiction was the device which allowed him to come to terms with his own past and with Scottish History. It might be said, as with another Scottish writer, that for Stevenson it was a case of 'out of the world and into Balwearie'.[71] Another device which he employed was temporal and spatial dislocation with which ideas, it was suggested above, he began to experiment in *The Master*. Such manipulation implies a highly confident sense of History.

In his *Humble Remonstrance* Stevenson wrote that the art of narrative is the same whether it is applied to the selection and illustration of a real series of events or an imaginary series. Henry James had insisted on the sanctity of truth for the novelist, but to Stevenson truth was a word of very debatable propriety, not only for the labours of the novelist, but for those of the historian as well. No art can successfully 'compete with life' – the phrase is James's – 'not even History built indeed of indisputable facts ... The real art that dealt with life directly was that of the first men who told their stories round the savage camp-fire'.[72]

This chapter has attempted to argue that Robert Louis Stevenson was profoundly influenced by his sense of Scottish History and that his greatest literary achievements were fuelled by deeply-rooted preoccupations with the Scottish past. It could be further argued that such was Stevenson's historical consciousness that it is pointless, as so many critics have done, to separate his Literature from his History. In 'Pulvis et Umbra' he exclaimed,

> Ah if I could show you this! if I could show you these men and women, all the world over, in every stage of history, under every abuse of error, under every circumstance of failure, without hope, without help, without thanks, still obscurely fighting the lost fight of virtue, still clinging, in the brothel or on the scaffold to some rag of honour, the poor jewel of their souls![73]

In such attractive aspirations Louis showed himself to be the soul-mate of his hero, Robert Burns, who could look upon the foibles of his fellow human beings with a brother's eye. History was, for Stevenson, like Literature, an exploration of the human predicament. In 1868 he had written that 'five square miles of a Scotch hillside would take a man a lifetime to describe'.[74] A career of writing and travelling took him far from Scotland to many exotic locations and experiences which he captured with his pen in essay, story and novel, but at the end of his short life he was still trying to describe that hillside. At the same time, like Scott before him, he was artfully constructing his own history; as he told Bob Stevenson, his letters would 'form a history of myself', along with his numerous publications. That history was never completed because, when death struck his life was unfinished. Although he was on the brink of achieving reconciliation between his own and Scotland's past the quest was not yet quite fulfilled. He once wrote that 'the worst historian has a clearer view of the period he studies than the best of us can hope to form of that in which we live'.[75] When Stevenson's life truly took on meaning at Vailima so too did his understanding of the past. Great epochal change was not what fascinated him but rather 'the essential identity of man'; historiography was to him less interesting than historical sources which, like fiction, could elucidate 'the truly mingled tissue of man's nature, and how huge faults and shining virtues cohabit and persevere in the same character'.[76] History for Stevenson was most attractive when it was most personalised, when it embraced the experience of his own folk, a limited vision perhaps, but one which in his case marked the acquisition of some historical understanding, which might in turn, had he been spared, have led to some profound historical insights as his family expanded to include the native peoples of the South Seas as well as his world-wide readership. He once fancied that he had opposed Agricola, had stood with the Picts, had rallied round MacBeth, had participated in the siege of St Andrews castle, had engaged on border raids with the Elliots, had assisted in the Fifteen rebellion, had established a plantation in St Kitts, had accompanied Scott to Shetland and had helped to build the Bell Rock lighthouse.[77] So close to the Scottish past was he, so much was it a part of his very being, that it informed all of his greatest work whether Scottish in theme or otherwise. To be Scots was indeed erysipelatous and incurable. On the Isle of Apemama in 1889 he experienced the recurring vision of his beloved Pentland Hills and the view over his native Edinburgh to the towns of Fife. Once again the calls of his ancestors invited him to step into their History and his own, an overture which, throughout his life, he found irresistible,

> The voice of generations dead
> Summons me, sitting distant, to arise,
> My numerous footsteps nimbly to retrace,
> And, all mutation over, stretch me down
> In that devoted city of the dead.[78]

Notes

An earlier version of this paper was presented at the Association for Scottish Literary Studies Annual Conference in May 1994 in the Advocates' Library, Edinburgh. The theme was 'From Edinburgh to Samoa. The Shifting Identities of Robert Louis Stevenson'.

1. Robert Louis Stevenson, *Collected Poems* (ed.) Janet Adam Smith (2nd edn. London 1971) 326.
2. *The Letters of Robert Louis Stevenson* (eds.) Bradford A. Booth and Ernest Mehew, 8 vols (New Haven and London 1994–5) 810,817. £250 was the notional annual allowance which RLS received from his father, Frank McLynn *Robert Louis Stevenson A Biography* (London 1993) 183. His financial dependency had long been a source of anxiety and embarrassment, *Letters* 176.

3. *Letters*, 810. On the chair see also 813–4, 818–21, 823–5.

4. *Letters*, 715, 718, 719, 721.

5. *Letters*, 749, 764, 765. By 1894 he considered that 'the most philosophical language is the Gaelic . . . and the most useless'. *Letters* 2782.

6. J.G. Mackay, 'The Misrepresentation of Highlanders and their History' *Glasgow Highland Association* (Glasgow 1882)

7. W.H. Murray, *Rob Roy MacGregor his life and times* (Edinburgh 1982) *passim*.

8. Edward Burt, *Letters from a Gentlemen in the North of Scotland* 2 vols. (London 1754, rep. 1974).

9. Donald McNicol, *Remarks on Dr. Johnson's Journey to the Hebrides* (Edinburgh 1779).

10. *Letters*, 765.

11. In the heady weeks of December 1880 RLS requested an impressive range of books in preparation for the project. In addition to those mentioned above, others included were *Culloden Papers Comprising An Extensive and Interesting Correspondence from the year 1625 to 1748* (London 1815), Mark Napier *Memorials of John Graham of Claverhouse, Viscount Dundee* 3 vols (Edinburgh 1862), Sir James Dalrymple *Memoirs of Great Britain and Ireland (1681–1692)* (Edinburgh 1788), Martin Martin *A Description of the Western Islands of Scotland* (London 1703), John Macculloch *A Description of the Western Islands of Scotland* 3 vols.(London1819), John Knox *A View of the British Empire, More Especially Scotland* 2 vols. (London 1785), David Stewart *Sketches of the character, manners, and present state of the Highlanders of Scotland* 2 vols. (2nd. edtn. Edinburgh 1822), Thomas Pennant *A Tour in Scotland and Voyage to the Hebrides* (Chester 1772), Sir George Mackenzie *General View of the Agriculture of the Counties of Ross and Cromarty* (Edinburgh 1813), *Report on the Trial of Patrick Sellar* (Edinburgh 1816), John Walker *An Economical History of the Hebrides and Highlands of Scotland* 2 vols. (Edinburgh 1808), James Robertson *General View of the Agriculture of the County of Inverness* (Edinburgh 1808), John Smith *General View of the Agriculture of the County of Argyll* (Edinburgh 1798), *Spalding Club Miscellany Three* (Aberdeen 1846), James Brome *Travels over England Scotland and Wales* (London 1700), *The Correspondence of Robert Wodrow* (ed.) Thomas MacCrie 3 vols. *Wodrow Society* (Edinburgh 1842–3), Alexander Auld *Ministers and Men in the Far North* (Wick 1868), John Kennedy *Days of the Fathers in Ross-shire* (Edinburgh 1861), Hugh Miller *Sutherland As it Was and Is: or How a Country May Be Ruined* (Edinburgh 1843) as well as various volumes of *The Statistical Account of Scotland* (ed.) Sir John Sinclair 21 vols. (Edinburgh 1792–9), *Letters* 748, 750–1, 758, 763.

12. *Letters*, 862, 865, 867, 2624. The volume in question was *The Trial of James Stewart in Aucharn in Duror of Appin, for the Murder of Colin Campbell of*

Glenure ... (Edinburgh 1753). It is bound with *A Supplement to the Trial of James Stewart By a By-stander* (London 1753) and *An Authentick Copy of the Dying Speech of James Stewart*. It is now at Princeton. He also possessed Hugo Arnot *A Collection and Abridgement of Celebrated Criminal Trials in Scotland from ad 1536 to 1784* (Edinburgh 1785) and J.H. Burton *Narratives from Criminal Trials in Scotland* (Edinburgh 1852), see *Letters* 865 and note.

13. *Letters*, 854 and n., 865 and n.; David B. Morris *Robert Louis Stevenson and the Scottish Highlands* (Stirling 1929) 62–72, 130; J.A. MacCulloch *Robert Louis Stevenson and the Bridge of Allan* (Glasgow 1927) 83–5. See also the supplementary information supplied to RLS by Professor A. C. Fraser, a descendant of Campbell of Glenure's brother, *Letters* 1659, 1717.

14. *Letters*, 3, 246 n.

15. *Letters*, 1928, 1518.

16. *Letters*, 1527, 1528, 1533, 1554 and note, 1605, 1614.

17. Jenni Calder, *R.L.S. A Life Study* (London 1980) 84, 117. See too Andrew Noble 'Highland History and Narrative Form in Scott and Stevenson' in *Robert Louis Stevenson* (ed.) Andrew Noble (London 1983) 134–187.

18. *Letters*, 254, 279, 1201.

19. *Letters*, 39, 57. James Aikman *Annals of the persecution in Scotland: from the Restoration to the Revolution* (Edinburgh 1842), Robert Wodrow *The history of the sufferings of the Church of Scotland from the Restauration to the Revolution* 2 vols (Edinburgh 1721). RLS probably used the more recent edition, 4 vols. (Glasgow 1828–30). Two other works by Wodrow to which he made reference were – *Collections upon the lives of the reformers and most eminent ministers of the Church of Scotland* 2 vols. Maitland Club (Edinburgh 1842) and *Analecta, or, Materials for a history of remarkable providences mostly relating to Scotch ministers and Christians* 4 vols. Maitland Club (Edinburgh 1842–3). He was also familiar with Patrick Walker *Biographia Presbyteriana* (Edinburgh 1827) and John Howie *The Scots Worthies* (Edinburgh 1775) which he described as 'a rotten book', *Letters* 547, 554.

20. *Letters*, 89.

21. *Letters*, 184.

22. *Letters*, 234.

23. *Letters*, 198, 225, 424, 438. He was also, of course, at the same time sampling many other works British and foreign, literary and historical. He later considered editing Robert Henryson, James I's 'Scots Quhair' and Gavin Douglas for the *English Poets* series, *Letters* 632.

24. A writer with whom RLS can be constructively compared is his slightly older contemporary, Andrew Lang (1844–1912) whose literary endeavours embraced essays, poetry, ballads, reviews, fairy tales, mythology, anthropology

and much editorial work. In later life he turned to Scottish history in such works as the four volume *A History of Scotland* (1900–1907), *James VI and the Gowrie Conspiracy* (1902) and *John Knox and the Reformation* (1905). He also wrote about Jacobite topics as well as Scott and Scottish Literature and he provided an introduction to the Swanston edition of the *Works of RLS* (1911). The two men were friends and correspondents. See Roger Lancelyn Green *Andrew Lang A Critical Biography with a Short-title Bibliography of the Works of Andrew Lang* (Leicester 1946).

25. Christopher Harvie, 'The Politics of Stevenson' 116–22, J.C. Furnas 'Stevenson and Exile' 138 in *Stevenson and Victorian Scotland* (ed.) Jenni Calder (Edinburgh 1981).

26. Calder, *R.L.S.*, 84.

27. Douglas Gifford, 'Stevenson and Scottish Fiction: The Importance of The Master of Ballantrae' in *Stevenson and Victorian Scotland* 68.

28. McLynn, *Stevenson* 302–3.

29. *Familiar Studies of Men and Books* 7. Unless otherwise indicated all references to Stevenson's *Works* are to the *Vailima Edition* 24 vols. (London 1922).

30. *Letters*, 1562.

31. *Letters*, 2542, 2231.

32. *Letters*, 1148.

33. *Letters*, 2322.

34. *Letters*, 1974, 2009, 2132, 2153 and note.

35. David Daiches, 'Stevenson and Scotland' in *Stevenson and Victorian Scotland*.

36. *Robert Louis Stevenson: The Critical Heritage* (ed.) Paul Maixner (London 1981) 352.

37. *Robert Louis Stevenson: The Scottish Stories and Essays* (ed.) Kenneth Gelder (Edinburgh 1989) 5–10.

38. S.R. Crockett, 'The Apprenticeship of R. L. S.' in *Robert Louis Stevenson. A Bookman Extra Number* (London 1913) 70–1.

39. Gifford, 'Stevenson and Scottish Fiction', 86.

40. For a discussion of Scottish historiography in Stevenson's time see Colin Kidd '*The Strange Death of Scottish History* revisited: Constructions of the Past in Scotland, c. 1790–1914' *Scottish Historical Review* lxxvi, 1 (April 1997) 86–102.

41. *Collected Poems*, 284. For an important, sympathetic account of Crockett see Islay M. Donaldson *The Life and Work of Samuel Rutherford Crockett* (Aberdeen 1989).

42. J.C. Furnas, *Voyage to Windward. The Life of Robert Louis Stevenson* (London 1952) 241–2.

43. *Letters*, 2389, 2755, 2782.
44. *Letters*, 2152 and note, 2357.
45. *Letters*, 2367, 2368, 2378, 2408.
46. *Records of a Family of Engineers*, 411.
47. J.H. Stevenson was best known as an editor of texts; possibly his best-remembered work is *Scottish heraldic seals: royal, ecclesiastical, collegiate, burghal, personal* (Glasgow 1940). J.R.N. MacPhail was editor of four volumes of *Highland Papers* (Edinburgh 1914–34) for the Scottish History Society. Herbert Maxwell published a number of books on Scottish History including *Scottish Land-names: their origin and meaning. Rhind Lectures in Archaeology 1893* (Edinburgh 1894).
48. W.F. Skene, *Celtic Scotland* 3 vols 2nd. edtn. (Edinburgh 1886–90). He earlier produced *The Highlanders of Scotland* (Edinburgh 1836). 'Tell some of your journalist friends with a good style to popularise old Skene; or say your prayers and read him for yourself; he was a Great Historian – and I was his blessed clerk and did not know it; and you will not be in a state of grace about the Picts till you have studied him'. *Letters*, 2782.
49. *Letters*, 2629, 2744.
50. *Letters*, 545, 1579, 1827A, 1831, 1832. See also the curiously detached 'Thomas Stevenson Civil Engineer' which originally appeared in *The Contemporary Review* (June 1887) and was later collected in *Memories and Portraits*.
51. *Critical Heritage*, 371.
52. *Collected Poems*, 227; *Letters* 1827.
53. 'The Coast of Fife', 291–2.
54. 'Picturesque Notes on Edinburgh', 27.
55. 'A Gossip on Romance', 189–192, 201–2; *Letters* 76, 323.
56. *Letters*, 2621, 2704. In addition to *The Decisions of the Lords of Council and Session from June 6 1678 to July 30th 1712 collected by the Honourable Sir John Lauder of Fountainhall* (Edinburgh 1759–61) his reading included Robert Law *Memorialls; or, The Memorable Things that Fell Out Within this Island of Britain from 1638 to 1684* (Edinburgh 1819), *A Cloud of Witnesses for the Royal Prerogatives of Jesus Christ: or, The Last Speeches and Testimonies of those who have suffered for the Truth in Scotland since the year 1680* (Glasgow 1714), Alexander Shields *A Hind Let Loose* (Glasgow 1687) and *The Life and Death of Mr James Renwick; with a Vindication of the heads of his dying testimony etc.* (Edinburgh 1724), J. Murray Graham *The Annals and Correspondence of the Viscount and First and Second Earls of Stair* (Edinburgh 1875), Hugh Mackay of Scourie *Memoirs* Bannatyne Club (Edinburgh 1833), Alexander Fergusson *The Laird of Lag* (Glasgow 1886). In researching *Heathercat* he requested *The Darien Papers: Being a Selection of original Letters and Official Documents Relating*

to the Establishment at Darien by the Company of Scotland . . . 1695–1700 (Edinburgh 1849), *State papers and Letters Addressed to William Carstares* . . . (Edinburgh 1774), *A Selection from the Papers of the Earls of Marchmont . . . Illustrative of Events from 1685 to 1750* (ed.) Sir G.H. Rose (Edinburgh 1831), *Correspondence of George Baillie of Jerviswood, 1702–1708* (ed.) Gilbert Elliot, Earl of Minto (Edinburgh 1842) and *Family papers at Caldwell 1496–1853* (Glasgow 1854).In this same period he purchased E.W. Robertson *Scotland Under Her Early Kings* 2 vols. (Edinburgh 1862) and considered joining the Scottish History Society. See *Letters* 2610, 2652, 2665, 2666, 2805 and notes.

57. *The Story of Grettir the Strong* (London 1869), *Three Northern Love Stories and other tales* (London 1875). Of the volumes translated by Morris and Magnusson and collected in the *Saga Library* series, the following had appeared before Stevenson's death: *The Story of Howard the Halt. The Story of the Banded Men. The Story of Hen Thorir* (London 1891), *The Story of the Ere-Dwellers (Eyrbyggja Saga) with The Story of the Heath-Slayings (Heidarviga Saga)* (London 1892) and *The Stories of the Kings of Norway Called the Round World (Heimskringla)* (London 1893)

58. William Morris, *The Story of Sigurd the Viking and the Fall of the Nibelungs* (London 1876), *Letters* 872, 873; *The Story of Burnt Njal* Translated with an Introduction by George Webbe Dasent (Edinburgh 1861), *Letters* 1539.

59. *Letters*, 2413, 2658.

60. 'The Waif Woman' *in Robert Louis Stevenson The Complete Short Stories. The Centenary Edition* (ed.) Ian Bell 2 vols. (Edinburgh 1993) 2, 391–406. The passage which inspired the story is in Morris and Magnusson *The Ere-Dwellers* 136–152. For RLS's interest in the sagas see additionally *Letters* 2339, 2496 and note.

61. Julian D'Arcy, *Scottish Skalds and Sagamen. Old Norse Influence on Modern Scottish Literature* (East Linton 1996) 17–36, Edward J. Cowan 'Icelandic Studies in Eighteenth and Nineteenth Century Scotland' *Studia Islandica* 31 (Reykjavik 1972) 109–151.

62. *Letters*, 2315.

63. *Letters*, 2315, 2347, 2479.

64. *Letters*, 1169.

65. *Robert Louis Stevenson: Weir of Hermiston* (ed.) Catherine Kerrigan (Edinburgh 1995).

66. Heathercat, in Robert Louis Stevenson, *Weir of Hermiston Some Unfinished Stories* Tusitala Edition (London 1924) 143.

67. *Family of Engineers*, 408–411.

68. *Letters*, 2316.

69. Heathercat, 161.

70. *Letters*, 2744.
71. Lewis Grassic Gibbon, *Sunset Song* (1932) in *A Scots Quair A Trilogy of Novels* (London 1950 edtn.) 23.
72. 'A Humble Remonstrance', 210–12.
73. 'Pulvis et Umbra', 320.
74. *Letters*, 72.
75. 'The Day After Tomorrow', 451.
76. 'Books Which Have Influenced Me', 473.
77. 'The Manse', 162–3.
78. *Collected Poems*, 270.

10

John Buchan's Lost Horizon: An Edinburgh Celebration of the University of Glasgow

Owen Dudley Edwards

A Man at my time of life sees old age not so very far distant, and the nearer he draws to the end of his journey the more ardently he longs for his receding youth . . . he clothes all his youth in a happy radiance and aches to recapture the freshness and wonder with which he then looked at life . . .

'. . . There's such a thing, remember, as spiriting away a man's recollection of his past, and starting him out as a waif in a new world. I've heard in the East of such performances, and of course it means that the memory-less being is at the mercy of the man who has stolen his memory. That is probably not the intention in your case.'

– *The Three Hostages* (1924), chapter vi

John Buchan, born in Perth on 26 August 1875, son of a Free Church minister (called to Pathhead, Fife, in 1876, and Glasgow in 1888), entered the University of Glasgow in 1892, graduating in 1895. During his days as a Glasgow student he finished one novel, started another, introduced, edited and published an anthology of Bacon's essays and apophthegms, and wrote several essays and short pieces. The novel, *Sir Quixote of the Moors*, was written in his last weeks at Glasgow University and published before he entered Oxford in October 1895. On 4 May 1896 the *Glasgow University Magazine* announced:

> It will be of interest to our readers that Mr Buchan has almost completed a long historical romance, of which the hero is a Platonist and soldier who attended this University in the times of Charles II. *Scholar-Gipsies*, a volume of essays, and *The Face of Proserpina*, a collection of stories, will be published before *John Burnet of Barns*. Mr Buchan's stories treat of Scotsmen in a way that might be expected from one who has a thorough knowledge of the importance of their character and surroundings.

Buchan was so well known at his first University that even after his departure he was identifiable without his Christian name. While at Glasgow he had taken notes from Highland drovers and others whence to draw in essays and stories, folk material in the tradition of Walter Scott and Robert Louis Stevenson. His fellow-students at Glasgow may have known of more drafts of his stories than would appear in his books: if 'The Face of Proserpina' was a short story, it is (like its archetype) hidden from us.[1]

The University of Glasgow was thus maternity ward to the first published novel of one of its country's leading novelists. Few universities anywhere in the world can rival such a claim, especially for a writer of ultimate achievements as perfect as the urban thriller *The Power House* (*Blackwood's Magazine* 1913, enlarged for book publication 1916), the rural thriller *The Thirty-Nine Steps* (1915), the historical novel *Witch Wood* (1927), and the posthumously published novel of life and death *Sick Heart River* (1941). Buchan had to wait long for a biography, but when Janet Adam Smith produced it in 1965, she made it very clear how deep were Buchan's debts to his first university, and as her own work is a masterpiece of its kind, she governs future biographical investigation. But the life-story of Buchan for his posthumous mass readership was the one anonymously dictated by his son, the Hon. William Buchan, as 'Note on the Author' published by Penguin Books in its 1956 edition of ten volumes selling over 900,000 copies by 1964.[2] It paid tribute to the city of Glasgow as the origin of Dickson McCunn and the Gorbals Diehards of *Huntingtower* (1922), but of the University it spake not a word. Instead it declared:

> At the age of nineteen John Buchan went, as a scholar, to Brasenose College Oxford, and at once began writing in earnest. His University work won him many prizes, culminating in a 'First' and including the Newdigate Prize for poetry, yet left him time to write and publish five books and a number of articles . . . As a result of these labours the young man who arrived at Oxford too poor to dine in Hall, became, in his own words, 'rather rich for an undergraduate'.

He was not an undergraduate, having graduated from Glasgow, but Oxford had insisted that he was, denying the degrees of other institutions as it did. John Buchan, unlike William Buchan, did not slight the Glasgow achievement: but his reputation as the publishing undergraduate of Brasenose had a little more gilt on its gingerbread if the preliminary baking in Glasgow was forgotten. It is a self-serving Oxbridge tradition to encourage amnesia in its students with respect to their previous histories. If they could not acquire amnesia, it was often obligingly contracted on their behalf. That Brasenose's most famous undergraduate novelist had won his laurels in his native university before arriving sounded as though Brasenose gained more than Buchan by his admission. (It probably did: his previous experience gave him the training to publish its history while still on its books.)

But Oxford's pre-eminence was most zealously trumpeted outside its walls (the Hon. William had in fact been sent down from New College, after which his father got him a job with Alfred Hitchcock). Penguin kept their jacket blurbs in tune with the Hon. William's, that of 1956 sending John Buchan to Oxford 'from his Glasgow grammar school'. By the 1980s, blurbs for the reprints allowed Buchan's attendance at 'Glasgow University (by which time he was already publishing articles in periodicals)' but 'his years at Oxford – "spent peacefully in an enclave like a monastery" – nevertheless opened up yet more horizons and he published five books and many articles . . . '. Scottish publishing houses (Edinburgh ones, anyway) continue to leave Glasgow University a lost horizon. 'After graduating at Glasgow University, Buchan took a scholarship to Oxford were' (pronounced Canongate Classics with a curiously anglophone illiteracy) 'he wrote his first two historical novels while still an undergraduate'. B&W Publishing have been Buchan's most adventurous and praiseworthy publishers in recent years, but their blurb excludes the University of Glasgow altogether: 'In 1894 [sic] he went to Oxford University and began to write, publishing several books and many articles while still a student'. The one publishing house which has been absolutely scrupulous in giving the University of Glasgow its due is Oxford University Press.[3]

The effect of this popular misconception (the *mot juste*, surely?) is to bring John Buchan to a much lesser, more unhistorical birth in the general mind. The Scottish writer may rise from the stepping-stones of his dead past to higher-priced things, but if we sink the stepping-stones we falsify the Scotland. What did the University of Glasgow mean to Buchan, how far did it condition his writing, and to what extent in space and time did he acknowledge it? We are at once brought up against a startling fact: within a few days of arrival at Brasenose, Buchan analysed his own situation as Glasgow graduate at Oxford, and indicted Glasgow for pushing him there. His protest was made as lead article in the first number of the *Glasgow University Magazine* for the new academic year:[4]

> . . . the University which has forgotten her traditions and has ceased to colour some tract of the country as her own, has already half capitulated in the struggle with commercialism. She must prepare to see not the least virile of her students uneasy in her atmosphere, troubled with errant fancies unsatisfied, and ready to listen to any call which appeals to their thwarted instincts. The case is made

desperate when that University encourages the ambition of her best pupils by offering the most honourable fellowship in her gift to the man who is most willing to desert her. He has been told that he is joining the long file of great Scotsmen who, from the days of Adam Smith to Edward Caird, have held the 'Snell'; he dreams a little of the shadow of the Magdalen Tower that has lain upon the Cherwell since the Middle Ages; he thinks of the room in the Balliol with its mullioned window and Virginia creeper, where [Thomas Hill] Green once worked, the gardens of 'New', and the secular trees which Verlaine sings of – and he goes.

John Snell (1629–79) had founded a scholarship to Oxford for 'further education' for Glasgow students: that this was interpreted by Oxford as meaning 'The Graduate as Freshman' (in the derisive title of Buchan's article) was self-contradiction. Victorian Oxford and Cambridge sustained their relatively recent intellectual pre-eminence partly by denying the degrees awarded by other institutions; in the alleged words of Al Capone 'it's a sweet racket, if you can keep the boys in line'. Oxbridge got away with it because graduates of other institutions lacked the courage to withstand the practice. Had the universities insulted under the system refused to recognise degrees from institutions which failed to honour theirs, all parties would have improved their perspectives rapidly: Oxbridge graduates would no longer rejoice in a system, however gratifying, which debarred them from academic posts elsewhere. But Scottish graduates who had dishonoured their origins by going under the yoke, and Oxbridge graduates who had obtained Scottish university posts, had common motives for resisting an end to the Scottish university cringe. At that time the Glasgow Buchan left was an institution probably intellectually superior to the Oxford he joined, could it but have respected itself. Buchan later warmed to Oxford, but an affectionate reminiscence in his autobiography notes that 'the lectures which I attended seemed jejune and platitudinous, the regime slack, after the strenuous life of Glasgow . . . being a year older than my contemporaries, I felt I had been pitchforked into a kindergarten.'[5]

What had he left? Let us begin with the non-fiction subject on which he had published a book while at Glasgow: Francis Bacon. In the year he brought out his anthology there died Glasgow's John Nichol (1833–94), retired in 1889 from the Chair of English Language and Literature he had held since 1862, a Crown appointment (no doubt facilitated by Nichol's having been educated at Balliol College, Oxford as well as Glasgow University). Nichol's last work, completed in the year of his retirement, was on Bacon, and had created the atmosphere – and no doubt the local research materials – whence Buchan could make his Baconian way.[6] Nichol also established American Literature as an academic discipline in

Britain, a significant milestone for the Glasgow student whose *Salute to Adventurers* (1915) fictionalised colonial Virginia and whose *The Path of the King* (1920) linked fictional vignettes imagining a royal (Viking) ancestry for Abraham Lincoln.[7] Buchan would also produce a remarkable short story reworking Shakespeare's *Coriolanus*, and that, no less than his sense of the character in general, had been profoundly inspired by Glasgow's A. C. Bradley whose *Shakespearean Tragedy* would establish its author as the greatest lecturer on Shakespeare of his time.[8] Bradley had warmly commended Buchan's undergraduate essay on Carlyle (whose biography by Nichol Buchan held in lifelong regard). Buchan's closest intellectual links with the Glasgow Faculty were with Gilbert Murray, to whom he dedicated *Sir Quixote*, and whose translations of Greek tragedy brought the classics before a wider English audience than they had ever known. What Buchan found at Glasgow was a clear expression of what George Davie has defined as 'the democratic intellect' and his own edition of Bacon asserted it. He thrilled to the idea of placing in the hands of students far beyond the walls of any university the text Oxbridge restricted to its elite. Buchan would later follow Glasgow University's insistence on making the classics accessible to the widest audience when he inaugurated 'Nelson's Sixpenny Classics'. Oxford did play a crucial part there: he met Tommie Nelson at Oxford. It was an invaluable place to meet people.[9]

But that friendship took some time to arrive, and in the meantime Buchan brooded darkly on the Glaswegians who sold themselves short by selling him into exile:[10]

> It is pitiably brave, but it is pitiably childish – this fascination of landscapes and traditions! For a few days the glamour of the place will be its own reward, and he will see before him a long vista of peace in which to dream and to find orientation. But before long there will press in upon him a spirit very alien to the idealism of Gothic towers. He will encounter something of the brute self-assertion of the young English gentleman, and he will miss the freedom and comradeship of his own University. The society in which he must move is stupidly exclusive . . . .
>
> He who goes to Oxford in the hope of finding there some new movement of thought, will encounter nothing but the stale gospels of the pulpits and the magazines. At Mansfield he may hear the Higher Criticism alloyed with Earnestness. At St Mary's, or St Barnabas, he may learn the latest new thing on the Sacraments and Socialism. In Balliol and Pembroke he will meet coteries of young men who study the 'Yellow Book', and talk with languor until moved by whisky or epigrams. They would fain have him believe that they spend their days in inventing strange sins, and their nights in perpetrating them; but he will probably set them down as mere amateurs in both branches . . .

> The Oxford don lives in a world perhaps as limited and as exclusive as that of the undergraduate. He is not an adventurer among ideas; he is before all things a 'socius' – a fellow in a society perhaps the most learned and refined in Europe. A high conception of his duty as a tutor separates him for ever after his election from the irresponsible student attitude to which he was bred. He has no high ambition to revolutionise his subject, to break new ground, or give an idea to the world – that would be inconsistent with the etiquette of the caste to which he belongs. He shows what Tacitus would call his 'civile ingenium', by preserving loyally the whole law and tradition of his school. He will never commit the impropriety of doing better what others can do as well . . .
>
> But there is much gain every way for the Scottish graduate who becomes an English freshman. He will make new friends, perhaps not least of all among many of his own contemporaries in Glasgow whose worth and abilities he never valued to the full in the press of the too sordid competition in which he met them first. In the colleges he will find a compensation for the isolation of the four years spent in a northern town which has no Latin Quarter, while he will return with love renewed for the way of life which permits a man to be a student and yet a citizen. But will his University encourage for ever this annual drain of emigration, while she professes to be busied with schemes for research-fellowships, and higher degrees? There is no rounded life which does not count its years of wandering; but here is a system which drugs by prolonged tutelage.

Buchan at this point wanted to become a professor in a Scottish university – in English literature or (as he fell under the influence of the Welsh philosopher at Glasgow, Henry Jones) in philosophy. But whatever the focus of his academic aim, his Glasgow preceptors seem to have made it clear it must turn on an Oxbridge degree, be its academic merits what they might: pushing him most strenuously of all was the most recent Oxonian import, the Professor of History, Richard Lodge, product of Balliol, tutor at Brasenose.[11]

Professor Christopher Harvie entitles his seminal analysis of Buchan 'Second Thoughts of a Scotsman on the Make':[12] the evidence of 'The Graduate as Freshman' makes it clear that these are First Thoughts, and basic. Buchan at Oxford 'resolved on a different career', as he put it later. But in doing so he settled for a life in alien territory; however much the association of their names might have disgusted him, he chose something akin to James Joyce's 'silence, exile and cunning'. It helps us understand why he became the greatest classical spy-story writer of his time. He himself *was* a spy, and always remained one, although at many points a double agent; as a son of the manse he preferred to call his hero-spies 'missionaries' notably in *Greenmantle* (1916), so that in his terms he was a missionary in danger of cannibalisation by his mission-field, a Jonah in his whale intermittently remembering to seek emetic relief by calling on the Lord. The theme only emerged in his work after departure to Oxford: his Glasgow novel, *Sir Quixote*, pitches a French chevalier into the midst of the Covenanter wars of the 1680s with every cause for dissimulation, but in fact the protagonist is frank to the verge of disaster. It was evidently inspired by Arthur Conan Doyle's early short stories of the Napoleonic soldier, Étienne Gerard, in the *Strand* during preceding months. Buchan's researches on the Covenanter wars, his derivations from Scott's *Old Mortality*, his obvious contrast of the affectionate and joyless facets (or were they moods?) of his Free Church parents and circle at home, his knowledge of the terrain from Ayrshire to Edinburgh, and even his resentment of well-to-do Glasgow University Church of Scotland complacency scorning the privations and honour of Free Church principle, had been in the assembly process already, but intended for *John Burnet of Barns* (1898). Conan Doyle gave him the kick-start as an historical fictionist just as Rider Haggard would do when he took to the present in *The Half-Hearted* (1900), a debt he acknowledges to both in *The Thirty-Nine Steps* when the literary innkeeper authenticates Richard Hannay's lies to him as 'all pure Rider Haggard and Conan Doyle'. The innkeeper's salute was also a proclamation: Buchan evidently realised he was now writing a masterpiece and, as a good publisher and propagandist, wished to tell the world in what league stood his boots. But the Edinburgh student of 1876–81, Conan Doyle, was the obvious model for his Glasgow junior's emulation with his tale of Puritan courage under persecution in the Monmouth Rebellion *Micah Clarke* (1889), his use of peril and flight from puritanically-spoken ruffians in *A Study in Scarlet*, and even his apotheosis of a slightly artificial chivalry in *The White Company* (1891). The more disreputable Edinburgh student of the earlier 1870s, Robert Louis Stevenson, inspired Buchan as he had Conan Doyle from afar, his death in December of 1894 almost passing a torch for Buchan to seize (not always wisely: the somewhat improbably chaste and unchaperoned man-and-woman domesticity of *Catriona* (1893) is innocently borrowed for *Sir Quixote*). Scotland – especially the University of Glasgow – had made John Buchan a novelist; Oxford made him a spy novelist.[13]

Buchan was never quite secure enough to write an Oxford novel, or even a novel with Oxford in it (apart from a few paragraphs to build up the biography of a hero sundered from his Scottish origins in 'The Far Islands'). For that matter his intensely political life produced no political novels, although *The Power House*, *John Macnab* (1925), *A Prince of the Captivity* (1933) and, in renunciation, *Sick Heart River*, contain able use of political ideas, the historical novels work out instructive political arguments, and *The Runagates Club* (1928) and *The Gap in the Curtain* (1932) have elegantly political short stories. The backstairs diplomacy and damnation by nuance, linking Oxbridge and politics as entities, were not for Buchan to enjoy freely; his ticket of admission gave him no entry to the inner enclosure, and he would not listen at doors. His strongest link to the establishment would be through his wife, Susan Grosvenor, and the clearest revelation of political diplomacy is through women's destruction of men's machinations, in *A Prince of the Captivity*. Occasionally Buchan seems to indict the political elite by whom he would strive to rise – Tommy Wratislaw in *The Half-Hearted* (1900) is a contemptible patron and party manager, priding himself on giving no help to protégés on whom he spies to wing his waspishness, Lord Lamancha in *John Macnab* is a pattern of the graceful, masterful, empty orator-statesman. Sometimes Buchan lashes out in brief but open anger at it – the young baronet Radical candidate gaining his social due of a parliamentary seat by recruiting as supporting speaker a complete stranger whom he has knocked over in his motor-car (*The Thirty-Nine Steps*), or the 'Duke of Angus . . . very old, highly respected, and almost wholly witless . . . Disraeli, it was said, had refused him the Thistle on the ground that he would eat it . . .As a chairman . . . was mercifully brief . . . told a Scots story, at which he shook with laughter, but the point of which he unfortunately left out' (*John Macnab*). In moments like this Buchan briefly blows his own cover, significantly in the context of the politics foisted on his own Scotland by the system he sought to exploit and which exploited him.[14]

Similarly Oxford is a theme disguised. *The Half-Hearted* is an indictment of its dilettantism, its Hamlet-like gentilities as an excuse for inadequacy, and in the final analysis its mental and moral cowardice, but we encounter these in an Oxford product on his native Scots heath. The spy theme emerges in several ways in the story. Buchan had used such a theme in his remarkable but neglected novel of the '45, *A Lost Lady of Old Years* (1899), inspired by the recent edition of the memoirs of Prince Charlie's traitor secretary John Murray of Broughton, published by the high Tory founder of student representative government in Edinburgh and thence in Glasgow and Britain at large, Robert Fitzroy Bell. Buchan's imaginary protagonist is more morally ambiguous than any he would ever use again, and attempts deception on both personal and political grounds, and the great historical personage of the novel is the most devious politician of the period, Simon Fraser Lord Lovat, remarkably well realised by the author. The *Half-Hearted* is almost a spy among novels: for a start, it spies out the contemporary novel for its creator, his first attempt as such. Initially, we see a great house in Scotland headed by very anglified aristocrats (using such instinctive English religious vocabulary as 'Nonconformist' and 'Churchman' regardless of the Presbyterian Church of Scotland, or its adversary the purer Presbyterianism of John Buchan's father). We spy out the landed Oxbridge society through the eyes of a girl (daughter of a bourgeois plutocrat) whose spiral of repulsion, acceptance, new repulsion, new acceptance, yet final divergence echo in some degree Buchan's own. (It is his fullest literary performance in drag: 'Alice' was subsequently the name given his daughter.)

> What merry haphazard people were these she had fallen among! At home everything was docketed and ordered. Meals were immovable feasts, the hour for bed and the hour for rising were more regular than the sun's. Her father was full of proverbs on the virtue of regularity, and was wont to attribute every vice and misfortune to its absence. And yet here were distinguished men and women who got on very well without it. She did not wholly like it. The little doctrinaire in her revolted and she was pleased to be censorious.
>
> . . . Competence, responsibility were words she had been taught to revere, and to hear them light-heartedly disavowed seemed an upturning of the foundation of things.
>
> . . . He spoke with a touch of the drawl which is currently supposed to belong only to the half-educated classes of England.
>
> . . . She . . . innocently and abruptly asked her if she had not found her companion at table amusing.
>
> Alice, unaccustomed to fiction, gave a hesitating 'Yes' . . .
>
> . . . The vigorous little democrat in her hated the exclusive . . . .
>
> . . . His name was Arthur Mordaunt, but because it was the fashion at the time for a certain class of people to address each other in monosyllables, his friends invariably knew him as 'John'.
>
> . . . Politics had always been a thing of the gravest import in her eyes, bound up with a man's duty and honour and religion, and lo! here was this Gallio who not only adorned a party she had been led to regard as reprobate, but treated the whole affair as a half-jocular business, on which one should not be serious. It was sheer weakness, her heart cried out, the weakness of the philanderer, the half-hearted.
>
> . . . 'But – but', he stammered, 'the chap isn't a gentleman, you know.'
>
> The words quickened her vexation. A gentleman! The cant word, the fetich of this ring of idle aristocrats – she knew the hollowness of the whole farce. The democrat in her made her walk off with erect head and bright eyes . . .

Buchan bridged the contradictions by a mordantly-observed if slightly heavy-handed brief skit on a tuft-hunting *bourgeoisie*, even more repulsive to Alice and owing much to Mrs Elton in Austen's *Emma*. But his own Oxford friends, when he made them, were mostly bourgeois.[15]

The novel ends in formal espionage whereby the hero saves the Empire at the cost of his own life, partly by acting the dilettante role which has irritated his associates and readers throughout, finally self-realised in a grand slaughter of invading tribesmen deployed in the Russian interest against the North-west Frontier of British India. The tribal chieftain's last reluctant salute to his dead foe derives from Conan Doyle's 'The Green Flag', where a self-indulgent performance by rebellious Irish agrarians becomes the basis for their self-sacrificial victory. But there are other forms of espionage. The hero's Radical rival 'had declined somewhat nervously to talk of his early life, though the girl, with her innate love of a fighter, would have listened with pleasure', and she has in any case already been told that

> Oh, he has done many things. He has been very brave and quite the maker of his own fortunes. He has educated himself, and then I think edited some Nonconformist paper. Then he went into politics, and became a Churchman. Some old man took a liking to him and left him his money, and that was the condition. So I believe he is pretty well off now and is waiting for a seat. He has been nursing this constituency . . . He has also written a lot of things and he is somebody's private secretary.

Social advancement may depend on espionage: and information damning in one quarter turns the key to fortune in another. The great international spy who first tricks and then is foiled by the half-hearted hero is a recurrent type in Buchan, the apparently faultless Englishman of decidedly alternative origins. This particular one is obsessively loyal to his first syllable ('He might call himself Constantine Marka, or Arthur Marker, or the Baron Mark – whatever happened to suit him.') but while Marka is, appropriately, the point of departure of Buchan's journey to Medina, he is also the parent of the unquestioned Englishry who defy Richard Hannay to unmask their German identities in *The Thirty-Nine Steps*:[16]

> 'Don't get flustered, Uncle,' he said. 'It is all a ridiculous mistake; but these things happen sometimes, and we can easily set it right. It won't be hard to prove our innocence. I can show that I was out of the country on the 23rd of May, and Bob was in a nursing home. You were in London, but you can explain what you were doing.'
>
> 'Right, Percy! Of course that's easy enough. The 23rd! That was the day after Agatha's wedding. Let me see. What was I doing? I came up in the morning from Woking, and lunched in the club with Charlie Symons. Then – oh yes, I dined with the Fishmongers. I remember, for the punch didn't agree with me, and I was seedy next morning. Hang it all, there's a cigar box I brought back from the dinner.' He pointed to an object on the table, and laughed nervously.
>
> 'I think, sir', said the young man, addressing me politely, 'you will see you are mistaken. We want to assist the law like all Englishmen, and we don't want Scotland Yard to be making fools of themselves. That's so, uncle?'

'Certainly, Bob.' The old fellow seemed to be recovering his voice. 'Certainly, we'll do anything in our power to assist the authorities. But – but this is a bit too much. I can't get over it.'

'How Nellie will chuckle', said the plump one. 'She always said that you would die of boredom because nothing ever happened to you. And now you've got it thick and strong', and he began to laugh very pleasantly.

'By Jove, yes. Just think of it! What a story to tell at the club. Really, Mr Hannay, I suppose I should be angry, to show my innocence, but it's too funny! I almost forgive you the fright you gave me! You looked so glum, I thought I might have been walking in my sleep and killing people.'

Hannay's terror that he will never break through this suffocating Englishness is the touch of genius. Hannay is defending 'England'; but he is not English, he is Scots-born South African, and tells on his first page 'the talk of the ordinary Englishman made me sick'. He himself can pass confidently as Australian and Scots, but Englishness becomes the enemy, the apparently impenetrable camouflage. Finally he successfully disputes the German spies' title to it, however 'confoundedly genuine' their patter ('Percy . . . Agatha . . . Woking . . . the club . . . Charlie Symons . . . [the worshipful company of] Fishmongers . . . punch . . . seedy . . . Hang it all . . . making fools of themselves . . . anything in our power . . . a bit too much . . . Nellie . . . die of boredom . . . thick and strong . . . What a story . . . it's too funny!'). Once the war is over, all this paraphernalia will be Hannay's, or a slight class-cut above it: and what a story *he* will then have to tell at *his* club. But to start with, it is the enemy spies who rule as clubland heroes, and Hannay – Buchan – must learn as scientifically as possible how to play that part.

Buchan worried consistently about the loss of his integrity akin to Esau's ('he was bidden sell his birthright for pottage, and affection could not gloze over the bargain'), and found a destiny somewhere between the polar opposites of his manse origin and his Oxbridgian success story ('There are two men only who will not be ashamed to look their work in the face in the end – the brazen Opportunist and the rigid Puritan . . . . If I had my pick my companions should either be the narrowest religionists or frank unashamed blackguards . . . .').[17] He lightly sketches in a triangle of antitheses in a story finished in his Oxford days, 'The Herd of Standlan', narrated by a Scotsman grown up on the borders alongside an English heir to wealth who toyed with sheepfarming, but the bulk of the story comes from a local shepherd talking freely and confidently: 'irresistable fate' had 'swept' the narrator 'southward to college', but we are to notice the frank and unceremonious freedom of speech of the herd himself. The herd has saved the life of the Englishman who then tries to reward him:

... Mr Airthur wad tak nae refusal but that I maun gang awa' doon wi' him to his braw house in England and be a land o' factor or steward or something like that. And I had a rale fine cottage a' to myself, wi' a very bonny gairden and guid wages, so I stayed there maybe sax month and then I gaed up till him. 'I canna bide nae longer', says I. 'I canna stand this place. It's far ower laigh, and I'm fair sick to get hills to rest my een on. I'm awfu' gratefu' to ye for your kindness, but I maun gie up my job.' He was very sorry to lose me, and was for gien' me a present o' money or stockin' a fairm for me, because he said that it was to me he owed his life. But I wad hae nane o' his gifts. 'It wad be a terrible thing', I says, 'to tak siller for daein' what ony body wad hae dune out o' pity'. So I cam awa' back to Standlan and I maunsay I'm rale contentit here. Mr Airthur used whiles to write to me and ca' in and see me when he cam North for the shooting; but since he's gane sae far wrang wi' the Tories, I've had naething mair to dae wi' him.

Ill-fated friendships solidified by rescue from drowning in the Black Linn recur in this period of Buchan's writing perhaps from autobiographical or at least reportorial origins: but the herd's hold on his birthright may contrast with the southern college man no less than with the defector to Toryism (Buchan had supported the Liberal candidate in the Glasgow University Rectorial election in 1894, raising the suspicion his Toryism may also have been acquired at Oxford).[18]

Entry into the world of Oxbridge contacts and London success cut Buchan off from security, and it bred fear. His immediate non-Oxbridge predecessors among the Scottish emigrant masters shared the quality: Stevenson, Conan Doyle, and even J. M. Barrie, find different ways of making a reader intimate with fear, notably through Jekyll's inability to shake off Hyde, Holmes's sight of the speckled band, or Captain Hook's discovery of Peter Pan's identity. Buchan's use of fear is simpler and more inevitable. It is one of his key-notes. Richard Hannay is full of self-reproach for supposed want of courage. The spiritual generosity of that repetition lifts Hannay far above the Bulldog Drummonds and James Bonds who leeched off his saga, but its intellectual strength is its subtlety:

> It is the type that makes dashing regimental officers, and earns V.C.s, and gets done in wholesale. I was never that kind. I belonged to the school of cunning cowards.
>
> A man's courage is like a horse that refuses a fence; you have got to take him by the head and cram him at it again. If you don't, he will funk worse next time. I hadn't enough courage to be able to take chances with it, though I was afraid of many things, the thing I feared most mortally was being afraid.
>
> ... there was no witness of my cowardice ... it is just as difficult to be a coward for long as to be a hero.

This is the work of a philosopher of fear, but of one who knows how to make his philosophy pay off in his best coin, propaganda. In his South African days Buchan had learned the monetary and status value of persuasive powers in the cause of his recent hosts. World War One produced the first three Hannay stories, putting Buchan's own anxieties to work far more effectively than prevailing militarist rant against the admission of fear as treasonable weakening of morale. Buchan had learned the meaning of fear from his life in alien country which could so easily prove enemy country: *The Power House* is a fascinating metaphor whose apparently friendly, familiar London streets and restaurants become assassins' nests. The protagonist's own badge of success and opulence – a chauffeur – becomes a means of his destruction. Buchan had a nervous collapse in 1907, and a duodenal ulcer by 1912 (he would make his readers ulcer-friendly in *Greenmantle* via John S. Blenkiron, another alien). Graham Greene during the enemy bombardment of London in 1941 'gratefully' admitted how well 'Buchan prepared us in his thrillers better than he knew for the death that may come to any of us, as it nearly came to Leithen [in *The Power House*], by the railings of the Park or the doorway of the mews'. Buchan was, nonetheless, too good a propagandist to leave fear simply to straightforward exposure to bombardment, well though he makes us feel it through Peter Pienaar in *Greenmantle*:

> Peter felt very sick. He had not believed there could be so much noise in the world, and the drums of his ears were splitting. Now, for a man to whom courage is habitual, the taste of fear – naked, utter, fear – is a horrible thing.
>
> It seems to wash away all his manhood. Peter lay on the crest watching the shells burst, and confident that any moment he might be a shattered remnant. He lay and reasoned with himself, calling himself every name he could think of, but conscious that nothing would get rid of that lump of ice below his heart.

Buchan took fear beyond the point of no return in polite fiction: he conscripted his readers into the terror of rape, as anticipated by Hannay from von Stumm in *Greenmantle*, and by Mary Lamington from von Schwabing in *Mr Standfast* (1919), written while the war still raged.[19]

The hint of heterosexual rape may be obvious enough for women in secret service work, and the infinite possibilities of enemy nastiness are axiomatic, but pre-Buchan convention gave little rope to such imagination:

> she was aware of a dark shadow lurking at the back of her mind, the shadow of the fear which she knew was awaiting her. For she was going into the unknown with a man whom she hated, a man who claimed to be her lover.
>
> '. . . To-morrow, my fairest one, fatigue will be ended.'

> There was no mistake now about the note of possession in his voice. Mary's heart began to beat fast and wild. The trap had closed down on her and she saw the folly of her courage. It had delivered her bound and gagged into the hands of one whom she loathed more deeply every moment, whose proximity was less welcome than a snake's. She had to bite hard on her lip to keep from screaming.

This is again Buchan writing in drag. The snake's contribution can be assessed as Biblical, mythological or Freudian, according to preference, but is strong meat on any interpretation. It is unusually sophisticated, disturbing, propaganda; in cruder forms the inter-war thriller market followed its lead. Buchan was probably the most persuasive evangelist among the embattled novelists of World War I. *The Thirty-Nine Steps* may be a bit crass:

> There was more in those eyes than any common triumph. They had been hooded like a bird of prey, and now they flamed with a hawk's pride. A white fanatic heat burned in them, and I realised for the first time the terrible thing I had been up against. The man was more than a spy; in his foul way he had been a patriot.

Conan Doyle does that sort of thing better, by endowing Holmes with the appropriate professionalism, generosity, and vanity:

> '. . . But you have one quality which is very rare in a German, Mr Von Bork: you are a sportsman, and you will bear me no ill will when you realize that you, who have outwitted so many other people, have at last been outwitted yourself. After all, you have done your best for your country and I have done my best for mine, and what could be more natural? Besides', he added, not unkindly, as he laid his hand on the shoulder of the prostrate man, 'it is better than to fall before some more ignoble foe . . . .'

But if Holmes and not Hannay is the professional spy, Buchan and not Conan Doyle is the professional propagandist, and his improvement may be measured by the touches in the Hannay stories still hailed by innocent admirers as counterweight to Buchan's propaganda work. He allows Hannay to reflect on the futility of war and the 'goodness' of some Germans. He paints a sympathetic portrait of the Kaiser at a time when he was reviled by the Allies, and only a year after Gallipoli pays tribute to the fighting skills of the Turk. These would have been the most effective passages in winning neutral readers to the Allied cause; persons immune to horror-stories of German brutality in Belgium in 1914 were not likely to be recruited by their fictional rewarming in 1916. To deny the 'fighting skills' of 'the Turk' would be to deny the shape of the earth. To portray the Kaiser as a guilt-haunted, hysterical Pontius Pilate inviting pity well mingled with contempt, was far more convincing than to parade him as a modernized

Attila. The beautiful episode of the fugitive Hannay among the German woodcutter's family at Christmastide specifically declares a much improved propaganda offensive:

> That night I realized the crazy folly of war. When I saw the splintered shell of Ypres and heard hideous tales of German doings, I used to want to see the whole land of the Boche given up to fire and sword. I thought we could never end the war properly without giving the Huns some of their own medicine. But that woodcutter's cottage cured me of such nightmares. I was for punishing the guilty but letting the innocent go free. It was our business to thank God and keep our hands clean from the ugly blunders to which Germany's madness had driven her. What good would it do Christian folk to burn poor little huts like this and leave children's bodies by the wayside? To be able to laugh and to be merciful are the only things that make man better than the beasts.

It was propaganda of real genius to win readers' affection for a German family as a means for strengthening the case that the German higher command were no better than beasts. Thus Buchan in *Greenmantle*; *Mr Standfast* turns an even neater trick by pacifist's evolution from a repulsive conscientious objector to a hero, dying in combat as a non-fighting runner for Hannay in mid-battle:

> 'Funny thing life. A year ago I was preaching peace . . . I'm still preaching it . . . I'm not sorry.'
> I held his hand till two minutes later he died.

This is as shrewd a recruitment of pacifism in a belligerent cause as one could find, even abler than the Irish pro-Germans who hijacked the late pacifist Francis Sheehy-Skeffington, murdered by a British officer during the Easter Rising. Buchan's subtlety came from the same source – as a recruit from the periphery, aware of the nuances of its different loyalties from those of the centre. *Mr Standfast* does clever demolition work on the anti-war Irish whom it condemns as blacklegs usurping soldiers' jobs in Scotland.[20] In the same episode Buchan's Glasgow self avenges his Oxford wrongs neatly enough in the Allied cause. An Oxbridge don is let loose on Glasgow workers:

> Tombs . . . was determined to speak, as he would have put it, to democracy in its own language, so he said 'hell' several times, loudly but without conviction. Presently he slipped into the manner of the lecturer, and the audience grew restless. 'I propose to ask myself a question – ' he began, and from the back of the hall came – 'And a damned sully answer ye'll get.' After that there was no more Tombs.

But the memory of Oxford pressed into service in *Greenmantle* with most emotive effect was covert:

> Stumm locked the door behind him and laid the key on the table. That room took my breath away, it was so unexpected . . . . At first sight you would have said it was a woman's drawing-room.
>
> But it wasn't. I soon saw the difference. There had never been a woman's hand in that place. It was the room of a man who had a passion for frippery, who had a perverted taste for soft delicate things. It was the complement to his bluff brutality. I began to see the queer other side to my host, that evil side which gossip had spoken of as not unknown in the German army. The room seemed a horribly unwholesome place, and I was more than ever afraid of Stumm . . . .
>
> His ugly sneering face was close above mine. Then he put out his hands and gripped my shoulders as he had done the first afternoon . . . .
>
> 'The weasel would like to bite', he cried. 'But the poor weasel has found his master. Stand still, vermin. Smile, look pleasant, or I will make pulp of you . . .'.

The subsequent fisticuffs, Stumm's half-trip 'over a little table', Hannay's knockout of his host and flight, are devices trembling on the frontier between the horrific and the hilarious, T.E. Lawrence possibly drawing on the first mode, P.G. Wodehouse certainly on the second. Hannay may reasonably flip his lid over the possible implications of Stumm's room, his own past not having included the occasional manly roll on the veldt with Boer, Briton, or Bantu. But Buchan's knowing gibes about Oxford to his Glasgow fellow-students ('They would fain have him believe that they spend their days in inventing strange sins and their nights in perpetrating them . . . mere amateurs in both branches') deny such innocence. At Walter Pater's Brasenose, however bereft of Pater (dead in 1894) and of any further return visits from his most famous (if Magdalen) disciple Oscar Wilde (in prison since May 1895), Buchan was still certain to encounter rooms in which 'there had never been a woman's hand' and which would inspire the Stumm aesthetics more fully than any hard information on the German higher command:

> In place of the grim bareness of downstairs here was a place all luxury and colour and light. It was very large, but low in the ceiling, and the walls were full of little recesses with statues in them. A thick grey carpet of velvet pile covered the floor, and the chairs were low and soft and upholstered like a lady's boudoir. A pleasant fire burned on the hearth and there was a flavour of scent in the air, something like incense or burnt sandalwood. A French clock on the mantelpiece told me that it was ten minutes past eight. Everywhere on little tables and in cabinets was a profusion of knick-knacks, and there was some beautiful embroidery framed on screens.

It combines rather too many schools, perhaps, the High Anglican jostling the luxurious, the opulent offsetting the spinsterlike, but one don could have managed all ('You will be *so* careful of my little treasures, Mr Buchan? And do you care for sugar?'). As for Stumm, he may have had all too much in common with such fellow-students as the 'six drunken gentlemen [who] . . . came into my bedroom' four nights after his arrival 'turned the table upside down and got inside it . . . wedged a chair across the door . . . carefully unscrewed the electric light globes and put them inside the fender . . . upturned the coal-scuttle into one of the presses . . . began a search for whisky in my cupboard and found methylated spirits.'[21]

But whatever amusement, embarrassment, involvement and/or fear Buchan may have gained from the sexual preferences of his fellow-Oxonians, the war effort required a rebirth of innocence. Buchan had been drawn into intelligence work – Professor Harvie suspects it may have been much greater than we know, particularly with the brilliant, unscrupulous Captain (later Admiral Sir Reginald) Hall of 'Room 40'. It was Hall who tracked Roger Casement from Germany to Ireland in the prelude to the Easter Rising, Hall who had Casement brought secretly to the Tower of London, Hall who deployed the 'Black Diaries' with their accounts of promiscuous homosexual activity to discourage the Pope, the King, the President of the United States and various other persons from appeal against Casement's sentence of death: all of this was contemporaneous with the writing of *Greenmantle*. If the homosexual matter in the diaries was forged, it was Hall's staff who did it: his recruitment was eclectic enough to ensure authority and indeed enjoyment in their preparation. Stumm buggering for Berlin was an obvious spin-off from the propaganda offensive, with Buchan neatly combining his Puritanism of origin with opportunism of environment.[22]

Professor Harvie suggests that 'Blinker' Hall's piercing eyes – eponymous for his biography – make him an obvious original for the masterspy of *The Thirty-Nine Steps*, and certainly Hall in his foul way had been a patriot. Similarly A.J. Balfour's cynical deployment of intellect in indifference to human convictions seems to have inspired the chilling master-criminal of *The Power House*. The deductions have formidable implications. Buchan had been recruited into the Tory ranks headed by Balfour, and subsequently into the war manipulative machinery whose supreme genius was undoubtedly Hall; he placed his literary talents at the service of the operations they directed; yet if they inspired visions of Lords of Misrule, Buchan's capitulation to the world that Oxbridge made bred undertones of moral as well as physical fear. It also suggests that Buchan, like other periphery-born supporters of the British metropolitan-directed war channelled his aversions against the British establishment into anti-Germanism: Shane Leslie, the Ulster Unionist convert to Roman Catholicism and Irish Home Rule, actually produced Allied propaganda for Irish Americans to this effect. Leslie was very clear about it: in fighting Germans you fight everything you dislike about the English. Buchan, with his career and marriage in English society, could not go to these lengths but the hypothesis is consistent with what we know of his first impressions of Oxford.

Three additional points may be noted. Firstly, the only successful sexual seduction by an enemy in Buchan's World War One novels is Hilda von Einem's amour with Sandy in *Greenmantle*, as his subsequent hysterics testify, but he finally rejects her offer of 'the greatest career that mortal has known . . . a task which will need every atom of brain and sinew and courage': 'You can offer me nothing that I desire . . . I am the servant of my country, and her enemies are mine. I can have neither part nor lot with you . . . .' Then she denounces him, leaves, and is killed, and he is nearly killed in reclaiming her body ('I did not know that anything could be so light'). Secondly, Stumm is killed by a mob he is heroically withstanding ('He was a brute and a bully, but, by God! he was a man'), exactly as the dilettantish Lewis Haystoun, the half-hearted, dies for the British Empire to the admiration of Fazir Khan, his enemy ('This thing was a man . . . This man was of the race of kings'). Finally, von Schwabing, master of a thousand disguises and dissimulations yet terrified of the guns, among whose roar he is held prisoner on the battlefront, runs towards his advancing fellow-Germans and is killed by their fire, under the chapter-title 'How an Exile Returned to His Own People'.[23]

The world war did not end in disillusion for Buchan, but it returned the exile to his own people by a somewhat circuitous route. Ex-soldiers in the USA voted for the near-neutralist Warren Harding, ex-soldiers in Ireland went into guerrilla warfare against their former colours, ex-soldiers in Britain helped vote an opponent of the war – the Scot, Ramsay MacDonald – into office as premier in 1924. Buchan, Nelson's historian of the war and his employer, friend and fellow-soldier Tommy Nelson's memorialist, did not repudiate the Allied cause although the hatred of war he had conscripted as propaganda in *Mr Standfast* now reappeared in John Heritage for his first fully Scottish thriller *Huntingtower*. The art-form which had sustained his special brand of war service so well rethought its priorities, to find hope in a retired Glasgow grocer and a pack of little working-class waifs from the Gorbals: significantly *Huntingtower*'s upper-class recruit from the social world now engulfing Sir Richard Hannay is Sir Archie Roylance, a minor if gallant figure, whose difficulty in finding reality in the story he is told symbolises his own increasing irrelevance to the Dickson McCunns and Gorbals Die-Hards from whom the future will be made. Buchan had returned to his Glasgow, in a spirit of comedy as well as tragedy, but with a realism dry-eyed in the ruins of the purple prose of propaganda:

> I do not know to whom the Muse of History will give the credit of the tactics of 'infiltration', whether to Ludendorff or von Hutier or some other proud captain of Germany, or to Foch, who revised and perfected them. But I know that the same notion was at this moment of crisis conceived by Thomas Yownie, whom no parents acknowledged, who slept usually in a coal cellar, and who had picked up his education among Gorbals closes and along the wharves of Clyde.

It is made very clear his education has been gained in great part from incessant warfare against the police. And his signature-tune is his comrades' watchword 'Ye'll no fickle Thomas Yownie'.[24]

Thomas Yownie disappears from the stories, to become a minister, acknowledging that his place in Buchan's roots now symbolised the paternal root. Thomas's next edition is in *John Macnab* where men at the head of Buchan's three non-literary professions (lawyer, businessman, politician) risk their careers for crowded hours of glorious life as a Scottish poacher, and Sir Edward Leithen, the nearest among them to a self-portrait, risks that risk to enter confederacy with a tinkler boy:

> 'Benjie', he said solemnly, 'there's a lot of things in the world that I don't understand, and it stands to reason that there must be more that you don't. I'm in a position in which I badly want someone to help me. I like the look of you. You look a trusty fellow and a keen one . . .'
> . . . He was in two minds as to whether he had done wisely in placing himself in the hands of a small ragamuffin, who for all he knew might be hand-in-glove with the Strathlarrig keepers. But the recollection of Benjie's face reassured him. He did not look like a boy who would be the pet of any constituted authority; he had the air rather of the nomad against whom the orderly world waged war. There had been an impish honesty in his face, and Leithen, who had a weakness for disreputable urchins, felt that he had taken the right course. Besides, the young sleuth-hound had got on his trail, and there had been nothing for it but to make him an ally.

It is the principle of Sherlock Holmes's 'Baker Street Irregulars' restored to the country which originally inspired them (Conan Doyle clearly owed something to Edinburgh recollection, being himself the product of infant street-gang warfare). Benjie, like the Gorbals Die-Hards, is a professional spy and trickster, unable to afford the luxury code of the sportsman: he deals in fish professionally, in contrast to Leithen's amateur work as piscator and poacher. He has the impatience of that other Scots creation, Sherlock Holmes, anent English bungling amateurs and their want of system. The English banker Palliser-Yeates (whose name typifies the amateur victim of professionals, drawn from Trollope's Plantagenet Palliser and Somerville & Ross's Irish R.M.), has tricked his way to illegal killing of a stag, but to persist after challenge from a woman 'isn't the game, you know'. Benjie is not playing a 'game':

> '. . . And look here – you're a first-class sportsman, and I'm enormously grateful to you. Here's something for your trouble.'
> Benjie's face grew very red as he swung his equipage round. 'I see', he said. 'If ye like to be beat by a lassie, dinna blame me. I'm no wantin' your money.'

The Cheviot, The Stag, and the Black, Black Oil could not show a firmer cleavage between the play-acting of lairds and realism of workers, between the throwaway small change of the haves and the ungracious integrity of the have-nots. Benjie does take money from Palliser-Yeates' victrix who remains wholly unaware that he had all but cheated her out of the stag she so gallantly defended from the mysterious poacher 'John Macnab':

> '. . . Now you're going to Mrs Fraser to have the best tea you ever had in your life, and you shall also have ten shillings.'
> 'Thank you kindly, lady, but I canna stop for tea. I maun awa down to Inverlarrig for my fish.' But his hand closed readily on the note, for he had no compunction in taking money from one who had made him to bear the bitterness of incomprehensible defeat.

She is his enemy, and he will take her money given him for guarding what he has done his best to steal. There is a Marxism in it, symbolising enmity from the laird class and their lackeys as his normal condition. What he cannot accept is recompense from an unworthy ally. Buchan, necessarily economising at Oxford, no doubt met *Punch*-type chaffing about Scots avarice: he must have enjoyed making the Scots tinker refuse the money of the English banker. Benjie's one real friend, the Buchanoid Leithen, is the only poacher to complete his capture of the game he kills, and he does so by literally pooling his own legerdemain with Benjie's. Leithen, and hence Buchan, is ultimately ambiguous in the war of professional hunters against landowners; in *Sick Heart River* he shows his new height of integrity in killing for food, not sport:[25]

> He had heard Lew say that they must get all the caribou they could, since it was necessary to take a load of fresh meat into the [Amerindian] Hares' camp . . . he felt a glow of satisfaction which he had not known for many a day. He was primitive man again who had killed his dinner.

The embrace of the primitive as the genuine is the ultimate in his return to Glasgow and its Gorbals boys, to Scotland and its Fish Benjies, to his folk-collecting origins of creative writing. Professor Harvie has shown Buchan's links with the sensational anthropology of Sir James Frazer, but while granting that, we must witness their common origins in the simple business of archetypal story-telling. Buchan's English Association address, 'The Novel and the Fairy Tale' (1931), an admirably straightforward celebration of the folk roots of fiction, silently indicates to his critics how deeply his own achievement depended on his folklore inheritance; and the stories he took down or at least listened to when on country rambles during his time at Glasgow University, shaped his long-term future. David Crawfurd is the imperialist Scots boy frustrating a black rising in South Africa, in *Prester John* (1910) which culminates in a phoenix-like emergence from the tomb whence the black nationalist leader the Rev. John Laputa has leaped downward to his death, having been mortally wounded by the false ally Henriques whom he then kills, and all harmonises with Frazer's use of the ancient tradition Buchan and he knew from their Macaulay:

> Those trees in whose dim shadow
>   The ghastly priest doth reign,
> The priest who slew the slayer,
>   And shall himself be slain;

but the simplicity of Buchan's original stories is even more important than our sophisticated explanations. Ostensibly a story in the How-young-John-foiled-the-Mad-Mullah tradition (the screw gaining a turn by this Mullah being also a minister in the hero's own Kirk), *Prester John*'s true appeal lies in growing mutual regard between Laputa and the boy Crawfurd: the relationships of Stevenson's boy heroes, Jim Hawkins and David Balfour, to Long John Silver and Alan Breck Stewart respectively, speed Buchan's creative plough, but the Buchan story depends subtly on unexpected similarities rather than Stevensonian contrasts, as when Laputa and Crawfurd find themselves exchanging data on the legend of the Trojan horse, and the Virgilian scholarship of a Scots professor. A deeper common resonance is the inheritance of the fairy-stories which dictate the novel itself: the folklore spun from the Biblical account of Solomon and the Queen of Sheba (1 Kings x. 1–13, 2 Chronicles ix. 1–12), and the legend of Prester John, King of Ethiopia and Christian priest, Presbyter John, according to the twelfth-century Otto of Freising, as Buchan would have known. The Rev. John Laputa is in one sense Prester John, as Presbyter John, and in another meaning Buchan would be following his own eponymous Scots story of 1897, which told of a mist-bedevilled narrator's rescue by an isolated shepherd, islanded by mountains, evidently working out his own salvation by his philosophy and folklore. The titles assert a private and personal road to God, bereft of conventional theology, and a majesty and priesthood in both figures. The effect is an almost deliberate self-diminution by the conventional narrator of both stories on his last sight of 'Prester John'. This goes two ways, firstly to a fascination with outlawed and vanquished religious culture, secondly in a celebration of the kingly qualities flourishing amongst ordinary people.

Buchan took up the latter idea in his first post-war fictional collection, *The Path of the King*, supposedly miniatures of a line of maternal ancestry for Abraham Lincoln, going back to a Viking king. It is a variant of the Irish Catholic 'me ancestors were kings in Ireland', occasionally a useful antidote to snobbery, or indeed to deference and social constraints at large: and Buchan, who disliked that (my) ethnic group, would presumably have disliked the linkage. But *The Path of the King* is essentially an anti-snob impulse if not a democratic one, and the comparability of peripheral questioning of English class and exclusiveness is instructive. Buchan did not make heroes of all of his Ur-Lincolns, merely gave them kingly moments in sometimes squalid lives. One, indeed, proves the critical influence in bringing Charles I to execution, partly by asking himself 'Were honest folk to be harried because of the whims of a man whose remote ancestor had been a fortunate bandit?' The final essays, on Lincoln, are impressively in tune with modern scholarship, much more so than was the Lincoln historiography published in Buchan's own time. Ironically, his case for Lincoln's maternal kingly descent was far stronger than he knew, for Lincoln derived from the great medieval Welsh kings Rhodri Mawr and Hywel Dda, and the sister of Owain Glyn Dwr, rulers obsessed by the need for their country's Union: but Buchan's Anglo-Scottish dialogue throughout his life was little affected by the third country of the island. The argument essentially demands the recognition of the kingly anywhere in human history, and in the most unpromising circumstances. As he himself would stress, the fairy story insists on the survival of the unfittest, whether idiot boys winning kingdoms or Cinderella finding her prince (Scots folklore seems not merely to emphasise the poor prospects of the ultimate victor, but often prefers him to be an alleged or actual simpleton). The Gorbals Die-Hards and Dickson McCunn are such figures; so is Leithen in *Sick Heart River*, where he has to show his kingliness despite the impediments to its discovery created by his own success in life.[26]

Buchan had become a best-selling novelist in the war effort: his thriller fiction, beginning with a Scottish imprint, went from Blackwood of Edinburgh (who paid 12½ per cent royalty for *The Thirty-Nine Steps*) to

London's Hodder & Stoughton (who paid 30% for *Greenmantle*), the deal made when Buchan met Ernest Hodder-Williams in 1916 as they worked on Government propaganda. He had dropped fiction for ten years after *The Half-Hearted*: now he was good for at least one fiction a year. Yet his service to the world whither Oxbridge had sent him (Milner's imperial service in South Africa, Nelson's, World War work) invited him to ask questions of his own servitude, enhanced by his use of the fairy-tale basis. Richard Hannay was his most popular figure, yet what was his value after World War I? Hannay having won his wife, his knighthood, his generalship, and his country-house, protests against more espionage, and presumably his author was tired of so limited a figure: so *The Three Hostages* got itself moving by a fairy-tale formula, a wicked enchanter who imprisons and transforms beyond recognition a lord, a wealthy maiden, a hero's son, their whereabouts being only discoverable by a rhyme kindly provided by their abductor. Buchan even indulges in deconstructionism at the beginning, to talk up his thin conjuring. But the story itself, a good thriller, has other work to do. Buchan confronts the unpleasant fact that the propaganda game has been made to work against Britain in Britain's imperial heartland: the Irish, led by brilliant English-born publicists such as Desmond FitzGerald and Erskine Childers, established the most demoralising enemy propaganda service in British history: Childers had shown Buchan how propaganda could work best in a thriller of literary stature, *The Riddle of the Sands* (1903) and had been an analyst of South Africa after the Boer War like himself. Macgillivray, in *The Three Hostages*, lays bare the propagandist's conscience, understandably alerted when facing his own weapons:

> '. . . Dick, have you ever considered what a diabolical weapon that can be – using all the channels of modern publicity to poison and warp men's minds? It is the most dangerous thing on earth. You can use it cleanly – as I think on the whole we did in the War – but you also can use it to establish the most damnable lies. Happily in the long run it defeats itself, but only after it has sown the world with mischief. Look at the Irish! They are the cleverest propagandists extant, and managed to persuade most people that they were a brave, generous, humorous, talented, warm-hearted race, cruelly yoked to a dull mercantile England, when, God knows, they were exactly the opposite.'

The story assumes an Irish master-criminal Dominick Medina, so English as to use 'un-English' as a term of reproach, and to make his mother fear he is 'forgetting your own land'. The plot is judiciously distanced from Ireland, even if Sandy Arbuthnot psychoanalyzes the villain on the basis of the inadequacies of Irish heroic mythology (not as daft as it sounds, given Pearse's obsession with Cú Chulainn and the mythical nomenclature of the Fenians). The hostage *motif* probably got in because of legendary Irish kings' hostage-taking as a (usually illusory) mark of their pre-eminence. But within the story Hannay pretends to fall under the villain's domination, with all the emblems of slavery, being returned to his South African origins in the process. He testifies as much by bitterness at 'this new possessory attitude, this hint of nigger-driving [which] had suddenly made me hate Medina'. Medina's supreme Englishness makes Hannay's soliloquies seem to speak for their author:

> I had been annexed by him as a slave, and every drop of free blood in my veins was in revolt; but I was also resolved to be the most docile slave that ever kissed the ground before a tyrant. Some day my revenge would come . . .

That revenge could take different forms, greatest of all in *Sick Heart River* where dying he anatomised the worthlessness of the gospel of success which had enslaved and abducted himself.[27]

The theme of kingliness among the people as against servitude, derived from a Scottish idea, a version of Glasgow cultural supremacy however lacking in Oxbridge polish. (Buchan, who had an English market to cultivate, sent the smallest Gorbals Die-Hard to Cambridge on Dickson McCunn's money.) The idea became fused with an echo of G. K. Chesterton's great populist poem on English history 'The Secret People' (1907): Buchan writes of a truly majestic underground people in *Midwinter* (1923) whose 'Naked Men' recall Chesterton's 'naked people under a naked crown'. In *The Blanket of the Dark* (1931) a rightful heir to the throne so grossly inhabited by Henry VIII ends by disappearing into a secret people. Buchan had offered the English a metaphor culled from Scots resentment at their own anglicisation. But the crowning example is more princely than kingly, *A Prince of the Captivity* having as epigraph

> As when a Prince
> Of dispers'd Israel, chosen in the shade,
> Rules by no canon save his inward light,
> And knows no pageant save the pipes and shawms
> Of his proud spirit.

Like Prester John, it is a well-laden title. One meaning is literal: the hero Adam Melfort, another Buchanoid, more highly-coloured than Leithen, lives out a life analogous to that of his own superior in World War One, Lassom alias Macandrew alias Meyer, a Zionist Jew running a spy network in Germany and ultimately killed. Adam will also die by German (in his case Nazi) hands at the book's end, many pages and years after his mentor's death, which had befallen[28] in the courtyard of a military prison in a certain Rhineland city, [where] a small man with a pointed beard and a nervous mouth had confronted a firing squad. On that occasion he did not look down, as had been his habit, but faced the rifles with steady, smiling eyes.

Lassom dreams of the restoration of his lost Israel, and when Adam tells him of his own dream of reunion with his dead son in a Scots Gaelic island, he understands: 'it is as I guessed. We have each our Jerusalem'.

One of the worst aspects of Buchan's sale of birthright for English establishment pottage had been his readiness to foster pro-Scottish sentiment by arousing the hostility of his new masters against other, and to him rival, ethnic groups or races. His chief targets were the Jews and the Irish Catholics, both formidable international forces as Buchan claimed for the Scots:[29]

> You will hear people talk of the 'Scottish nation'. Well, I am not so sure that we are a nation for that involves territorial boundaries. We are something greater than that. We are a race. We own no limits of land or water. Scotland is wherever Scotsmen are stamping upon the world the tradition which is our heritage.

That was spoken in 1921. Up to that point allusions to Jews in his novels were mainly hostile, sometimes in the mouths of unpleasant persons (Marka in *The Half-Hearted*), sometimes in those of sympathetic victims (Scudder in *The Thirty-Nine Steps*), sometimes gratuitously in those of persons we are to respect in all things (Blenkiron in *The Three Hostages*). The classic case is the doomed American spying for Britain, Scudder, with his conviction of a 'conspiracy . . . to get Russia and Germany at loggerheads':

> Everything would be in the melting-pot, and they looked to see a new world emerge. The capitalists would rake in the shekels, and make fortunes by buying up wreckage. Capital, he said, had no conscience and no fatherland. Besides, the Jew was behind it, and the Jew hated Russia worse than hell.
>
> 'Do you wonder?' he cried. 'For three hundred years they have been persecuted, and this is the return match for the *pogroms*. The Jew is everywhere, but you have to go far down the backstairs to find him. Take any big Teutonic business concern . . . if you're . . . bound to get to the real boss, ten to one you are brought up against a little white-faced Jew in a bath-chair with an eye like a rattlesnake. Yes, sir, he is the man who is ruling the world just now, and he has his knife in the Empire of the Tzar, because his aunt was outraged and his father flogged in some one-horse location on the Volga.'

This is utterly irrelevant to the plot, and critics have argued that it is to test Hannay in risking all for Scudder's possibly crazy cause, which might be true if Hannay had worried about the point. Secret Service Supremo Sir Walter Bullivant remarks that Scudder 'had a lot of odd biases too. Jews, for example, made him see red. Jews and the high finance'. But Bullivant's scepticism shrivels when Scudder's prophecy of the murder of Karolides is fulfilled. 'I apologise to the shade of Scudder' might seem to give a clean bill of health to the entire Scudder package, rattlesnake-eyed Jew included. Why Scudder's hatreds and Blenkiron's dislikes against all Jews are necessary, is inexplicable if not simply judicious propaganda against allegedly powerful rivals. Equally sympathetic figures, Andrew Amos and Macgillivray, perform the same service against the Irish Catholics, with comparable irrelevance to the plots. *A Prince of the Captivity*, a puzzling work for Buchan's less critical admirers, is surely a noble retraction. The thesis of a separate Jewish agenda in World War One is as strong as ever, but one now making for heroic isolation. Buchan recognises that love of Britain might be a stronger motive than hatred of Russia, and – he was writing in 1932 – that Germany might be a more logical enemy than Russia.[30]

In the 1920s Buchan's doubts about birthright and pottage were taking a more positive form regarding his lost horizon: he evangelised the Scots language in past and present, in prose and poetry. He met Hugh MacDiarmid and introduced his poems. He anthologised 245 Scots vernacular poems in *The Northern Muse* (1924). He had collected his own *Poems Scots and English* in 1917: 'practically all his nature poems (1911–17) are in Scots', remarked Kurt Wittig, 'while his English verse reads like exercises in a foreign language'. Was it a foreign language to him in some respects? He was not born into it. Jaikie Galt in *Castle Gay* (1930) late of the Gorbals Die-Hards, now at Cambridge, speaks 'with the slight sing-song which is ineradicable in one born in the West of Scotland, but otherwise . . . pure English for he had an imitative ear and unconsciously acquired the speech of a new environment': one doubts if his creator was as unconscious. But if Buchan's English poetry, like his more aristocratic English prose, was artificial (*The Half-Hearted* had self-mocked 'the boldness which comes from the use of a peer's name without the handle', prophetically), Buchan in the 1920s got down to work on a Scotsman whose life was spent speaking in one language and writing in another: Sir Walter Scott, whose most perfect prose Buchan also found in pure Scots, 'Wandering Willie's Tale' recorded in the vernacular by the folklorist Darsie Latimer in *Redgauntlet*. Scott's great novels Buchan held to be his major Scots novels, but saw elsewhere no less 'great drama [proceeding] from the clash of character . . . also epic [showing] the conflicts of history sublimated and focused by a triumphant imagination, [stirring] the blood like wine and trumpets':

[in] one of the lesser novels, *Ivanhoe* . . . suddenly comes something different. – 'And now', said Locksley, 'I will crave your Grace's permission to plant such a

mark as is used in the North Country.' What has happened? The horns of Elfland are blowing. What we have had before has been the good stock machinery of romance, but now the horizon is suddenly enlarged to embrace the greenwood, and Old England is summoned to the rescue.

Buchan manages this himself in *A Prince of the Captivity* when Lassom speaks of Jerusalem: the horizon is enlarged to embrace the Holy Land, and old Judaea is summoned to the rescue, and for the horns of Elfland we hear the harp of David. His growing peace with himself, his recovery of Scotland and new justice to its supposed rivals (including England) as opposed to jostling for a place in the English sun, gave him his reward.[31]

The propagandist was turning towards justice. It might be seen in his comments on historians when fleshing out Nelson's *History of English Literature* (1923):

> Carlyle as a historian stands alone. He can never be imitated, and should not be followed. His style and his habits of thought are not conducive to the discovery or exposition of historical truth, but beyond doubt his was one of the greatest minds than ever applied itself to history.
>
> ... The critics complain that [Macaulay] lacked qualities which he never claimed to possess. But his work remains one of the great possessions of the British people – an introduction to historical study for the ordinary reader, and also one of the most brilliantly coloured and artistically composed reconstructions of the past in any literature.
>
> Froude as a historian is less inaccurate than Macaulay, but more essentially unfair.

And the old professional recognised his fellow when his *Julius Caesar* (1932) summed up *De Bello Gallico*: 'primarily an electioneering pamphlet, the most brilliant known to history'. He was less able to see through the propaganda of Julius Caesar's great-nephew and heir when he came to write his *Augustus* (1937), but there he had no counterpart of his own confections to confront, merely the results of brilliant and diversified lost scribes. He was ready enough to confront his own former propaganda, as in his revisions and tacit admissions of bias when his *Montrose* (1928) sought to undo the partisanship of its predecessor (1913).[32]

A Prince of the Captivity also opened up Buchan's own sense of limits. He had bought his way to success; he had sold himself into captivity. The novel is his metaphor. Adam's 'Jerusalem', as Lassom calls it, his Gaelic island, is an old theme in Buchan, but is also a repossession of the Scotland he has left, and the Scotland his Scots background had initially sealed off from him. It is Gaelic Scotland, Catholic Scotland, Scotland part of a Communion of Saints in which Adam can find the soul of his dead son. It is Buchan's equivalent of the Christ-quest of the young MacDiarmid, of the Catholic conversion which would overtake Compton Mackenzie and Moray MacLaren and 'Fionn MacColla' (Tom Macdonald). But it also involves embrace of what the Scots Calvinists insisted the Reformation was about: the survival of Paganism, whether in Roman Catholicism or popular custom and belief. Formally Catholicism hides below the surface in *A Prince of the Captivity*, where Adam proclaims the justice of Catholic statesmen: the actual Cosgrave of Ireland who ruled from 1922 to 1932, the Catholic Karl Brüning driven by the Nazis from power in Germany in 1932 and disguised as Loeffler in the novel written as he was falling. *Prince* has been called 'misplaced' because Hitler (and de Valera) had come to power when it was published: but it was obviously written in such expectation. Buchan produced the first great anti-Nazi novel in English literature. It chronicles how its hero, Adam, schemes and is frustrated on the brink of success, repeatedly, usually through female intrigues cutting across his hopes, how his peacetime successes dwindle down to one coup which can be little more than a desperate hope for whose fulfilment he sacrifices his life. But he is already a figure emasculated and crippled by his own compromises with integrity, however altruistic they may appear. He has been imprisoned, taking the blame for his wife, just as Buchan had been taken prisoner in Oxford whither his lost University of Glasgow had sold him. It is in prison that Adam has the first vision of his lost island and his dead child, although in life boy and place had never known one another. It savours of enchantment and its ambiguities, as previously confronted by Buchan, notably in his major historical novel *Witch Wood*.[33]

The historical novel, short story, play or film, gets in history's way if the author merely wishes to use the past in place of the imagination or use imagination to defy the past. It may by constructive falsification achieve a deeper truth, as do the insights in *1066 and All That*, or *'Don't, Mr Disraeli!'*, but in the main the historian's best hope must be that historical fiction will illuminate the parts of the past which formal history cannot reach. The historian should finish reading a successful piece of historical fiction feeling that it may well have been so, and that after looking through this fictional glass certain problems of the past begin to make more sense. The young Buchan at least gave readers of *Sir Quixote* the chance to confront the romantic and repulsive faces of the Covenanter victims of Charles II through one pair of eyes, albeit a pair borrowed from Conan Doyle and transported 150 years backward. Likewise, he made readers of *A Lost Lady* experience the companionship of Simon Fraser, Lord Lovat, at the end of his life. *Salute to Adventurers* may well be unrivalled in showing how well the Scots in the early American colonies made themselves respected and reprehended. *The Path of the King* is frequently probable in its vignettes, such as a view of Titus Oates and his criminal circle, or the mentality of the mercenary spy in the first months of George I, neither of which are readily available as straight fact.[34]

But *Witch Wood* is something else. Here Buchan takes the Calvinist vs Catholic (= Pagan) equation and shows how in certain circumstances it may become Calvinist = Pagan. The impulse will have some anachronism, just as Scott could show: it is all very well to take personal experience or folk tradition and assume it plucks a thread running without break to the point of historical enquiry. Buchan's love-hate relationship with the Covenanters clearly grew out of filial affections and rational reappraisals of the Free Church in its totems and taboos. But the initial stimulus for his novel was less Montrose's true Scottishness surviving his transition from Covenant to King – a question with all too much relevance to Buchan's Scottishness in transition between Glasgow and Oxbridge-London – than childhood memory of local folk-tale anent the vanished minister whom Buchan would resurrect as his protagonist in *Witch Wood*. Had he been abducted by the Devil, or by the Fairies? The infant Buchan discovered conflict-traditions among his contemporaries when he visited his grandfather's Peebles. The quest is a profound one, for historians no less than Frazerians: how far could ordinary Fairylore be misread as devil-worship? Buchan was no intimate of Yeats, whose Sinn Féin politics he must have loathed: but he would have respected Yeats's quotation of the Irish countryman who denied believing in fairies while adding that of course 'they're there'. The zeal of the Calvinist to eradicate diabolism could throw out the Divine with the Devil. *Witch Wood* turns on the point. It is the theist as opposed to the atheist critique of witchhunting, the recognition that the Devil is best served by those who persecute in the name of God: it also insists that the victims of persecution are liable to be transformed into the likeness of their enemies, once a chance of power comes their way.

Mixed with it is the theme of the losers in history: the pagans, the Picts, the native Africans, the native Americans, the Jews, the Catholics, the Jacobites, a theme linking all Buchan's work from the early stories 'No-Man's-Land' (written at Oxford) and 'The Grove of Ashtaroth' (*Blackwood's* June 1910), to the self-sacrifice of Leithen in *Sick Heart River* to save the Hare Amerindians from destruction. In the early stories it is the admission that Pagans and Picts have been obliterated unheard, despite our debts to their imprint. It is the undertow of the imperial propaganda, resulting in Laputa's ending as hero when he had so obviously been cast as villain. It grew stronger as the post-war Buchan questioned the triumphalism in which he had been enlisted: *Midwinter* celebrates the Jacobites of '45, unearthing their English identity to include the most English figure of the time, Samuel Johnson. *Montrose* and *Witch Wood* mourn the lost cause of fortitude against intolerance; even *Oliver Cromwell* (1934) is the story of a loser incapable of building a state to outlive himself, whence his name was held chiefly in horror for almost two centuries. Yet Buchan's immediately preceding historical work retold the most savage of all persecutions of the Jacobites, *The Massacre of Glencoe* (1933). Buchan may include even the Fairies among his sympathetic losers: in *Witch Wood* the alleged Fairies abducting the minister prove soldiers of fortune persuading him to join them, a reminder of the fairy stories lying behind the Buchan hero stories. But the accumulative effect is to qualify the gospel of success-worship so long fastened on Buchan. If it was his reason for making his exile from Scotland permanent, then the mass of his writing became his own self-indictment. He, no less than Shane Leslie, rejoiced in the idea of sublime failure and made its cultivation a point of patriotic pride.[35]

Yet it would be unfair to leave Buchan's debt to the University of Glasgow on a note so negative, however salutary. We do have a final word to his old University, delivered on 30 October 1933, on 'Principles of Social Service', and it shows how profoundly he knew his real Alma Mater regardless of the offers he could not refuse from his Oxonian Godmother:

> I am speaking not only to the members of a University, but to a Scottish University, my own University. Here you have one tremendous advantage. The older English Universities are a little apt to be what Americans call 'hand-picked', and the life there to be what Stevenson called 'a half-scenic life of gardens'. A young Oxford or Cambridge man too often is a little out of touch with the ordinary world. I see a good deal of them, and many of them consult me who are proposing to embark on a political life. My first advice to them is always to go out and get to understand something of the people of Britain.
>
> But you in Glasgow are different. You cultivate the Muses in close contact with a busy industrial world. And this juxtaposition should keep you free from pedantry and broaden your outlook and strengthen your hold upon realities. There was a famous seceder minister in Edinburgh in the early part of last century whose life work was a great edition of St Paul's Epistles. He was known to inform his friends in confidence that he 'found *Tom Jones* grand stuff for taking the taste of the Apostle out of his mouth'. You have many opportunities here in Glasgow for getting the taste of the class-rooms out of your mouth. But remember you must take them; you can segregate yourselves just as much in Glasgow as you can in Oxford or Cambridge. So in addition to the moral duty which lies upon you because of your privileges, you have this direct personal interest if you are to complete your education. Books are only part of that education; mixing with your own fellow-students is only a part of it. Before

you are really educated men or women you have still to rub shoulders with a wider and rougher and in some ways a richer world.

For it is the great achievement of the University of Glasgow that it is more responsive to its immediate hinterland than any of the other ancient universities of these islands can claim to be, Dublin being too colonial, St Andrews too cut-off, Aberdeen with too huge a hinterland to epitomise, Edinburgh too conscious of its elite and frontier status, Oxford and Cambridge too self-sufficient. It gave John Buchan the means of discovering what to make of the community whence he had emerged, and how his listening to its people could make a writer of him, as similar experience had made Scott and Stevenson and Conan Doyle writers. But while Edinburgh University had trained them, its training had not been in their craft as folklore conservators, analysts and consequent fictionists, however much Scott learned from Edinburgh historians, and Stevenson from Edinburgh academic gossip, and Conan Doyle from Edinburgh medical personalities and peculiarities. The University of Glasgow did train Buchan as a writer to the point that it started his publishing career. And it was as a writer that his intellectual value was acknowledged sufficient to ensure his sale. As Professor Sir Richard Lodge recalled:

> I wrote to my late colleagues at Brasenose and urged them not to pay excessive attention to Buchan's Latin Prose or even to his translations, but to read carefully his Essay and General paper, and, if they were really good, to elect him in spite of possible defects in his other papers.

The examiners duly acknowledged the professionalism which Buchan had attained at the University whose degrees they did not recognize, his essay seeming to them 'just like a bit out of Stevenson'. It never seems to have occurred to anyone that in so doing they bowed their heads in acknowledgement of the genius of the University of Glasgow, which had taken a man from his people and shown him how to make that people live in his pages.[36]

Notes

1. The major biographical source for Buchan is Janet Adam Smith, *John Buchan: A Biography* (London 1985[1965]), but Andrew Lownie, *John Buchan: The Presbyterian Cavalier* (London 1995), is useful and eager. Robert G. Blanshard, *The First Editions of John Buchan: A Collector's Bibliography* (Hamden Conn., 1981), has a value far beyond its limited title. *Scholar-Gipsies* was duly published on 25 September 1896 (with three short stories among the essays), but *John Burnet of Barns* was serialised in *Chambers's Edinburgh Journal* from

4 December 1897 to 23 July 1898 with book publication 3 June 1898, well before the first short story collection *Grey Weather*, 29 March 1899. Proserpina was the Latin version of Persephone, Goddess of Spring and Queen of the Underworld (Buchan's classicism was firmly Roman rather than Greek). Was Buchan working up an abortive ghost story or was he simply more literary about the weather than in his later title? It might have been a very early version of what eventuated as 'The Grove of Ashtaroth' (*Blackwood's* 1910) set in Africa.

2. The Penguin ten of 1956 were the five Hannay novels (*The Thirty-Nine Steps, Greenmantle, Mr Standfast, The Three Hostages,* and *The Island of Sheep*), the Dickson McCunn three (*Huntingtower, Castle Gay,* and *The House of Four Winds*), *Prester John* and *John Macnab*. For sales, see Smith, *Buchan*, 295–97, for attribution of the anonymous 'note on the author', Lownie, *Buchan*, 287–88: as the device of a 3-page biographical note in addition to its customary back-of-jacket photograph-cum-sketch-of-life was quite exceptional for Penguin, the Buchan estate would seem to have suggested, if not insisted on, its use (Buchan's widow, Susan Lady Tweedsmuir (*née* Grosvenor) would have approved, or perhaps commanded, the arrangement, and the sketch would have embodied her views). Penguin were still using the 'note' for many, though not all, of the titles by 1988 (Susan Tweedsmuir died in the late 1970s, aged 94).

3. Canongate Classics 17: *Witch Wood* (with an instructive introduction by Christopher Harvie) (Edinburgh 1988): the excellent collection *The Watcher by the Threshold – Shorter Scottish Fiction*, Canongate Classics 79 (ed. Andrew Lownie (Edinburgh 1997)) corrects 'were' to 'where' but otherwise leaves the blurb unchanged. B&W have identical blurbs on their editions of *The Free Fishers* (Edinburgh 1994) and *A Lost Lady of Old Years* (Edinburgh 1995), and presumably many others. Oxford's integrity is ensured by the detailed biographical chronology given in its World's Classics series. For the Hon. William Buchan at Oxford, see Lownie, *Buchan*, 233.

4. 'The Graduate as Freshman', *Glasgow University Magazine*, vol. VIII, no. 1 (Wednesday, October 30, 1895), anonymous but firmly identified by Blanshard, *Buchan Bibliography*, D. 11. One of its most singular qualities is self-description as though the author is another being: the first literary assertion of Buchan's Glasgow-Oxford schizophrenia.

5. Buchan, *Memory Hold-the-Door* (London 1940), 47–48.

6. The 18-year-old produced his introduction at speed, judicious and beguiling as it is. The first paragraph begins impressively 'The two decades between 1550 and 1570 are marked, perhaps, more than any other in the history of our literature by the birth of famous men': he meant English literature, writing for a London publisher and audience, but his alien origin emerges two sentences later – 'Mary was dead, and her sister Elizabeth had mounted the throne', events of 1558. So Oxford had something left to teach him, viz. the dates of the English rulers.

7. Nichol (1833–94) was the son of Glasgow's Professor of Astronomy John Pringle Nichol (1804–59). John Nichol *American Literature An Historical Sketch 1620–1880* (Edinburgh 1882), on Lincoln seems an anticipation of *The Path of the King* in the sphere of rhetoric:

   . . . Gettysburg . . . gave rise to the few paragraphs of consummate natural eloquence, in which the rail-splitter of Illinois, raised on the surge of a great moral and patriotic tide, recalled the address of Pericles over his Athenian dead . . . (141–42).

   On John Nichol, see the invaluable collection by Professor Andrew Hook of Glasgow, *From Goosecreek to Ganderclough – Studies in Scottish-American Literary and Cultural History* (East Linton, 1999) 6–7, 218–32.

8. Bradley's allusions to *Coriolanus* in *Shakespearean Tragedy* (1904) are few though frequently profound, but his British Academy Shakespeare Lecture (1912), *'Coriolanus'*, was reprinted in his *A Miscellany* (1929). Five years later the composite volume *Six Stories from Shakespeare* featured Buchan's *Coriolanus* with its fascinating use of new characters to discuss Coriolanus's having 'gone barbarian', even in his death. The idea relates both to Buchan's Scottishness weakening in England, and to Britishness endangered by German example in wartime. The other five essays are little more than worthless paraphrases: *Julius Caesar* (Winston Churchill), *The Merchant of Venice* (Philip Snowden), *Hamlet* (Francis Brett Young), *The Taming of the Shrew* (Clemence Dane), *King Lear* (Hugh Walpole). They had previously been run in the *Strand*, Buchan's appearing in January 1934. Buchan had probably heard Bradley on *Coriolanus* at Glasgow.

9. There is an agreeable tribute to Tommie Nelson in *Memory Hold-the-Door*, 137–39. His Rugby Football 'Blue' may account for Jaikie's performance at the outset of *Castle Gay*, though as Buchan's future employer and the heir of an ancient and powerful Edinburgh publishing house, he was no Gorbals Die-hard. He was killed at the battle of Arras, in 1917.

10. 'The Graduate Freshman'. A few other passages suggest themselves for quotation:

    He may sit for a year beside the same man in a lecture room, who will make no attempt to fraternise, and who will receive any effort on his part by exhibit – a side view of a sturdy pair of shoulders, fashionably draped. If he should be fortunate enough to obtain an introduction to their owner, he will find his behaviour coldly courteous, unless by this time he has learned to take his share in the sporting talk of the 'Varsity', or, better still, to irrigate his speech with wantonness . . .

    . . . It is a startling but not an inexplicable fact that from Bacon to Bradley no great English philosopher has taught in either Oxford or Cambridge, if we except T. H. Green; and that with the single exception of Hume, Scotland has never failed to attract her own thinkers to her University chairs.

    [The 'Bradley' in question was F. H. Bradley, brother of A. C. Bradley.]

11. Smith, *Buchan*, 29–45. Lownie, *Buchan*, 31–37.

12. 'Second Thoughts of a Scotsman on the Make: Politics, Nationalism and Myth in John Buchan', *Scottish Historical Review* (April 1991), 34.

13. Everything written by Professor Harvie on Buchan is inspirational, and in some respects I am but varying his theme. See introduction to *The Thirty-Nine Steps* (Oxford, World's Classics 1993); 'For Gods are Kittle Cattle: J. G. Frazer and John Buchan' in Robert Fraser (ed.), *Sir James Frazer and the Literary Imagination* (ed.) Robert Fraser (London 1990), 253–69; *The John Buchan Journal* (Winter 1989), 14–26; *The Centre of Things: Political Fiction in Britain from Disraeli to the Present Day* (London 1991); 'Political Thrillers and the Condition of England' in *Literature and Society* (ed.) Arthur J. B. Marwick (London 1989). Our only serious divergences are on Buchan's anti-Jewish attitudes (which he denies but I detect) and on his anti-Gaelic attitudes (which he detects but I deny). The Conan Doyle stories of Gerard ran in the *Strand* as follows: 'The Medal of the Brigadier' (December 1894), 'How the Brigadier Held the King' (April 1895), 'How the King Held the Brigadier' (May 1895). The later stories appeared when *Sir Quixote* had been completed. The last story (appearing late in April) is in fact concerned with Gerard adrift on the moors (of Devon) as a fugitive from Princetown Prison. Buchan's obituary of Stevenson appeared in the *Glasgow University Magazine* 9 January 1895, discussed Smith, *Buchan*, 33.

14. The narrator of 'No-Man's Land' (written at Oxford in 1898) is supposedly a Fellow of 'St Chad's', Oxford, but the University's only relevance is to exacerbate his death by its 'polite scorn' for his discovery of surviving Picts. Of the political short stories, 'A Lucid Interval' is simply party propaganda fictionalised with cunning but less bite than Saki, 'Tendebant Manus' is a telepathic ghost story turning ably on a political theme which it nobly transcends, the political stories in *The Gap in the Curtain* include a delicious political satire 'The Right Honourable David Mayot' which suggests that Buchan's social insecurity lost us one outstanding political novel. (Its Tory leader is obviously Lloyd George and its Labour Prime Minister is equally clearly Stanley Baldwin.)

15. *Memorials of John Murray of Broughton* (ed.) R. Fitzroy Bell (Edinburgh 1898). I use the 1920 Hodder and Stoughton 'cheap edition' of *The Half-Hearted* whose quotations above are, sequentially, 22, 23, 26, 29, 44, 52, 93, 125.

16. *The Half-Hearted*, 29–30. Is the name of 'Medina' (a very odd one for an Irishman passing as English) in *The Three Hostages* a conceit privately acknowledging Marka as sufficiently close to 'Mecca' to make him the original form of a character matured over a quarter-century, recalling Mohammed's journey from Mecca to Medina? Has anyone a better explanation? It is another proof of the seminal, experimental place of *The Half-Hearted* in Buchan's writing, and a further instance of his readiness to

return to the dilemmas and counter-attractions of his Scottish-Oxford youth. The quotation from *The Thirty-Nine Steps* is only a few paragraphs before the end of the story, a fascinating choice for the final, greatest obstacle for the hero to overcome.

17. Esau is from *The Path of the King*, 116, the king-spirit in this chapter ('The Wood of Life') is a crusader, who rejects a safe stay-at-home destiny, but the passage has obvious permanent relevance for its author. For further examples of the Esau complex, see for instance *The Thirty-Nine Steps*, chapter 1, first five paragraphs, *John Macnab, passim* (even for Lamancha when the navvy scorns his attempt at bribery, chapter 14), the character of Lombard in *The Island of Sheep*, the character of Gaillard – and more profoundly that of Leithen – in *Sick Heart River*, esp. Part III, section 1, end. *A Prince of the Captivity* in which the hero loses birthright for a frivolous wife, is pure Esau. The 'two men only' are identified by the manipulative Wratislaw in *The Half-Hearted*, 176–77: it is as though Buchan sees his own market-value from his dilemma, bringing two antithetical vantage-points to his own recruitment. But the recruit's misgivings make for reappraisals of the horns of his dilemma: if his defence of his opportunism seeks to give it a moral dimension, his retreat to the Puritan origins requires the growth of generosity in the process.

18. 'Linn' is from the Gaelic, meaning 'pool' ('Dublin' similarly means 'Blackpool'). 'The Herd of Standlan' was published in *Black and White* (June 1896), went into *Grey Weather* and is conveniently available in *The Watcher by the Threshold* (ed. Lownie). Buchan's Glasgow politics are thus stated in *Memory Hold-the-Door*: 'I acquired the corporate spirit only at a rectorial election, when, though a professed Tory, I chose to support the Liberal candidate, Mr Asquith, and almost came by my end at the hands of a red-haired savage, one Robert Horne, who has since been Chancellor of the Exchequer' (33). The profession of Toryism may be no more accurate than the preceding 'As a student I was wholly obscure': it is, admittedly, a pretty compliment to Glasgow to see an undergraduate book-author and short-story writer as 'wholly obscure'. The style of the *Glasgow University Magazine*'s form of allusion to him says otherwise.

19. The Hannay cowardice allusions are from *Mr Standfast* (paragraph 4 from end, chapters 5, 13, 16). *The Power House* was considerably enlarged from its Blackwood's long short story status for its book appearance: the 1913 version featured Leithen's pursuit from his home to the friendly Embassy [presumably Russian] at the conclusion, the 1916 text *inter alia* introduces for the first time the Antioch St restaurant ambush and the Oxford St attempts at abduction. Hannay's perils in London stem from the law-abiding citizenry (*The Thirty-Nine Steps* chapter 8, *Mr Standfast* chapter 10). It was clearly an ongoing nightmare. Graham Greene, 'The Last Buchan', 1941 (*Collected Essays* (London 1969)). *Greenmantle*, chapter 20.

20. *Mr Standfast*, chapter 18. *The Thirty-Nine Steps*, fourth paragraph from end. A. Conan Doyle, 'His Last Bow', in *His Last Bow* (1917). The 'Counterweight to Buchan's propaganda' argument is Lownie, *Buchan*, 140. Christmastide is *Greenmantle* chapter 7, but the passage and the theme are chapter 8. The death of the pacific Launcelot Wake is chapter 21, *Mr Standfast* and its anti-Irish diatribe chapter 4.

21. Tombs is *Mr Standfast*, chapter 4. Stumm is *Greenmantle*, chapter 6. Lawrence, *Seven Pillars of Wisdom*, the rape at Deraa, is the possible derivation, Wodehouse, *The Code of the Woosters*, chapter 7, the definite one. Wodehouse in 1938, wanting the most merciless attack he could make on Oswald Mosley's Black Shirts and their pro-German posturing, invented Spode as an English Stumm with the Black Shorts. If Buchan produced the first major British anti-Nazi novel, Wodehouse used him to make the finest anti-Mosleyite one. For Buchan at Oxford, Smith, *Buchan*, 47, and for his own perceptions see his *Brasenose College* (London 1898), 139: 'specially famous, too, were the dinners which, . . . he used to give to undergraduates in his quaint green-panelled rooms'. The book met some jealous Oxford criticism, all the more because its author was the only College historian of its series still nominally an undergraduate. It would have increased Buchan's alienation, and the need to conceal the wounds. Buchan's reference to 'Earnestness' at Mansfield College in 1895 is also curious. 'Ernest' at that date was code for 'homosexual', whence Wilde, *The Importance of Being Earnest*.

22. If the diaries were forged, it was presumably not by interpolation but by the use of a set of blank diaries requisitioned from the makers of the actual Casement diaries in Hall's possession into which Hall's forger could then copy matter from the real diaries together with salacious matter, moderate at first and increasing as the forger warmed to his work: the silence of the makers whose file copies had been obtained would be ensured under D.O.R.A. The prime candidate as forger is the future Professor Sir Frank Ezra Adcock, Fellow of King's, Cambridge, and editor of the *Cambridge Ancient History*: he was of course gay, as others of Hall's staff seem to have been.

23. 'Such eyes as the man has!' (US Ambassador Walter Hines Page, quoted as epigraph for Admiral Sir William James, *The Eyes of the Navy* (London 1955): see also James's notice of Hall in the 1941–50 *D.N.B.* Shane Leslie, *The Celt and the World* (New York 1917). *Greenmantle*, chapters 15, 19, 21, 22. *The Half-Hearted*, last lines. *Mr Standfast*, chapter 21. Harvie, introduction to *The Thirty-Nine Steps*, xvi.

24. *Huntingtower* (Edinburgh 1978), my introduction, and chapter 15.

25. *John Macnab*, chapter 3, chapter 5. *Sick Heart River*.

26. Buchan, *Scholar Gipsies* (London 1896) both in fiction and essays shows the young Buchan in action as folk collector; for his use of folk evidence in literary criticism, 'The Country of *Kidnapped*', *Academy* 7 May 1898, followed

by what seem ungenerous rejoinders by Andrew Lang (who had him to dinner when Buchan migrated to London in 1900, and whom Buchan made a contributor to *Nelson's Scottish Review* in 1908–08) on 14 May, with subsequent appropriate snipings at both from inevitable Stewarts and Camerons (but not Balfours) on 21 May. 'The Novel and the Fairytale' after separate pamphlet publication was included in the later edition of *Homilies and Recreations* (Hodder & Stoughton, 1939) (whose earlier, Nelson, edition (1926) contains essays on 'The Muse of History', 'The Great Captains', 'A Note on Edmund Burke', 'The Judicial Temperament', 'Catullus', and 'The Literature of Tweeddale' dropped later). The Macaulay pre-Frazer verse is from 'The Battle of Lake Regillus' stanza X (*Lays of Ancient Rome*). Buchan's earlier 'Prester John' story was published in *Chambers's Edinburgh Journal* (June 1897) and thence in *Grey Weather*: see *The Watcher by the Threshold*, (ed. Lownie). On Lincoln's path of the Welsh kings, see *Burke's Presidential Families of the United States of America*, 'The Descent of President Lincoln from Edward I, King of England': the Edwardian descent is in fact doubtful, but that from Gruffudd Fychan II, Lord of Glyndyfrdwy and father of Owain Glyn Dwr (*anglice* Owen Glendower) is definite, and both Grufudd and his wife Elen descended from Hywel and his grandfather Rhodri, John Davies, *A History of Wales* (London 1990, 1993) 82–83. On the Scots tradition of the victorious simpleton, see A. J. Bruford and D. A. MacDonald, *Scottish Traditional Tales* (Edinburgh 1994), esp. 'Silly Jack and the Lord's Daughter', 'The Three Feathers', 'The Green Man of Knowledge', &c.

27. Smith, *Buchan*, 292–93. *The Three Hostages*, chapters 4 and 8.
28. Chesterton's 'The Secret People' first appeared in E. Nesbit's Socialist periodical *Neolith*, no. 1 (1907); it would later reappear in his *Poems* (1915) and subsequent collections. However Socialist its first audience neither Chesterton nor Buchan were Socialists: they had strong common ground, however little they acknowledged it, and both acknowledged a duty to address the Socialist agenda, however critically. Both seem to have been alert to a false Messiah's use of Socialist priorities, thus immunising them to the appeal of an Oswald Mosley. Buchan, bitterly critical of the ineptitude with which all parties responded to the unemployment crisis (House of Commons, January 1930: see Smith, *Buchan*, 314–15), expertly dissects its fuel to the political opportunists (*The Gap in the Curtain*, chapter 3 and 5). The epigraph to *A Prince of the Captivity* is unascribed, and could be Buchan's own: I, at all events, have failed to discover it. See also *Prince*, Book 1, chapter 2.
29. Buchan, address to the Vernacular Circle of the London Burns Club, 1921, quoted by Alasdair Hutton, 'John Buchan and the Union of 1707', *John Buchan Journal* no. 17 (August 1997), 19. The subversive implications of *John Macnab* naturally asserted themselves in the modern sequel by the poet Andrew Greig, *The Return of John Macnab* (London 1996), an excellent thriller apparently written from a left-wing nationalist feminist sympathy.

Greig scores a neat point in differentiating the politics of the participants, where Buchan seems to make them all Tories (Leithen may be in Opposition and Lamancha is certainly in Government but Leithen is Tory from *The Power-House* and Lamancha would hardly be Claybody's choice if he were Labour or in Government if he were Liberal: *The Power-House* produces a Tory-Labour partnership potentially inspirational to Greig). But Buchan develops character distinctions (destined to serve him well in *Sick Heart River*) where Greig's are implicit from the first. Greig is closer to *John Macnab* than he admits: Crosby, the pressman, anticipates some (though by no means all) of the contribution of Greig's presswoman Kirsty. Where Buchan outflanks him is with Fish Benjie, although Greig does use a small child as future archivist of the affair. But in two startling ways Greig's novel is in itself subversive of its own radicalism. Casual authority figures are much more human than in Buchan, notably police and state security (contrast Greig's Sergeant Jim MacIver, and Ms Ellen Stobo of 'The Corridor', with the police and A.P.M. pursuing or arresting Hannay in *The Thirty-Nine Steps* and *Mr Standfast*, Greig creating loveable instruments of authority, Buchan some deliberately hateful ones – in *The Power-House*, indeed, Leithen is chased by a policeman who is one of the great anarch Lumley's minions). The other distinction is even more curious. Although Buchan would actually be made George V's representative at the Church of Scotland General Assembly and later in Canada, his subversive views on kingly descent determine *The Path of the King*, where Greig makes the living Charles Prince of Wales the *deus ex machina* of a book which logically should end in the state security forces' destruction of the four major participants in the new John Macnab. The portrait of Charles is realistic within firmly affectionate contours (other evidence suggests far less tolerance regarding challenges to his agrarian seigniorial claims). Monarchy has been declared the pivot of state reactionary forces in the United Kingdom by the most profound of modern Scottish nationalist thinkers, Tom Nairn (*The Enchanted Glass*): it is somewhat disturbing to find Buchan in this respect more progressive than his self-appointed reinterpreter for more nationalist times. It would matter much less if *The Return of John Macnab* were not such a good book.

30. Anti-Jewish allusion in Buchan persists as late as *Sir Walter Scott* (London 1932), 309–10. I am most grateful to Professor David Daiches for this reference, and for support on the general question, and would point out to those who scout the idea of anti-Jewish intent in early Buchan that Professor Daiches has the advantage of them, whoever they are, both scholastically, and ethnically. I have discussed Racialism in Buchan in my 'John Buchan and South Africa', in Brian Filling and Susan Stuart (eds.), *The End of a Regime?* (Aberdeen 1991), 93–116. Presumably the logic of anti-Jewish attitudes in *The Thirty-Nine Steps* is that 'the Jew' is opposed to Russia and hence to Britain's wartime allies (the book was written shortly *after* the declaration of war during the writer's illness: if he wished to pursue this

particular theme in his subsequent propaganda work it was evidently discouraged). Buchan, *The Half-Hearted*, 231 (but see 233 where the 'objective' author's own voice speaks of 'certain Jewish gentlemen, members of the great family who have conquered the world, engaged in the pursuit of their unlawful calling' which seems to legitimize the otherwise deplorable Marka); *The Thirty-Nine Steps*, chapters 1 and 8. *The Three Hostages*, chapter 2 ('Blenkiron, who didn't lie his race, had once described him to me as 'the whitest Jew since the Apostle Paul': apart from its Grand Slam in racialist terms, this is disturbingly akin to Buchan's own 'E. Phillips Oppenheim – the greatest Jewish writer since Isaiah' (Smith, *Buchan*, 178), which professes its author's right to pronounce on Jewish literature since Isaiah no more convincingly than Blenkiron's claims to knowledge of the morality – and pigmentation – of Jews since Paul.

31. K. Wittig, *The Scottish Tradition in Literature* (Edinburgh 1958), 277. Wittig has the advantage of approaching both Scots and English from the perspective of a foreigner. *The Half-Hearted*, 141. 'Sir Walter Scott', *Homilies and Recreations* (1926) 21, (1939) 21 (coincidentally).

32. *A History of English Literature from Chaucer to the end of the Nineteenth Century with an introduction by Sir Henry Newbolt* (ed. John Buchan (London 1923)) 517, 519. Buchan, *Julius Caesar*, chapter 8.

33. Lownie, *Buchan*, 248, notes 'bouts of depression' for both Buchan and his wife chiefly in 1934: how far her masterful character, and her unease (to put it mildly) with his Scottish antecedents, affected Buchan's tensions physical and mental, or impelled the characterization and plot of *A Prince of the Captivity* we cannot say. All of their children are now dead, and hence the subject is no longer taboo to decent people.

34. By now, alas!, it is necessary to point out that the authors of *1066 and All That* were W. C. Sellar and R. J. Yeatman, and that those of *'Don't, Mr Disraeli!'*, were Caryl Brahms and S. J. Simon: their works remain indispensable to the historian.

35. Shane Leslie, *Studies in Sublime Failure* (1932).

36. The University of Glasgow published Buchan's essay as a pamphlet: the quotation is from the penultimate lines. John Buchan, *Principles of Social Service: Address to the Students of the University of Glasgow During Social Service Week, 30 October 1933* (Glasgow 1933), 15–16. Lodge's remarks were made at a Brasenose dinner in 1935, after Buchan's appointment to the Governership General of Canada, which no doubt exacerbates their colonial missionary spirit. (Smith, *Buchan*, 41). Compare Dr Samuel Johnson: 'Much may be made of a Scotchman, if he be caught young'.

My grateful thanks are due to Ted Cowan, Christopher Harvie and Andrew Hook, for encouragement in the making of this chapter.

11

The Roots of the Present: Naomi Mitchison, Agnes Mure Mackenzie and the Construction of History

Kirsten Stirling

Naomi Mitchison's 1947 novel *The Bull Calves* is invested with a great many of her own personal concerns of the period 1940 to 1947. She was prompted to write the novel by the loss of her baby in 1940, and as she worked on it throughout the war years, the shadow of the second world war and contemporary concerns is cast over it. The novel also marks her emergence as a Scottish writer. By writing a Scottish historical novel based on her own family history and set in an uncertain political climate, she constructs a fictional compound of kinship, history and nationality. But at the same time as constructing a Scottish identity and a Scottish context for herself, she also draws attention to the fact that all history is necessarily a construction.

The poem 'Clemency Ealasaid' which prefaces *The Bull Calves* makes explicit the parallel between the death of Mitchison's new-born baby daughter in July 1940 and her reading of history. Her diary describes the birth and death of the baby; and her reading of Scottish history is a part of this narrative. Mitchison writes:

> They said she should not come to me but must stay warm all day; I was rather sad about it but began reading Agnes Mure Mackenzie's history of Scotland; . . . I had got to the chapter on the Bruce when the Nurse came in saying Baby's not so well.[1]

The co-existence of her baby and Agnes Mure Mackenzie's history book at this point serves as an indication of the link between the relative impersonality of history and Mitchison's personal grief. In the poem 'Clemency Ealasaid', Mitchison explores her grief at the loss of her baby and makes some attempt to come to terms with her own personal loss by setting it in the context of the worldwide losses incurred during the second world war. The death of her baby is paralleled with the death of French soldiers at Oran on 3rd July (the day before the baby died). She contextualises her loss by imagining it as a small event in a history book which is as yet unwritten, and looks a hundred years into the future to see a time when she will be subsumed in the virtual anonymity of history, existing only as a name in the index of a history book. She attempts to put her personal grief, the death of her baby, into perspective by comparing it with 'history' in two ways. She compares it with both the magnitude of the Second World War, a major historical event which she is living through; and also with the sense of distance inherent in reading a history book, both due to the remoteness in time of what is described and the subsequent narrativisation of events.

In *The Bull Calves* Mitchison writes her own family history into the major historical narrative of the Jacobite uprisings. She also writes her present into this same narrative: there are obvious parallels between the aftermath of the Second World War in Europe and the aftermath of the Jacobite rebellion in Scotland. The past is thus to a certain extent seen through the eyes of the present; at the same time, she distances herself from the events of the twentieth century by writing them into a 'history book'.

The Bull Calves marks the reincarnation of Mitchison as a Scottish writer. Naomi Mitchison's ancestors on both sides were Scottish. Her father's family were Haldanes[2] and her mother was a Trotter and her early summers were spent on the Haldane estate of Cloan in Perthshire. But her identity as a Scottish writer really began with her move to Carradale in the late 1930s. In the 'self-portrait' which she wrote for the Saltire Self-Portraits series, she traces the development of her sense of Scottishness and describes how moving to Carradale: 'strengthened my growing feeling of being a Scot and a Haldane at that.'[3] In her diary she records her pleasure at being regarded by the librarian at the National Library:

> as part of Scottish history, descendant and representative of the Haldanes and indeed of all the great families whose blood is mixed in mine.[4]

Mitchison's position is interesting because she has made a conscious decision to be Scottish. No-one in 1999 would dispute the fact that Naomi Mitchison is an important Scottish writer; but had she stayed in London and not moved to Carradale in 1939, had she not started writing definably Scottish books, she would no doubt still exist on that hazy margin of Scottishness reserved for good writers with Scottish parentage. This perhaps serves to illustrate how fluid the idea of 'being Scottish' is. However, she makes the decision to be Scottish: in her long poem 'The Cleansing of the Knife' she asserts her position, saying . . . 'I am a woman of Scotland'. As her biographer Jenni Calder puts it, Naomi Mitchison wanted to write her way into Scotland[5] and we can see this both in 'The Cleansing of the Knife' and in *The Bull Calves*. She draws attention to her status as 'a part of Scottish history' by confusing the personal and the political: her writing about history is paralleled, both in her autobiographical and in her fictional works, by an element of personal history. The death of her baby left Mitchison feeling somewhat adrift. She writes in 'Clemency Ealasaid' and in her diary that the baby was 'meant to be a kind of binding' between herself and Carradale, but without the baby she could not for a while summon any enthusiasm for running the estate at Carradale. It seems legitimate to regard her 'writing herself into Scotland' as an alternative method of binding. Her doctor suggested to her, four days after the baby's death, that she should start writing a book. 'As though one could turn on the tap', Mitchison wrote in her diary. 'If only I had my baby I wouldn't need to write a book that probably nobody wants to read'.[6] But she starts considering the possibility of writing a history of Kintyre, and also adds that she has finished Agnes Mure Mackenzie's book.

Agnes Mure Mackenzie wrote a series of six books published between 1935 and 1941, comprising a history of Scotland from the earliest times to the present day.[7] Mackenzie's emphasis throughout the series is on the continuity of Scottish nationhood and the importance of understanding history as a process. By bringing Scottish history right up to date she was emphasising the continuing existence of the Scottish nation up to the present day. She was also aiming to contextualise the famous stories of Scottish history. Due to the lack of Scottish history being taught in schools, many Scots learned their history in the form of stories – Bruce, Wallace, Mary Queen of Scots, Bonnie Prince Charlie – passed down from generation to generation. Because these stories are placed in no general context, there is no sense of how they fit together, with the result that they tend to merge in the mind. Thus there is a tendency for Scottish history to exist as a medley of stories with no sense of the passage of time or historical development. Scotland's past, Mackenzie wrote, 'must be recalled and understood, not as a series of highly coloured stories but as a consecutive process of event.'[8] Rosalind Mitchison writes in the preface to the Saltire Society volume *Why Scottish History Matters* (1991):

> Scotland's sense of national identity has survived the lack of serious study of national history because a limited amount of knowledge of it has percolated through the educational system to most people.[9]

The point Mackenzie was making in 1938, however, is that this limited amount of knowledge is not a very sound basis for national identity. She sees the historian's project as being to set the highly coloured stories of history in a context, so her history covers every age of Scottish history from pre-history to modern times. In the preface to her history of modern Scotland she claims to be writing the first *general* survey of the period although more specialised histories had been written.[10] Mackenzie says that we need a general background in which to root the 'close-up' histories and the highly coloured stories; some sense of continuity is essential to make the past seem relevant to the present. In the General Preface to her series, Mackenzie wrote:

> History is more than a study of things past. It is a study of the roots of the present, of the seeds of the future. No man can guide present or future who forgets it, and one major cause of Scotland's unhappy present is that, though her sense of the past is still keen and vivid, she recalls it only confusedly and in part.[11]

Naomi Mitchison wrote in her diary on 27th July 1940:

> Went on reading history and having some slow ideas about what kind of book I could write . . . I wonder whether perhaps the book should be written completely backwards: whether I should take the village first, take an incident, and hunt back to what it was really about. I could make a fascinating book that way; I would call it *The Roots of the Present*.[12]

Mitchison's use of this phrase of Mackenzie's, 'the roots of the present' indicates the main parallel between the two: their determination to make Scotland's history relevant to Scotland's present and indeed future.

Mackenzie identifies the tendency to relate Scottish history in terms of highly-coloured stories; Mitchison goes further by pointing out that the stories of Scottish history tend to be based upon famous disasters. Our confused and partial recollection of Scotland's past privileges a somewhat defeatist perspective. The 'roots of the present' extract from Mackenzie's preface can indeed be read as a blueprint for Mitchison's long poem 'The Cleansing of the Knife'[13] in which she constructs a confused and imperfect summary of Scotland's past in order to point out the limitations of such a world-view. She distils the famous disasters of popular Scottish history into an exceedingly defeatist and melancholy view of Scottish history. In Part One of 'The Cleansing of the Knife' almost every verse presents us with a notable misfortune in Scottish history, among them the death of Wallace; exile; emigration; the Highland clearances; Calvinism[14]; the Union; concluding with the state of Scotland today. Each verse begins with the line 'Tears in the glen, tears' and ends with the idea of drinking to forget, a structure which reflects an episodic and pessimistic grasp of Scottish history. Even the positive elements of Scottish history which creep into this catalogue of failure are given the most pessimistic clothing: Bruce is mentioned; however, he is mentioned in the most negative way possible: 'Bruce that died too soon'; similarly Scottish literature is encapsulated by the line 'the makars who are dead'. Thus Scotland's golden ages, of various kinds, are seen as ultimately useless because they came to an end. It seems that death and failure are the best to which any Scot can aspire.

Ernest Renan suggests that the construction of national unity is better served by suffering in common than by joy:

> Where national memories are concerned, griefs are of more value than triumphs, for they impose duties, and require a common effort.[15]

Mitchison however challenges the pessimistic view of history she has encountered in Scotland. She points out that national griefs tend to involve Scots adopting the position of victim and seeing history merely as something that was done to us, in which we accept no responsibility for the state of the nation. We must, she says, find a different way in which to look at the past. The end of 'The Cleansing of the Knife' brings Scottish history right up to date and looks into the future. The appearance of Tom Johnson, the Labour politician, in the latter part of the poem, anticipates a socialist future for Scotland. Like Agnes Mure Mackenzie, Mitchison sees history as a 'consecutive process of event', rather than something complete and confined to the past. She too sees the past as 'the roots of the present'.

It is very tempting to consider *The Roots of the Present* as an alternative title for Mitchison's *The Bull Calves*. The novel is set on two days in June 1747 in the aftermath of the Jacobite rebellion. There is a 'plot' which involves the sheltering of a fugitive Jacobite, Robert Strange, in Gleneagles, the Haldane family home. We also, however, witness certain tensions between the older protagonists in the book, which are slowly explained through stories told by various characters in conversation. About half the book is composed of these stories and it is in these that the real drama lies – particularly in those told by the two principal characters, Kirstie Haldane and her husband, William Macintosh of Borlum. Kirstie tells her life story to her niece Catherine, but omits from this narration a part of her life which she tells only to William: that she became involved with witchcraft and believed herself to be responsible, by witchcraft, for the death of her first husband, Andrew Shaw of Bargarran. William, on the other hand, keeps from Kirstie part of the story of his life: the fact that at the time of their marriage he was already married to an American Indian woman and that therefore his marriage to Kirstie is invalid and their child is illegitimate. He tells this not to Kirstie but to her brother Patrick. The telling of these stories traces the roots of the present-day tensions within the family. This plot development, explaining the present in terms of the past, corresponds to what Mitchison said she wanted to do in her projected book *The Roots of the Present*: to 'take an incident, and hunt back to what it was really about'.

In the same preface from which the phrase 'roots of the present' comes, Agnes Mure Mackenzie states:

> I have also tried, consistently, to deal with things, people and actions, not with forms of words.[. . .] History was never made by the alphabet, in any permutation or combination, but by what men were and valued and believed.[16]

Her point is to make the past more immediate and human; she wants the reader of her books to be aware that the people she talks about existed as flesh and blood, rather than merely as words on a page. However, while she asserts that history was never made by the alphabet she at the same time demonstrates, in her style and in what she says, that narrative and the forms of words are, on the contrary, crucial to the construction of history, since 'History' is the manner in which the events of the past are narrated.

Agnes Mure Mackenzie was a novelist before she turned to writing history, which could be one reason why she is not in general taken very seriously as a historian. Her histories are very readable; in fact her style is in places exceedingly 'story-like'. The opening line of *The Kingdom of Scotland* (1940) is 'There was once a great river, running to the north'.[17] It is also ironic, given Mackenzie's resistance to the idea that history is made by the alphabet, that in an article entitled 'Woman of Letters', in which he was defending her against charges of being unscholarly, Alexander Reid proclaimed that the beauty of Mackenzie's style was the proof that what she wrote was 'on the line of truth'.[18] There is an ambivalence about Mackenzie's attitude to history versus narrative. She shuns the notion of history being taught as 'a series of highly coloured stories' in favour of 'a consecutive process of event'.[19] Yet despite this opposition of 'story' and 'event', she acknowledges elsewhere that the writing of history is an essentially narrative process:

> [The decision to make each volume of the history self-contained] proved to possess the great advantage that to each of these separate volumes could be given the literary form its contents required. [. . .] In any narrative writing, the first requirement . . . is to choose the stance from which one best may perceive the pattern and significance of the action.[20]

History books are texts and their persuasiveness lies not in the 'facts' which they present but in the way in which those facts are presented. History is constructed by narrative. Mitchison was evidently fascinated by this idea. Through the stories in *The Bull Calves* she explores this construction of history; and charts the progression from history as event to history as narrative.

A.J. Youngson's book *The Prince and the Pretender: a study in the writing of history*[21] begins with the phrase 'All perception is selection'. In this book Youngson writes two separate histories of the Jacobites, one from a Hanoverian and one from a Jacobite point of view, drawing on the same core of 'facts' for each. The Jacobite cause is an excellent example of the potential for the historian to select facts according to his or her belief, because each side had such fixed opinions on what was right. The maxim 'all perception is selection' can be applied to any historian, any historical period. It is interesting, however, that *The Bull Calves* is set in the shadow of the '45, and that besides the stories of Kirstie and William, many of the present day tensions in the Haldane family which are exorcised in the course of the two days are related to the roles played by family members in the Jacobite risings. As 'stories' are told about the Jacobite risings we are witnessing the narrativisation of the events of the past two years. The duality of perception regarding the Jacobite risings[22] functions as an excellent backdrop to Mitchison's questioning of the reliability of the narratives of history and her exploration of the gap between history as event and history as story.

In *The Bull Calves*, the plot of the present day is presented to us as 'action'. We are advised at the start of the book that: 'The action of this book takes place on June 16th and 17th 1747, in and about the house of Gleneagles, on the northern slopes of the Ochils.'[23] 'The action', or the events of these two days is clearly contrasted with the telling of stories. The key stories are told by Kirstie to her niece Catherine, and by Kirstie to her husband William; by William to Kirstie, and by William to Kirstie's brother Patrick. We can read these stories as representing history itself. The gap between past and present is represented clearly in *The Bull Calves* as generational. At first it is the younger members of the family who are involved in the sheltering of the Jacobite outlaw – the 'action' of the present day – and the older family members are excluded, shut off in a world of the past which seems to have no relevance to the younger ones. Catherine is initially resistant to the idea of listening to Kirstie's stories:

> Aunt Kirstie would begin to talk, to ramble and remember, and all the older ones would join in and there they would be blethering away about what had nothing at all to do with nowadays or the things the young ones were after . . . [24]

That is, history – history as narrative – is seen to have no relevance to the present. But Kirstie's stories to Catherine form a bridge between the words of the past and the actions of the present.

To describe these narrations as 'stories' might appear a somewhat vague term. The semantic development of the word 'story', however, is important to this argument. The words history and story come from the same root, and in almost all languages except English there is only one word for both concepts. In English the earliest senses of the word story relate it to history, but the word is most commonly used today to the narration of (usually fictitious) events. Colloquially, the word story is also used to denote a lie.[24] Mitchison herself uses the word to describe the narrations of her characters, fully aware of the shifting connotations of the term.

Catherine says to Kirstie 'But after supper there will be the end of the story?' [134] and Patrick says to William: 'Go on with your story, William' [280] – these seem fairly innocent uses of the word. However the word 'story' is also used explicitly to mean something false. William tells a 'story' to Kirstie's eldest brother Mungo which is a categorical falsehood. In order to discredit the villain of the piece, Lachlan Macintosh of Kyllachy, William creates a fiction that Kyllachy once tried to rape Kirstie. We as readers know this particular story of William's to be untrue, yet it has the same status as the other stories told within the book. It is contained within quotation marks, told by one character to another. The word 'story', applied to this narration of William's, is used specifically to indicate the falsehood of the narration: in William's mind 'the story image died out and the real one took its place'. [242]

Perhaps the most telling use of the word 'story' is when Kyllachy, whose plans to cause trouble on this occasion have come to nothing, contemplates fictionalising events for his future amusement:

> nor would this stop him from making a grand story out of it amongst his own cronies; he could see himself telling it and putting a touch on it here and there where it had not turned out as it should in reality. [387]

Thus we see the potential for 'the action' of these two days to become narrative, and consciously distorted narrative at that. This casts doubt back on the veracity of all the 'stories' in the book. The narration of history must always be inaccurate, even if the truth is not intentionally perverted, as in the story Kyllachy plans to tell. Words can never adequately represent actions.

The key stories in the book do not adequately represent the events to which they relate in a variety of ways. William disguises the fact that he married an Indian woman by telling Kirstie instead about other minor crimes and indiscretions. Kirstie's narration to Catherine, on the other hand, is characterised by fractures. As soon as she comes close to speaking about the death of her first husband there is an abrupt halt in her narration, illustrated in one instance by a dash [90], and in another by the phrase: 'Kirstie stopped speaking suddenly, as though she had come against a stone wall.' [132] There are parts of her history which are not told to Catherine, though she fills in the gaps for the reader by telling them to William. Her narration to Catherine is one version of her history, and probably the version that will be passed down to later generations, and her history is incomplete. However the fractures in her narrative mean that her history is obviously incomplete. As Foucault says in *The History of Sexuality*, silence is a part of discourse:

> Silence itself – the things one declines to say, or is forbidden to name, the discretion that is required between different speakers – is less the absolute limit of discourse, the other side from which it is separated by a strict boundary, than an element which functions alongside the things said, with them and in relation to them within over-all strategies. There is no binary division to be made between what one says and what one does not say; we must try to determine the different ways of not saying such things.[25]

What Kirstie does not say is as much part of her history as what she does say. The silence which fractures her narration to Catherine is a telling silence.

The Russian formalists' distinction between story and plot can here be applied to *The Bull Calves*. In the formalist sense story means more than simply narration: story is the sequence of events as they 'actually' happened and the 'plot' is the way in which these events are narrated in the text; the chronology of events may differ, there may be prolepses and analepses rather than a blow by blow account of events. The way in which the events are narrated affects the way in which we understand events.

In *The Bull Calves* we are presented with narratives within the text as a whole: what the structuralist Gerard Genette terms metadiegetic narrative. Genette adds a third component to the equation: as well as story – the events; and plot – what is actually said; he identifies the narrating instance as important. This is crucial in *The Bull Calves* because the way in which the story is narrated depends upon whom the story is being told to. Foucault too made the point that what is said is very much dependent on who is being spoken to. The fact that Kirstie is telling her story to her niece Catherine influences what she feels able to reveal. Likewise, William speaking to Kirstie cannot tell her of his previous marriage. Neither Kirstie nor Patrick hear the full truth from William. To no one person within the text is the full account of events made available. We are able to piece together fragments and come to some approximation of what happened in the past but we are outside the world of the text. Kirstie's story to

Catherine is fractured by silences; as William's story to Kirstie covers up unpalatable facts.

Russian formalists related their theory of narrative to theories of history. As Robert Scholes puts it: 'The facts of life are to history as the story is to the Plot. History selects and arranges the events of existence, and plot selects and arranges the events of the story'.[26] We can legitimately regard the stories told in *The Bull Calves* as representing history. As well as being the life-histories of their narrators, they function as metaphors for the macro-narrative of History with a capital 'H'.

The elisions in Kirstie's story can be seen as elisions in history; and when reading history too we have to bear in mind that the audience affects what is said. Kirstie's story to Catherine is, so to speak, a primary source, and yet it is incomplete and therefore inaccurate. We always try to be aware of the possible bias of primary sources; what we are perhaps less aware of are the silences operating alongside discourse within history books. Agnes Mure Mackenzie says that Scotland recalls the past 'only confusedly and in part' and that this is part of the reason for Scotland's unhappy present. Her project is to fill in the elisions in Scottish history. She says:

> I have tried to put back again into the picture certain elements that for the last two hundred years have frequently been for practical reasons omitted from the official teaching of the subject, thus considerably distorting the common impression.[27]

Mackenzie wants to establish this coherent Scottish history partly to emphasise the continuing existence of the Scottish nation; her project is at least partly political. If she wants to fill in the gaps in Scotland's history in order to make Scotland's present more happy, then her objectivity is to a certain extent compromised by present-day concerns. Both twentieth-century Scottish nationalism and the second world war intrude into her text in footnotes: for example, when writing about the migration of races in Europe she takes the opportunity in a footnote to debunk any notion of 'pure' races.[28] According to the Russian formalist Boris Eichenbaum:

> History is, in effect, a science of complex analogies, a science of double vision: the facts of the past have meanings for us that differentiate them and place them, invariably and inevitably, in a system under the sign of contemporary problems . . . History in this sense is a special method of studying the present with the aid of the facts of the past.[29]

This applies to Mitchison as much as to Mackenzie and is most relevant when applied to her use of contemporary language. As Kirstie says to Catherine:

> None of yon words are making my meaning right, none ava! And every generation has its own words, new minted, and the old words must be cast out onto the midden of past thought that's ever growing at the door of human experience. It is only actions that show. [78]

That is, the past must necessarily be narrated in the language of the present if it is to be understood at all. And as the language of the present is geared to contemporary modes of thought, the past is narrated in terms of contemporary problems.

Mitchison devotes a section of her Notes to 'The historical use of words', and writes that the 'moral structure of society is temporal in history . . . and held together by words'. [457] That is, the modes of thought and behaviour which characterise a society and an era, are expressed through, and therefore to a certain extent created by, words. Mitchison suggests that:

> one way of getting the feel of a historical period is by the correspondence between society and the words in which the organization of society, in personal and group relationships, is expressed. [459]

Mitchison also makes the point that what we believe — even what we believe about ourselves — is constructed by the words of others. In *The Bull Calves*, William tells Kirstie that no matter what she may have thought, she is *not* responsible for the death of her first husband by witchcraft, and Kirstie believes him and tells Patrick so:

> It is as well you have your belief in him [Patrick says to her] but mind you this. Supposing the Kirk session had found you guilty of witchcraft and they with all the power and weight of the respectable behind them, then thon would have been the ones you'd be forced to believe, you poor bitch, and to hell you would have gone, in your own mind and fancy. [352]

While Mackenzie claims that history was never made by the alphabet, Mitchison seems to claim the opposite and has a healthy respect for the power of words. Mackenzie stated that seeing history in terms of words rather than actions was a deadly habit of mind; Mitchison rather sees words as a way of getting a handle on history.

The Bull Calves is basically written in West Coast, Kintyre, Carradale dialect, (despite being set in Perthshire) rather than authentic eighteenth-century Scots. Mitchison directs the reader who wants to know how people spoke in the eighteenth century to the novels of Scott and Ferrier, and to contemporary memoirs, saying:

> I could have made my book people talk that way, but, because I was not actually thinking or imagining it, that would have been artificial, a barrier between myself and them, as also between them and the reader. [410]

This 'anachronistic' mode of writing is not restricted to *The Bull Calves*. Naomi Mitchison discussed her use of modern language with reference to her first novel *The Conquered*, claiming that she was the first person to have so used it:

> Oddly enough I was the first to see that one could write historical novels in a modern idiom: in fact it was the only way I could write them. Now everybody does, so it is not so interesting.[30]

In the case of *The Bull Calves*, Mitchison ties her use of modern speech forms in her representation of the eighteenth century to a more general parallel between the two centuries: she writes in the notes to the novel:

> Two hundred years ago, in the mid eighteenth century, Scotland was in a transitional period. There was much questioning, much research and experimentation in science . . . philosophy and literature. I think this makes it more possible to get the feel of eighteenth century Scotland in words and phrases which come easily now to us in another transitional and experimental period . . . [464–5]

Mitchison's use of contemporary language illustrates the way in which she ties the eighteenth century to the twentieth. She also does this by writing her 20th-century self into the character of Kirstie. The small cameo of Kirstie and William which appears on the title page of the novel bears a strong resemblance to Mitchison herself and her friend Denny Macintosh. Many of Mitchison's principal female characters bear a striking similarity to herself or at least to her projection of herself – Erif Der in *The Corn King and the Spring Queen*, for example. But this cameo serves as a concrete illustration of Mitchison's imposing of the twentieth century upon the eighteenth.

As we have seen in the extracts from Mitchison's diary, the book was originally conceived of in 1940, and it was published in 1947. The parallels between 1747 and 1947 are obvious – both are periods of recovery after conflicts. The emphasis on *rebuilding* Scotland which runs through *The Bull Calves* has obvious relevance for contemporary Scotland. The dénouement of *The Bull Calves* is a pseudo-tribunal held by Duncan Forbes of Culloden, the Lord President, which resolves both the present-day problem of the Jacobite outlaw and the tensions which have been aroused due to the telling of old stories. Culloden winds up proceedings with this speech:

> We in Scotland have been over much battered to be able to spare any man who will set his hand and mind to the future. Aye, or any woman, Kirstie! We must act together and build ourselves up slowly and surely, by way of the peaceful arts and trades through commerce and agriculture, until we are well of our wounds. [389]

Thus the successful outcome of the problems faced by the Haldane family in *The Bull Calves* symbolises a hope for the healing of the whole country; and the resonances of this speech for post-World War Two Scotland and Europe are unmistakable.

The emphasis on agriculture here points to the importance in *The Bull Calves* of the growing of both trees and turnips to the rebuilding of Scotland. In the poem 'Clemency Ealasaid', Mitchison talks of the trees she planted while pregnant, which her daughter now will not see fully grown. In *The Bull Calves* William thinks of his plantations as 'a comforting crop . . . tying you into a rotation away beyond your own temporal life, something nearer eternity.' [208] Trees represent the passing of time; human life-spans fade into insignificance beside them. And yet they are a 'crop': they are planted by humans; like history they are shaped by humans. And as the stories within the text function as 'the roots of the present' in terms of family history, so the family tree at the start of the book very literally illustrates that notion.

The cycles of agriculture too function as a metaphor for the regeneration of Scotland. As Kirstie's brother Mungo muses:

> It was strange the way [thoughts about agriculture] came to him during the reading of theology. Yet indeed they were both of them equally profound subjects when taken with all their implications. Aye, aye, Scotland would rise again like a muckle turnip from the seed. [156]

The turnip is thus elevated from the ridiculous to the sublime. The home of Kirstie and William, Borlum, occupies an almost utopian space in the novel; and the new agricultural methods practised there by Kirstie and William, including the growing of turnips, symbolise hope for the nourishing of Scotland in the future and an alternative to war. A large section of the notes is devoted to a discussion of agricultural methods and this too connects with Mitchison's own life at Carradale, where, in an unorthodox move for a laird (particularly a female laird), she personally took on the working of the estate rather than tendering it out.

The link between agriculture and patriotism is personified by William's late father, Brigadier William Macintosh of Borlum (Red William), admired by Kirstie's brothers, despite being a Jacobite, as 'a true lover of his country and its agriculture . . . [29] William's father, unlike Kirstie and William, is a real historical figure. He wrote the *Essay on Ways and Means of Enclosing* by *A Lover of his Country*[31] while he was in prison. Mitchison writes in the notes that she identified with his essay as being the same sort of thing she was trying to do in Carradale – and what she envisaged for Scotland as a whole.

I first read the book myself, in the Signet Library in Edinburgh, and of a sudden I found myself in tears, thinking of the way it was written, only a few hundred yards away in space . . . but too far off in time for me ever to speak with the man who had written of it and tell him how some of us are yet working his way . . . [478–9]

This incident makes its way into *The Bull Calves* as Margaret, another of Kirstie's nieces, describes to Catherine how she burst into tears while reading the book

'There was a gentleness about the writing, a fashion of love, oh you would never have guessed that the author was in prison and never like to see a tree again in his life! . . . [he] had written his books out of pure love for Scotland and the poor folk of Scotland.' Again her eyes filled with tears and she wiped them with a corner of her shawl. 'Amn't I a silly besom to be crying over an old dead Tory, Catherine . . .' [189]

The notes to the novel illustrate, as in this case, the extent to which Mitchison has written herself into her novel. Because *The Bull Calves* is based on her own family tree, anecdotes of family history become written into it, present-day family nicknames become applied to ancestors. Mitchison writes that she herself finds this process of cross-fertilisation between past and present quite fascinating. The notes are such an integral part of the novel that Susanne Hagemann suggests that the voice of the notes might more properly be called 'the narrator' rather than 'Naomi Mitchison', implying that there is an element of fictionality about the notes and emphasising the theme of treating all representation of fact as narrative.[32] The notes detail the way in which Mitchison has turned history into fiction. She has constructed her micro-history of Scotland out of both secondary sources like Agnes Mure Mackenzie's history and primary sources like William Mackintosh's *Essay on Ways and Means*, family history and twentieth-century insights. It is an excellent insight into the way in which a writer's mind works – maybe 'a writer' is wrong – the way in which *her* mind works, particularly with reference to the writing of a historical novel.

Historical novels are allowed, in fact expected, to bend the truth to meet dramatic purposes. For many people, historical novels function first as a gateway into history. Because they are more dramatic, more narrative, than a history book, they make history itself seem interesting. Once interest is kindled there is pleasure in trying to distinguish the historical facts from the historical fiction. *The Bull Calves* has a different dynamic. It draws attention to its own fictionality, partly because of the notes and partly through the 'narratives' which form its own internal structure. History with a capital H, for example, the Jacobite risings, is paralleled by the personal histories told by Kirstie and William. The book draws attention to the construction of history itself. Since Kirstie and William were real names from Mitchison's family tree but those of children who died young, they, and their stories, exist very obviously on the boundaries of fictionality and history.

Notes

1. Naomi Mitchison *Among You Taking Notes . . . : the wartime diaries of Naomi Mitchison 1939–145* (ed.) Dorothy Sheridan (London 1985) 71.
2. Most of the characters in *The Bull Calves* are her father's ancestors.
3. *Saltire Self-Portraits 2: Naomi Mitchison* Saltire Society (Edinburgh 1986).
4. Mitchison, *Among You Taking Notes* 169.
5. Jenni Calder, *The Nine Lives of Naomi Mitchison* (London 1997) 149.
6. Mitchison, *Among You Taking Notes* 73.
7. The six books in the series are: *The Foundations of Scotland* (1938), *Robert Bruce, King of Scots* (1935), *The Rise of the Stewarts*, (1935), *The Scotland of Queen Mary and the Religious Wars* (1936), *The Passing of the Stewarts* (1937); *Scotland in Modern Times 1720–1939* (1941). There is also a single-volume history *The Kingdom of Scotland* (1940) which must have been, incidentally, the book Mitchison was reading at the time she learned of her baby's death. She also published the four-volume *A Scottish Pageant* (1946–50).
8. Agnes Mure Mackenzie, 'General Preface' *The Foundations of Scotland* (Edinburgh 1938) vii.
9. *Why Scottish History Matters*, (ed.) Rosalind Mitchison, Saltire Society, (Edinburgh 1991) ix.
10. Agnes Mure Mackenzie, *Scotland in Modern Times 1720–1939* (London & Edinburgh 1941) viii.
11. Mackenzie, *The Foundations of Scotland* vii.
12. Mitchison, *Among You Taking Notes* 76–7.
13. 'The Cleansing of the Knife 1941–1947', in Naomi Mitchison, *The Cleansing of the Knife and other poems* (Edinburgh 1978).
14. The status of Calvinism as a misfortune is of course debatable.
15. Ernest Renan, 'What is a nation?' in *Nation and Narration* (ed.) Homi K. Bhabha (London & New York 1990) 19.
16. Mackenzie, *The Foundations of Scotland* vii–viii.

17. Agnes Mure Mackenzie, *The Kingdom of Scotland* (Edinburgh 1947) 2.
18. Alexander Reid, 'A Woman of Letters' *Scotland's Magazine* v. 53 (November 1957) 47.
19. Mackenzie, *The Foundations of Scotland* (1938) vii.
20. Mackenzie, *Scotland in Modern Times* (1941) vii.
21. A.J. Youngson, *The Prince and the Pretender: a study in the writing of history* (London 1985) 9.
22. The use of the phrase 'Jacobite rising' aptly illustrates the way in which the historian's use of words influence the reader's perception. Youngson's Hanoverian history is titled 'A History of the Rebellion' and his Jacobite one is called 'The Jacobite Rising' – the choice between the use of the word rebellion and the use of the word rising is a choice between representing an unlawful insurrection or a justified revolution.
23. Naomi Mitchison, *The Bull Calves* (London 1947) All page references will appear in parentheses in the text.
24. *OED*, 2nd ed. vol. xvi 797–8.
25. Michel Foucault, *The History of Sexuality Volume One: An Introduction* (trans.) Robert Hurley (Harmondsworth 1990) 27.
26. Robert Scholes, *Structuralism in Literature* (New Haven & London 1974) 80.
27. Mackenzie, *Foundations of Scotland* viii
28. Mackenzie, *The Kingdom of Scotland* 12.
29. Boris Eichenbaum, in *Readings in Russian Poetics*, (eds.) Ladislav Matejka and Krystyna Pomorska (Cambridge, Mass. and London) 56. Quoted in Scholes op.cit. 79.
30. Naomi Mitchison, *You May Well Ask* (London 1986) 163–4.
31. William Mackintosh, *An Essay on Ways and Means for inclosing, fallowing, planting* (Edinburgh 1729).
32. Susanne Hagemann, 'Woman and Nation', in *The History of Scottish Women's Writing* (eds.) Douglas Gifford and Dorothy McMillan (Edinburgh 1997) 324.

12

A World at the End of History? A History Maker by Alasdair Gray

Johanna Tiitinen

This essay aims to examine the concepts of history dramatized by Alasdair Gray in the post-historical world of *A History Maker*.[1] I will argue that by constructing a historyless future world, Gray stresses the vital role of history in understanding the present and, at the same time, theorizes and criticizes history as a universal objective science. To better illustrate how Gray views history, I will compare his utopian novel with Francis Fukuyama's main theses in *The End of History and the Last Man*,[2] a book among many others in the 1990s that declared the end of science, nature or other fields or concepts as we know them. This chapter intends to study how Gray can be seen to challenge Fukuyama's notion of the end of history and the possibility of writing a universal history.

It may, at first, seem paradoxical to study concepts of history in a novel set in the future. History-writing is, however, inherently connected with the future,[3] as will be demonstrated in this chapter. The first section will parallel the novel with Fukuyama's *The End of History* in order to better illustrate the political statements explicit and implicit in Gray's utopia which reaches beyond Fukuyama's notion of liberal democracy. More importantly, attention will be drawn to the complex ways in which Gray dramatizes the implications of a post-historical world; in other words, to whether Gray in fact believes in the possibility of the end of history. Why is the 'utopian' world in his novel forced to historical awareness and what does this indicate about the relation of utopia and history? And most importantly, how does Gray conceive of history: as a Universal Directional History, as Fukuyama argues, or as a culturally conditioned narrative, like Hayden White?[4]

The second section will deal with these questions by focusing on the many-layered, metafictional narrative structure of Gray's novel. The novel contains two retrospective stories: Wat Dryhope's autobiography is encased in his mother's pedantic notes, which create a historical continuum for it. As both stories claim to be true historical accounts, their relationship must be studied carefully: what kind of history is being written, and more importantly, by whom? As White asks,

> What is involved, then, in that finding of the 'true story,' that discovery of the 'real story' within or behind the events that come to us in the chaotic form of historical records? What wish is enacted, what desire is gratified, by the fantasy that real events are properly represented when they can be shown to display the formal coherency of a story?[5]

This question must also be extended to the novel as a whole as, after all, the novel is the author's imaginary construct, as several metafictional devices point out. I will argue that by drawing parallels between history and fiction, Gray is emphasizing the view of history as narrative, and by including several authentic histories within the novel, emphasizing the view of history as one of many culturally, socially and historically conditioned narratives. In the end, we need to ask who is truly making history in this novel?

Alasdair Gray is a writer much concerned with different aspects of history. This has been noted by Christopher Harvie, who characterizes Gray's works as 'theoretical histories . . . synoptic, though also very subversive',[6] and Willy Maley, who compares Gray to James Kelman, in that they both 'play with and parody the genres of historiography and political theory'. As a whole, Maley sees Gray's oeuvre as offering a mythopoetics of history.[7] Furthermore, Douglas Gifford sees Gray's first novel, *Lanark* (1981), as breaking with the anti-historicism of much postwar, urban literature in Scotland, embracing a totality of vision in its understanding of how Scotland has developed through history till now.[8] An intriguing addition to the discussion is Cairns Craig's idea of *Lanark* playing with the theme of being caught between the progressive historical world and the secure, static historyless one.[9] Apart from these remarks and Maley's essay, the role and representation of history in Gray's works have not yet attracted much attention, let alone full-length studies.[10]

In his later works, history gains an even more central place, particularly in *A History Maker* and in his Victorian pastiche, *Poor Things* (1992), which is a hilarious resurrection of Mary Shelley's *Frankenstein* (1818). The characters in *Poor Things* are a mixture of fictional and historical: for instance, Bella is simultaneously Frankenstein's monster, Mary Wollstonecraft and her daughter, Mary Shelley. The strange surgical genius, Godwin Bysshe Baxter, who resurrects Bella from death and replaces her brain with that of her unborn baby, combines Victor Frankenstein with both William Godwin and Percy Bysshe Shelley. The main point of this wonderful shambles is to draw attention to the similarities between history and fiction and to discuss the nature of a literary construct. And to further complicate the story, Bella Caledonia can be interpreted as an allegory of Scottish history – a constructed nation.[11] *Poor Things* is a perfect example of Linda Hutcheon's rather cumbersome, but useful term, historiographic metafiction, since in his self-reflexive novel Gray problematizes representation and yet at the same time 'lays claim to historical events and personages'.[12]

More topical for the purposes of this chapter is the debate between the novel's two competing stories which also juxtaposes fiction-writing and historiography. The two stories within the novel are the fantasy written by Archie McCandless and the realistic letter written by his wife, Victoria (Bella). The editor, fiction-writer Alasdair Gray defends the truth and historical value of the first story against the claims of the historian Michael Donnelly, who is not convinced by the mostly fictional evidence the editor provides to support his case. Neither of the stories is given as the 'true' version but the reader is left with two competing accounts. This is a good illustration of what Ernst Breisach has termed 'history merging into fiction as the merits of historical accounts could not be evaluated by measuring them against reality'.[13]

This theme is continued in *A History Maker,* a more recent novel published in 1994, which, however, has not raised as much attention and critical acclaim as Gray's previous works. This may be connected with a failure to understand Gray's utopian vision in this novel: the world the reader meets seems utopian at first, even its people call it 'democratic utopia'. But as the story proceeds the utopian world is revealed as a halted world inhabited mostly by bored people. This chapter will discuss how and why this static, post-historical society is forced back to the historical movement and change so that, paradoxically, the real utopia is established at the end of the novel. Fukuyama's theses are helpful in the sense that they allow one to pinpoint more carefully some of Gray's concerns that in turn will shed light on the nature of utopia and history in the novel.

A History Maker is set in the Ettrick Forest, in the Borders of Scotland in *circa* AD 2230. This is a peaceful period which the world has finally achieved after the so-called historical era. The world has survived the global cataclysm caused by our capitalist, postmodern era. This is how Kate Dryhope, the writer of the 'pedantical lang-nebbed notes', as she refers to them herself,[14] sums up our age:

> Postmodernism happened when landlords, businessmen, brokers and bankers who owned the rest of the world had used new technologies to destroy the

power of labour unions. Like owners of earlier empires they felt that history had ended because they and their sort could now dominate the world for ever. This indifference to most people's wellbeing and taste appeared in the fashionable art of the wealthy. Critics called their period postmodern to separate it from the modern world begun by the Renaissance when most creative thinkers believed they could improve their community. Postmodernists had no interest in the future, which they expected to be an amusing rearrangement of things they already knew. Postmodernism did not survive disasters caused by competitive exploitation of human and natural resources in the twenty-first century.[15]

What is post-historical for Fukuyama is still historical in Gray's world; Gray shows how postmodernity, understood as late capitalism, or liberal democracy, as Fukuyama would call it, has led the world to its near destruction. This is in contrast to Fukuyama who argues that liberal democracy 'remains the only coherent political aspiration that spans different regions and cultures around the globe'.[16] For him we live in the post-historical age in the developed countries because we have reached the end point beyond which mankind will not evolve ideologically.[17] Liberal democracy which rests on 'the twin principles of liberty and equality' is the final form of government because we cannot imagine any radically better form of government, though the ideal differs from the practical, since stable democracies in the West are not without injustices and social problems.[18]

While not criticizing the ideals of liberty and equality, Gray's novel can be seen to attack Fukuyama's notion of free trade and capitalism as an essential part of liberal democracy. In his future world, Gray imagines a world that has reached beyond capitalism and beyond liberal democracy. In Gray's new world economics has acquired its original Greek meaning, as the author tells the reader at the very beginning of the novel:

> *Economics*: Old Greek word for the art of keeping a home waterproof and supplied with what the householders need. For at least three centuries this word was used by British rulers and their advisers to mean political housekeeping – the art of keeping their bankers, brokers and rich supporters well supplied with money, often by impoverishing other householders. They used the Greek word instead of the English word because it mystified folk who had not been taught at wealthy schools. The rhetoric of plutocratic bosses needed economics as the sermons of religious ones needed the Will of God.
> – From *The Intelligence Archive of Historical Jargon*.

The criticism that is obvious in these quotes is directed at capitalism and right wing conservatism, as represented by Fukuyama, for instance. By insisting that capitalism divides people into to those who exploit and those who are exploited, Gray's criticism comes from the Left. In Fukuyama's own words,

> The Left would say that universal recognition in liberal democracy is necessarily incomplete because capitalism creates economic inequality and requires a division of labour that . . . implies unequal recognition.[19]

Fukuyama sees the mechanism of economic development as one of the forces behind Universal History. For him, the West has achieved economic and democratic freedom in its liberal democracy and history has ended. Gray's novel shows how liberal democracy 'continues to recognize people unequally'[20] and is thus not the final form of government, as Fukuyama argues. While Fukuyama sees all mankind following in the footsteps of the developed West and progressing towards liberal democracy and capitalism, this march in Gray's world was towards greater inequality, speculation and greed, to a near global destruction.

However, in Gray's imagined world, global destruction is prevented and the world created anew. None of our familiar institutions exist in this highly technological global village where economic well-being is evenly spread and people's basic needs seem satisfied. Wat Dryhope tries to explain to himself why he should prefer this world instead of the historical one; 'it was luxury to fear the ill opinion of the Ettrick aunts more than an empty belly, to worry about an unfair blow struck in a war between willing fighters'.[21] This 'utopian' world has turned its back on our historical era. In this 'mild matriarchy' women hold the power as they are in charge of powerplants which produce all the energy, food and consumer goods that can be desired. Lacking any other role except fathering children, men are excluded from household economics.

There is a more sinister element to this powerplant system too: bodies are recycled into food and energy. This is a 'gentler' version of the metaphor made real in the much more violent and gloomy atmosphere of *Lanark*, where people have become cannibals without realizing it. The motto repeated over and over again in *Lanark*, 'Man is the pie that bakes and eats itself and the recipe is separation',[22] applies likewise to *A History Maker*. Most of the bodies in *A History Maker* come from the battlefields; as a matter of fact, there seems to be a connection with wars and the production of food and energy. Perhaps wars are necessary so that the supply for the mysterious powerplant system can be guaranteed?

In this society, men are mostly warriors. Wars have become a highly regulated game of sports, rather than fighting for territorial gains. For Fukuyama, these wars would be form without content, art without social purpose:

A World at the End of History?

> For most of post-historical Europe, the World Cup has replaced military competition as the chief outlet for nationalist strivings to be number one . . . the object has ceased to be an historical one, and is now purely formal . . . For where traditional forms of struggle like war are not possible, and where widespread material prosperity makes economic struggle unnecessary, thymotic individuals begin to search for other kinds of contentless activities that can win them recognition.[23]

'The motor of history' for Fukuyama is not only economics and modern natural science but man's struggle for recognition – *thymos* – his desire to be recognized by other men, for example his willingness to risk his own life for the sake of abstract ideals.[24] To claim that such a thing as a Universal History exists, Fukuyama needs to base his argument on universal human nature which transcends cultural and social contexts.[25]

Gray's post-historical world parallels, in several ways, Fukuyama's vision of the world after the end of history. The world we meet at first is a model example of the society of the last men characterized by boredom and nostalgia for the historical. In order to maintain stability as well as to foster people's belief in this particular form of government as utopia (the goal of man's perfection), the leaders of Gray's world have declared it post-historical. As the world has now reached its highest stage of development, there is no need for change, improvement or any kind of significant movement that would alter the principles on which this new form of government relies.

The leaders, who are very hard to pinpoint, see, very much like Fukuyama, the historical era as an age of wars, violence and nation-states, in other words a nightmare of chaos. It is in their interest to control people's thoughts about history and present it as a negative, destructive force which would threaten the static security of the historyless world. As people in Gray's novel live in 'utopia', there is no need for the improvement of society and therefore no more need for history. This is the same kind of error that Kate Dryhope accused of 'postmodernists' of committing; these leaders are likewise indifferent to the future which they expect to be the same as the present. There is no need for history as a progressive force because the goal of progress has now been reached.

In fact, interest in the past and future are inseparable. History, as E.H. Carr states, is a synthesis of past and future.[26] The trouble makers in *A History Maker* are those who yearn for the historical age, want know more about the past and wish to see their static world dynamic again. The protagonist, Wat, is one of these trouble makers.

Wat's story begins with the depiction of the Battle of the Standard, a war game where the Geneva Council for War Regulation Rules are broken as men begin to fight like Fukuyama's first men seeking recognition, risking their lives for values like courage. Wat is one of the survivors of this new battle and is hailed as a hero who will lead the world back to the dynamics of history. The boredom, or as Kate Dryhope puts it, 'a widely spread male phenomenon', quickly changes into a fast spreading 'epidemic of military enthusiasm',[27] which seeks to re-establish nation-states, borders, national armies and all the familiar institutions of the historical age. This reminds us once again of Fukuyama, who claims that liberal democracy will be most severely criticized by the fact that man will always strive to be superior to others and refuse to live as one of many in the society of last men, 'men without chests'.[28]

Interestingly enough, the battle that triggers off the new militarism bears the same name as a famous Scottish defeat at the hands of the English, the 'Battle of the Standard' in 1138. Perhaps this is Gray's way of telling us how easily the Ettrick county, or the society of last men, is drawn into the cycle of history and the repetition of earlier destructive historical events. The words of General Shafto to Wat are left to echo in the reader's mind: ' . . . yes, Scotland will be a nation again and who but Wat Dryhope is fit to lead it? By gum, the Scots and Sassenachs can look forward to some grand scrimmages again'.[29]

Let us take this idea a bit further. Perhaps Gray rewrites Scottish (and world) history by showing us how the road to the horrendous wars of our centuries and to our present system of government could have been avoided. In this sense, the novel can be seen as a theoretical, synoptic and subversive history, as Harvie argues. In this utopian novel, the cycle of history will not be repeated as the military epidemic is prevented from spreading, the peace restored and a more equal world established. The powerplants are destroyed by a virus, which in turn forces men and women to unite and work together for the common good and survival of their families. Recognition is no longer sought in battlefields but in work with a purpose. What is more, this time the utopian world will maintain its connection with the narrative of history through Kate's notes. By editing her son's notes, she hopes to show the world the dangers of a 'easy-oasy habit of thinking the modern world at last a safe place, of thinking the past a midden too foul to steep our brains in'.[30] In a sense, then, it could be said that, paradoxically, the utopia thus reached is dynamic instead of static. It is not the final goal of man's perfection but a society that seems to be moving forwards.[31] Below I will discuss other ways in which the novel is connected with the past.

As noted before, the novel is divided into two stories – the hero's autobiography and the notes written by his editor who is also his mother, Kate Dryhope. In her foreword, Kate claims that four-fifths of Wat's story is proven by fact and then goes on to provide more historical facts, some related, some not, to back up the story. Kate reminds the reader of the editor in *Poor Things* who goes to extremes to prove that the story is based on facts, not fiction, and is therefore true and reliable.

It is important to notice, as Willy Maley has done, that while Gray's fiction gets footnoted and is clothed with all kinds of 'trappings of scholarship', his history remains a story without claims of academic objectivity.[32] Both Gray's political pamphlet, *Why Scots Should Rule Scotland 1997* and its earlier edition from 1992, are brief, subversive and openly biased histories of Britain focused on proving why, on the basis of historical events, Scots should indeed rule Scotland.

What I see this to mean is that Gray wants to emphasize history as a subjective narrative, not as objective science. Paradoxical as it may seem, this position does not subvert Gray's political intentions. On the contrary, the strength of his politics, of his story, comes from the recognition of the existence of other stories. As F. R. Ankersmit argues, with only one story or one interpretation of some historical topic, there is no interpretation. 'An interpretative way of seeing the past can only be recognized as such in the presence of *other* ways of seeing the past. Narrative interpretations mutually define each other and therefore owe their identity to their "intertextual" relations.'[33] It is therefore the narrative voice arranging the historical events into a coherent line that must be studied. In Gray's history the bias of the narrator is openly revealed while the narrators in his novels try to hide their motives and pretend to write objective accounts of historical events, as Kate does here. By confusing our traditional views of history and fiction, Gray demonstrates how, ultimately, the only thing that sets fiction and history apart is their truth claim.

A study of the different meanings of the title, *A History Maker*, will show us that there are as many history makers as there are views of history in this novel. Truly, this novel is a good illustration of what Maley calls a 'mythopoetics of history' as Gray draws attention to the myths of historiography, especially by playing and parodying the myth of a Universal objective History.

In its most stereotypical sense, Wat Dryhope seems to be the first history maker in this novel. At first his story seems one of the many stories of god-like heroes, the Great Men whose portraits fill our histories. His reluctance to be the next leader vanishes as he sees himself heading for glory, making history like the mythical war heroes before him. 'Then he remembered George Washington's troops – Napoleon's generals – Ulysses S. Grant –

Leon Trotsky – Che Guevara. The world would be watching him with these in mind, a wonderful, fearful thought.'[34] At first his goal seems indeed high and noble but as the story unravels itself we realize that Wat is one of Gray's ambivalent Holy Fools, as Douglas Gifford has called them, 'wise and foolish, flawed human beings and conscientious citizens'.[35] Wat is an easy prey for Delilah/Meg, 'a ferocious female',[36] who is the mastermind behind the wave of militarism. Wat's noble thoughts for the good of his community become insignificant in his desire and love for Delilah. He is willing to risk the world peace for her love. His autobiography ends on a note of impending disaster and the title, 'A History Maker', is thus meant to be ironical and he refers to his notes as 'an apology for a botched life'.[37] Wat is hardly one of Fukuyama's bloodthirsty first men.

His action nevertheless seems to have triggered a change and movement in the static society although the story as a whole does not make him the heroic human agent making history. According to Kate, Wat's story 'tells of seven crucial days in the life of a man with all the weaknesses that nearly brought the matriarchy of early modern time to a bad end, yet all the strengths that helped it to survive, reform, improve'.[38]

Kate's role makes her a history maker on several levels of the story. It is she who summons up the 'grannies', who then prevent the virus of militarism from spreading. On one hand, their action stops the world lapsing into the historical era of uncontrollable wars and nation-states, while on the other, they manage to reform and improve the world collectively – thus drawing the world back to the historical movement, or to making history. As Cairns Craig notes, 'history as a medium would make no sense in a society that did not change but, equally, would make little sense in a society that did not see change as the fundamental structuring category of its existence'.[39]

Another sense of making history becomes apparent if we look at Kate's role as the editor in the novel. I indicated in the beginning that Kate's notes provide a historical context for Wat's autobiography. Her notes are written in the third person and with this more neutral effect than in the prologue she hopes to give them an authentic and objective air. The reader will soon find out how they are at totally irrelevant places, constructing a world of their own, like Kinbote's commentary on John Shade's poem in Vladimir Nabokov's *Pale Fire*. Her notes make broad sweeps of the history of the world, which are hardly objective in tone; as the earlier quote about postmodernism reveals, they are truly synoptic and subversive histories. There are plenty of references to the present-day politics, particularly in the British Isles, and Kate's political voice blends with that of Alasdair Gray, which has been described as 'documentary-didactic voice'.[40] However, this fierceness, familiar to us from Gray's other works, is once again balanced by his sense of humour. As Gray has said,

> If I start talking about the things I don't like in contemporary social and political society, my voice goes up and I become intense and I become repetitive and I realize that a tape-recording is unwinding from my mouth and I have heard it before. I try to take steps not to get angry because as soon as you start yelling at people they naturally start doing it back and nobody learns. No ideas are communicated.[41]

Kate differs from most of the people in this utopian world in the sense that she has always stressed the importance of remembering the past, no matter how violent or unpleasant at times, so that the present can be more easily understood. As she states in the foreword, she is on a mission to make the past known so that this utopian society can see where it comes from and then be able to move forward. She could be said to provide a link to the past that has been missing and in that sense trying to re-establish a sense of self and belonging in that community. She could be called a historian in the sense that she establishes 'the value of the study of the past, not as an end in itself, but as a way of providing perspectives on the present that contribute to the solution of problems peculiar to our own time.'[42]

By juxtaposing the two stories with their different approaches to history writing, I believe Alasdair Gray is, first of all, showing how deeply sceptical he is of historical truths. This is also the purpose of drawing parallels between history and fiction, as Gray does in the novel. Kate's notes, for example, contain nonsensical fictional evidence side by side with historical facts. The reader's attention is thus drawn to the way these facts have been chosen to weave a coherent narrative line of history. After all, Kate is 'the hero's mother' and her 'objective' account of her son's action must necessarily be weighed against her biased motives as a mother.

Kate's notes and Wat's story differ in tone, emphasis and perhaps even purpose from one another. They force the reader to take a closer look at how histories are constructed. Yet they do not compete with one another for the truth value as do the two stories in *Poor Things*. Any attempt, therefore, to write a Universal History necessarily excludes many other histories. As Fukuyama himself – surprisingly – states, 'the Universal Historian must be ready to discard entire peoples and times as essentially pre- or non-historical, because they do not bear on the central "plot" of his or her story'.[43] The comment is strange as it shows how untenable Fukuyama's entire notion of writing a Universal History is. His Western, conservative perspective cannot and should not speak on behalf of the rest of the world.

For Gray to acknowledge the silencing of other stories while still pretending to be a Universal Historian is simply impossible. It is an act of cultural colonialism. When writing history, we necessarily project our own idealism and preoccupations to the ways we 'represent' the world.

Although Gray is sceptical of historical truths, I would argue that history as a whole is not presented as a negative force in the novel. Neither does history suddenly stop existing nor its value diminish even though it is shown as a human construct.[44] The ultimate history maker in this novel is of course the creator of imaginary worlds, the fiction-writer Alasdair Gray. In Scots 'makar' means poet.

His writing is not 'form without content or art without social purpose' but political and historical in its aims. Paradoxically, Gray brings art from the pure aesthetic realms to 'real' life. One of his ways in doing this is parody.[45] The numerous intertextual references, familiar from his other works, also draw our attention to the nature and origins of the fictional construct. The novel recalls the world of Border ballads, Sir Walter Scott and, most importantly, the world and writings of the Ettrick Shepherd, James Hogg. The geographical setting is explicitly that of the Hogg country. Moreover, the structure of the novel with its different narrators remind the reader of *The Private Memoirs and Confessions of a Justified Sinner* and the story could be seen to elaborate the title of Hogg's other novel: *The Three Perils of Man: War, Women and Witchcraft*.

The novel is Gray's construct, his utopia and criticism of the politics of today's world. As the map maker in Jorge Luis Borges's story saw his map taking the shape of his own face, the story in *A History Maker* reveals Gray's own idealism and preoccupations. It is significant that the mode he has chosen in this novel is science fiction utopia, as utopia is 'desire for a different, better way of being'.[46] This is Gray's utopia which arises from the particular social conditions of his present-day environment: post-Thatcherite Britain and liberal democracy. Surely it is no accident that Delilah's name, Meg, alludes to the 'ferocious female' of recent British politics, Margaret Thatcher.

Gray thus shows the impossibility of history coming to an end, on the plot level, as the utopian world is forced back to the historical movement, in other words back to change and improvement, and as well as on the metafictional level, where Gray's own cultural, historical and social contexts are blended with the fictional world of the novel. Both Fukuyama's and Gray's histories could be characterized as utopias: Fukuyama's vision of the end of history implies that we have now arrived at a utopian stage in the developed West and the rest of the world is progressing towards the same goal. In his fictional prediction of the future of the West, Gray on the other hand demonstrates the dangers involved in forgetting the past and in believing that the present is in no need of improvement and change. *A History Maker* is Alasdair Gray's attempt to combine history and future into one narrative, which reflects his own face, his own utopian vision. To rephrase Oscar Wilde: 'There can be no true history of the world which does not contain utopia'.[47]

Notes

1. Alasdair Gray, *A History Maker* (London 1994, paperback edition 1995).
2. Francis Fukuyama, *The End of History and the Last Man* (London 1992). I am indebted to both Prof. Douglas Gifford and Eilidh Whiteford for giving me this idea. I do not know whether Gray has in fact read Fukuyama's thesis and is responding to it directly.
3. E.H. Carr, *What is History?* (London 1961, reprinted 1970), 122.
4. For example, Hayden White *Tropics of Discourse. Essays in Cultural Criticism.* (Baltimore and London 1978), and *The Content of the Form. Narrative Discourse and Historical Representation* (Baltimore and London, 1987).
5. White, *The Content of the Form* 4.
6. Christopher Harvie, *Scotland and Nationalism. Scottish Society and Politics 1707–1994.* Second edition. (London 1994), 233.
7. Willy Maley, 'History's Mandate: Alasdair Gray and the Art of Independence,' *The Glasgow Review* 3 (1995), 49.
8. Douglas Gifford, 'The Return to Mythology in Modern Scottish Fiction,' *Studies in Scottish Fiction: 1945 to the Present* (ed.) Susanne Hagemann (Frankfurt 1996), 34.
9. Cairns Craig, 'The Body in the Kit Bag,' *Out of History: Narrative Paradigms in Scottish and English Culture* (Edinburgh 1996), 51–54.
10. Eilidh Whiteford's recent Ph.D thesis on Gray (for the University of Glasgow) deals with the politics of the representation of history to some extent. My forthcoming doctoral dissertation, 'Making and Unmaking History in Alasdair Gray's Fiction' for the University of Helsinki focuses more on the concepts of history in Gray's work.
11. I have discussed the implications of interpreting Bella Caledonia as an allegory of Scotland in my unpublished Master's Thesis, 'The Fiction of Alasdair Gray and the Question of Scottishness' (University of Helsinki 1996). Resurrection of *Frankenstein* is the topic of two of my forthcoming conference papers; the first concentrating on the creation of female identity, linking Gray's work with its intertextual source text and the historical characters looming in the background. The second paper focuses on the

mixture of fact and fiction by comparing Gray's version of *Frankenstein* with a Finnish novel *Frankensteinin muistikirja* ('Frankenstein's Notebook') by Juha K. Tapio (1996).

12. Linda Hutcheon, *A Poetics of Postmodernism. History, Theory, Fiction* (London 1988) 5.
13. Ernst Breisach, *Historiography: Ancient, Medieval & Modern. Second Edition*, (Chicago and London 1994) 335.
14. Gray, *A History Maker* xv.
15. Gray, *A History Maker* 203.
16. Fukuyama, *The End of History* xiii.
17. Fukuyama, *The End of History* xi.
18. Fukuyama, *The End of History* xi.
19. Fukuyama, *The End of History* xxii.
20. Fukuyama, *The End of History* xxii.
21. Gray, *A History Maker* 61.
22. Gray, *Lanark: A Life in 4 Books* (London 1981, paperback edition 1991) 411.
23. Fukuyama, *The End of History* 319.
24. Fukuyama, *The End of History* 162–170.
25. Ruth Levitas, *The Concept of Utopia*, (Hemel Hempstead 1990) 181–182.
26. Carr, *What is History?* 122.
27. Gray, *A History Maker* 205.
28. Fukuyama, *The End of History* xxii.
29. Gray, *A History Maker* 155–156.
30. Gray, *A History Maker* xiv.
31. This kind of sceptical utopia is common in contemporary utopias, particularly in feminist utopias, and worth further study.
32. Maley, 'Alasdair Gray and the Art of Independence' 49.
33. F.R. Ankersmit, 'The Dilemma of Contemporary Anglo-Saxon Philosophy of History,' *Knowing & Telling History: The Anglo-Saxon Debate. History and Theory* Beiheft 25 (1986), 25.
34. Gray, *A History Maker*, 97.
35. Douglas Gifford, 'Author's Postscript Completed by Douglas Gifford' Alasdair Gray *Unlikely Stories, Mostly* (Edinburgh 1997) 284.
36. Gifford, 'Author's Postscript' 288.
37. Gray, *A History Maker* ix.

38. Gray, *A History Maker* x–xi.
39. Craig, *Out of History* 209.
40. Christopher Harvie, 'Alasdair Gray and the Condition of Scotland Question' in *The Arts of Alasdair Gray* (eds.) Robert Crawford and Thom Nairn (Edinburgh 1991) 81.
41. Kathy Acker, 'Alasdair Gray Interviewed,' *Edinburgh Review* 74, 89.
42. White, *Tropics of Discourse* 41.
43. Fukuyama, *The End of History* 139.
44. Hutcheon, *A Poetics of Postmodernism* 7.
45. Hutcheon, *A Poetics of Postmodernism* 24.
46. Levitas, *The Concept of Utopia* 181.
47. I have replaced the word 'map' with 'history'.

13

'Out of the World and into Blawearie': The Politics of Scottish Fiction

Douglas Gifford

I begin with Walter Scott and Robert Louis Stevenson. These two writers represent the opposite ends of the spectrum in political attitudes in Scottish fiction; Scott with his ambitious yet doomed attempts to forge a new historical and unionist myth for Scotland, and Stevenson, later in the century, with a disenchanted view of what he saw increasingly as the sordid reality of Scottish history and politics.

After dealing with the self-inflicted agonies of Scotland in the great civil wars of religion and Jacobitism in the seventeenth and eighteenth centuries, in *Waverley* and *Old Mortality* in 1814 and 1816 respectively, with mixed success, Scott turned his attention from attempting to heal these old wounds to the regeneration of more contemporary Scottish social and political life. Neither of the previous two novels had succeeded in linking their main protagonists with any kind of successful engagement with politics; Edward Waverley is throughout his Scottish adventures far more the passive victim of others' ploys than heroic initiator, and, for all his greater integrity and initiative, Henry Morton has to flee Scotland, its religious affairs unresolved. There is thus for Scott a discrepancy between his heroes (admitted by Scott to be insipid), and the politics of their times. Unlike, say, Disraeli in his *Young England* fiction, Scott has a major problem in aligning his apparently heroic protagonists with movement towards politicial decision-making and fulfilment, presumably since Scottish history disallows final victory for so many of its home causes.

In *The Heart of Midlothian,* published in 1818, Scott presents a deeply ironic but in the end essentially supportive picture of Scottish union with England. The novel is set in Scotland, just after the Union of 1707, and the nation – if it can still be called a nation – is seen as unhappy about its loss and wary of its new partner. New national and civic corruption sits uneasily and vindictively alongside old native habits. To London and Westminster Scotland appears barbaric in its anachronistic smuggling and the excessive number of its illegitimate births, and monarchy and government over-react with draconian measures to both. To reassert – or re-invent – the essential decency of the Scottish nation, Scott embodies traditional Scottish virtues in an innovative fictional symbol, 'the cowfeeder's daughter', Jeanie Deans, the simple peasant girl whose honesty and decency is seen throughout that novel as the redemptive essence of Scotland. Confronted by a magistracy and legal system in Edinburgh which is motivated by expediency rather than natural justice, a weak military, and finally by a corrupt Westminster and British monarchy, Jeanie falls back on 'nature's voice' rather than the advice of lawyers, ministers and politicians to guide her through the temptations put in her way by civil riots, her sister's trial for child murder, her bigoted sectarian father. Her biggest temptation is to tell the expediential lie to save her sister Effie from the gallows for suspected child-murder. Jeanie refuses to compromise with wordly politics, and wins her sister's pardon through asserting a grass-roots decency, an instinctive morality which makes her the outstanding exemplar of the essential and core beliefs of Scottish common-sense philosophy as developed in the eighteenth century by thinkers like Francis Hutcheson and Thomas Reid.

She is the outstanding exemplar, but there are many more. Before Scott, Henry MacKenzie's *The Man of Feeling* (1771) presented a somewhat incredible – and English – model of the type in Harley, who wept copiously throughout the novel to show his empathy with human suffering. In Scott's lifetime Galt presented a range of Men of Feeling, from his minister Micah Balwhidder to his sycophantic and unsufferable sentimental Scottish adviser to fashionable Anglo-Scottish aristocracy, Andrew (to become Sir Andrew) Wylie.[1] Later in the century Stevenson, William Alexander, and George Macdonald all presented recognisable variants on the type, enduring David Balfours, Johnny Gibbs, and Malcolms.[2] This tradition of presentation of the location of ultimate Scottish worth in simple and usually peasant integrity attained its culmination in 1932 in Chris Guthrie, heroine of Lewis Grassic Gibbon's *Sunset Song*; which presented the iconic figure of a Scottish peasant girl set against a background of rural decline and First World War political and social corruption.[3]

Scott had created the mould for generations of the archetype; but in so doing he had arguably dissociated the most important tradition of the Scottish novel from engagement from mature political involvement at the most significant national and international levels. Jeanie, successfully negotiating her trials and saving her sister from the gallows, receives her reward from the very source of the political corruption she has been opposing, from diseased monarchy in London, and from the wordly and Westminster-based Duke of Argyll. From patronising and London-based decisions, she and her patron-appointed minister husband are given the island [sic] of Roseneath to administer and civilise, in a way which Scott means to stand as a microcosm of what Scotland could be if peaceful union between Scotland and England was allowed to flourish. It may be significant that Scott mistook Roseneath for an island. To make such a mistake, if it is a mistake, would demonstrate what would be for Scott an unusual lack of knowledge of Scottish topography. Did Scott exploit poetic license and simply wish Roseneath into being an island, since it fitted so well his desire to will a new Scotland into being? What is certain is that Scott's creative manipulation of Roseneath, in its 'out-of-the-world', anachronistic idealism, anticipates later Kailyard and Brigadoon visions of a dissociated, simplistic, rural and a-historical Scotland.

It is true that, on a superficial reading, many of these later writers apparently use their symbolic Scottish protagonists to engage with issues of their time. Galt's minister Balwhidder and provost Pawkie, Alexander's tenaciously effective small farmer, Johnnie Gibb, Macdonald's fabulous missing heir, Malcolm – all appear to stimulate their communities to reformative and regenerative action, in matters of manners, trade, religion; but upon examination their activities can be seen to be limited to their immediate communities, with these communities ultimately seen as saved to a greater or lesser extent by their humble leaders from corrupting engagement with national Scottish political activity. While these fictions should not be considered as early Kailyard versions, since their realism and subtlety transcend the stereotypification of the classic Kailyard, it is true that, for all their sophistication of depiction of ministers, provosts, and farmers, and for all that distant and macrocosmic events have their effects on their parishes, illustrating the effects of central government, foreign wars, new taxation, the Patronage controversy and the Disruption of 1843, these people and places are seen as passive recipients of change, and – with a worthy exception in the case of Johnny Gibb, who makes some effective practical local changes, and allowance being made for the noble but less credible influence of young Malcolm – hardly ever the active contributors to significant change in national politics and ideology.

And with this, together with earlier versions of Kailyard escapism from political and social reality as found in Burns in 'The Cottar's Saturday Night' and even Galt in *Annals of the Parish*, is – with due respect for William Donaldson's brave argument to the contrary – part of well over a hundred years of evasion of treatment of the political issues of industrialisation,

Highland Clearance, and Scottish responsibility in decision making.[4] It may surprise that I have chosen to include John Galt's 'theoretical histories' among these parochial fictions, since Galt is often seen as an honourable exception, in his portrayals of members of parliament, radicals, and small town ministers and provosts; but in his most successful 'histories' Galt continually works in a reductive idiom to cut his provosts, ministers and lairds down to size, so that their dealings are seen to be indeed parochial, and usually egotistical or simple-minded. When Galt has his provost introduce the first chapter of his egotistical account of his political career over fifty years, pompously boasting of his attainment of 'the highest station of life', and how he has been 'made an instrument to represent the extreme power and authority of majesty, in the royal burgh of Gudetown', Galt clearly intends comically to diminish our sense of Pawkie's political importance. Despite Galt's undoubted success in making Gudetown represent innumerable small communities of Scotland in transition, and however accurate his record of the changes to roads and lighting, trade and commerce, customs and manners, Pawkie and Gudetown are small beer.

Recurrently, when fiction presents a picture of an essential Scotland throughout the nineteenth and early twentieth century, that Scotland is to be found in an exemplary small community, remote from central power and cities ('out of the world and into Blawearie', as Gibbon puts it), in endless Roseneaths, in sleepy villages and towns, in fantasy. 'Naebody's nails can reach as far as Lunnon' says an angry and impotent Mrs Plumdammas, one of Scott's colourful Edinburgh High Street worthies in *The Heart of Midlothian*; and that humble perception of the distancing of Scotland from the centres of political power is a keynote of all Scott's fictional dealing with the idea of Britain.[5] And most of his fictional inheritors, however brilliant they may be in presenting deep psychological divisions in novels like Hogg's *The Private Memoirs and Confessions of a Justified Sinner* (1824) or Stevenson's *The Master of Ballantrae* (1886), are content to accept – or to deliberately create and exploit – this perspective and political agenda which distances Scotland from the reins of power. (And if fiction thus parochialised Scotland, even more so did the poetry of the period. Radical poets like Alexander Wilson and Alexander Rodger were sidelined by Scottish publishers and journals like *Blackwood's Magazine* in favour of the presentation of a more anodyne Scotland. From Scott and Hogg to William Tennant and Robert Pollock, the poetry which found most acceptance evaded engagement with current affairs, seeking either comic escape or profound and boring metaphysical musing. Great national epics, like Barbour's *Brus* or Lindsay's *Ane Satyre of the Thrie Estaitis*, or the heroic political satires of Allan Ramsay and Robert Fergusson, are not for this age.)

It is in fiction we expect representation of reality. And here the example of Stevenson's *Catriona* is strikingly representative of Scottish fiction's thematic malaise. *Catriona* was the continuation of Stevenson's *Kidnapped*, the first published in 1886, the second in 1893. Stevenson usually seems to have lacked either the interest or the talent to work at sustained or epic novels; his fictional output is made up of short stories, novellas and short novels – and many unfinished stories. It is revealing that in this epic of two volumes, centred around David Balfour, he persevered over seven years to complete the Scottish adventures and fortunes of David – like Jeanie Deans, representative of the simple and ordinary Scottish human being, and whose fortunes were perhaps meant to stand for those of Scotland herself. David's journey is a quest, like Jeanie's; he journeys, trapped by enemies, waylaid by political opponents, around Scotland, struggling to return to his inheritance. Like so many of Scott's trapped heroes, he is the means through which Scottish affairs are seen in warring perspective. But why did Stevenson need to continue David's story in *Catriona*? Most of David's adventures were complete in the first novel – his miser grandfather dead, David himself safely returned to his inheritance. What was there to continue? What remained unsettled, of course, was the story of the affair of the 'Red Fox', the murder of the hated Campbell agent committed outside Ballachulish in the mid-eighteenth century, which has remained since as the subject of intense historical speculation. In its typically Scottish and ferocious reflection of internecine tensions, here between Campbells and their Highland neighbours in Argyllshire, the affair stood alongside the Jacobite Rebellions for Stevenson as a kind of test case of schizophrenic Scottish politics. What is continued in *Catriona* are David's efforts to bear witness that James of the Glens did not murder the Red Fox. But since for British government and Campbell dominance of the Highlands the hanging of James of the Glens is expediential (echoing the intention of government to use Jeanie Deans's sister Effie as political scapegoat) it is crucial that David be sidelined in his efforts to bear witness to James's innocence in Inverary. Such are the complications of politics at the time that David is indeed sheltered and accepted into the families of the very judges and spies who are bent on James's destruction; and David's realisation two-thirds of the way through *Catriona* that his politicking has had no effect seems to me to stand also as a concluding statement from Stevenson himself regarding the validity of political life in Scotland after the Union:

> So there was the final upshot of my politics! Innocent men have perished before James and are like to keep on perishing (in spite of all our wisdom) till the end of time. Until the end of time young folk (who are not yet used with the duplicity of life and men) will struggle as I did and make heroical resolves and

take long risks; and the course of events will push them upon the one side and go on like a marching army. James was hanged; and here was I dwelling in the house of Preston Grange, and grateful to him for his fatherly attention. He was hanged; and behold when I met Mr. Simon in the causeway, I was fain to pull off my beaver to him like a good little boy before his dominie. He had been hanged by fraud and violence, and the world wagged along and there was not a penny weight of difference; and the villains of that horrid plot were decent, kind, respectable fathers of families, who went to kirk and took the sacrament!

But I had had my view of that detestable business they call politics – I had seen it from behind, when it is all bones and blackness; and I was cured for life of any temptation to take part in it again. A plain quiet private path was that which I was ambitious to walk in , when I might keep my head out of the way of dangers and my conscience out of the road of temptation. For, upon a retrospect, it appeared I had not done so grandly, after all; but with the greatest possible amount of big speech and preparation, had accomplished nothing . . .[6]

Stevenson was to be involved in the politics of Ireland and to be an early critic of colonialism in the South Seas; but as far as he envisioned Scotland's place as a political entity in the world, it would appear that, as with Buchan after him, he saw little potential for significant action. For them, Scotland remains as a periphery, a place of old intrigues, if, paradoxically, a place to seek spiritual renewal or freedom in flight from centralised powers. The imagery which remains in the reader's mind from Stevenson's Scottish fiction is that of the wind-blown moorlands of Scotland, with curlews crying; this for him has become the essence of Scotland, and full-bodied participation in British and world politics is, as with Buchan, left for exiles for whom Scotland remains as a nostalgia, a yearning detached from mature business.

This de-politicising of Scotland owes much to the Disruption of the Church of Scotland in 1843. As Professor Christopher Harvey has argued, before 1843 the annual General Assembly of the Church of Scotland looked 'more like a parliament than many of the provincial assembles of continental Europe, and acted as a *locus* for a type of transactional politics', being consulted by politicians and used by politicians as a sounding board before inflicting Westminster decisions upon the country.[7] But with the fatal and schizophrenic split of the Church in 1843 that remaining central arena for politics in Scotland was lost, and thereafter for a full hundred years it would appear that Scottish political life, as reflected in its fiction and culture generally, is somehow dissociated from the rest of Britain. Christopher Smout's great study, *A Century of the Scottish People 1830–1950*, covering the period from the beginning of Victoria's reign to the middle of the twentieth century, refuses to discuss any achievement in Scottish culture, such is Smout's disgust at its dissociation from the horrid social realities of Scottish urbanisation and industrialisation.[8]

With great respect for Smout's dark view of the century (or one hundred and twenty years), I believe he is wrong to ignore cultural achievement (apart from the odd reference to Carlyle, or Hugh Miller, or William Alexander, whom he wrongly terms a 'kailyard' novelist). The Scots wrestled endlessly with issues of industrialisation and social alienation, especially in the period 1770–1850, as George Davie has shown.[9] William Donaldson has also shown how the popular press and local newspapers grew enormously and increased their involvement with issues of the day after the repeal of the Stamp Act in 1855.[10] And thinkers like Carlyle and Miller contributed immensely to Victorian debate, with poems and fiction like Thomson's *The City of Dreadful Night* (1874) and Stevenson's *Dr. Jekyll and Mr. Hyde* (1886) becoming authoritative metaphoric and exemplary statements about the decline of religious belief and moral and social hypocrisy in Victorian Britain. That said, it must be admitted that from the death of Scott till Stevenson's fiction in the 1870s there was a period when Scots seemed to lose their sense of Scottish, as opposed to British (or even English) national identity. Moreover, when Scottish writing in 'another spring' began 'heaving again', as the German critic Kurt Wittig perceived it, for well-nigh fifty years it was marked by its sense of disillusion and its ironic perspectives on Scottish life and character – a process of bitter and necessary re-assessment found outstandingly in the work of writers like George Douglas Brown, Neil Munro, John Davidson, John MacDougall Hay, Marion Angus and Violet Jacob.[11] These are fine writers, and their work is steadily being re-assessed in ways which increasingly reveal that Scotland was far from being culturally benighted before the so-called 'Scottish Renaissance' associated so closely with the contribution of Hugh MacDiarmid and his group; but their disillusion with what Scotland has become is everywhere obvious. Scottish political affairs, when dealt with at all, were dealt with satirically and parodically, represented as matters of internecine historical feuding and betrayal, or small-town chicanery, envy and gossip.

There is indeed a great school of Scottish fiction, from Scott to Gibbon, in which writers like George Macdonald and Margaret Oliphant deal with insight and satirical effect through realism and fantasy with Scottish character and social life, identifying and symbolically representing what Edwin Muir described as a 'dissociation of Scottish sensibility', a destructive split in Scottish language, mind and literary values which he claims began with the Reformation in 1560, but which recent critics, including the present writer, see as being wider and multi-sourced, to be described in terms which are less simply dualistic, and as less negative in its results for Scottish literature than Muir argued.[12] But this school of fiction is essentially rural-based, and arrives at bleak and negative conclusions in its analysis of deformed Scottish character. With the exception of a vein of 'urban Kailyard' fiction in the Scottish popular press, later nineteenth century Scottish fiction was slow to engage with the industrial and social realities of Scotland from 1850 to the Great Depression of the 1930s.[13] We have to wait until 1934 for Lewis Grassic Gibbon's *Grey Granite* before we are given a fundamentally serious attempt to analyse the political and social workings of a major Scottish industrial city, and we have to wait until the novels of Neil Gunn (beginning with *Butcher's Broom* in 1932) for any substantial political analysis of what really happened in the Highland Clearances. From Scott's death and the Disruption eleven years later, indigenous Scottish culture and radical political activity was perceived by the great Tory dominated periodicals of the day as something to be kept down. *Blackwood's Magazine* stood as the ruling Tory authority, with its editor, John Wilson, an immensely influential figure, with his inherited wealth, his chair in Moral Philosophy at Edinburgh University, his poetry, essays, and fiction, and his friendship with Wordsworth and the Lake school of poets. As the uncrowned king of Scottish literature after Scott's death in 1832, and a hugely powerful figure in the world of literature and publishing generally, he ruled over a North British culture which had all but atrophied in its view of Scotland as a pre-Kailyard pastoral and idyllic backwater of British life. Wilson's own melodramatic and sentimental fiction was unashamed propaganda designed to ensure that the Scottish peasant classes remained subservient and docile through dangerously subversive years.[14] There is a clear line of descent running from these rural idealisations of John Wilson and *Blackwood's Magazine* down through *The British Weekly* of William Robertson Nicoll in the later nineteenth century to the idylls of *The People's Friend* and *The Sunday Post*, the last bastions of this retreat into a timeless Scotland of weavers' cottages, of sentimental gruff elders, and small-town parish worthies, their timelessness perhaps finding its last incarnation in the unchanging adventures of Oor Wullie and The Broons.

And when trenchant criticism of Scottish social mores and town life finally came, outstandingly with George Douglas Brown's *The House with the Green Shutters* in 1901, it was to be marked with a sense of sardonic futility which hardly stands as effective counterblast to the ailments of Scottish society, as perceived by authors like Douglas Brown, James Barrie, John MacDougall Hay (in his monumental Highland version of *The House with the Green Shutters* in *Gillespie* in 1914) and even Neil Munro's caustic and ironic pictures of west Highland life in his great satirical novels (rather than the marine kailyard adventures of *Para Handy*). Munro's neglected achievement stands at the end of the nineteenth century and immediately prior to the Great War as a representative summary of how major Scottish writers from Stevenson to Davidson viewed their country, as tormented by its internecine history and betrayed by its involvement in the politics of British imperialism and commerce. Munro's first stories in *The Lost Pibroch* of 1896 were too easily read as part of a romanticised Celtic Twilight, when they were essentially bitter and ironic stories about loss of innocence, tradition and community, and about tragic self-betrayal brought about by fatal flaws of Highland character induced by destructive and hierarchical clan politics and corruption. *John Splendid* (1898) developed the analysis further, presenting in the subtle, complex and apparently dashing Highland hero a figure shown, as the wars of Montrose and Argyll in the seventeenth century engulf the country, to have feet of clay, and to be the arch-representative of the cancer at the heart of Highland decay. *Gilian the Dreamer* (1899) turned from examining the diseased soldier-clansman to analysing the cultural and creative decay of Highland community and its once-great oral tradition, now, in the nineteenth century, reduced to being the tattered fringe of British imperialism. In this portrait of Inveraray as a town of pensioned-off officers and would-be army gentlemen, pathetically hoarding memories of the peninsular wars and tartan regiments, the greatness of talent of the (literally and symbolically) orphaned boy, Gilian, is utterly ignored. The Scottish town is perceived as dissociated from either worldly reality or creative energy, and instead as moribund and remote. And while Munro – a hugely influential and respected journalist in Glasgow, writing in his newspapers from 1880 about the enormous variety of activity taking place in the second city of the empire for fifty years, from industry to art, from literature to war – tried with some success in his final great novel, *The New Road* (1914), to suggest a drive towards positive change, brought about by the actual new road through the Highlands being built by General Wade in the aftermath of Culloden in 1746, and through the new roads of opportunity and trade which were finally bringing the old chicaneries of the clans to book, the final impression of the novel is once again of its protagonists, the young Aeneas MacMaster and his friend, a mature and far less romantic version of Alan Breck, Ninian Macgregor Campbell, secret agent for the Duke of Argyll, in the end retreating to out-of-the-world Inveraray, disliking the implications of the very new roads they have helped to open up.

It is as though writers such as these could accurately and effectively analyse the deficiencies of Scottish character in relation to municipal and national politics when they wished, but preferred to focus on other figures, and to symbolise these central characters, from Stevenson's ferocious hanging judge, Lord Weir of Hermiston, to Douglas Brown's giant town merchant, John Gourlay, to Munro's bull-necked pensioned soldiers – and, outstandingly, his portrait of the most corrupt of Highlanders, Simon Lovat, the dreaded and bloated spider at the heart of all Northern corruption, the anachronistic worshipped-and-hated *MacShimi* – as monuments to an older, brutal, materialistic, and unfeeling Scotland. These are anachronistic figures of an older past, who stand in antagonism against their feckless sons to the point where the father destroys the son and the son destroys the father. This recurrent symbolic representation, from Stevenson and Brown down to MacDougall Hay's Argyllshire version in his grasping merchant Gillespie Strang (admittedly more forward-looking in his greed, but portrayed as the unconscious agent of an older evil), and the later merchant-tyrant of A.J. Cronin's *Hatter's Castle* (1931), seems to me to symbolise a deadlock in Scottish culture, and to illustrate the way in which the authoritarian and materialistic side of Scottish society checkmates and destroys any sensitive creative cultural response in the symbolic figures of the doomed younger generation, so often the tragic sons of their tyrant fathers. Archibald Hermiston senior destroys and presumably would have been destroyed by Archibald Hermiston junior, in Stevenson's unfinished family tragedy; John Gourlay senior destroys and is destroyed by John Gourlay junior. And so it goes, down through so many of our major Scottish novels. So recurrent is the pattern of internecine family struggle, that the reader of Scottish fiction from Scott to the 'Scottish Renaissance' 1920s might be forgiven for thinking that, if these versions of Scottish life hold truth, the implicated generations of this dark century were too busy quarrelling amongst themselves to allow productive assessment of where they had come from, where they now were, and how they might develop as a homogenous society.

This disengagement from politics continues through the so-called 'Scottish Renaissance', for all its apparently prominent political agenda. Hugh MacDiarmid's fiery political statements stand somewhat apart from the major successes of his poetry. It is significant that his early lyrics, drawing so strongly from the works of Marion Angus and Violet Jacob, celebrate the timeless tragedies of local Scottish peasants in Scotland, from the mother whose child has died to the passing of giant local worthies, and from the bonnie broukit bairn to the dead patriarchs buried at Crowdieknowe. Even MacDiarmid's celebrated *A Drunk Man Looks at the Thistle* in 1926, for all its occasional involvement with issues of General Strike and England, and its recurrent condemnations of Scottish psyche and society, prefers to explore European metaphysics, rather than make explicit comment upon how Scots might re-engage with a healthy political life. It is revealing that MacDiarmid chose to edit out some of the most explicit and ambitious political statements of his age, when he edited his friend and fellow-poet William Soutar's poems after his death. In 1948 MacDiarmid brought out what is now recognised as a limited and biased edition of Soutar's poems, omitting – through envy? professional jealousy? – the very poems we might have expected him most to admire, like the huge visionary and political epic modelled on older Scottish political epic, 'The Auld Tree', and the comparable envisioning of Scottish political and national rebirth in 'The Whale'.[15] And although MacDiarmid and others like Neil Gunn and Lewis Grassic Gibbon were extremely active in their own lives in a range of politics which spans Communism, Socialism and Nationalism, repudiating the dominating Tory ethos of the nineteenth century, almost invariably every major author from MacDiarmid to Eric Linklater and Edwin Muir in the end retreated from involvement in politics.

It seems that, however much the Renaissance writers wished to engage with regenerative politics, they were condemned to work within self-imposed psychological limits (often, ironically enough, diagnosed by themselves as applying to their country's creativity – Muir's theory of 'dissociation of sensibility', in its historical analysis of how Scots are creatively split, may differ in important respects from MacDiarmid's racially-based theories of antisyzgy, but it shares with it the final identification of a dualism at the core of Scottish thought). For all the commitment to modernisation and radical change to be found in fiction of the Scottish Renaissance, the sad fact is that virtually all the novelists end in suggesting withdrawal to eternal rhythms of season and rural consolation, or end in ironic despair in regard to the possibilty of change. Gibbon, Gunn, Edwin Muir, 'Fionn MacColla' (Tom Macdonald), George Blake, Ian Macpherson and Eric Linklater – all of these important Renaissance novelists in the end retreat from the Scotland whose cause they initially espouse.

And here it's worth using as exemplars Eric Linklater and his magnificient and Rabelaisian satire of 1934 on Scottish politics at the time of MacDiarmid's 'Renaissance', *Magnus Merriman,* and the most ambitious of surveys of the state of Scotland around the time of the Great War, Lewis Grassic Gibbon's great trilogy of 1932–34, *A Scots Quair.* Linklater, of all the Renaissance writers, seems to be the man of the world, with his various and often illustrious careers as journalist, soldier, dramatist, novelist – and would-be politician. Like MacDiarmid, Linklater was actively involved in Renaissance and nationalist politics, standing as a candidate for the Scottish Nationalist party in 1933. The very variety of careers and personas, represented at their extermities on the one hand in his role as a northern military gentleman, on the other by his habitual self-reductive description of himself as 'an old peasant with a pen', yet again illustrates something of that dualism and internal conflict which bedevils so many Scottish writers, incapacitating any sustained and consistent vision of a valid contributing personal place in national affairs.

It is just this theme of incapacitation from larger events through fundamental fragmentation of character which Linklater, simultaneously mocking himself and Scottish Renaissance, produced in his masterpiece, *Magnus Merriman*. The novel has the liveliest of Renaissance protagonists, the eponymous Magnus, whose oxymoronic names suggest that Linklater wished to capture Magnus's descent from Orkney's patron saint – but wished to indicate the contradictory aspects of his personality by placing any association the reader might make between Magnus and saintly idealism alongside a reductive humanism (echoing the strikingly antisyzygical imagery of *A Drunk Man*, with its grinning gargoyles juxtaposed with saints) and confirmed when Magnus suggests that the Merrimans have tinker connections. Magnus – like his creator, perhaps – is a set of contradictions which prevent synthesis; he is a prose version of MacDiarmid's and Smith's notion of 'the Caledonian antisyzygy'.[16] Magnus initially hurls himself into the new nationalism, standing for parliament and participating in gloriously silly debates in a wonderful satire on the bizarre complexities of Scottish politics in the period; but is finally forced to withdraw from politics ignominiously, finding fulfilment and peace – so predictably! – in the beauty, the certainties and rhythms of Orkney landscape. His political activities and his constant changes of political loyalty are exposed as a sham and a comic delusion. Linklater here is partly mocking, partly celebrating, MacDiarmid's own position, satirising MacDiarmid's constant willingness to change political allegiances on a sixpence throughout the 'thirties and 'forties; but he is also mocking his own experience of politics, in which he lost his deposit as a candidate.

Without self-mockery, and even more distrustful of contemporary 'Scottish Renaissance', the most political of all the Renaissance fictions, Lewis Grassic Gibbon's *A Scots Quair*, moves in two opposed directions. On the one hand there is Chris Guthrie's movement from wordly action to withdrawal to the rhythms of the land and ancestral time; echoing that of Jeanie Deans. On the other, there is the movement of her son Ewan down to London where he feels he can have some impact upon politics – a movement which most critics agree is far less credible and satisfying. Virtually all critics agree that the mythopoetic power of the trilogy lies with Chris, and Gibbon's evocation of her conscious and unconscious bonds with older Scotland and its language, with even older communities and their legacy, and with the Land as a living entity. And although Gibbon in fact undercuts this bond between Chris and the Land in the end, by suggesting that she recognises even more potent and permanent forces in Change and Death, this deeper recognition, far from moving Gibbon closer to political engagement with Scotland and Britain, actually moves him even further from it. In this he is comparable to MacDiarmid, who similarly withdrew from engagement with Scots language after *A Drunk Man*, moving, like Gibbon, to a contemplation of vast aeons of geological time in which humanity's existence and its validity was often seen as microscopic. And looking beyond Gibbon, it would be fair to say that, for all the magnificent achievement of Scottish Renaissance novelists and poets – and even with William Soutar, so positive and ambitious in his great poems of spiritual rebirth for Scotland in the early thirties, who turned away from political to local and community themes in his dying years – there is almost always in the end an underlying retreat either to the past and to the traditions and imagined consolations of an older country, or to the vast impersonality of inhuman time.

The values of the Scottish literary Renaissance of the twenties and thirties were undercut by the disgrace of National Socialist ideologies in the defeat of Germany in 1945. To the extent that certain agendas had been shared – a belief in answers lying in a return to the soil, a belief in ideologies of race, and the significance of ancestral memory, and the belief in the importance of an essential rural origin of modernity – these could no longer be seen in the 1950s as valid contributions to a world disillusioned and distrustful of simplistic and radical non-urban ideologies. But with the exception of the work of Naomi Mitchison, whose *The Bull Calves* in 1947 does seem to me to be simultaneously an echo of the Scottish Renaissance and a precursor of new ways of thinking about Scotland, the 1950s and 1960s in Scotland were hardly to offer agendas of political optimism. Outstandingly the work of novelists like Dorothy Haynes and Robin Jenkins, and later George Friel, were to offer mocking pictures of small lowland towns and the big cities which were debased versions of older rural Scottish communities. Now, from James Bridie's *Mr Gillie* in drama to Muriel Spark's *The Prime of Miss Jean Brodie* and Friel's *Mr Alfred MA* in fiction, serious Scottish writing is dominated by analyses of failed teachers and political idealists, people whose dreams to bring their children into the light from slum, poverty and ignorance are to end in disappointment, madness and suicide.[17] With a slight change of wording the ironic poem written by the reviewer of George Douglas Brown's novel in 1901 could still be applied to Scottish fiction;

Paint village hell where sadist monster mutters
Till Scotland's one mad House with its Green Shutters
Depict the lust that lurks in hall and hovel.
And build thereon a Scottish national novel.[18]

With Jenkins, Spark, Kennaway, Friel, McIlvanney and so many more the Scottish national novel did indeed seem to continue to prefer negativity, identification of warped psychological and sociological strains, and endings of universal gloom, to any indication of the viabilities of positive political action, in attitudes substantially different from those found in English fiction and literature. In the work of Dickens, Disraeli and Mrs Gaskell, the industrial had been painted relentlessly, and yet with a range of suggestions as to how social and political change might be brought about, from philanthropic reform of the human heart suggested by Dickens to overt regeneration of Tory philosophy as suggested by Disraeli; the Scots, in contrast, had little to contribute beyond their sense of terminal decline.

And it is true to say that since the work of Jenkins and Friel much of Scottish fiction has persevered down that cul-de-sac of introspective disillusion, removing its protagonists from any relevance to a world of political change, and from any enablement of personal choice in that social change. In studies of Scottish character after the war like that of Colonel Jock Sinclair in James Kennaway's *Tunes of Glory* (1956), and in the early 'sixties such as those of Jean Brodie, or Dougal Douglas in *The Ballad of Peckham Rye* by Spark, once again it is the overwhelming negativities which dominate such characterisation rather than the suggestion that somehow Scottish character could rescue itself and reform in order to address brave new possibilities.[19] And in the poetry and fiction of Norman MacCaig, Iain Crichton Smith, George Mackay Brown, and even James Kelman and Irvine Welsh, there is a detachment from history and politics which is virtually complete. MacCaig's poetry continually refuses to acknowledge the existence of myth or of any sense of Scotland moving through any historical process. He is content to be bewildered by his senses, and his poetry is the analysis of a man looking simply at himself within his surroundings. Crichton Smith seems on first reading to be interested in the processes of history and some kind of social politics in his novel of 1968 set in the time of Highland Clearance, *Consider the Lilies*; but deeper scrutiny reveals that his ultimate diagnosis is not of the roots, rights and wrongs of the Highland Clearances themselves but of the interior and Calvinistic clearances of the mind, which his novel argues are far more significant than land clearance. The novel is thus a part of his recurrent analysis of the traumatic effects of Calvinism upon the Scottish mind. The magnificent work of George Mackay Brown, in poetry and fiction, can stand forever as a memorial to his beloved Orkney; but even the most sympathetic of readers would not claim that Mackay Brown's underlying mythology of the significance of Saint Magnus Cathedral as exemplar of the Christian message, set within a curiously pagan and Scandinavian islandscape, has much truck with a contemporary Scotland facing political challenge and immense social change – indeed, throughout Brown's work there is an explicit hostility to Progress, identified as a destroyer of the simplicity and harmony of small communities.

The culmination of this antagonism towards a mythologised Scottish past, with its insistence on the dominance of a bleak and warped Scottish present, can be found in the work of James Kelman, Irvine Welsh, and Duncan McLean. Kelman is apparently the outstanding representative of the bleak hopelessness of the dispossessed, the counterpart in fiction of the Glasgow poet Tom Leonard; yet it seems to me in the end his statement has more in common with the philosophical alienation of the Outsider of Albert Camus than any message of politically motivated anger suggesting positive ways of changing a corrupt system. With all due respect for the compelling accuracy of Kelman's representation of the predicaments of ordinary urban people (whether they be in Glasgow or anywhere in the west of Europe) it would appear that there lurks behind Kelman's apparent political activism an undercutting metaphysical pessimism which ultimately places his disaffected chancers and down-and-outs in a self-chosen position of dissociation from a world of positive action. Going further, Welsh's work shows his central characters (some of whom have university education and therefore chances) sharing an ideology which boils down to laconic oneliners – life is a bitch, we didn't ask to be born, let's live for now in as self-interested and hedonistic a fashion as is possible in our debased and impoverished circumstances; while McLean's aim in recent fiction has been to show that rural community has been blighted irredeemably by commerce and levelling out of institutions and manners in a bleak international modernism.[20]

So does the line of descent through Scottish fiction from Scott through Stevenson and *Green Shutters* lead to the bleakest of dead ends in stagnant Drumchapel burns and the desolate bleak slum clearance flats of the Leith of Irvine Welsh? Is all Scottish fiction to be seen as a movement from disappointed history, the lesson of which is that other non-Scottish centres of power make our crucial decisions for us, as recognised by Scott, down to a placing of modern Scots as children of the dead end? The answer I would like to suggest is an emphatic No. It seems to me that some very significant changes of Scottish attitudes began in 1980 with Alasdair Gray's

Lanark. Thereafter, fiction and drama of the 1980s and 1990s spell out some very different agendas for Scottish literature. Gray's *Lanark*, with its astonishing mixture of genres from science fiction to realistic *bildungsroman* does indeed diagnose the limitations of Scottish culture and the self-alienation of the artist in a materialistic urban society; but it is shot through with moments of positive assertion, moments which in Gray's later fiction such as *Janine, 1982* and *Poor Things* are to be developed into positive representations of personal decision-making. Suicidal alcoholic Jock McLeish finally takes up the broken ends of his life to manipulate them into something positive, and in *Poor Things*, in the Mary Shelley-and-Stevenson derived presentation of a man-created new woman, Bella Caledonia, Gray presents what women could be if the ancient patriarchal mould of Scottish womanhood were to be broken and fashioned anew. All Gray's novels since *Janine* have embossed on their outside covers overtly political messages requiring the reader to work as though they were living in the early days of a better nation, and repudiating the disappointments of the Devolution Referendum of 1979. Gray continues to produce books urging Scots towards home rule.[21] And if Gray has been the leader, he is far from being alone; the new Scottish poetry inspired by Edwin Morgan (and outstandingly in 1984 with his huge collage of visions of Scotland past, present and future in *Sonnets From Scotland*) and Liz Lochhead, and drama such as Lochhead's *Mary Queen of Scots Got Her Head Chopped Off* (1987) have consistently engaged with large and panoramic pictures of Scotland in history and in science fiction speculation in ways which have liberated Scottish literature from its introspective pessimism.[22] The work of William McIlvanney, in essays and in recent award-winning novels such as *The Kiln*, has consistently committed its protagonists to rejection of the political status quo and by implication to the construction of a new Scotland. And the evidence of newer Scottish writing, in especial the work of newer writers such as Janice Galloway, Alison Kennedy, Iain Banks, and Carl McDougall, steadily suggests that there is a quite deliberate artistic intention to emphasize the positive in personal and social development. Titles of recent novels such as *Looking For the Possible Dance* and *The Lights Below* contain the symbolism of old, hidden rhythms and sources of illumination which can revivify and inspire protagonists whose lives have been deadened by the effects of urban decay and by apathy of vision regarding their country and its possibilities.[23] These novels end with a fusion of the rural and the urban, suggesting that we must refashion and reintegrate Scotland in our imaginations as an inspiring landscape with potentially enriching cities, working towards something that can be seen and lived in as a whole rather than as fragmented parts. The fiction of Iain

Banks shows this reassembly of crow roads, places of nature, with city streets, of modern mechanics of oil and cars and computers with a love of ancient rural place. Women and women writers are to the fore, in Gray and Banks's focus on modern Scottish sexual and gender dilemmas in novels like *Janine* and *Whit,* in the sensitive analyses of women by Ronald Frame, and in the rise of splendid new satirical yet implicitly politically conscious work by Janice Galloway and Alison Kennedy. The political agenda is never strident, but very much present in the confident, comical, surrealist, and constantly changing genres of the new Scottish literature – fantasy from Margaret Elphinstone and Sian Haytoun, mature international satire from William Boyd, and Alan Massie, and a host of young short story writers of radically new imagination and attitude.[24] Add to this an exciting and similarly varied and adventurous scene in poetry, in drama, in painting and music, and a clear sense of bold new possibilities of Scottish identities emerges, a sense of constant experimentation and rising confidence, devoid of political reticence. The reasons for this are many and complex, ranging, I believe, from the belated fruiting of the Welfare State to the singular success of the Scottish Arts Council, as well as the dawning recognition by Scots that they are in danger of being left behind, economically, culturally and historically, if they don't at last speak out. All this is still more promise than reality, but I think many contemporary Scots would admit that from education to art, from fiction to reality, change is in the air.

I finish with a question regarding what seems to me to be one of modern Scotland's oustanding paradoxes. Why was it that, in the 1920s and 1930s with the Scottish Renaissance in full flight, and Scottish culture vigorous in assertion of ancient identity and political rights, no political gains resulted in terms of membership of parliament? Yet, in the 1970s, when Scottish writers from McIlvanney to Mackay Brown were repudiating Scottish literary traditions and insisting on the non-Scottish and international roots of their work, nigh a dozen Scottish nationalist members of parliament resulted? Is it perhaps the case that Scottish culture and Scottish politics are doomed forever to be at loggerheads, or – at last – are we witnessing the reintegration of all the many split and divided traditions of our cultural and social life? Can we hope that with our re-creation of a new Scottish parliament that we will also see the re-creation – or perhaps, more simply, the creation – of new voices which will, while maintaining our traditions of flyting and debate, speak with a greater willingness to involve themselves with possible new Scotlands?

Notes

1. John Galt, *Sir Andrew Wylie of That Ilk* (Edinburgh 1822).

2. David Balfour is of course hero of both *Kidnapped* and *Catriona* (Edinburgh 1886 and 1893 respectively); while Johnny Gibb is the central figure in William Alexander's *Johnny Gibb of Gushetneuk* (Edinburgh 1875), and Malcolm MacPhail, finally Marquis of Lossie, the central figure of George Macdonald's *Malcolm* and *The Marquis of Lossie* (London, 1875 and 1877 respectively).

3. Lewis Grassic Gibbon (pen-name of J. Leslie Mitchell) created the trilogy *A Scots Quair*, comprising the three novels *Sunset Song*, *Cloud Howe*, and *Grey Granite* (London 1932, 1933, 1934 respectively).

4. In *Popular Literature and Victorian Scotland* (Aberdeen 1986) (and in valuable editions of the work of William Alexander) Donaldson argues that historians of Scottish fiction have failed to take into account the large amount of fiction dealing with Scottish urbanisation and industrialisation of the nineteenth century (as well as the large amount of writing in Scots). I have taken issue with this in my essay 'Myth, Parody and Dissociation: Scottish Fiction 1814–1914' in Douglas Gifford (ed), *The History of Scottish Literature Volume Three; Nineteenth Century* (Aberdeen 1988), 235–236.

5. The phrase 'out of the world and into Blawearie' is cited as the voice of community in *Sunset Song* describing the sense of remoteness of John Guthrie's small farm of Blawearie, even more distanced from wordly affairs than its isolated near community, Kinraddie. (*Sunset Song*, 'Prelude; The Unfurrowed Field'; in the Jarrolds edition of the trilogy (London 1946), 23.

6. Chapter Twenty, *Catriona*; Robert Louis Stevenson, *The Scottish Novels* (Canongate Classics edition, Edinburgh 1995) 173.

7. Christopher Harvie, 'Industry, Religion, and the State of Scotland', in *The History of Scottish Literature; Volume Three; Nineteenth Century*, 31.

8. T.C. Smout, *A Century of the Scottish People 1830–1950* (London 1986), 7

9. George Davie, 'The Social Significance of the Scottish Philosophy of Common Sense' (*The Dow Lecture*, University of Dundee, 1972.)

10. William Donaldson, *Popular Literature and Victorian Scotland*; Donaldson exemplifies his argument that the popular press increasingly engaged with the major national and international issues of the day after the repeal of the Stamp Act in 1855 in his anthology *The Language of the People; Scots Prose from the Victorian Revival* (Aberdeen, 1989). A succinct version of his arguments can be found in his essay 'Popular Literature: The Press, the People, and the Vernacular Revival', *The History of Scottish Literature; Volume Three; Nineteenth Century*, 213–216.

11. Kurt Wittig, *The Scottish Tradition in Literature* (Edinburgh and London 1958) 254ff.

12. Muir's theory of dissociation in Scottish culture is argued throughout his *Scott and Scotland: The Predicament of the Scottish Writer* (London 1936). For my qualification and extension of Muir's argument see 'Myth, Parody and Dissociation' in *The History of Scottish Literature; Volume Three; Nineteenth Century*, 217–260.

13. The term 'urban kailyard' is borrowed from Moira Burgess, who uses it in her recent study of fictions of Glasgow, *Imagining a City: Glasgow in Fiction* (Glendaruel, Argyll 1998) to describe nostalgic and patronisingly emollient representations of the industrialised Scottish History.

14. Wilson's fiction comprises *Lights and Shadows of Scottish Life*, *The Trials of Margaret Lyndsay*, and *The Foresters* (Edinburgh 1822, 1823, and 1825 respectively). For a critical analysis of Wilson's place in Scottish culture, see Andrew Noble's essay 'John Wilson ("Christopher North")' in *The History of Scottish Literature; Volume Three; Nineteenth Century*, 125–152.

15. The reasons for MacDiarmid's exclusion of so many of the most important political poems of Soutar are unclear. MacDiarmid was extremely angry at those who attacked him for his omissions, and his defence is put forward in a long letter dated 25/11/48 to Douglas Young. See Alan Bold (ed.) *The Letters of Hugh MacDiarmid* (London 1984), 602–604 .

16. The first use of the term 'the Caledonian antisyzygy' is in George Gregory Smith's *Scottish Literature; Character and Influence* (London 1919); MacDiarmid thereafter deployed the term.

17. For examples of such reductive fictions of Scottish industrialised and small-town community in the work of Haynes, Jenkins and Friel, see Haynes's *Winter's Traces* (London 1947), Jenkins's *The Thistle and the Grail* (London 1954), and Friel's *Mr. Alfred MA* (London 1972).

18. The poem describing Scotland's 'village hell' is quoted by Angus MacDonald in his essay 'Modern Scots Novelists' in H.J.C. Grierson (Preface), *Edinburgh Essays on Scots Literature* (Edinburgh and London 1933), 165.

19. *The Ballad of Peckham Rye* (London 1960); *The Prime of Miss Jean Brodie* (London 1961).

20. For examples of the work of Kelman, Welsh and McLean with regard to my argument, see Kelman's *The Bus Conductor Hines* (Edinburgh 1984), Welsh's *Trainspotting* (London 1993), and McLean's *Blackden* (London 1991).

21. Alasdair Gray, *Lanark*; *Janine, 1982*; *Poor Things* (Edinburgh 1981; London 1984; London 1992 respectively).

22. Edwin Morgan's *Sonnets From Scotland* can be found in his *Poems of Thirty Years* (Manchester 1982); Liz Lochhead's *Mary Queen of Scots Got Her Head*

Chopped Off and *Dracula* were published together by Penguin (London 1989).

23. Examples of the new writers cited here can be found in William McIlvanney, *The Kiln* (London 1997), Janice Galloway, *The Trick is to Keep Breathing* (Edinburgh 1989), Alison Kennedy, *Looking For the Possible Dance* (London 1993) and *So I am Glad* (London 1995) Iain Banks, *The Bridge* (London 1986), *The Crow Road* (London 1992), and *Whit* (London 1995); Carl MacDougall *The Lights Below* (London 1993).

24. Further examples of contemporary Scottish writing cited include (in order of reference in the text) Ronald Frame, *Winter Journey* (London 1984) and *Watching Mrs. Gordon* (London 1985); Margaret Elphinstone, *The Incomer* (London 1987) and *Islanders* (Edinburgh 1997); Sian Haytoun, *Cells of Knowledge* (Edinburgh 1989); William Boyd, *A Good Man in Africa* (London 1981) and *The New Confessions* (London 1987); Alan Massie, *The Last Peacock* (London 1986) and *Augustus* (London 1986). A fuller description of the contemporary scene in fiction can be found in my essay,'Imagining Scotlands: The Return to Mythology in Modern Scottish Fiction', in Susan Hagemann (ed.), *Studies in Scottish Fiction: 1945 to the Present* (Frankfurt am Main 1997), 17–50.

Index

Adomnán, 2, 39–57
   Life of Columba, 2, 39–57
Áed Dub, 50
Áed Sláine, 50
Áedan mac Gabráin, 48–51
Alexander III, 2, 201
Alexander, William, 285, 290
   Johnny Gibb of Gushetneuk, 286
Aneirin, 1
   The Gododdin, 1
Anglo-Scots, 80–81
Angus, Marion, 290, 293
Aonghas nan Aoir, 137
Aonghas Òg, 138
Arbuthnot, Alexander, 79
Arens, W., 158
   The Man-Eating Myth, 158
Arthur, 200
Athanasius, 40
   Life of Antony, 40

Bacon, Francis, 218
Baíthéne, 41, 47, 54–56
Balfour, A.J., 231
Baliol, John, 90
Ballads, 201
   'Sir Patrick Spens', 201
   'The Bonnie Earl o Moray', 201
Banks, Iain, 299–300
Bannockburn, battle of, 3, 61, 62–63, 65–66, 69, 71–72, 75, 100, 102
Barbour, John, 2, 3, 4, 5, 9, 62–65, 66–72, 88, 90–91, 95, 100, 102, 287
   The Bruce, 2, 5, 62, 66, 68–69, 75, 88–89, 90, 92, 99, 102, 287
Barker, Elspeth, 159, 167
   O Caledonia, 159
Barnett, T. Ratcliffe, 172
   The Road to Rannoch and the Summer Isles, 1924, 172
   The Land of Lorne and the Isles of Rest, 133, 172
Barrie, J.M., 204, 226, 291
   Peter Pan, 226
Bassadyne, Thomas, 79
Bell, Henry, 177
Bellenden, John, 7
Black Book of Taymouth, 114, 116, 124
Blackwood's Magazine, 287, 291

Blake, George, 294
Blair, Hugh, 12, 162–163, 169
   Critical Dissertation on the Poems of Ossian (1763), 162
Blind Harry, 4, 5, 6, 9, 68, 75, 77–78, 80, 84–85, 87, 90–91, 95–97, 101–102
   Wallace, 4, 68, 75–75, 77–80, 82–83, 89–90, 99–100, 102
Boece, Hector, 6, 7
   Scotorum Historiae (1527), 6
Book of the Dean of Lismore, 136–137
Boswell, James, 12, 171, 189, 190, 194
Bower, Walter, 3, 4
Boyd, William, 300
Bradley, A.C., 219
   Shakespearean Tragedy, 219
Brendon of Clonfert, 52–53
Bridie, James, 296
   Mr Gillie, 296
Brontës, 14
Brown, George Douglas, 14, 290–291, 293, 296
   The House with the Green Shutters (1901), 14, 291, 298
Brown, George Mackay, 297–298, 300
Bruce, Edward, Earl of Carrick, 62, 64, 66, 69
Bruide son of Derile, 51
Buchan, John, 15, 215–245, 289
   Augustus, 241
   A Lost Lady of Old Years, 222, 242
   A Prince of the Captivity 221–222, 240–242
   A Study in Scarlet, 221
   Castle Gay, 240
   Greenmantle, 220, 227, 229–232, 237
   Huntingtower, 216, 231
   John Burnet of Barns, 221
   John Macnab, 221–222, 233–234
   Julius Caesar, 241
   Micah Clarke, 221
   Midwinter, 238, 244
   Montrose, 241, 244
   Mr Standfast, 227, 229, 231
   Oliver Cromwell, 244
   Poems Scots and English, 240
   Prester John, 235
   Salute to Adventurers, 219, 242
   Sick Heart River, 216, 221, 234, 236, 238, 243

Index

Sir Quixote of the Moors, 215, 242, 219, 221
The Blanket of the Dark, 238
The Gap in the Curtain, 222
The Half-Hearted, 221–222, 237, 239–240
'The Herd of Standlan', 225
The Massacre of Glencoe, 244
The Northern Muse, 240
'The Novel and the Fairy Tale', 235
The Riddle of the Sands, 237
The Runagates Club, 222
The Thirty-Nine Steps, 216, 221–222, 224, 228, 236, 239
The Three Hostages, 237, 239
The Path of the King, 219, 236, 243
The Power House, 216, 221, 231
The White Company, 221
Witch Wood, 216, 242–244
Buchan, Nichol, 219
Buchan, Hon. William, 216–217
Buchanan, John L., 191
   Travels in the Western Hebrides from 1782 to 1790 (1793), 191
Buchanan, George, 7, 194
Burns, Robert, 6, 8, 22, 24, 29, 75, 83, 85, 178, 194–195, 201, 204, 207, 286
   'Tam o' Shanter', 201
   'The Cottar's Saturday Night', 286
Burton, John Hill, 188

Caesar, Julius, 11
Cainnech of Achad Bó, 47, 52
Calderwood, David, 7
Calvinism, 78–79, 195
Caledonian Antisyzgy, 1
Calgacus, 1
Calvinism, 242, 243, 257, 297
Campbell, Alasdair of Barbreck, 126
Campbell, Cailean Liath, chief of the Glenorchy Campbells, 114, 117, 119–124, 128, 130–131, 134, 137
Campbell, Donnachadh, 129
   Reminiscences and Reflections of an Octogenarian Highlander, 129
   Griogal Cridhe, 115–116, 118, 122, 124, 127–129, 132, 134–137
Campbell, Donald, Sir 136
Campbell, Duncan of Glen Lyon, 124
Campbell, Gilleasbuig, Earl of Argyll, 119, 121, 132
Campbell, Lachlann, 126
Campbell, Marion, 8, 124–125, 127–129, 131–137
Griogal Cridhe, 115–116, 118, 122, 124, 127–129, 132, 134–137
Carlyle, John, 14, 219
Carlyle, Thomas, 32, 241, 290
Cash, C.G., 171–2
   A Contribution to the Bibliography of Scottish Topography, 171, see also Mitchell, Sir Arthur
Catholic, Catholicism, 6, 78–79, 241–243
Catriona, daughter of Domhnall Gorm Òg, 136
Cawdor, Iain of, 119
Celt, Celtic, 191, 199–200
Chambers, Robert, 158
Charles I, King of Scots and King of England 91, 236
Charteris, Henry, 76
Chaucer, 5
   Canterbury Tales, 89
Chaseabout Raid, 121
Chesterton, G.K., 238
   'The Secret People', 238
Childers, Erskine, 237
Chronicle of Fortingall, 114, 116, 130
Clark, Edward, 175
Claverhouse, 10
Clearances, 27, 257, 286–287, 291
Clydeside, 199
   Clydesideism, 23
Cogitosus, 46
   Life of Brigit, 46
Colmán mac Beógnae, 48
Columba, 39–57
Colvin, Sydney, 187, 205
Comgall of Bangor, 52–53
Commonsense philosophy, 285 Conall, mac Comgaill, 51
Cooper, James Fenimore, 14
Cormac Ua Liatháin, 39
Covenanters, 7, 10, 11, 13, 14, 28
Crockett, S.R., 157–158, 197, 204
   The Grey Man (1896), 157
Crofters' Act of 1886, 180
Cronin, A.J., 293
   Hatter's Castle, 293
Cumméne Find, 43
   Book of the Miraculous Powers of Columba, 43
Cunningham, Alison, 188, 204

David II, King of Scots, 70
Davidson, John, 290, 292

Davie, George, 219, 290
Diarmait mac Cerbaill, of Tara, 49–50, 52
Devolution Referendum, 299
Diarmait, servant of Columba, 56–57
Disruption of 1843, 24, 286, 289, 291
Divine Right, 96
Domhnall Gorm, Òg, 137
Donnchadh Dubh, 117, 119, 124, 130–131, 134
Donnchadh Rhadh, of Glen Lyon, 120, 124–125, 128, 130–131, 137
Donaldson, William, 286, 290
Dorbbéne, 40
Douglas, Archibald, 70
Douglas, Gavin, 5
Douglas, George, 176–177
Douglas, James, 'Black Douglas', 62–72
Douglas, William, 65
Drummond, William of Hawthornden, 8
   The History of Scotland (1655), 8
Donaldson, M.E.M., 172, 182–3
   Wanderings in the Western Highlands and Islands (1921), 172, 182
Donnan of Eigg, 53
Doyle, Arthur Conan, 221, 226, 228, 233, 245
   Sherlock Holmes, 233
   The Green Flag, 224
Dunbar, William, 5
   'The Golden Targe', 5
   'The Thrissell and the Rose', 5
Duncan I, King of Scots, 182

Edward I, King of England, 101
Elizabeth I, Queen of England, 162
Elphinstone, Margaret, 300
Enlightenment, 11, 13, 16, 19, 23–24, 30, 162–163, 169, 174
Ernán, 41

Falkirk, battle of, 92
Feradach, 50
Fergusson, Robert, 6, 12, 82–83, 85, 194, 287
Findchán, Abbot 52
Finsnechta, Fledach, 50
Fintán Munnu, 47
Flaubert, 14
Fordun, John of, 2, 3
   Chronicle of the Scottish Nation, 2
Foucault, Michel, 262
   The History of Sexuality, 262
Freebairn, Robert, 81–82, 95–97

   Wallace, c.1714–30 edition, 81, 89, 96
   Bruce, 95–96
Free Church, 180, 221
Freeman, E.A., 198
   Old English History for Children (1869), 198
Friel, George, 296–297
   Mr Alfred M.A., 296
Frye, Northrop, 34
   The Anatomy of Criticism, 34
Fukuyama, Francis, 270, 272–276, 278–279
   The End of History, 270

Gibbon, Lewis Grassic, 6, 19, 285, 290–291, 294–296
   A Scots Quair, 294–295
   Gray Granite, 291
   Sunset Song, 285
Gaels, 40–42, 46, 52
Gaelic, 115, 195, 198, 241
Galloway, Janice, 299–300
Galt, John, 10, 14, 19, 37, 286–287
   Annals of the Parish, 14, 287
   The Provost, 14
Garnett, Thomas, 174
George I, King of Great Britain, 243
Godwin, William, 272
Gordon, Duchess of, 176
Gordon, Patrick, 85, 91, 101
   The Famous History of . . . Robert, sirnamed The Bruce, King of Scotland . . . (1613), 90, 91
   Britain's Distemper, 91
Graham, James, first Marquis of Montrose, 91
Graham, Sir Patrick, 90
Gray, Alasdair, 15–16, 157, 163, 165, 167, 270–276, 278–281, 298, 300
   A History Maker, 15, 270–272, 274–275, 277–278, 280–281
   Janine, 299–300
   Lanark, 165–167, 271, 274, 298–299
   Poor Things, 157, 271–272, 277, 279, 299
   Whit, 300
Gray, Sir Thomas of Heton, 63
   Scalacronica (1355–59), 63
Gregory of Tours, 41
Gregory the Great, 44
   Dialogues, 46
Grierson, Rev. Thomas, 180
Griogair, Ruadh, (Gregor Roy), 115–118, 120–128, 130–131, 134–135

Index

Grosvenor, Susan, 222
Gunn, Neil, 6, 19, 291, 294
  Butcher's Broom, 291

Haggard, Rider, 203
  Eric Brighteyes, 203
Haldane, Sir John, 132
Hamilton, William of Gilbertfield, 75–6, 81–83, 86, 91–93
  Wallace, 1722 edition, 84, 85, 88, 92, 101
Hart, Andrew, 78–79, 89, 95
  Bible, 1610 edition, 79, 81
  The Wallace, 1618 edition, 78–81
Hart, Francis, 14
  The Scottish Novel (1976), 14
Harvie, Christopher, 25, 26, 195, 220, 231, 271, 289
Harvey, John, 86, 91–94
  The Life of Robert Bruce King of Scots (1729), 86, 92–94, 98
Hay, John MacDougall, 290, 293
  Gillespie, 291
Haynes, Dorothy, 296
Haytoun, Sian, 300
Henryson, Robert, 5, 6
  'The Testament of Cresseid', 5, 6
History and Chronicles of Scotland (1565), 7
Hogg, James, 6, 10, 14, 19, 37, 196, 280, 287
  The Brownie of Bodsbeck, 10
  The Private Memoirs and Confessions of a Justified Sinner, 1, 196, 280, 287
  The Three Perils of Man, 10, 280
Hollinshead, Raphael, 69, 71, 159–160
  Chronicle, 159
Holmes, Ronald, 156–157, 161
Hume, David, 11, 13, 19, 36, 194
  History of England to the Revolution of 1688 (1763), 11, 13
Hume of Godscroft, 69
Hutcheson, Francis, 285

Iain Dubh, 128
Iain Ruadh, 119
Icelandic sagas, 2, 203
  Eyrbyggja Saga trans. by Eirikr Magnusson, 203
  The Story of Burnt Njal by George Dasent, 203
  Volsunga Saga trans. by William Morris, 203
Iseabal Ní Mhic Cailein, 138
  Atá fleasgach ar mo thí, 138
  Is mairy dá ngalar an grádh, 138

Jacob, Violet, 290, 293
Jacobite, 20, 23, 28, 76, 81–82, 90–91, 94–95, 97–98, 192–193, 195, 197, 244, 255, 258, 260, 265–267
James III, King of Scots, 75
James IV, King of Scots, 5, 9
James V, King of Scots, 5
James VI and I, King of Scots and King of England, 5, 8, 9, 77, 91, 154, 162
James, Henry, 11, 14, 203, 207
Jenkins, Robin, 296–297
Johnson, Captain Charles, 156
Johnson, James, 177
Johnson, Samuel, 171, 174–175, 189, 244
Jones, Henry, 220
Joyce, James, 220

Kailyard, 204, 286
  pre-Kailyard pastoral, 291
  'urban Kailyard', 291
Kelman, James, 271, 297–298
Kidd, Colin, 28–32
Kennaway, James, 297
  Tunes of Glory, 297
Kennedy, Alison L., 299–300
  Looking for the Possible Dance, 299
Knox, John, 7, 11, 22, 25, 28, 79, 160, 168, 194–195
  History of the Reformation in Scotland (1559), 7

Laisrén of Durrow, 54
Lanercost Chronicle, 63, 69
Lawrence, T.E., 230
Leavis, F.R., 32
Leonard, Tom, 298
Leslie, John, 7
Leyden, Dr. John, 173
Life of Adomnán, 49
Lindsay, Robert of Pitscottie, 7, 160–161, 165–166, 168
  History and Chronicles of Scotland (c.1570), 160
Linklater, Eric, 294–295
  Magnus Merriman, 294–295
Lockhart, John Gibson, 27, 193, 196
  Life of Scott, 193
Lochhead, Liz, 299
  Mary Queen of Scots Got her Head Chopped Off, 299
Lodge, Richard, 220
Loingsech mac Óengusso, 50
Lowland Scots, 132

Lukacs, George, 13, 32–33, 35
Lyndsay, Sir David, 5, 194, 287
   Ane Satyre of the Thrie Estaitis, 5, 287
   The History of Squire Meldrum, 6

Paruig Mac an Tuairneir, 115, 124, 129–133
Macbeth, 9, 182, 208
MacCaig, Norman, 297
MacColla, Fionn, see Tom MacDonald
MacCrie, Thomas, 11, 194
MacCulloch, John, 179
MacDiarmid, Hugh, 1, 6, 24, 240, 242, 290, 293–296, 300
   A Drunk Man Looks at the Thistle, 293, 295–296
   The Voice of Scotland, 24
Macdonald, Flora, 189
Macdonald, George, 285, 290
Macdonald Tom ('Fionn MacColla'), 242, 294
MacGregor, Alistair Alpin, 172
   Behold the Hebrides! Or Wayfaring in the Western Isles (1925), 172
   The Haunted Isles (1933), 172
MacGregor, Gregor, 124
Macintosh, Brigadier William, 266–267
   Essay on the Ways and Means of Enclosing by a Lover of his Country, 266–267
Mackay, Professor Aeneas, 187
Mackenzie, Agnes Muir, 15, 254–268
   The Kingdom of Scotland, 259
Mackenzie, Compton, 242
MacKenzie, Henry, 285
   The Man of Feeling, 285
MacLaren, Moray, 242
Maclean, Lachlan, 182
MacLean, Sorley, 115
MacMhuirich, Cathal, 136
MacMhuirich, Neil, 8
   'Book of Clanranald', 8
   'The Lament for Griogair Ruadh MacGregor of Glen Strae', 8
Macpherson, James, 7, 12, 162, 176, 178
   Fragments of Ancient Poetry (1760), 12
   Ossian, 7, 29, 163
McDougall, Carl, 299
   The Lights Below, 299
McIlvanney, William, 299–300
   The Kiln, 299
McLean, Duncan, 298
Máel Ruba, 53

Mair, John, 6, 7
Malt Tax, 100
Marx, Marxism, 33, 234
Mary Queen of Scots, 9, 20, 28, 121, 256
Massie, Alan, 300
Menzies, Pàdraig, 134
Menzies, Railbeat of Comrie, 133–135
Menzie, Robert, 134
Menzies, Ulleam, 134
Merlin, 200
Middle Ages, 129, 198
Middle Scots, 78, 80
Mill, James, 32
   History of British India (1818), 32
Miller, Hugh, 290
Mitchell, Sir Arthur, 171–2
Mitchison, Naomi, 15, 254–268, 296
   'Clemency Ealasaid', 254–256, 266
   The Bull Calves, 15, 254–256, 258–260, 263–267, 296
   'The Cleansing of the Knife', 256–258
   The Conquered, 265
   The Corn King and the Spring Queen, 265
   The Roots of the Present, 258–259
Moderate party, 12
Mo Luag of Lismore, 53
Monro, Dean, 182
Mons Graupius, 1
Monteith, Sir John, 101
Montgomery, Alexander, 8
Morgan, Edwin, 299
   Sonnets from Scotland, 299
Montrose Wars, 8
Motherwell, William, 9
Moubray, Elizabeth, 133
Muir, Edwin, 14, 21–22, 25–26, 29, 290–291, 294
Munro, Neil, 6, 14, 290–293
   Gilian the Dreamer, 292
   John Splendid, 292
   Para Handy, 292
   The Lost Pibroch, 292
   The New Road, 292
Murray, Gilbert, 219
Murray, Sarah, 177

Nabokov, Vladimir, 278
   Pale Fire, 278
Napier, Archibald, 132–133
Napier Commission, 180
Nationalist, 294
   National Socialist, 296

Index

Nelson, Tommie, 219
Niall Òg, 137
Nichol, Thomas, 172
   By Mountain, Moor and Loch to the Dream Isles of the West (1931), 172
Nicol, John, 218
Nicoll, William Robertson, 291
Nicholson, John, 154–162, 164–165, 167, 169
   Historical and Traditionary Tales connected with the Sout of Scotland of 1843, 154
Noakes, Monsignor, 167–168

Oliphant, Margaret, 290
Orygynale Cronykil of Scotland c. 1420, 3
Osbourne, Fanny, 200
Ossian, 162, 176, 179, 181, 182, 184, 189
Oswald, King of Northumbria, 43, 49

Pennant, Thomas, 174–175, 182
Pennecuik, Alexander, 84
Pennell, Joseph and Elizabeth, 179
Pict, 2, 39, 45, 48–49, 50–52, 200, 243
Pinkerton, John, 80
   Wallace, 3rd edition 1790, 80
Pococke, Richard, Archdeacon of Dublin, 173
Pollock, Robert, 6, 287
Pont, Timothy, 133
Presbyterianism, 79, 223
Protestantism, 6, 78

Ramsay, Allan, 6, 8, 78, 82–85, 194, 287
   'A Vision', 6
   'The Ghaists', 6
Ramsay, John, 89
Randolph, Thomas, Earl of Moray, 65
Ranke, Leopold von, 13
Reformation, 5, 8, 78, 242, 290
Reid, Thomas, 36, 285
Revolution of 1688, 96
Rizzio, David, 121
Righ gur mór mo Chuid Mhulaid, 116–117, 123–125, 127, 135–137
Robert I (Bruce), King of Scots, 2, 28, 62–63, 66, 76, 88, 90–96, 98, 100–102, 256, 258
Robert II, King of Scots, 70
Rob Roy, 9, 189, 190–191
Robertson, William, 12, 19
   An Historical Disquisition . . . of India (1791), 12
   History of America (1777), 12
   History of the Reign of Emperor Charles V (1769) 12
   History of Scotland (1759), 12
Rodger, Alexander, 287
Russian Formalism, 262–263
Ruthven, Lord William, 130
Ruthven, Katherine, 130–131

Sacheverell, William, Governor of Man, 174
Saracens, 14
Sawney Bean, 9, 154–162, 164–167
Scott, Walter, 6, 8, 10, 13–16, 19, 22, 24, 27, 29, 31–32, 34–35, 37, 162–163, 167, 173, 176, 178–179, 190, 192–194, 202, 204, 216, 221, 245, 280, 284, 286–287, 290, 298
   Guy Mannering, 193
   Old Mortality, 10, 14, 221, 284
   Redgauntlet, 240
   Rob Roy, 193
   The Fortunes of Nigel, 193
   Tales of a Grandfather, 13, 198
   The Antiquary, 193, 202
   The Heart of Midlothian, 284, 287
   The Lady of the Lake, 176
   The Letters of Malachi Malagrowther (1826), 13
   'The Two Drovers'
   Waverley, 162, 176, 193, 199, 284
Scotichronicon, 3
Scottish Enlightenment, 5
Scottish Renaissance, 6, 290, 293–296, 300
Scottish Wars of Independence, 2, 201
Severus, Sulpicius
   Life of Martin, 40
Shakespeare, William, 9, 182, 219
   Coriolanus, 219
Shelley, Mary, 271, 299
   Frankenstein, 271
Shelley, Percy Byshe, 272
Smith, Adam, 11, 12, 201
Smith, Captain Alexander, 156
   A Complete History of the Most Notorious Highway-men . . . (1719), 156–157
Smith, Gregory, 1, 295
   'Caledonian Antisyzygy', 295
   Scottish Literature: Character and Influence, 1
Smith, Iain Crichton, 297
   Consider the Lilies, 297
Smith, Janet Adam, 216
Smollett, Tobias, 12, 19
Snell, John, 218

Soutar, William, 6, 294
   'The Auld Tree', 294
   'The Whale', 294
Spark, Muriel, 296–297
   The Ballad of Peckham Rye, 297
   The Prime of Miss Jean Brodie, 296
Spottiswood, Archbishop 7
'Standart Habbie', 83
Stamp Act repeal of 1855, 290
Stevenson, Robert Louis, 6, 11, 14, 15, 187–208, 216, 221, 226, 235, 245, 284–285, 289–290, 292–293, 298–299
   'A Gossip on Romance', 202
   'A Humble Remonstrance', 11
   'An Old Scots Gardener', 204
   Catriona, 15, 200, 288
   Footnote to History, 202
   Heathercat, 205–206
   Humble Remonstrance, 207
   Jekyll and Hyde, 196, 290
   Kidnapped, 15, 191–193, 195, 288
   Memories and Portraits (1897), 11
   'Pastoral', 204
   Prince Otto, 195
   'Pulvis et Umbra', 207
   The Beach of Falesa, 202
   'The Body Snatchers', 190
   'The Foreigner at Home', 205
   'The Manse', 204
   The Master of Ballantrae, 14, 195–197, 206, 287
   'The Merry Men', 190
   The Pirate, 193
   'The Scot Abroad', 205
   The Young Chevalier, 202
   'Thrawn Janet', 190, 205–206
   Treasure Island, 190, 195
   Weir of Hermiston, 200, 202, 205, 293
Stewart, Charles Edward, 97
   Bonnie Prince Charlie, 9, 97, 189, 256
   Pretender, 98
Stewart, James, 97, 191
   Pretender, 81, 97
Stewart, Sir David of Rosyth, 3
Stewart, Walter, 62, 64–66, 70–72
Stuart, Gilbert, 12
Suibne mac Colmáin, 50
Sutherland, Halliday, *Hebridean Journey* (1939), 172

Tacitus, 1
   Life of Agricola, 1
Tait, Harry, 161, 163, 165–167
   The Ballad of Sawney Bean (1990), 161, 165, 167
Tennant, William, 6, 287
Terain son of Ainftech, 50–51
'The Cherrie and the Slae', 8
'The Gaberlunzie Man', 9
Thomson, James, (1700–48), 12, 85
   'Rule Britannia', 12
   The Seasons, 12
Thomson, James, 290
   The City of Dreadful Night, 290
Tudor, Margaret, 5

Union of the Crowns, 78, 100
   Treaty of Union, 99
Union of 1707, 12, 13, 85, 98–100, 157–159, 188, 257, 284, 288

Walker, Rev. John, 173
Wallace, William, 4, 6, 9, 75–6, 78, 86–88, 95–97, 100–102, 256
Wallace, Sir Thomas, 98
Watson, James, 82, 91
   Choice Collection of Comic and Serious Scots Poems, 82
Watson, John, 8
Wedderburn, Robert, 5, 6
   'Dame Scotia', 6
   The Complaynt of Scotland, 5
Welsh, Irvine, 297–298
White, Hayden, 10, 270–271
   Metahistory: The Historical Imagination in Nineteenth Century Europe (1973), 10
Wilde, Oscar, 230, 281
Wilson, Alexander, 287
Wilson, John, 291
Winter, William, 182
   Old Shrines and Ivy (1892), 182
Wittig, Kurt, 290
Wordsworth, William, 176, 178, 291
   'The Lake School', 291
Wyntoun, Andrew, 3, 4

Yeats, W.B., 15
Youngson, A.J., 15, 260
   The Prince and the Pretender, 260